ARIS & PHILLIPS CLAS

MENANDER

The Shield (*Aspis*)
and
The Arbitration (*Epitrepontes*)

Edited and Translated by

Stanley Ireland

Aris & Phillips Classical Texts
are published by
Oxbow Books, Oxford

ISBN 978-0-85668-897-3 cloth
ISBN 978-0-85668-833-1 paper

A CIP record for this book is available from the British Library

This book is available direct from

Oxbow Books, Oxford, UK
Phone: 01865-241249; Fax: 01865-794449

and

The David Brown Book Company
PO Box 511, Oakville, CT 06779, USA
Phone: 860-945-9329; Fax: 860-945-9468

or from our website

www.oxbowbooks.com

Cover image (paperback only):
Mosaic from the 'House of Menander' Mytilene
Epitrepontes *Act II: The Arbitration Scene*
Showing l. to r.: Daos, Smikrines, Syriskos

Printed and bound in Great Britain by
TJ International, Padstow, Cornwall

CONTENTS

PREFACE

Following on from the earlier edition of Menander's *Dyskolos*, the present volume is designed to provide ready access to two more fragmentary, but no less important, plays, especially for those with limited experience of the original text. For this reason I have tried to provide a translation which is both readable and yet gives some help in understanding the essential fluidity of Menander's text. On another level I have sought to incorporate into the commentary, founded for the most part on the translation, those factors significant for the modern reader rather than delving constantly into the history of textual interpretation, especially where later discoveries have rendered otiose ideas that were once put forward. Where notes do deal with matters more relevant to the original Greek (often inserted to assist those less experienced in the language), I have generally signalled this by placing them in square brackets.

In producing a work such as this I know only too well that I am standing on the shoulders of giants, and it is with especial gratitude that I recognise the contributions of scholars like Sandbach, Arnott, Jacques and Martina to our understanding of the plays, not least the sophistication that the playwright so often injected into his work. There is much, of course, that the format and ethos of the present series precludes, but pointers to further investigation may perhaps be found in the bibliography. In reaching the text's present state I have also been fortunate to have the close advice of the series editor, Prof. Chris Collard, whose perceptive sense highlighted a number of areas where revisions were needed. Those errors that remain are, of course, my own.

The appearance of Furley's edition of *The Arbitration* came too late for me to take full cognisance of his careful review of the complex evidence of the play. I have, however, taken the opportunity to insert a number of references to his thinking.

THE SHIELD: INTRODUCTION

The Plot and its Reconstruction

(Act I) While campaigning in Lycia in an effort to secure enough wealth to provide a suitable dowry for his sister, the young man Cleostratos has reportedly been killed in a surprise night attack on the Greek camp by the natives. His ex-tutor Daos has returned home bringing much of the booty that had been secured, together with a shield, the only means by which the young man's body was identified. On his arrival he is met by Cleostratos' elder uncle, Smikrines, whose interest in the booty becomes all too evident, and soon the old man is plotting to secure it by invoking the law allowing a family member to claim Cleostratos' heiress-sister in marriage. His justification for this, the neglect he claims he has suffered from the rest of his family (principally his younger brother, Chairestratos), results in a paranoid determination not to let them get their hands on his own estate after his death, something he can ensure by marrying the girl and thereby producing a male heir. His first move in achieving this, an attempt to win over the support of Daos, is rebuffed by the claim that a slave has no role in such matters, which are properly the concern of free men, and that his antipathy to what Smikrines is suggesting stems from his Phrygian origins, where things are done differently.

(Act II) The correctness of Daos' thinking is soon confirmed when Chairestratos intervenes, pointing out the age differential between Smikrines and his niece, the fact that the girl is already betrothed to Chairestratos' step-son, Chaireas, (preparations for the wedding celebration, scheduled for that very day, have had to be cancelled – much to the disgust of the cook involved at the end of Act I), and offering to cede to Smikrines the booty in return for allowing the wedding to go ahead. None of this is of any interest to Smikrines; in fact, he sees in Chairestratos' offer to cede the booty a future legal liability. Faced by his hopes for the future now in ruins Chairestratos collapses in despair. Daos, in contrast, aware that he will himself become the property of Smikrines if the old man gets his way, suggests an escape route: Chairestratos is to succumb to his current depression by feigning death. His own daughter would then become 'heiress' to her father's much larger

estate, thus diverting Smikrines' attention away from Cleostratos' sister and (presumably) allowing Chaireas to marry her instead.

(Act III) In order to convince Smikrines that his brother's 'imminent demise' is a reality, a sham-doctor is brought in, prepared for by a histrionic display of despair by Daos reporting Chairestratos' collapse. Smikrines is evidently convinced by both aspects of the deception ...

While the main text of the play ceases at this point, fragments of the final two Acts, along with references in Acts I–III, and Menander's dramatic technique in other plays provide some indication of subsequent developments:

From the tattered remains of the end of Act IV it is clear that Chairestratos' 'death' is announced; by whom is not clear, though the other character involved in the dialogue at this point is presumably Smikrines. Subsequently the stage is cleared and Cleostratos returns home. Those fragments from the beginning of Act V mention preparations for a double wedding (presumably that between Chaireas and Cleostratos' sister and between Cleostratos and Chairestratos' daughter earlier referred to by her father). The wording used would tend to suggest that the speaker is Daos, who then summons Chaireas and informs him that Cleostratos has returned and awaits him. If interpretation of subsequent references is correct, Smikrines, still unaware of the radical change of situation, attempts to induce Chaireas to resume his original wedding plans but is brought face to face with both his ignorance of the truth and the results of his selfish avarice.

There remain, however, a number of loose ends derived mainly from references in earlier Acts and the general emphasis upon natural justice that is a feature of Menander's work:

1. How is Smikrines dealt with and by whom? The reference at 538 'I make (him) better behaved' echoes Getas' words at *Dyskolos* 903, 'At all events we've got to tame the man', spoken just prior to the cook and slave taking their revenge on Knemon for his earlier treatment of them.[1] Given that the plan to thwart the old man's schemes originated with the slave Daos, it would seem appropriate that he continues this by revealing to Smikrines the truth and its implications. But does he act alone in this? Arnott (1979a, p. 90) suggests a role in this for a re-emergent cook, on the analogy of *Dyskolos*, but we have to admit that evidence for this is slim.

---

[1] Cf. Onesimos' treatment of Smikrines at *Epitrepontes* 1080ff., where the old man is brought to realise that his attempts to remove his daughter from her husband are futile and irrelevant to the real situation.

2. What is Smikrines' ultimate fate? At 146 Chance predicts that 'he'll end up where he was before'. Does this mean that he will return to his previous lifestyle, living on his own and estranged from his family, or is there the possibility of some re-integration of him into the family as occurs, albeit reluctantly, in the case of Knemon in *Dyskolos*?[2] While the depiction of Smikrines is extreme and gives no evidence of redeeming features, the analogy of Plautus' Roman adaptation *Rudens*[3] may not be irrelevant – if, that is, Plautus chose to reproduce the evidence of the Greek original by Diphilus, and if Menander and Diphilus shared a common approach in this respect.[4] For at the end of the Plautine play the pimp Labrax, whose behaviour has been far worse than that of Smikrines, is invited to dinner by Daemones, despite the pimp's earlier treatment of Daemones' daughter.

3. Does Daos receive a reward for his actions? Menander's evident concern with natural justice suggests the distinct possibility that Daos' hopes for a restful retirement, mentioned at 11–12, become reality with the granting of his freedom and a continuing honourable place within Cleostratos' household.[5]

Stage Setting

By convention the stage of New Comedy depicted a street scene with a backdrop representing between one and three buildings, depending upon the requirements of the individual plot, each with a separate door.[6] To each side of the stage there were also projecting structures, *paraskenia*, which formed additional routes by which entrances and exits could be made. By convention too the exit to the audience's right led to the city or harbour, that

---

[2] Contrast Gaiser (1973) p. 126 who sees Smikrines' faults as so ingrained that redemption is impossible.

[3] Though the pimp Labrax has promised to sell his slave-girl Palaestra to her young lover Plesidippus, he absconds by ship with both the girl and the deposit paid for her. Through the intervention of the star-god Arcturus, however, the ship is wrecked off the very coast where Palaestra's long-lost father, Daemones, lives. Palaestra and her maid struggle ashore and take refuge in a nearby temple, but are menaced by Labrax until rescued by the intervention of Daemones. Recovery of a trunk containing Palaestra's trinkets leads to recognition of father and daughter, who can now marry her lover.

[4] That Diphilus' comedy was more vigorous than that of Menander is well known, see Astorga, Damen.

[5] Cf. Habrotonon's hopes for freedom at *Epitrepontes* 548–9, though once again the fragmentary nature of the play's ending removes all indication of whether the hope became reality.

[6] So, for instance, all three doors are needed in *Dyskolos*, only two in *Epitrepontes* (presumably the middle door in such cases was either neglected or disguised). The Roman plays *Captivi* and *Amphitryo* need only a single door, and this was probably the case also with their Greek originals.

to the left the country or foreign parts.[7] The actual number of stage doors required was normally evident from either the situation depicted, *e.g.* two families interacting with one another presupposes two houses, or from internal references in the text. Thus, the existence of a third building between the houses of Knemon and Gorgias in *Dyskolos* is clear from Pan's reference to it in the prologue, as is the fact that Knemon's house lies to the audience's left, his step-son's to the right. The stage requirements of *The Shield*, however, and the relationship of the houses to one another are to some extent uncertain, and need to be established from the context of the action. On the analogy of *Dyskolos* we might expect the ogre of the play, Smikrines, to occupy the house on the left, furthest away from the city centre, as befits his unsociable nature, with that on the right occupied by his more affable brother, Chairestratos. This arrangement, advanced by Jacques,[8] also envisages use of the central third door to represent the shrine of Chance,[9] from which she emerges to deliver the prologue at 97. While not universally accepted,[10] such an arrangement does have several attractive advantages: 1) it avoids an ostensibly less effective entry by the goddess either through one of the wing-entrances (Frost p. 23) or on the roof of one of the houses, the *theologeion*, as employed in a number of Euripides' tragedies; 2) it allows a lasting reminder of the goddess's role throughout the action, reinforcing those verbal references that occur. However, whether this is sufficient to guarantee the use of the third door in the absence of a specific reference to the building such as one gets at the beginning of *Dyskolos* must remain a matter of speculation.

Considering the initial procession itself commentators are divided as to whether Daos leads or follows the line of prisoners and booty. The latter is accepted by Arnott 1979a, p. 12, Blanchard 1983, p. 149 n. 59, Frost p. 21 and Blume p. 147. However, as Beroutsos p. 21 n. 25[11] cogently observes, it is more logical that Daos should lead, since only he knows their intended destination, and a leading position would immediately focus attention from the outset on both him and the battered shield that he carries.

---

[7] For suggested variations see Frost p. 103 n. 5, Wiles p. 45.
[8] 1998a, p. 2, n. 1, 33 n. 1, cf. Beroutsos p. 21. One disadvantage of such an arrangement is that the opening procession, coming from the harbour, *i.e.* through the right-hand wing-entrance, will immediately arrive at its presumed destination, Chairestratos' house. The dramatic weakness of this, however, could be easily avoided by supposing that it proceeded to centre-stage, where for maximum effect Daos delivered his monologue.
[9] Jacques (1998a) pp. XXIV–VI.
[10] Thus, Arnott (1979a) p. 12 specifies only two doors, cf. Dworacki (1973b) p. 37.
[11] Cf. Katsouris (1975a) p. 106.

The Opening of the Play

The beginning of a play is always a critical moment, and for a play in antiquity, set in a theatre with no means of highlighting the stage or darkening the auditorium, where there was always a greater degree of audience self-awareness and a greater fragility of the dramatic illusion than is the case today, this was especially so.[12] If a play was to succeed, its opening required particular care if it was to fulfil both its dramatic and theatrical functions. On a theatrical level there was the immediate need to attract and retain the attention and goodwill of the audience. In other plays this might be achieved through direct address to the audience delivered by an opening prologue speaker, the so-called *captatio benevolentiae*.[13] In *The Shield*, on the other hand, that seizing of attention is achieved not by interaction with the audience, but its opposite, a silent procession in sombre mood, which initially denies information rather than provides it.[14] On a dramatic level Menander shows the same width of approach. For plays that were conventionally short the demands of economy in terms of introducing the situation upon which the plot was founded and the characters involved were often filled by an expository prologue delivered either by an omniscient deity such as Pan in *Dyskolos* or by one of the humans involved in the situation, as in *Samia*.[15] *The Shield*, in contrast, employs what might be seen as a more sophisticated technique, one more naturally attuned to the dramatic situation portrayed, which in many respects is the very antithesis of comedy.[16] For

---

[12] The problems that a playwright might face are graphically described, if in a Roman context, by Terence in the prologues to his *Hecyra*.
[13] Thus, Pan's invitation to the audience in *Dyskolos* to 'Imagine the setting is in Attica...', followed at the prologue's end by the appeal, 'the details you'll see, if you wish – and do make it your wish' or Moschion's quasi-confidential address in *Samia*. More blatant approaches, including direct banter with the audience, occur in the prologues of Plautus' Roman adaptations, *e.g. Amphitryo*, *Captivi*, and *Poenulus*. In *Aspis* such direct reference to the audience is restricted to the fragmentary statement '[Anyone who pays attention] will realise this' at line 100 and 'That's enough information for you on that' at 113f.
[14] See further, Arnott (2001).
[15] Though the use of such a prologue may appear highly artificial, it is not an uncommon feature within the history of drama and is certainly more entertaining than modern programme notes. In addition, as Gomme-Sandbach aptly observe p. 133, it neatly avoids 'the difficulty of smuggling into the dialogue facts needed more for the audience's sake than for that of the characters'.
[16] Borgogno (2002) indeed sees the play as dominated by a series of contrasts and oppositions: happiness/unhappiness, life/death, gain/loss, generosity/greed, youth/age.

while genre expectations require a happy ending, this play opens with a tragedy, the implications of which for the family involved are revealed in the opening monologue from the slave Daos.[17] Only when the audience has been tantalised by this and the implications of Smikrines' subsequent intervention, does the introduction of a deferred expository prologue convert that tragedy into misapprehension, breaking the tension earlier built up and allowing the injection of New Comedy's major effect, dramatic irony, where the audience's superior knowledge enables it to appreciate the mistaken thought processes and resultant embarrassment of the stage characters.[18] In this way the interest of the play lies not in the actual dénouement (logically there is only one possible route to a happy ending and this is explicitly given in the prologue[19]) but in the obstacles placed in the way of that ending and the efforts made to circumvent them.

The Legal Background to the Play

While founded on the premise of Cleostratos' reported death, the plot of *The Shield* is centred rather upon the danger that this event poses for the young man's sister, specifically the fact that her new status as *epikleros* makes her a target for the grasping avarice of her elder uncle, Smikrines. The term itself, normally used in the context of a girl whose father died leaving no direct male issue, is often translated as 'heiress', though in Attic law it did not, in fact, carry with it implications of direct inheritance, even if she and the estate became an inseparable entity. Rather, a woman who found herself in the position of *epikleros* was regarded as the conduit through which an estate might be passed on from its previous male owner to the next, her own male offspring.[20] And to ensure that an estate did not pass from the orbit of the wider family unit, she could be claimed in marriage by the nearest male

---

[17] Compare *Perikeiromene*. Though the actual opening of the play is lost, later references suggest a scene of serious domestic discord between the soldier Polemon and his mistress Glykera that cannot have been rich in comedy. Groton p. 40, in contrast, claims that the audience, realising they were watching a comedy, would not take Daos' tragic message at face value, cf. Dworacki (1973a) p. 35.

[18] As well as *Perikeiromene* such deferred prologues are posited with some degree of certainty for *Epitrepontes*, and *Heros*, and suggested for *Georgos*, *Misoumenos* and *Synaristosae* (see further Groton p. 27 n. 29).

[19] Cf. *Perikeiromene* 162–7 where Misapprehension shows that she has engineered the situation so that Glykera might be reunited with her family and, as a result, gain her rightful place in society.

[20] Harrison (1968) p. 113.

relation of the deceased father through the process of *epidikasia* (recognition and sanctioning of the claim by the archon), or if he chose not to exercise this right, by the next in line.[21] Such a husband did not himself become the outright owner of the estate in question,[22] but was required to manage it until any male offspring attained two years after puberty, *i.e.* 18.[23] The legal issue of the play, therefore, seems at first sight to be straight-forward enough, but has in fact been the centre of considerable discussion[24] caused by our only partial understanding of Attic law in its totality, but also by the facts: 1) that much of that understanding stems from the court cases themselves, which predictably present a one-sided picture, and 2) that *The Shield* is a play, not an academic study, and therefore as capable of distortion in terms of the law, as it is of anything else.[25] Particular concern, in fact, has centred upon those issues of inheritance on which the play appears to throw new light, the problems created for interpretation of that law in general, and the question of whether the play presents a thinly veiled criticism of the law dealing with *epikleroi*.

[21] MacDowell (1978) p. 95f., Harrison (1968) p. 10f., 132f. Such claims would normally come into play if the girl in question were unmarried or if, though married, she had produced no male issue. In that case the family claimant could effect a divorce, and even divorce his own wife to facilitate such a claim. If, on the other hand, the married *epikleros* had produced male issue, she was no longer subject to a claim on her person.

[22] Schaps p. 27, citing Isaeus, asserts that the property was legally in the hands of the *epikleros*, though as a woman she had no right to dispose of it or even manage it, cf. MacDowell (1978) p. 95.

[23] Demosthenes 46, 20: 'If someone be born the son of an *epikleros*, two years after he has grown to manhood he assumes control of the estate and makes provision for his mother's maintenance'.

[24] The literature on the status of *epikleroi* is large; among the most relevant studies here are: Harrison (1968) pp. 132–8, Karabelias (1970), Gaiser (1973) pp. 130–2, Karnezis (1977), Schaps (1979) pp. 25–42, MacDowell (1982), Groton (1982) pp. 16–18, Brown (1983), Jacques (1998a) pp. LXX–LXXV. That the theme of the *epikleros* was a popular one for Greek playwrights is shown by the number of plays with that title – two by Menander alone – or the associated title *Epidikazomenos* (*The Claimant*).

[25] Karnezis' brief study of the legal aspects of the play presents a telling, if somewhat extreme, summary of possible distortions; see further below.

New Issues[26]

1. The transfer of guardianship: Since all females were deemed to be legally incompetent, *i.e.* they had no independent standing in law, they each needed a guardian or *kyrios* to be responsible for them. Upon his departure for service abroad, therefore, Cleostratos, his sister's *kyrios*, had left her with his younger uncle, Chairestratos, who subsequently took it upon himself to betroth her to her step-cousin, Chaireas. Since betrothal was the responsibility of a *kyrios*, it is inferred that the play shows that this status could be transferred to another in the event of a temporary absence by the true legal guardian. The fact that Smikrines nowhere questions this is taken as indicative of its validity,[27] though, equally, the apparent ease with which Smikrines sweeps aside the marriage that Chairestratos has already arranged[28] and appropriates the right to marry the girl himself can be interpreted as indicating either that Chairestratos has exceeded his power,[29] or that a transfer of *kyrios*-status was rendered void by the death of the *kyrios* who effected the transfer, *i.e.* that on Cleostratos' death a new set of rules came into play.[30]

2. Claims upon an *epikleros* were governed by the principle of primogeniture, that is, the eldest of the nearest relations had first claim upon her.[31] This is given substance by the emphasis that both Chance and Smikrines himself place upon his status as the older brother (Chance: 142f. Smikrines: 172, 255), but it is clear that in other matters of inheritance there was no such principle.[32]

---

[26] These are summarised by Brown (1983) p. 418 in his examination of MacDowell's paper, though some are of doubtful relevance.

[27] Groton p.119f., who emphasises rather Chairestratos' altruistic motivation in arranging the marriage.

[28] At 297f. Chaireas specifically states that the law will make someone else (*i.e.* Smikrines) her *kyrios*, though this may be no more than part of the young man's hyperbole of despair.

[29] Thus Karnezis p. 153f., cf. Karabelias p. 368.

[30] Karabelias p. 367.

[31] Karabelias pp. 375–8, MacDowell (1978) p. 95, (1982) p. 47; contrast Karnezis p. 154.

[32] So, for instance, an estate would be shared out equally by claimants (see Commentary on 170–1), though as Schaps points out p. 34, division of an *epikleros* herself among potential claimants would not be easy, and Scafuro p. 284 observes that the principle of primogeniture may have been governed more by custom than by law (cf. Brown 1983 p. 418). At the same time, however, Smikrines' apparent belief that he has an *automatic* claim upon the girl is itself incorrect, since it was the function of the Archon, through the process of *epidikasia*, to determine which nearest relation (*anchisteus*) should be awarded an *epikleros*. Since the prime purpose of the process was the procreation of heirs, a claimant was excluded from consideration if he was deemed to be too old for this (*i.e.* incapable of either engaging in sex at least three times a month or siring offspring as laid down by Solon: Plutarch *Solon* 20, cf. Lane Fox p. 225). However, we need to be careful not to inject into the play factors the playwright never intended to raise (cf. Karabelias p. 380f.).

3. A girl could become *epikleros* to her brother's estate as well as that of her father. At 265 Chairestratos' offer to give Smikrines 'all this stuff' in exchange for allowing the girl to marry Chaireas presumably relates not only to any property Cleostratos inherited from his father but also (and perhaps more immediately) to the booty Daos brought back from Lycia. The fact that Smikrines rejects the offer suggested to MacDowell (1982, p. 48) that the booty formed part of the property covered by the *epikleros* law and that Smikrines recognised the danger of subsequent legal proceedings against him by any child born to the young couple. In consequence MacDowell argued that a sister could become *epikleros* to her brother's estate as well as that of her father, whereas previously it had been claimed that a sister inherited from a brother in her own right and not as the means of transferring such property to any offspring. However, Karabelias (p. 372–5) had already suggested that the evidence of *Aspis* does not allow for so clear-cut an interpretation. Rather, the two inheritances, that which was ancestral and that coming from Cleostratos' booty, were essentially separate and would devolve by different processes, even if the end result were the same. In addition, as Brown argues, Smikrines' rejection of the offer may be caused simply by his apprehension over a law suit, not the status of the offered property.[33]

4. Once Smikrines has been diverted away from Cleostratos' sister to Chairestratos' daughter, as providing 'richer pickings', Daos declares that the old man will be willing to hand the girl over to the first man who asks for her, presumably Chaireas (353–5). MacDowell argues that this would only be possible if the girl belonged to the *thetic* class, the lowest in Athens,[34] and that the girl must belong to this since it was income that determined class, not capital, and Cleostratos' inherited estate was known to be small (line 132). In the case of more affluent classes the girl would simply be available for claim by the next blood relation in line. This then becomes the basis for Macdowell's subsequent assertion (p. 49) that to avoid Smikrines returning to his claim on Cleostratos' sister once the sham of Chairestratos' death is revealed, the play must be evidence that such a course of action on Smikrines' part cannot be possible in the context of someone in the *thetic* class. As Brown points out, however,[35] there is no real evidence that social class was determined by income, and the problem of

---

[33] Brown (1983) pp. 418–9, cf. Scafuro p. 298, who notes that if Chairestratos' offer relates to transmissible estate (*i.e.* is attached to the girl as *epikleros* rather than her own property), then he is himself breaking the law in offering to dispose of it to someone other than the father of the girl's future issue. Again, however, this is an issue that is never developed in the play.

[34] (1982) p. 48f., cf. (1978) p. 96. Demosthenes 43, 54: 'As regards *epikleroi* of the *thetic* class, if the nearest relative does not wish to have her, let him give her away'. The law goes on to specify the size of any dowry to be given to the girl, commensurate with the wealth of the nearest relative.

[35] (1983) p. 414f., 419.

Smikrines' reaction to his brother's 'resurrection' is never investigated, being overtaken and rendered irrelevant by the return of Cleostratos.

In addition to providing new evidence for Attic law the play also raises issues and apparent illogicalities that have invited investigation and elucidation.

1. At 279–81 Chairestratos expresses the now futile hope that his step-son Chaireas would marry Cleostratos' sister, as he had already planned, while Cleostratos himself would marry Chairestratos' daughter, and that both young men would become heirs to his estate. In law, however, Chairestratos' estate would have passed solely to his daughter, who would have herself been an *epikleros*, for transmission to her offspring, while Chaireas, the step-son, would not figure at all in any inheritance. In other circumstances Chairestratos might have avoided his daughter becoming an *epikleros*, and thus a potential prey to Smikrines (as Daos soon proposes should happen at 348f.), by adopting a son and marrying the girl to him. However, the obvious choice, Chaireas, is ruled out since both he and the daughter have the same mother, and any such union would be deemed incestuous. An alternative solution, and one enacted at *Dyskolos* 731–2, would entail Chairestratos adopting Cleostratos, who, as the girl's *kyrios* after Chairestratos' death, could legally dispose of her in marriage to an appropriate suitor.[36] However, while the text records Chairestratos' hopes, it makes no effort to investigate the rationale behind what is said. As a result it may well be that in the context of a drama the audience was simply not expected to question the logicality of the statement but simply to absorb its emotional impact.

2. In the event of Chaireas finally marrying Cleostratos' sister any male issue would, in fact, belong to Chaireas' family, thus potentially threatening the existence of Cleostratos' line (if he were really dead). That Attic law actively aimed to prevent this is advocated by some,[37] and to avoid it a male child might be posthumously adopted by its maternal grandfather, thus continuing his line, though this could of itself then threaten the existence of its father's line unless there were more than one male child born.[38] Again, it is a problem that is never considered by the play.

---

[36] A similar solution, adoption, is advanced by MacDowell (1982) p. 44f. to explain Smikrines' claim at 170f. that Cleostratos would have been heir to the old man's total estate, in ostensible violation of the normal rules of inheritance. See further, Commentary ad loc.

[37] Schaps pp. 32–3, investigates the potential and the problems inherent in such a system.

[38] Lane Fox pp. 226–7. The various methods of avoiding the disruption of a marriage by an *anchisteus* (the nearest male relative to the deceased) even if there were no issue (*e.g.* the relatives did not challenge it or the *anchisteus* was bought off, as Chairestratos ostensibly attempts to do with Smikrines, cf. Isaeus 10) are discussed by Schaps p. 29f.

Menander's Verdict on the Epikleros *Law*

The fact that Smikrines is consistently condemned for exercising his rights in strict application of the law concerning *epikleroi* is taken by some as *prima facie* evidence that the playwright intended his work also to be a condemnation of the law itself.[39] On the other hand, as Brown (1983) argues, the play cannot be taken as providing a fully accurate picture of Attic law. Commentators have long recognised that the need to present a situation and its solution within a relatively short time-frame frequently led to obscurities of detail, an aspect of dramatic economy found in Menander and, indeed, every other playwright.[40] As a result the question inevitably arises why the representation of a legal situation should fare any differently, especially when the audience itself may not have been totally expert in the finer points of such cases. Thus, in view of the fact that Menander's aim was the presentation not of a legal tract but of characters' reaction to the situation in which they found themselves, we would hardly be justified in extending any verdict on the actions of those characters to the wider ambit of the situation presented: Menander's condemnation is of Smikrines' insistence upon applying the law to his own selfish benefit and that is all. As Lane Fox observes (pp. 226, 230),[41] the law gave him a right, not a duty. The fact that he chose to represent it as a duty (186–7), despite the alternative offered by his brother and others that existed, suggests it was his application of the law that was at fault, not the law itself. But in the end the whole question of *epikleroi* in the play proves to be an irrelevance; Cleostratos' return, allowing the 'resurrection' of his uncle, removes all problems, and the law that Smikrines hoped to exploit becomes the means by which, as Chance makes clear (145–6), his discomfiture is assured.

---

[39] Karabelias pp. 384–7, MacDowell (1982) p. 51, cf. (1978) p. 98, Turner (1979) p. 120, cf. Jacques (1998a) p. LXXIVf., though J. also recognises that comedy 'n'est pas un genre réaliste', Hurst (1990) p. 120.

[40] Brown (1983) pp. 416–18. The insertion of what might be termed deliberate shortcuts in the presentation of a situation is suggested indeed by the very fact that commentators have been exercised by such factors, here the inconsistencies of law within the action.

[41] Cf. Brown (1983) p. 414, Blanchard (2007) p. 77f. who perceptively points out that Menander uses the *epikleros* element to develop the classic comedy theme of conflict between two brothers, not the playwright's stance on a particular law.

The Characters

'The characters...lack depth and originality' (Gomme-Sandbach p. 62); 'Smikrines is wholly bad...Daos by comparison seems rather too faultless' (Arnott 1979a, p. 5).[42] These two verdicts in many ways encapsulate the general opinion of a majority of commentators, but are they the whole story? In approaching the composition of a play the playwright makes a number of decisions: the complexity of his plot and its formation, the range of characters to be involved and their relationships,[43] the extent to which an initial revelation of information will preclude or accommodate surprise developments, the manner in which the dénouement will be brought about and where in the play this will occur. The list could go on, but in terms of character it is clear that Menander has here deliberately chosen to represent types who remain within the parameters expected of their type, *i.e.* there is no one like Knemon in *Dyskolos*, whose portrayal develops from the totally antisocial figure described in the prologue to a man who has chosen to isolate himself from what he regards as the selfishness of society, and whose desire for self-sufficiency would strike a chord of sympathy, and even admiration, with many in the audience. Yet while moderating characteristics may be absent in the case of a figure like Smikrines, we must not conclude that variety is altogether absent; rather, they are replaced by a no less interesting range of components that constitute the total picture.

Smikrines: Identification of the stock type of unsympathetic and money-oriented old man is assisted by the very name given to the character with its connotations of small-mindedness.[44] As Jacques pertinently indicates (1998a, p. XLVIIIff.), the old man displays a range of characteristics, many of them well established or associated with the stock figure of the miser: *aischrokerdeia*, defined by Aristotle (*Nicomachean Ethics* 1122a2)[45] as typifying those who will 'put up with any reproach for the sake of profit, even if this is small' (cf. Chance's description at 117–20); *aneleutheria*, again defined by Aristotle (ibid. 1119b28) as a slavish obsession with money; suspicion – the belief that others wish to do one harm (cf. 153, 175–

---

[42] Cf. Jacques (1998a) p. LXV (speaking of virtuous slaves) 'il (sc. Daos) en est même le représentant le plus proche de la perfection', Vogt-Spira p. 81 'Menander hier im Unterschied zu anderen Stüken weniger differenzierte und komplexe Charaktere zeichnet'.

[43] On the nature of Menander's characters see further Arnott (1979a) p. xxxiiff.

[44] cf. *Epitrepontes*, *Sikyonios*, MacCary (1970) pp. 278–82, (1971) pp. 306–12.

[45] Cf. Theophrastus' *Characters* 30, where the type is characterised more by his meanness.

80, 270–3, 391–8); gullibility in the face of trickery – born of Smikrines' obsession with gain, despite an otherwise acute understanding of his rights; dissimulation and hypocrisy, the pretence that the situation is other than we know it to be (*e.g.* his denial of any interest in the booty when it is clear this is at the forefront of his thinking, 85–6, 149–53, his so-called regrets at the reported death of his nephew); calculating parasitism, *e.g.* his attempt to secure Daos' participation in his scheme (187–9); an egocentric approach (Feneron p. 18, 'He (*i.e.* Smikrines) uses the first person twice as frequently as anyone else in the *Aspis*', cf. Gaiser 1973, p. 124–6) which sweeps aside any consideration for others (*e.g.* his total disregard for the wedding already arranged). Clearly such features display little scope for the injection of mitigating factors, but the point at issue is not whether Menander should have taken this route, but to recognise that what we have is the result of deliberate choice on his part. Our task, therefore is to understand why, at the same time recognising that we have only half the total evidence.

Daos: Daos' role in masterminding the plot against Smikrines and its execution is aptly founded upon his role as *paidagogos* to his young master (see Commentary on line 2). Yet while he may be regarded as a paragon of virtue, skilfully avoiding being drawn into the old man's scheme, his approach is not one of unmitigated altruism towards his owners.[46] Already in his opening monologue he mentions a factor of self-concern: his now ruined expectation for an easy retirement, dependent as it was upon the success of his master. Later at 213–15 the prospect of becoming Smikrines' property fills him with dread, and while this is not mentioned subsequently, the seed of motivation for his later actions is planted in the audience's mind. As Lombard aptly observes (p. 142), when Daos becomes the 'personal victim of the leading character's baseness', we see the introduction of a slave character who is not totally bound up with his master's welfare – his own is a significant factor too (cf. Habrotonon in *Epitrepontes*).

Chairestratos: Despite his description in the prologue as 'a really good character' (125, 130), one marked out by his generosity towards his niece in the grant of a dowry from his own resources, Chairestratos represents the most complex of all the figures in the play. This same man at 338–9 is described by Daos as having 'a gloomy side...one prone to depression'. Can the two be reconciled? The answer is likely to be 'no', unless one is prepared to stray beyond the boundaries of the text and to envisage factors

---

[46] Krieter-Spiro p. 120, cf. Gaiser (1973) p. 127.

not underpinned by our evidence. Yet inconsistency *per se*, such as ostensibly occurs here, is not restricted to this play; nor should we attribute it to the play's being an early product of the playwright, the sign of still immature control of dramatic technique as many suggest;[47] rather, it is a factor of all drama, a recognition that characters at times speak and act in accordance with the needs of the moment, a part of dramatic economy without which plays at times could not function.

Chaireas: In some respects Chaireas' name ('he that rejoices') seems deliberately designed to contradict the depiction of him within the first half of the play, though without doubt its implications will have become more prominent in the resolution of the problems facing him that figure in the last two Acts.[48] The minor role the young man fulfils in the extant text, however, can be accounted for by the emphasis the play places upon the older generation, and the fact that he represents in his very person the pathos of those threatened by Smikrines' machinations (see further, Commentary on 284ff.).

Cook: Like other 'professional' characters injected into Menander's plays the cook provides an element of broader comedy, serving at times to lighten what might otherwise be scenes of excessive pathos (*e.g.* the expulsion of Chrysis at *Samia* 369ff.). In the present case his entry rounds off Act I with a theme that mirrors the play's opening, but one that views Cleostratos' supposed death through quite different eyes. As often with such professional types, however, Menander seems deliberately to reverse what might be regarded as the stock themes normally attached to them, usefully detailed by Beroutsos p.73f.[49]: rather than being seen arriving (*e.g. Dyskolos* 393ff.), he is forced to depart; rather than his normal tendency to boast about his culinary expertise,[50] he here complains about his bad luck; rather than mentioning his pilfering tendencies,[51] Menander concentrates upon the failure of the

---

[47] Jacques (1998a), p. LXXXIIIff. provides an incisive defence of Menander's technique in the play; contrast Arnott (1979a) pp. 5–7.

[48] Groton p. 11 points to the incongruity inherent in the names of all three victims of Smikrines' greed: Cleostratos ('fame of the army'), and Chairestratos ('rejoicing in the army')

[49] Cf. Jacques 1998a, p. 16 n. 2, p. 17 n. 1.

[50] *E.g.* Philemon's *Stratiotes* fr. 82 K-A, 'What a tender fish I had, how I served it, not smothered with cheese or decked out with ornament, but even when cooked it was just like it had been when alive…', Alexis' *Lebes* fr. 129 K-A, *Pannychis* fr. 178 K-A, Hegesippus' *Adelphi* fr. 1 K-A, Dionysius *Thesmophoros* fr. 2 K-A, Plautus' *Pseudolus* 804ff.

[51] *E.g.* Dionysius fr. 3.5ff. K-A 'I'm taking you into enemy territory; take courage and rush

assistant Spinther to capitalise on the opportunity by not filling his oil-flask from the stores inside (cf. Arnott 1975, p. 149); rather than a character from the lower rungs of society, he demonstrates a degree of verbal sophistication (contrast Sikon in *Dyskolos*). As Brown 1987, p. 187f. observes, indeed, Menander may well have relied on the audience's knowledge of such figures' stock behaviour to point the contrast injected here.

Waiter: A rough-and-ready figure clearly designed both to complement the cook and to contrast with him: complement in his disappointment of a hiring, contrast in the crudity of his thinking when interacting with Daos, itself an incongruous factor in someone who must interact closely with his clients. In other contexts his function is detailed by Photius 598.84ff. as 'the character who is in charge of everything to do with a drinking party: the tables, settings, libations, music'.[52] The fact that elsewhere it is the cook who has charge of some of these tasks (cf. Menander's *Kolax* fr. 1, Athenion fr. 1.40 K-A 'We cooks begin things; we make the sacrifices, the libations') may account for the rivalry between them. (See further Krieter-Spiro p. 31f.)

Doctor: Appreciation of the character suffers as a result of extensive damage to the text, but clearly his role, or rather the role of Chaireas' friend who plays the part, is designed largely to enhance the depiction of Smikrines' gullibility seen in the Act's opening scene. At the same time it is important, especially when he first emerges from Chairestratos' house to announce his diagnosis, that his words have a degree of credibility sufficient to convince the old man that his brother is on the point of death, and thus achieve its aim of deflecting attention away from Cleostratos' sister. It is only later, in private conversation with Smikrines, that the full potential for burlesque appears.

---

in. They give you meat they've measured out and keep an eye on you; once it's cooked and tender, disguise the amount. There's a nice fat fish – the innards are yours, and if you can put a slice of something to one side, that's yours as well', Euphron fr. 1.13ff. K-A 'I...was the first to discover how to filch', *Fr. Adesp.* 1073 K-A, 1093.221ff. K-A, Plautus' *Mercator* 741ff.

[52] Cf. Antiphanes fr. 150 K-A 'I went and hired this waiter. He'll wash the place-settings, get the lamps ready, make the libations and whatever else is his job', Hesychius τ 1256 L, 'Waiter: not the cook but the one who takes care of all the preparations for drinking parties', Pollux III 41 'the man who takes care of everything connected with banqueting'.

The Role of Chance in the Play

Though Chance makes it clear at the end of the prologue that it is she who controls and directs the situation, the play itself operates very much upon the level of human motivation and action. True, the human characters are caught up in a situation that is not of their making, but within this they remain totally responsible for their actions and behaviour; they are no more puppets of the divine than Sostratos is in *Dyskolos*, or Polemon in *Perikeiromene*,[53] despite the passing references to chance that pervade the text.[54] As Vogt-Spira p. 77f., for instance, observes, one might restrict Chance's intervention to the mistaken identification of Cleostratos' body through the shield, hence the prominence given to the theme of misapprehension at 99–110, while what we actually see is the reaction of the human characters to this initial event. Further influence by Chance, however, may be detected in the timing of Cleostratos' return at the end of Act IV, though its relationship to the crisis of Chairestratos' death and Smikrines' interest in his second niece are unfortunately masked by severe loss of text.[55]

That chance (*tyche*) was a potent factor in contemporary thinking, however, needs little demonstration. It was already a factor centuries earlier, mentioned in Hesiod's *Theogony* 360 and the *Homeric Hymn to Demeter* 420. By the fourth century there was a shrine to Good Chance in Athens. It was analysed in Aristotle's *Physics* II, 4–6, and in many ways it seemed to dominate the very history of the period, which saw the world turned upside-down by Macedonian conquests, as Demetrius of Phaleron's discourse *On Chance* makes clear: 'If one were to take, not an infinite span of time or many generations, but only the last fifty years, one would recognise the harsh nature of Chance. Do you think that fifty years ago, if a god had foretold the future to them, the Persians or the king of Persia or the Macedonians or

---

[53] In *Dyskolos*, though Pan explains how he has made Sostratos fall head over heels in love with Knemon's daughter, we are immediately presented with a scene that emphasises instead the human aspect of that love, and it is this human aspect that subsequently dominates development of the theme (Ireland 1995 p. 20f.). In the case of *Perikeiromene* Polemon's hot temper is used by Misapprehension to begin the process of reuniting a family and converting Glykera's status from concubine into wife, but the goddess cannot be said to control its progress.

[54] See Commentary on line 18. Daos' plaintive outburst at 213–5 against the injustice of Chance apparently dooming him to be owned by a character like Smikrines, while apposite in its context, retains a comic element in the contrast it presents to the goddess' true intentions.

[55] See further, Vogt-Spira pp. 86–8.

the king of Macedon would ever have believed that by the present day not even the name of the Persians would survive, though they then ruled the whole inhabited world, while the Macedonians, whose name was previously unheard of, would control the world? Yet Chance, which is unconnected to our lives and changes everything contrary to our expectations, and reveals her power through surprises, even now, it seems, is showing everyone that though she has endowed the Macedonians with the wealth of the Persians, she has merely lent them this bounty until she decides to do something else with it' (Fr. Gr. H. II, 228.39, cited in Polybius XXIX, 21).

In other contexts Chance was frequently depicted as blind or blindfolded, indicative of the often inscrutable and irrational nature of events,[56] a theme that Daos himself gives voice to in his address to the audience at 248f. 'The ways of chance are uncertain'. In the present case, however, it is clear that Menander has chosen to emphasise something else: the goddess' active and beneficent side, actually intervening to promote and reward virtue.[57]

The Text of Aspis

Major sources:

Papyrus Bodmer IV (B).[58] *Aspis* occupies the third place (after *Samia* and *Dyskolos*) in this papyrus codex of the 3rd–4th century AD originally containing a larger selection of the playwright's works.[59] The extant text occupies seven sheets, 13 pages, 27.5 cm high and 13 cm wide, all of them suffering some form of damage at top and bottom, with occasional further loss of text at line beginnings and ends (*e.g* 34–9, 421–31, 452–63) caused by damage to the margins. Following 468 there is a major loss of two whole sheets before the resumption of text with a sheet that provides only the line beginnings of 469–508 and endings of 509–544. Minor improvement to

---

[56] Cf. Menander fr. 682 K-A 'Chance is blind and wretched', fr. 683 K-A 'Nothing that Chance does happens logically', fr. 853 K-A 'Oh Chance who delights in all manner of changes, it is a matter of reproach for you when this just man encounters undeserved misfortune', Diogenes Laertius V, 82 'He (Demetrius) said that not only was Wealth blind but Chance too, who was Wealth's guide.' The theme is inherent in Smikrines' own first reaction at line 18 to the news Daos brings, 'what an *unexpected* turn of events'.

[57] See further, Vogt-Spira pp. 75–88, Zagagi (1990) pp. 64–71 = (1994) pp. 143–9, Jacques (1998a) pp. XXI–XXIV, Groton p. 9f.

[58] *Papyrus Bodmer XXVI, Ménandre Le Bouclier*, eds R. Kasser and C. Austin, Cologny-Genève 1969.

[59] See further, Ireland (1995) p. 23f.

B was made possible by the later discovery of two fragments which had become separated from it and provide additional letters for 482–97 and 520–35 (= P. Cologne 904), as well as 487–498 and 525–35 (= P. Robinson inv. 38).[60] In all B provides evidence for lines 1–146, 149–400, 405–82, 497–520, 535–44.

Codex Florentinus (F). A fragment of papyrus dating from the first half of the 5th century AD and the first substantial evidence of the play to be discovered (1913). It contains lines 120–35, 145–60, 378–408, 410–29.

P. Oxy. 4094 (O). Found at Oxyrhynchus in Egypt and dated to the second half of the 5th century AD, this fragment of a papyrus codex contains lines 170–231 either wholly or partially preserved, with the exception of 189, which is omitted.[61]

In addition to textual loss, which can sometimes be ameliorated by restoration if this involves only parts of words, is the problem of interpretation. The text of our most important source, B, is written for the most part in small capitals which, apart from some orthographic confusions and omissions, present few difficulties. However, it was the practice of antiquity not to separate words by spaces and to be sparing in the use of punctuation and diacritical marks such as accents and breathings. In addition it is often only at the beginnings of Acts or where a new character enters the scene that a name is supplied in the margin or (more rarely) in the space between lines. More usually a change of speaker is only marked by 1) a *paragraphus*, a line drawn under the first one or two letters in a line to indicate that a change will take place somewhere within it or at the end, 2) a *dicolon* (:) at the actual position of the change. However, just as there are numerous occasions where, through carelessness or a failure to understand his original, the copyist has introduced or transmitted textual corruptions, so there are places where *paragraphi* and *dicola* have been omitted, wrongly placed, confounded with neighbouring letters or confused with punctuation. In addition to marking changes of speaker there are also times when the *dicolon* appears to indicate a change of addressee, *i.e.* the speaker turning form one person to another, or even a change of topic. Needless to say, editors are often divided as to the extent of such variation from normal usage.

---

[60] See further, Willis (1990), Gronewald (1992).
[61] See further, Jacques (1998a) pp. XCI–CXI.

The text printed here, while based on the Oxford Text of Sandbach's 2nd edition, has taken advantage of additions to the text made since the initial publication of the Bodmer papyrus in 1969, together with numerous alternative suggestions by editors and commentators.

Textual marks

1. Speakers

Δᾶος   Name given in the manuscript

(Δᾶος)   The manuscript indicates a change of speaker without identification

[Δᾶος]   A change of speaker lost in damage to the text

<Δᾶος> A change of speaker not given by the manuscript but supplied by conjecture

2. Text

[ ]   Material lost through damage to the manuscript

< >   Material inserted into the text to restore sense and metre

.   An in-line dot to indicate the vague sign of an extant letter or a letter lost

3. Translation

[ ]   Restoration of text lost in the manuscript or indicating the loss of text

( )   *Stage directions added to assist the reader: they do not occur in the manuscript.*

In Act IV *paragraphi* (__) and *dicola* (:) have been added to the Greek text, and in Act V *dicola*, in order to signal the evidence for a change of speaker.

Metre[62]

Iambic Trimeter

Apart from 516–44 the extant text of *Aspis* is written in iambic trimeters, its basic pattern created by alternation of long and short syllables:

$$v - v - \mid v - v - \mid v - v -$$

---

[62] More detailed analysis of Menander's metres can be found in Handley (1965) pp. 56–73, Gomme-Sandbach pp. 36–9, Raven pp. 31–5.

However, since the use of so rigid a pattern would not only result in a very stilted effect but would also create problems for the use of some words, it was open to variation in a number of ways:

1. The initial short syllable of each metron (*i.e.* each unit of v – v –) was regarded as anceps (i.e it could be either long or short) and could thus result in a spondaic (– –) effect, producing a metron of – – v –. Similarly, the final syllable of each line, though naturally long, could be replaced by a short syllable.
2. Resolution of a long syllable into two shorts could introduce either an anapaestic rhythm (v v –) at any point in the line with the exception of the second half of the final metron, or a dactyl (– v v) in the first half of each metron, or a tribrach (v v v) at any point except the second half of the final metron.
3. Regular insertion of a formal break between words (caesura) after either the first or third syllable of the second metron: v – v – | v // – v // – | v – v –, though this is not invariable and occasionally a mid-line caesura is found.
4. The law against a word-break after the first long syllable of the third metron producing a final cretic (– v –), observed in tragic trimeters (Porson's law), is not valid for comedy.

In a number of these features Menander, in common with other comic playwrights, adopts a freer approach to the trimeter than was the norm for tragedy. On occasion, though, the playwright clearly returns to the greater rigidity of the tragic pattern either to reinforce the atmosphere he seeks to produce, as at *Aspis* 1–9, or to parody it.

Trochaic tetrameter catalectic (516–44)
This reverses the iambic pattern to produce

$$- v - v \mid - v - v \mid - v - v - \mid - v -$$

with the possibility of the second short in each metron being anceps (*i.e.* either long or short) and diaeresis between the second and third metra. Naturally long syllables (*i.e.* the first and third in each metron), except for the last in the line, are open to resolution producing either tribrachs (v v v) or anapaests (v v –). Normally, as here, this metre was used to produce a lively effect.

MENANDER

THE SHIELD

ΑΣΠΙΣ

ΑΣΠΙΣ

Dramatis Personae

ΔΑΟΣ
ΣΜΙΚΡΙΝΗΣ
ΤΥΧΗ
ΜΑΓΕΙΡΟΣ
ΤΡΑΠΕΖΟΠΟΙΟΣ
ΧΑΙΡΕΣΤΡΑΤΟΣ
ΧΑΙΡΕΑΣ
ΙΑΤΡΟΣ
ΚΛΕΟΣΤΡΑΤΟΣ

ΧΟΡΟΣ

[ΔΑΟΣ] [   ] ἡμέραν ἄγω
ὦ τρόφιμε, τὴν [νῦν], οὐδὲ διαλογίζομ[αι
παραπλήσι᾽ ὡς τό[τ᾽ ἤλ]πισ᾽ ἐξορμώμεν[ος.
ᾤμην γὰρ εὐδο[ξο]ῦντα καὶ σωθέντα σ[ε
ἀπὸ στρατ<ε>ίας ἐν βίῳ τ᾽ εὐσχήμονι   5
ἤδη τὸ λοιπὸν καταβιώσεσθαί τινι,
στρατηγὸν ἢ σ[ύμ]β[ο]υλον ὠνομασμένον,
καὶ τὴν ἀδελφήν, ἧσπερ ἐξώρμας τότε
ἕνεκα, σεαυτοῦ νυμφίῳ καταξίῳ
συνοικιεῖν ποθ<ε>ινὸν ἥκοντ᾽ οἴκαδε,   10
ἐμοί τ᾽ ἔσεσθαι τῶν μακρῶν πόνων τινὰ
ἀνάπαυσιν εἰς τὸ γῆρας εὐνοίας χάριν.
νῦν δὲ σὺ μὲν οἴχει παραλόγως τ᾽ ἀνήρπασαι,
ἐγὼ δ᾽ ὁ παιδαγωγός, <ὦ> Κλεόστρατε,

---

3.   ἤλ]πισ᾽ Lloyd-Jones
4.   εὐδο[ξο]ῦντα Sandbach
11.   μακρῶν Austin, μακαρων Β

THE SHIELD

Characters (reconstructed from the text in order of appearance)

DAOS	One-time tutor to Cleostratos
SMIKRINES	Cleostratos' elder uncle
CHANCE	The goddess
COOK	
WAITER	
CHAIRESTRATOS	Cleostratos' younger uncle
CHAIREAS	Chairestratos' step-son
FALSE DOCTOR	A friend of Chaireas
CLEOSTRATOS	A young man, supposed dead

CHORUS

Non-speaking parts

A crowd of prisoners with pack animals, part of Cleostratos' booty
Spinther: An assistant to the cook
Doctor's assistant
Slaves

Act I

(*An urban street-scene showing two houses with perhaps a shrine between. The house on the right belongs to Chairestratos; that on the left to Smikrines. Daos, an aged slave and tutor, enters carrying a battered shield and accompanied by a sombre procession composed mainly of slaves and pack-animals. He addresses his absent master, whom he believes to be dead.*)

DAOS [ ] This is a [sorry] day for me, young master. I don't see things being remotely like I hoped when I set out. I thought you'd come back from the campaign safe and covered in glory, [5] that you'd live out the rest of your life in some style and dignity, with the title of General or Counsellor, and that you'd see your sister, for whose sake you went off on campaign, married to a man worthy of yourself, [10] once you returned home to the family eagerly waiting for you. And in my own case I thought there'd be some rest from my long labours in my old age in return for my services. But as it is, Cleostratos, you're gone, snatched away against all expectation,

24   *Menander*

τὴν οὐχὶ <σώ>σασάν σε τήνδ' ἐλήλυθα   15
ἀσπίδα κομίζων ὑπὸ δὲ σοῦ σεσωμένην
πολλάκις· ἀνὴρ γὰρ ἦσθα τὴν ψυχὴν μέγας,
εἰ καί τις ἄλλος.
ΣΜΙΚΡΙΝΗΣ   τῆς ἀνελπίστου τύχης,
ὦ Δᾶε.
(ΔΑ) δεινῆς.
(ΣΜ)   πῶς δ' ἀπώλετ', ἢ τίνι
τρόπῳ;
(ΔΑ) στρατιώτη, Σμικρίνη, σωτηρίας   20
ἔστ' ἔργον εὑρεῖν πρόφασιν, ὀλέθρου δ' εὔπορον.
(ΣΜ) ὅμως διήγησαι τὸ πρᾶγμα, Δᾶέ, μοι.
(ΔΑ) ποταμός τίς ἐστι τῆς Λυκίας καλούμενος
Ξάνθος, πρὸς ᾧ τότ' ἦμεν ἐπιεικῶς μάχαις
πολλαῖς διευτυχοῦντες, οἵ τε βάρβαροι   25
ἐπεφεύγεσαν τὸ πεδίον ἐκλελοιπότες.
ἦν δ' ὡς ἔοικε καὶ τὸ μὴ πάντ' εὐτυχεῖν
χρήσιμον· ὁ γὰρ πταίσας τι καὶ φυλάττεται.
ἡμᾶς δ' ἀτάκτους πρὸς τὸ μέλλον ἤγαγε
τὸ καταφρονεῖν· πολλοὶ γὰρ ἐκλελοιπότες   30
τὸν χάρακα τὰς κώμας ἐπόρθουν, τοὺς ἀγροὺς
ἔκοπτον, αἰχμάλωτ' ἐπώλουν, χρήματα
ἕκαστος ε[ἶ]χε πόλλ' ἀπελθών.
ΣΜ.   ὡς καλόν.
(ΔΑ) αὐτὸς δ'] ὁ τρόφιμος συναγ<αγ>ὼν χρυσοῦς τινας
ἑξακοσί]ους, ποτήρι' ἐπιεικῶς συχνά,   35
τῶν τ' αἰχ]μαλώτων τοῦτον ὃν ὁρᾷς πλησίον
ὄχλον, ἀπο]πέμπει μ' εἰς Ρόδον κα<ὶ> τω ξένω
φράζει κ]αταλιπεῖν ταῦτα πρός θ' αὑτὸν πάλιν
τάχιστ' ἀ]ναστρέφειν.

16. σεσωσμενην B, corr. Sandbach
20. στρατιώτῃ Austin, στρατιωτης B, στρατιώτην Stobaeus *Ecl*. IV,12,6, Sisti
22. διηγησασθαι B, corr. Austin
33. ἀπελθών Austin, ἀπελθεῖν B, Sisti, Σμ. Ἄπολλον, ὡς καλόν conjectured by Austin
34. suppl. Jacques, ἐνταῦθ' Austin; οὕτως δ' Sisti
35. ἑξακοσί]ους for restoration of the number cf. 83.
36. suppl. Kasser-Austin, ὄχλον αἰχ]μαλώτων Borgogno, Jacques
37. ὄχλον suppl. Kasser-Austin; ἀπο]πέμπει Kassel, δια]πέμπει Arnott
38. suppl. Kassel, κ]αταλιπόντ' αὐτὰ Pieters, Arnott; προσεαυτον B, corr. Kassel
39. suppl. Austin

while I, your tutor, [15] I'm the one who's come, bringing this shield which failed to save you, though often enough you brought it back safe. Yours was a gallant soul, if ever there was one.

(*An old man comes forward*)

SMIKRINES   Ah Daos, what an unexpected turn of events.

DAOS   Tragic!

SMI.   How did he die? What happened?

DAOS   [20] For a soldier, Smikrines, it's hard finding a reason for staying alive; a reason for dying is easy.

SMI.   Even so, Daos, tell me the facts.

DAOS   There's a river in Lycia called the Xanthos. We'd been successful there [25] in a fair number of engagements – the natives had taken to flight and abandoned the plain. But not being totally successful can be an advantage, so it seems. Someone who's taken a knock is also on his guard, but in our case over-confidence led to slack discipline in the face of what was to come. [30] Many men had left the protection of the camp and were looting the villages, laying waste to the fields, selling their booty. Everyone came back loaded with money.

SMI.   Splendid!

DAOS   Master [himself] had got together some [six hundred] gold coins, [35] quite a few cups, and that [crowd] of prisoners you see over there. He was sending me over to Rhodes and [told] me to leave them with a friend and get [straight] back to him again.

(ΣΜ)   τί οὖν δὴ γίνεται;

(ΔΑ) ἐγὼ μὲν ἐξώρμων ἔωθεν, ᾗ δ᾽ ἐγὼ   40

ἀπῆρον ἡμέρα λαθόντες τοὺς σκοποὺς

τοὺς ἡμετέρους οἱ βάρβαροι λόφον τινὰ

ἐπίπροσθ᾽ ἔχοντες ἔμενον, αὐτομόλων τινῶν

πεπυσμένοι τὴν δύναμιν ἐσκεδασμένην·

ὡς δ᾽ ἐγένεθ᾽ ἑσπέρα κατὰ σκηνάς θ᾽ ἅπαν   45

ἦν τὸ στρατόπεδον, ἔκ τε χώρας ἄφθονα

ἅπαντ᾽ ἐχούσης, οἷον εἰκὸς γίνεται·

<ἐ>βρύαζον οἱ πλεῖστοι.

(ΣΜ)   πονηρόν γε σφόδρα.

(ΔΑ) ἄφνω γὰρ ἐπιπίπτουσιν αὐτοῖς μοι δοκεῖ.

(ΣΜ) . .] . . . . . [. . .] . . . υσ . . φα . . [. .] . [50

(one or two lines missing)

[ΔΑ]   ] . . υπ[. . . .] . εγω

[   ]τα περὶ μέσας δ᾽ ἴσως

νύκτας φυλακ]ὴν τῶν χρημάτων ποούμενος

τῶν τ᾽ ἀνδραποδίων περιπατ[ῶ]ν ἔμπροσθε τῆς   55

σκηνῆς ἀκούω θόρυβον, οἰμω[γ]ήν, δρόμον,

ὀδυρμόν, ἀνακαλοῦντας αὐτοὺς ὀνόματι,

ὧν καὶ τὸ πρᾶγμ᾽ ἤκουον· εὐτυχῶς δέ τι

λοφίδιον ἦν ἐνταῦθ᾽ ὀχυρόν· πρὸς τοῦτ᾽ ἄνω

ἠθροιζόμεσθα πάντες, οἱ δ᾽ ἐπέρρεον   60

ἱππεῖς ὑπασπισταὶ στρατιῶται τραύματα

ἔχοντες.

(ΣΜ)   ὡς ὤνησ᾽ ἀποσταλεὶς τότε.

(ΔΑ) αὐτοῦ δ᾽ ἔωθεν χάρακα βαλόμενοί τινα

ἐμένομεν· οἱ δὲ τότε <δι>εσκεδασμένοι

ἐν ταῖς προνομαῖς αἷς εἶπον ἐπεγίνοντ᾽ ἀεὶ   65

ἡμῖν, τετάρτῃ δ᾽ ἡμέρᾳ προήγομεν

48–9.   πονηρόν...δοκεῖ given to Smikrines by Gallavotti, Jacques; dicolon after σφόδρα in B
54.   suppl. Kassel
58.   εκτυχως B, corr. Austin, ἐκ τύχης Turner, Jacques
63.   βαλλομενοι B, corr. Reeve
64.   suppl. Kassel
65.   επαιτιμοντ᾽ B, corr. Sandbach
66.   θ᾽ B, προσηγομεν B, corr. Sandbach

SMI.   So what happened next?

DAOS   [40] I set out at dawn and the day I left the natives began taking up position with a hill in front of them, unseen by our look-outs. They had learned from some deserters that our forces were scattered about. [45] When evening came and all those in the camp were in their tents, back from a countryside that had everything in abundance, the inevitable happened: most of our men were celebrating.

SMI.   Disgraceful!

DAOS   Yes, they must have made a sudden attack on them, I think.

       [50] [*c. three lines missing or seriously damaged in which Daos presumably refers to setting up camp after a day's travel*] It was about mid[night], and I was standing [guard] over the booty [55] and the prisoners, patrolling in front of the tent, when I heard an uproar: men crying out, running, wailing, shouting one another's names. It was from them I heard what had happened. Fortunately, there was a little hill there, a rallying point. [60] We all flocked up to it; then the wounded came streaming in – cavalry, guardsmen, infantry.

SMI.   How lucky you'd been sent away.

DAOS   At dawn we threw up a palisade, and there we stayed. Those who'd been away scattered about [65] on the raids I mentioned kept coming in to join us. Three days later we started out back again; we'd learned

πάλιν, πυθόμενοι τοὺς Λυκίους εἰς τὰς ἄνω
κώμας ἄγειν οὓς ἔλαβον.
(ΣΜ)   ἐν δὲ τοῖς νεκροῖς
πεπτωκότ᾽ εἶδες τοῦτον;
(ΔΑ)   αὐτὸν μὲν σαφῶς
οὐκ ἦν ἐπιγνῶναι· τετάρτην ἡμέραν   70
ἐρρι<μ>μένοι γὰρ ἦσαν ἐξῳδηκότες
τὰ πρόσωπα.
(ΣΜ)   πῶς οὖν οἶσθ᾽;
(ΔΑ)   ἔχων τὴν ἀσπίδα
ἔκειτο· συντετριμμένην δέ μοι δοκεῖ
οὐκ ἔλαβεν αὐτὴν οὐδὲ εἷς τῶν βαρβάρων.
ὁ δ᾽ ἡγεμὼν ἡμῶν ὁ χρηστὸς καθ᾽ ἕνα μὲν   75
κάειν ἐκώλυσεν διατριβὴν ἐσομένην
ὁρῶν ἑκάστοις ὀστολογῆσαι, συναγαγὼν
πάντας δ᾽ ἀθρόους ἔκαυσε, καὶ σπουδῇ πάνυ
θάψας ἀνέζευξ᾽ εὐθύς· ἡμεῖς τ᾽ εἰς Ῥόδον
διεπίπτομεν τὸ πρῶτον, εἶτ᾽ ἐκεῖ τινας   80
μείναντες ἡμέρας ἐπλέομεν ἐνθάδε.
ἀκήκοάς μου πάντα.
(ΣΜ)   χρυσοῦς φὴς ἄγειν
ἑξακοσίους;
(ΔΑ)   ἔγωγε.
(ΣΜ)   καὶ ποτήρια;
(ΔΑ) ὁλκὴν ἴσως μνῶν τετταράκοντ᾽, οὐ πλείονος,
κληρονόμε.
(ΣΜ)   πῶς; οἴει <μ᾽> ἐρωτᾶν, εἰπέ μοι,   85
διὰ τοῦτ᾽; Ἄπολλον. τἆλλα δ᾽ ἡρπάσθη;

---

68.   οὓς Austin, οις B, ὅσ᾽ Borgogno
73.   punctuation before συντετριμμένην Sandbach, after Jacques; δέ μοι Sandbach, διεμοι
B, δ᾽ ἐμοὶ Handley, διό μοι Kassel, Jacques
75.   ὁ δ᾽ Kassel, ουδ᾽ B
76.   κάειν Kassel, κλαιειν B, κλάειν Jacques,
77.   ἑκάστους Kassel
84–5.   <Σμ> οὐ πλείονος; <Δα> Kassel, Jacques

that the Lycians were taking their prisoners to their villages in the hills.

SMI.   And you saw him lying there among the dead?

DAOS   It wasn't possible to identify him [70] with any certainty since they'd been lying out for three days and their faces were all bloated.

SMI.   So how did you know it was him?

DAOS   He was lying with his shield. It was all buckled; that's why none of the natives had taken it, I suppose. [75] But that fine commander of ours didn't let us carry out individual cremations, realising that for each of us to gather the ashes individually would cause delay. So he heaped them all together and cremated them *en masse*, and once he'd given them a very speedy burial, he immediately broke camp. First, we slipped away to Rhodes, [80] then, after staying there a few days, we sailed here. That's the whole story.

SMI.   You say you've got six hundred gold coins?

DAOS   Yes.

SMI.   And drinking cups?

DAOS   Weighing in the region of forty minae, no more, [85] your 'inheritance'.

SMI.   What? Tell me – do you think that's why I'm asking? Apollo! Was the rest taken?

(ΔΑ)   σχεδὸν
τὰ πλεῖστα, πλὴν ὧν ἔλαβον ἐξ ἀρχῆς ἐγώ.
ἱμάτι' ἔνεστ' ἐνταῦθα, χλαμύδες· τουτονὶ
τὸν ὄχλον ὁρᾷς οἰκεῖον.
<ΣΜ>   οὐθέν μοι μέλει
τούτων· ἐκεῖνος ὤφελε ζῆν.
(ΔΑ)   ὤφελε.   90
παράγωμεν εἴσω τὸν ταλαίπωρον λόγον
ἀπαγγελοῦντες τοῦτον οἷς ἥκιστ' ἐχρῆ<ν>.
(ΣΜ) εἶτ' ἐντυχεῖν βουλήσομαί τι, Δᾶέ, σοι
κατὰ σχολήν· νυνὶ δὲ καὐτός μοι δοκῶ
εἴσω παριέναι σκεψόμενος τίν' ἂν τρόπον   95
τούτοις προσενεχθείη τις ἡμερώτατα.

ΘΕΟΣ ΤΥΧΗ
ἀλλ' εἰ μὲν ἦν τούτοις τι γεγονὸς δυσχερές,
θεὸν οὖσαν οὐκ ἦν εἰκὸς ἀκολουθεῖν ἐμέ.
νῦν δ' ἀγνοοῦσι καὶ πλανῶνται· τοῦτο δ[ὲ
[ὁ προσέ]χων μαθήσετα[ι   100
[..]ν .... [.] . [...] . [
ξ]ένος ἄλλος ὡς . [...]τοκαι[
ἥ τ' ἐπίθεσις τῶν βαρβάρων[ἐπεγένετο
ἐπέχων ἐσήμαιν', ἐξεβοήθου[ν αὐτίκα
ὁπλιζόμενοι <τὸ> παρὸν ἕκαστος πλησίον.   105
οὕτως ὁ μὲν παρὰ τῷ τροφίμῳ τούτου τότε
ὢν ἐξεβοήθει τήνδ' ἔχων τὴν ἀσπίδα
εὐθύς τε πίπτει· κειμένης δ' ἐν τοῖς νεκροῖς
τῆς ἀσπίδος τοῦ μειρακίου τ' ᾠδηκότος
οὗτος διημάρτηκεν· ὁ δὲ Κλεόστρατος   110

89. οὐθέν...ζῆν given to Smikrines by Kassel
92. ἔχρην Arnott, ἥκιστα χρῆν many, χρη B
93. σοι Austin, συ B; ησυχη in r. margin of B
94. δοκει B, corr. Kassel
100. ὁ προσέ]χων suppl. many
102. ὡς δ[' οὖν] τὸ κακ[ὸν αὐτοῖς ἐπέπεσεν suggested by Jacques
103. [ἐπεγένετο Jacques, [ἐγένετο καί Gronewald, [προσέρχεται Sbordone
104. [αὐτίκα Austin, [τ' αὐτίκα Jacques
105. τὸ suppl. Kassel

DAOS Pretty well most of it, except what I got at the outset. There's clothes in there, and cloaks; then there's this crowd you see – family property.

SMI. I'm not interested in them. [90] If only *he*'d survived!

DAOS If only. But let's get inside and tell this sad news to those who least deserve it. (*Daos begins to lead the prisoners and animals into Chairestratos' house*)

SMI. (*As Daos departs*) And then I'll want to have a talk with you about something, Daos – when you've time. (*To himself, now alone on stage*) But now I think [95] I'll go inside myself to work out how one might deal with these people – most gently.

(*Smikrines departs into his own house. The goddess Chance emerges onto the stage*)

CHANCE If something unpleasant had happened to these people, it wouldn't have been feasible for a goddess like me to come on next. As it is they're labouring under a misapprehension and are way off course. [100] [Anyone who pays attention] will realise this. [*one line almost totally absent*] another mercenary. When [the trouble broke out] and the attack by the natives [came], the alarm kept sounding; they rushed out [straight away] [105] armed with whatever each man had to hand. That's how the man who was next to this fellow's master at the time rushed out with the shield you've seen and was immediately cut down. What with the shield lying among the dead, and the young man all bloated, [110] this fellow came to completely the wrong conclusion. Cleostratos rushed out from there with someone

ἐκεῖθεν ἑτέροις ἐκβοηθήσας ὅπλοις
γέγον᾽ αἰχμάλωτος, ζῇ δὲ καὶ σωθήσεται
ὅσον οὐδέπω. ταυτὶ μὲν οὖν μεμαθήκατε
ἱκανῶς. ὁ γέρων δ᾽ ὁ πάντ᾽ ἀνακρίνων ἀρτίως
γένει μὲν αὐτῷ θεῖός ἐστι πρὸς πατρός,   115
πονηρίᾳ δὲ πάντας ἀνθρώπους ὅλως
ὑπερπέπαικεν· οὗτος οὔτε συγγενῆ
οὔτε φίλον οἶδεν, οὐδὲ τῶν ἐν τῷ βίῳ
αἰσχρῶν πεφρόντικ᾽ οὐδέν, ἀλλὰ βούλεται
ἔχειν ἅπαντα· τοῦτο γινώσκει μόνον,   120
καὶ ζῇ μονότροπος, γραῦν ἔχων διάκονον.
οὗ δ᾽ εἰσελήλυθ᾽ ὁ θεράπων ἐν γειτόνων
ἀδελφὸς οἰκεῖ τοῦδε τοῦ φιλαργύρου
νεώτερος, ταὐτὸν προσήκων κατὰ γένος
τῷ μειρακίῳ, χρηστὸς δὲ τῷ τρόπῳ πάνυ   125
καὶ πλούσιος, γυναῖκ᾽ ἔχων καὶ παρθένου
μιᾶς πατὴρ ὤν· ᾧ κατέλιπεν ἐκπλέων
ὁ μειρακίσκος τὴν ἀδελφήν· σύντροφοι
αὑταί θ᾽ ἑαυταῖς εἰσιν ἐκτεθραμμέναι.
ὧν δ᾽, ὅπερ ὑπεῖπα, χρηστὸς οὗτος μακροτέραν   130
ὁρῶν ἐκείνῳ τὴν ἀποδημίαν τά τε
οἰκεῖα μέτρια παντελῶς, τὴν παρθένον
αὐτὸς συνοικίζειν νεανίσκῳ τινὶ
ἔμελλεν, ὑῷ τῆς γυναικὸς ἧς ἔχει,
ἐξ ἀνδρὸς ἑτέρου, προῖκά τ᾽ ἐπεδίδου δύο   135
τάλαντα· καὶ ποιεῖν ἔμελλε τοὺς γάμους
νυνί. ταραχὴν δὲ τοῦτο πᾶσιν ἐμπεσὸν
τὸ νῦν παρέξει πρᾶγμα· τοὺς ἑξακοσίους
χρυσοῦς ἀκούσας οὑτοσὶ γὰρ ἀρτίως
ὁ πονηρός, οἰκέτας τε βαρβάρους ἰδών,   140
σκευοφόρα, παιδίσκας, ἐπικλήρου τῆς κόρης
οὔσης κρατεῖν βουλήσετ᾽ αὐτός, τῷ χρόνῳ
προέχων. μάτην δὲ πράγμαθ᾽ αὑτῷ καὶ πόνους

117.   ουτως B, corr. Page
123.   ἀδελφὸς van Leeuwen, Arnott, Jacques, ἀδελφὸς Koerte, Sandbach
127.   εκπλεων B, ετι νεαν F.
129.   αὑταί many, αὐταί Jacques
130.   ων δ᾽υπερ υπειπα B, corr. Kassel
133.   αυτος B, ουτος F

else's arms and has been taken prisoner. He's alive and will come back safe and sound – but not just yet. That's enough information for you on that. The old man, though, the one who was asking all the questions just now, [115] is his uncle on his father's side, and he's the last word in villainy. He recognises neither family nor friend, has never given a thought to the wickedness of his life; instead, he wants [120] everything for himself. That's the only thought he has. He lives like a hermit with an old serving woman. Next door, where the servant went in, is where this money-grubber's younger brother lives. He's the same relation [125] to the young man, but he's a really good character, as well as rich, with a wife and one daughter. It's in his charge that the young man left his sister when he sailed abroad, and the two girls have been brought up together. [130] As I said before, he's a good man, and when he saw the young man's absence would be rather long and his resources very modest, he planned to marry the girl to a young man, his wife's son [135] by her previous husband, and was providing a dowry of two talents. He was intending to have the wedding today, but this blow that's now befallen them all will upset everything. This scoundrel, who's just heard about the six hundred gold coins [140] and seen the foreign slaves, pack-animals, and female slaves, he'll want to get his hands on the girl himself now that she's an heiress, and because his age gives him prior claim. But once he's caused himself a lot of toil and tribulation to no purpose,

πολλοὺς παρασχὼν γνωριμώτερόν τε τοῖς
πᾶ[σ]ιν ποήσας αὑτὸν οἷός ἐστ᾽ ἀνὴρ   145
ἐ]πάνεισιν ἐπὶ τἀρχαῖα. λοιπὸν τοὔνομα
το]ὐμὸν φράσαι· τίς εἰμι, πάντων κυρία
τούτων βραβεῦσαι καὶ διοικῆσαι; Τύχη.

ΣΜ. ἵνα μή τις εἴπη μ᾽ ὅτι φιλάργυρος σφόδρα,
οὐκ ἐξετάσας πόσον ἐστ<ὶν> ὃ φέρει χρυσίον   150
οὐδ᾽ ὁπόσα τἀργυρώματ᾽, οὐδ᾽ ἀριθμὸν λαβὼν
οὐδενός, ἑτοίμως εἰσενεγκεῖν ἐνθάδε
εἴασα· βασκαίνειν γὰρ εἰώθασί με
ἐπὶ παντί· τὸ γὰρ ἀκριβὲς εὑρεθήσεται
ἕως ἂν οἱ φέροντες ὦσιν οἰκέται.   155
οἶμαι μὲν οὖν ἑκόντας αὐτοὺς τοῖς νόμοις
καὶ τοῖς δικαίοις ἐμμενεῖν· ἐὰν δὲ μή,
οὐθεὶς ἐπιτρέψει. τοὺς δὲ γινομένους γάμους
τούτους προειπεῖν βούλομ᾽ αὐτοῖς μὴ ποεῖν.
ἴσως μὲν ἄτοπον καὶ λέγειν· οὐκ ἐν γάμοις   160
εἰσὶν γὰρ ἥκοντος τοιούτου νῦν λόγου.
ὅμως δὲ τὴν θύραν γε κόψας ἐκκαλῶ
τὸν Δᾶον· οὗτος γὰρ προσέξει μοι μόνος.
ΔΑ. πολλὴ μὲν ὑμῖν ταῦτα συγγνώμη ποεῖν,
ἐκ τῶν δ᾽ ἐνόντων ὡς μάλιστα δεῖ φέρειν   165
ἀνθρωπίνως τὸ συμβεβηκός.
ΣΜ.   πρός σ᾽ ἐγὼ
πάρειμι, Δᾶε.
(ΔΑ)   πρὸς ἐμέ;
(ΣΜ)   ναὶ μὰ τὸν Δία.
ὤφελε μὲν οὖν ἐκεῖνος, ὃν δίκαιον ἦν,
ζῆν καὶ διοικεῖν ταῦτα καὶ τεθνηκότος
ἐμοῦ γενέσθαι τῶν ἐμῶν κατὰ τοὺς νόμους   170
κύριος ἁπάντων.
ΔΑ.   ὤφελεν. τί οὖν;
(ΣΜ)   τί γάρ;
πρεσβύτατός εἰμι τοῦ γένους. ἀδικούμενος

---

161. εἰσὶν Winnington Ingram, Henrichs, ἔστιν B, Sandbach

and makes it abundantly clear [145] to everyone what kind of a man he is, he'll end up where he was before. All that remains is to tell you my name. Who am I – in control of directing and managing all this? Chance.

(*As Chance departs, Smikrines emerges from his house*)

SMI.   So that no one can say that I'm totally fixated with money, [150] I didn't check how much gold it is he's bringing or how many items of silver; I didn't take an inventory of anything; I simply let them take it in here. They're always saying malicious things about me. The exact amount can be discovered [155] so long as those transporting it are slaves. I think they'll be willing to abide by the law and justice. If they don't, no one will let them get away with it. This wedding they're putting on, I intend to give them notice to call it off. [160] Perhaps it's out of place even to mention it. When news like this comes, people don't think of weddings. All the same, I'll knock at the door and call Daos out. He's the only one who'll pay any attention to me.

(*Smikrines approaches Chairestratos' door, but before he can knock, it opens and Daos emerges speaking to those inside*)

DAOS   It's perfectly understandable that you should behave like this, [165] but you should make every effort to bear what's happened as humanly as circumstances allow.

SMI.   It's you I'm here for, Daos.

DAOS   Me?

SMI.   Yes, by Zeus. If only he were alive! He was the right man to deal with these things and [170] be in charge of my whole estate after my death, in accordance with the law.

DAOS   Yes, if only. So?

SMI.   So? I'm the eldest in the family, but I have to put up with being

ἀεί τε πλεονεκτοῦντα τὸν ἀδελφόν τί μου
ὁρῶν ἀνέχομαι.
ΔΑ.   νοῦν ἔχεις.
(ΣΜ)   ἀλλ', ὦγαθέ,
οὐδὲ μετριάζει, νενόμικεν δὲ παντελῶς   175
οἰκότριβά μ' ἢ νόθον τιν', ὃς νυνὶ γάμους
ἐποίει διδοὺς οὐκ οἶδ' ὅτῳ <τὴν> παρθένον,
οὐκ ἐπανενεγκών, οὐκ ἐρωτήσας ἐμέ,
ἐμοὶ προσήκων ταὐτό, θεῖος ὢν ὅπερ
κἀγώ.
(ΔΑ) τί οὖν δή;
(ΣΜ)   πάντα ταῦτ' ὀργίζομαι   180
ὁρῶν. ἐπειδὴ δ' ἐστὶν ἀλλοτρίως ἔχων
πρὸς ἐμέ, ποήσω ταῦτ' ἐγώ· τὴν οὐσίαν
οὐχὶ καταλείψω τὴν ἐμὴν διαρπάσαι
τούτοις, ὅπερ δὲ καὶ παραινοῦσίν τινες
τῶν γνωρίμων μοι, λήψομαι τὴν παρθένον   185
γυναῖκα ταύτην· καὶ γὰρ ὁ νόμος μοι δοκεῖ
οὕτω λέγειν πως, Δᾶε. ταῦτ' οὖν ὃν τρόπον
πράττοιτ' ἂν ὀρθῶς καὶ σὲ φροντίζειν ἔδει·
οὐκ ἀλλότριος <εἶ>.
ΔΑ.   Σμικρίνη, πάνυ μοι δοκεῖ
τὸ ῥῆμα τοῦτ' εἶναί τι μεμεριμνημένον,   190
τὸ "γνῶθι σαυτόν". ἐμμένειν τούτῳ μ' ἔα
ὅσα τ' οἰκέτῃ δεῖ μὴ πονηρῷ ταῦτ' ἐμοὶ
ἀνάφερε καὶ τούτων παρ' ἐμοῦ ζήτει λόγον
χ[. .]ί[. .]ε.
(ΣΜ) ὡς [ὑπ]εστάλη[ς ἄρα   193a
ΔΑ. σῶν δ' εἴ με δο[ῦν]αι πρα[γμάτων βούλει λόγον,
πᾶν τὰς θεραπαίας ἐστι[ν ἀνακρίνειν τά τε   195

173. τ' εμου B, corr. Handley
174. ἔχεις. many, ἔχεις; Arnott
175. οὐδὲν West, Jacques, ουδε BO
177. suppl. Austin
182. ταῦτ' Del Corno
189. suppl. Sandbach
193a. suppl. Handley, Jacques
194. suppl. Handley, Jacques
195. π[.] . τας θεραπαινα . [Ο, πάντας θερά[ποντ]ας Kasser-Austin, πᾶν τὰς Handley, Jacques; line-end suppl. Jacques

done down and seeing my brother always taking advantage of me.

DAOS Quite.

SMI. Well, my dear chap, [175] he doesn't even meet me half way. He clearly takes me for some slave or illegitimate offspring, the way he was just now arranging a wedding, giving the girl to goodness knows who, and without consulting me or asking my opinion. He's the same relation as me, her uncle just like [180] I am.

DAOS So?

SMI. Seeing all this makes me angry. So, since he's behaving like a stranger to me, this is what I'll do. I'll not leave my estate for them to plunder. On the contrary, as some people [185] I know advise, I'll marry the girl here myself. In fact, it seems to me more or less what the law states, Daos. You yourself should have been thinking how this might be done correctly. You're not uninvolved.

DAOS Smikrines, it very much seems to me [190] that saying 'Know yourself' is the product of careful thought. So let me practise it. Anything that concerns an honest slave you can refer to me and seek my opinion on [ ].

SMI. How [remarkably] restrained [ ].

DAOS If [you want me] to give [an account] of your things, [195] you can

σώματα μεθ' ὦ[ν] ἐλάμβανον τὸ χ[ρυσίον·
σημεῖ' ἔπεστιν· [ὅσα σ]υνήλλαξέν τισι‹ν›
ἐκεῖνος ἀποδημῶν ἔχω φράζειν ἐγώ·
ταῦτ', ἂν κελεύῃ τίς με, δείξω καθ' ἕν, ὅπου,
πῶς, τοῦ παρόντος. περὶ δὲ κλήρου, Σμικρίνη,   200
ἢ νὴ Δί' ἐπικλήρου γάμων τε καὶ γένους
καὶ διαφορᾶς οἰκειότητος μηκέτι
Δᾶον ἄγετ' εἰς μέσον· τὰ τῶν ἐλευθέρων
αὐτοὶ δὲ πράττεθ' οἷς τὸ τοιοῦτον ἁρμόσει.
ΣΜ. δοκῶ δέ σοί τι πρὸς θεῶν ἀγνωμονεῖν;   205
(ΔΑ) Φρύξ εἰμι· πολλὰ τῶν παρ' ὑμῖν φαίνεται
καλῶν ἐμοὶ πάνδεινα καὶ τοὐναντίον
τούτων. τί προσέχειν δεῖ σ' ἐμοί; φρονεῖς ἐμοῦ
βέλτιον εἰκότως.
(ΣΜ)   σὺ νυνί μοι δοκεῖς
λέγειν ὁμοῦ τι· "μὴ πάρεχέ μοι πράγματ'" ἢ   210
τοιουτότροπόν τι. μανθάνω. τούτων τινὰ
ὀπτέον ἂν εἴη πρὸς ἀγορὰν ἐλθόντι μοι,
εἰ μή τις ἔνδον ἐστίν.
ΔΑ.   οὐδείς. ὦ Τύχη,
οἵῳ μ' ἀφ' οἵου δεσπότου παρεγγυᾶν
μέλλεις. τί σ' ἠδίκηκα τηλικοῦτ' ἐγώ;   215

ΜΑΓΕΙΡΟΣ
ἂν καὶ λάβω ποτ' ἔργον, ἢ τέθνηκέ τις,
εἶτ' ἀποτρέχειν δεῖ μισθὸν οὐκ ἔχοντά με,
ἢ τέτοκε τῶν ἔνδον κυοῦσά τις λάθρᾳ,
εἶτ' οὐκέτι θύουσ' ἐξαπίνης, ἀλλ' οἴχομαι
ἀπιὼν ἐγώ. τῆς δυσποτμίας.

196. suppl. Handley
197. ὅσα Del Corno
198. punctution after ἐγὼ Arnott; before, Sandbach
201. γαμων B, γαμου O
205. αγνωμονειν O, αμαρτανειν B
209. dicolon before σὺ in B; σὺ given to Daos by Jacques; traces of what might have been
Smikrines' name in r. margin of O
210. πράγματ' ἢ Handley, πράγματα B,O, Sandbach
219. οὐκ ἐπιθύουσ' Gallavotti

[interrogate] the slave girls and the people I brought the [gold] with about everything. The seals are there. [Any] contracts *he* made with people while abroad *I* can indicate. If instructed, I'll go through them point by point, indicating the place, [200] the circumstances, the witness. But as to inheritance or – goodness – an heiress, marriage, family, and degrees of kinship, don't ever involve Daos in them, Smikrines. Things that concern free men you deal with yourselves – you're the right people for such matters.

SMI. [205] For heaven's sake, do you think I have no feelings?

DAOS I'm from Phrygia. Many of the things that are fine to you seem dreadful to me and vice versa. Why take my views into account? Yours are naturally better than mine.

SMI. You seem [210] almost to be saying 'don't bother me' or something like it. I understand. (*Indicating Chairestratos' house*) I'd better go and see one of these people at the market, if there's no one inside.

DAOS No, no one. (*Smikrines exits to the right, leaving Daos on his own*) Oh Chance, what a master you're getting ready to hand me over to after the one I had! [215] What dreadful wrong have I done you?

(*A cook and his assistant appear from Chairestratos' house*)

COOK If ever I do get a booking, either someone dies – then I have to trot off without my fee, or one of the household has a baby after a hush-hush pregnancy – then all of a sudden the party's cancelled and [220] I'm off and away. What rotten luck!

ΔΑ.   πρὸς τῶν θεῶν,   220
μάγειρ', ἄπελθε.
ΜΑ.   νῦν δὲ τί δοκῶ σο[ι] ποεῖν;
λαβὲ τὰς μαχαίρας, παιδάριον, θᾶττόν ποτε.
δραχμῶν τριῶν ἦλθον δι' ἡμερῶν δέκα
ἔργον λαβών· ᾤμην ἔχειν ταύτας· νεκρὸς
ἐλθών τις ἐκ Λυκίας ἀφῄρηται βίᾳ   225
ταύτας. τοιούτου συμβεβηκότος κακοῦ
τοῖς ἔνδον, ἱερόσυλε, κλαούσας ὁρῶν
καὶ κοπτομένας γυναῖκας ἐκφέρεις κενὴν
τὴν λήκυθον; μέμνησο καιρὸν παραλαβὼν
τοιοῦτον. οὐ Σπινθήρ', Ἀριστείδην δ' ἔχω,   230
ὑπηρέτην δίκαιον· ὄψομαί σ' ἐγὼ
ἄδειπνον. ὁ δὲ τραπεζοποιὸς καταμενεῖ
εἰς τὸ περίδειπνον τυχὸν ἴσως.

ΤΡΑΠΕΖΟΠΟΙΟΣ   δραχμὴν ἐγὼ
ἂν μὴ λάβω, κοπτόμενος ὑμῶν οὐδὲ ἓν
αὐτὸς διοίσω.
ΔΑ.   πρόαγε· τοῦτον οὐδ . [.] . ς   235

(at least one line missing)

<ΤΡ> Δᾶος πάρεστι· τί ποτ' <ἀπ>αγγέλλων ἄρα;
[ἄ]νθρωπ[', ἄφ]ραστα.
(ΔΑ)   πάνυ μ[ὲν οὖν.
[ΤΡ] κακὸς κακῶ]ς ἀπόλοιο τοίνυν νὴ Δία
τοιό]νδ[ε π]εποηκώς, ἀπόπληκτε· χρυσίο[ν
ἔχων τοσοῦτο, παῖδας, ἥκεις δεσπότῃ   240
ταῦτ' ἀποκομίζων κοὐκ ἀπέδρας; ποταπός π[οτ' εἶ;
(ΔΑ) Φρύξ.

221. σο[ι] O, omitted in B
232. καταμενεῖ Austin, καταμένει Lloyd-Jones
235. οὐδὲ εἷς Austin; οὐδ' ὁρᾷς Handley
236. Δᾶος πάρεστι / προσῆλθε· τί ποτ' <ἀπ>αγγέλλων ἄρα; Gaiser from Fr. Adesp. 287 K
237. suppl. Koenen, Gaiser
239. suppl. Austin; τοιαῦτα Jacques; colon after ἀπόπληκτε Sandbach, Arnott, before
Austin, Jacques
241. suppl. Austin

DAOS In God's name, cook, push off.

COOK What do you think I am doing right now? (*He turns to his assistant*) Take the knives, boy, and quick about it. After ten days I land a job worth three drachmas and arrive. I thought it was money in the bank. Then some corpse [225] comes from Lycia and snatches them away. (*Noticing his assistant's lack of 'liberated' items from inside*) You useless article, those inside suffer a disaster like this; you see the womenfolk weeping and beating their breasts, and you still leave with an empty oil-flask. Think what a chance you had. [230] It's an honest assistant I've got, an Aristeides not a Spinther. I'll see you get no dinner. As for the waiter – he'll probably be staying for the funeral tea.

(*The cook and his assistant exit to the right. As they do, a waiter emerges from Chairestratos' house*)

WAITER If I don't get my drachma, I'll be just as cut up [235] as you lot are.

DAOS On your way. This [ ].

[*at least one line missing*]

WAITER Here's Daos; what news is he bringing then? [ ] marvellous, fellow.

DAOS Absolutely.

WAITER Be damned [to perdition] then, by Zeus, if [that's what] you've done, you idiot. [240] You had all that gold, and slaves, and you came back with them for your master? You didn't run off? Where [on earth are you] from?

DAOS Phrygia.

(ΤΡ)   οὐδὲν ἱερόν· ἀνδρόγυνος. ἡμεῖς μόνοι
οἱ Θρᾷκές ἐσμεν ἄνδρες· οἱ μὲν δὴ Γέται,
Ἄπολλον, ἀνδρεῖον τὸ χρῆμα· τοιγαροῦν
γέμουσιν οἱ μυλῶνες ἡμῶν.
ΔΑ.   ἐκποδὼν   245
ἀπαλλάγηθ' ἀπὸ τῆς θύρας· καὶ γάρ τινα
ὄχλον ἄλλον ἀνθρώπων προσιόντα τουτονὶ
ὁρῶ μεθυόντων. νοῦν ἔχετε· τὸ τῆς τύχης
ἄδηλον· εὐφραίνεσθ' ὃν ἔξεστιν χρόνον.

ΧΟΡΟΥ

ΣΜΙΚΡΙΝΗΣ
εἶέν. τί δή μοι νῦν λέγεις, Χαιρέστρατε;   250
ΧΑΙΡΕΣΤΡΑΤΟΣ
πρῶτον μέν, ὦ βέλτιστε, τὰ περὶ τὴν ταφὴν
δεῖ πραγματευθῆναι.
(ΣΜ)   πεπραγματευμένα
ἔσται. τὸ μετὰ ταῦθ', ὁμολόγει τὴν παρθένον
μηθενί· τὸ γὰρ πρᾶγμ' ἐστὶν οὐ σὸν ἀλλ' ἐμόν.
πρεσβύτερός εἰμι· σοὶ μέν ἐστ' ἔνδον γυνή,   255
θυγάτηρ, ἐμοὶ δὲ δεῖ γενέσθαι.
(ΧΑ)   Σμικρίνη,
οὐδὲν μέλει σοι μετριότητος;
(ΣΜ)   διὰ τί, παῖ;
(ΧΑ) ὢν τηλικοῦτος παῖδα μέλλεις λαμβάνειν;
(ΣΜ) πηλίκος;
(ΧΑ)   ἐμοὶ μὲν παντελῶς δοκεῖς γέρων.
(ΣΜ) μόνος γεγάμηκα πρεσβύτερος;
(ΧΑ)   ἀνθρωπίνως   260
τὸ πρᾶγμ' ἔνεγκε, Σμικρίνη, πρὸς τῶν θεῶν.
τῇ παιδὶ ταύτῃ γέγονε Χαιρέας ὁδὶ

---

244.   το B; τι Reeve
245.   ημων B, ὑμῶν Reeve; Jacques (following Reeve) gives τοιγαροῦν ... ἡμῶν to Daos
as an aside
255.   σοὶ Austin, συ B
256–9.   Webster assigned a speaking role to Chaireas

WAITER   Useless. A queer. It's only us Thracians are men. The Getae, by
           Apollo, real men! That's why [245] the mills are full of us.
DAOS   Push off, away from the door. (*The waiter leaves to the right*) There's
         another crowd of people here I see coming this way – drunk. You're
         the ones with sense. The ways of chance are uncertain. Enjoy
         yourselves while you can.

(*Daos disappears into Chairestratos' house as the chorus enter*)

CHORUS

Act II

(*Following the choral interlude Smikrines enters from the right accompanied
by two other figures, Chairestratos and Chaireas*)

SMI.   [250] Well, what do you say to me now, Chairestratos?
CHAIRESTRATOS   First, my good fellow, there's the funeral needs
           arranging.
SMI.   It'll be arranged. Afterwards, don't promise the girl to anyone.
          That's not your job but mine. [255] I'm the elder. You've a wife and
          daughter indoors. I need to get the same.
CH.   Smikrines, have you no sense of decency?
SMI.   Ha! And why's that?
CH.   Do you mean to marry a girl at your age?
SMI.   What age?
CH.   You strike me as being far too old.
SMI.   [260] Am I the only older man to be married?
CH.   Treat the situation like a human being, Smikrines, for God's sake.
          Chaireas here grew up with this girl and he's engaged to marry her.

σύντροφος ὁ μέλλων λαμβάνειν αὐτήν. τί οὖν
λέγω; σὺ μηδὲν ζημιοῦ· τὰ μὲν ὄντα γὰρ
ταῦθ᾽ ὅσαπέρ ἐστι λαβὲ σὺ πάντα, κύριος   265
γενοῦ, δίδομέν σοι· τὴν δὲ παιδίσκην τυχεῖν
καθ᾽ ἡλικίαν ἔασον αὐτὴν νυμφίου.
ἐκ τῶν ἰδ<ί>ων ἐγὼ γὰρ ἐπιδώσω δύο
τάλαντα προῖκα.
(ΣΜ)   πρὸς θεῶν, Μελιτίδη
λαλεῖν ὑπείληφας; τί φής; ἐγὼ λάβω   270
τὴν οὐσίαν, τούτῳ δὲ τὴν κόρην ἀφῶ
ἵν᾽, ἂν γένηται παιδίον, φεύγω δίκην
ἔχων τὰ τούτου;
ΧΑ.   τοῦτο δ᾽ οἴει; κατάβαλε.
(ΣΜ) "οἴει;" λέγεις; τὸν Δᾶον ὥς με πέμψατε
ἵν᾽ ἀπογραφὴν ὧν κεκόμικεν δῷ μοι.
(ΧΑ)   τί χρὴ   275
[   ]εμ᾽ ἢ τί <ποτε> ποι[εῖ]ν μ᾽ ἔδει;
(ΣΜ) . .] . μεν . . [
[. .]εστιν.
(ΧΑ)   ἐμὲ . [
ἀ]εὶ σὲ μὲν λαβ[όν]τα ταύτη[ν τὴν κόρην
αὐτὸν δ᾽ ἐκεῖνον τὴν ἐμὴν τῆ[ς οὐσίας   280
ὑμᾶς καταλείψειν τῆς ἐμαυτοῦ κυρίους.
ἀπαλλαγῆναι τὴν ταχίστην τοῦ βίου
γένοιτό μοι πρὶν ἰδεῖν ἃ μήποτ᾽ ἤλπισα.
ΧΑΙΡΕΑΣ
εἶέν· τὸ μὲν σὸν πρῶτον, ὦ Κλεόστρατε,
ἴσως ἐλεῆσαι καὶ δακρῦσαι κατὰ λόγον   285
πάθος ἐστί, δεύτερον δὲ τοὐμόν· οὐδὲ εἷς
τούτων γὰρ οὕτως ἠτύχηκεν ὡς ἐγώ.
ἔρωτι περιπεσὼν γὰρ οὐκ αὐθαιρέτῳ
τῆ[ς] σῆς ἀδελφῆς, φίλτατ᾽ ἀνθρώπων ἐμοί,

267.   αὑτῆς ἔασον / ἔασον αὑτῆς many
275.   δῷ μοι Austin; δη μοι B
276.   ποτε suppl. Sandbach
277f.   Sisti and Jacques assign the lines to Chaireas.
279.   ἀ]εὶ Austin; τὴν κόρην suppl. Arnott
280.   suppl. Handley, τῆς οἰκίας Austin

Here's what I suggest. No need for you to lose a thing. All this stuff,
265 take it, all of it; take title of it; we give you it. But the young
girl, let her find a husband of her own age. I'll give a dowry of two
talents from my own pocket.

SMI.   Good God! 270 Do you think you're talking to Melitides? What are
you suggesting? *I* take the goods and hand the girl over to *him* so
that, if they have a son, I should stand trial for having what's his?

CH.   Is that what you think? Forget it.

SMI.   'Think', you say? Send Daos to me 275 so that he can give me an
inventory of the things he's brought.

CH.   What must [ ] or what <on earth> should I have done?

SMI   [*one line badly mutilated*] (*Smikrines withdraws into his house*).

CH.   [*most of one line missing*]. [I] always [thought] you'd marry [the
girl] here 280 and he'd marry mine, and that I'd leave you both heirs
to my [estate]. Let me depart this life as soon as possible before I
see what I never thought I would (*With faltering steps he stumbles
to his door and disappears inside*).

CHAIREAS Oh well! I suppose it's only logical 285 to pity and mourn your
fate first, Cleostratos, and then my own, since none of these people
have suffered as much as I have. I didn't choose to fall in love with
your sister, you who were the dearest of humankind to me. 290 I did

οὐθὲν ποήσας προπετὲς οὐδ᾽ ἀνάξιον   290
οὐδ᾽ ἄδικον ἐδεήθην ἐμαυτῷ κατὰ νόμους
συνοικίσαι τὸν θεῖον ᾧ σὺ κατέλιπες
καὶ τὴν ἐμὴν μητέρα παρ᾽ ᾗ παιδεύεται.
ᾤμην δὲ μακάριός τις εἶναι τῷ βίῳ,
ἐλθεῖν δ᾽ ἐπ᾽ αὐτὸ τὸ πέρας οἰηθεὶς σφόδρα   295
καὶ προσδοκήσας οὐδ᾽ ἰδεῖν δυνήσομαι
τὸ λοιπόν· ἕτερον κύριον δ᾽ αὐτῆς ποεῖ
ὁ νόμος ὁ τοὐμὸν οὐδαμοῦ κρίνων ἔτι.
ΔΑ. Χαιρέστρατ᾽, οὐκ ὀρθῶς ποεῖς· ἀνίστασο·
οὐκ ἔ<σ>τ᾽ ἀθυμεῖν οὐδὲ κεῖσθαι. Χαιρέα,   300
ἐλθὼν παραμυθοῦ· μὴ ᾽πίτρεπε· τὰ πράγματα
ἡμῖν ἅπασίν ἐστιν ἐν τούτῳ σχεδόν.
μᾶλλον δ᾽ ἄνοιγε τὰς θύρας, φανερὸν πόει
σαυτόν· προήσει τοὺς φίλους, Χαιρέστρατε,
οὕτως ἀγεννῶς;
ΧΑ.   Δᾶε παῖ, κακῶς ἔχω.   305
μελαγχολῶ τοῖς πράγμασι<ν>· μὰ τοὺς θεούς,
οὐκ εἴμ᾽ ἐν ἐμαυτοῦ, μαίνομαι δ᾽ ἀκαρὴς πάνυ·
ὁ καλὸς ἀδελφὸς εἰς τοσαύτην ἔκστασιν
ἤδη καθίστησίν με τῇ πονηρίᾳ.
μέλλει γαμεῖν γὰρ αὐτός.
ΔΑ.   εἰπέ μοι, γαμεῖν;   310
δυνήσεται δέ;
(ΧΑ)   φησὶν ὁ καλὸς κἀγαθός,
καὶ ταῦτ᾽ ἐμοῦ διδόντος αὐτῷ πάνθ᾽ ὅσα
ἐκεῖνος ἀποπέπομφεν.
ΔΑ.   ὦ μιαρώτατος.
(ΧΑ) μιαρὸν τὸ χρῆμ᾽· οὐ μὴ βιῶ, μὰ τοὺς θεούς,
εἰ τοῦτ᾽ ἐπόψομαι γενόμενον.
Δα.   πῶς ἂν οὖν   315
τοῦ σφόδρα πονηροῦ περιγένοιτό τις;

295.   ἐλθεῖν Austin, ελθων B; πέρας Kassel, τερας B
300.   οὐκ ἔ<σ>τ᾽ Austin, ουκετ᾽ B

nothing rash or improper or wrong; I asked your uncle, in whose care you left her, and my mother, by whom she's being looked after, to give her to me in lawful marriage. I thought my life was blessed. [295] I really thought and felt I'd reached my very goal, but in future I won't even be able to see her. The law makes her someone else's and dismisses my claim out of hand.

(Daos appears at Chairestratos' door addressing the old man inside)

DAOS   Chairestratos, what you're doing isn't right. Get up. [300] You can't lie there in despair. *(Turning to address Chaireas on stage)* Chaireas, come and comfort him. Don't let him give up. All our futures pretty well depend on him. *(Turning to address Chairestratos again)* No, instead, open the doors and show yourself. Will you let your family down [305] with such feeble behaviour, Chairestratos?

CH.   *(Emerging from inside, assisted by slaves)* Daos, my boy, I'm in a bad way. These events have plunged me into depression. By God, I can't control myself. I'm within an inch of going completely out of my mind. My precious brother is driving me into such a state of distraction with his villainy. [310] He's planning to get married – him!

DAOS   Did you say married? Will he be able to?

CH.   That's what our fine gentleman says, and that's even though I'm offering him everything Cleostratos sent home.

DAOS   The blackguard!

CH.   Blackguard indeed. I'll die, by God, [315] if I see it happen.

DAOS   So how could one out-manoeuvre the foul villain?

48   *Menander*

<ΧΑ>   πάνυ
ἐργῶδες.
(ΔΑ)   ἐργῶδες μέν, ἀλλ' ἔνεσθ' ὅμως.
(ΧΑ) ἔνεστι;
<ΔΑ>   καὶ μὴν ἄξιον φιλονικίας,
νὴ τὴν Ἀθηνᾶν, τοὐργον.
(ΧΑ)   εἴ τις πρὸς θεῶν
ὥρμηκ[. . .] τωνδ' ε[320

(one or two lines missing)

<ΔΑ>   ]δύο τάλ[αντα
[   ]αυτῷ τιν' ἐλπίδ[
[   ] . φ[ε]ρόμενον εὐθὺς ἐπ[
προπετῆ, διημαρτηκότ', ἐπτ[οημένον
ὄψει μεταχειριεῖ τε τοῦτον εὐπόρω[ς.   325
ὃ βούλεται γὰρ μόνον ὁρῶν καὶ προσδοκῶν
ἀλόγιστος ἔσται τῆς ἀληθείας κριτής.
(ΧΑ) τί οὖν λέγεις; ἐγὼ γὰρ ὅ τι βούλει ποεῖν
ἕτοιμός εἰμι.
(ΔΑ)   δεῖ τραγῳδῆσαι πάθος
ἀλλοῖον ὑμᾶς· ὃ γὰρ ὑπεῖπας ἀρ[τίως   330
δόξαι σε δεῖ νῦν, εἰς ἀθυμίαν τινὰ
ἐλθόντα τῷ τε τοῦ νεανίσκου πάθει
τῆς τ' ἐκδιδομένης παιδός, ὅτι τε τουτονὶ
ὁρᾷς ἀθυμοῦντ' οὐ μετρίως ὃν νενόμικας
υἱὸν σεαυτοῦ, τῶν ἄφνω τούτων τινὶ   335
κακῶν γενέσθαι περιπετῆ· τὰ πλεῖστα δὲ
ἅπασιν ἀρρωστήματ' ἐκ λύπης σχεδόν

317.   paragraphus at beginning of line; *dicola* after πάνυ ἐργῶδες and ὅμως; attribution of
parts variously interpreted; πάνυ ἐργῶδες given to Chairestratos by Lloyd-Jones and Austin
318.   change of speaker after ἔνεστι suggested by Arnott, who gives καὶ μὴν ... τοὐργον to
Daos; Sandbach and Jacques assign to Chairestratos
324.   suppl. Austin
329.   δεῖ Austin, τε B
330.   ουκ'αλλοιον B, corr. Kassel, οἰκεῖον Ferrari, Jacques, οὐκ ἄλλο γ' Sisti

CH.   It won't be easy.

DAOS Not at all easy, but possible, nevertheless.

CH.   Possible?

DAOS Yes, and the task well worth the effort, by Athena.

CH.   By God, [320] if a man's made a start [ ].

[one or two lines missing]

DAOS [ ] two tal[ents] [ ] him some hope [ ]. You'll see him immediately carried along [ ] at full speed for [ ], totally on the wrong track, [carried away with excitement]. [325] And you'll easily deal with him. Someone who only sees and thinks what he wants will be a very poor judge of reality.

CH.   So what are you suggesting? I'm ready to do whatever you want.

DAOS You folk must put on a different tragic act. [330] What you just said, you must now pretend to happen: you've fallen into a state of despair at what the young man and his intended bride have suffered, and because you see Chaireas here, whom you've thought of as your own son, in total despair, [335] you've fallen victim to one of these sudden afflictions. Most ailments for people the world over stem

ἔστιν· φύσει δέ σ᾽ ὄντα πικρὸν εὖ οἶδα καὶ
μελαγχολικόν. ἔπειτα παραληφθήσεται
ἐνταῦθ᾽ ἰατρός τις φιλοσοφῶν καὶ λέγων   340
πλευρῖτιν εἶναι τὸ κακὸν ἢ φρενῖτιν ἢ
τούτων τι τῶν ταχέως ἀναιρούντων.
(ΧΑ)   τί οὖν;
(ΔΑ) τέθνηκας ἐξαίφνης· βοῶμεν "οἴχεται
Χαιρέστρατος" <καὶ> κοπτόμεθα πρὸ τῶν θυρῶν.
σὺ δ᾽ ἐγκέκλ<ε>ισαι, σχῆμα δ᾽ ἐν μέσῳ νεκροῦ   345
κεκαλυμμένον προκείσεταί σου.
(ΧΑ)   μανθάνεις
ὃ λέγει;
(ΧΑΙΡΕΑΣ) μὰ τὸν Διόνυσον, <οὐ> δῆτα.
<ΧΑ>   οὐδ᾽ ἐγώ.
(ΔΑ) ἐπίκληρος ἡ θυγάτηρ ὁμοίως γίνεται
ἡ σὴ πάλιν τῇ νῦν ἐπιδίκῳ παρθένῳ·
τάλαντα δ᾽ ἐ<σ>τὶ σοὶ μὲν ἑξήκοντ᾽ ἴσως,   350
ταύτῃ δὲ τέτταρ᾽, ὁ δὲ φιλάργυρος γέρων
ἀμφοῖν προσήκει ταὐτό –
(ΧΑ)   νυνὶ μανθάνω.
(ΔΑ) εἰ μὴ πέτρινος εἶ. τὴν μὲν εὐθὺς ἄσμεν[ος
δώσει παρόντων μαρτύρων τρισχιλί[ων
τῷ πρῶτον αἰτήσαντι, τὴν δὲ λήψεται –   355
(ΧΑ) οἰμώξετ᾽ ἄρα.
(ΔΑ)   – τῷ δοκεῖν. τήν τ᾽ οἰκίαν
πᾶσαν διοικήσει, περίεισι κλειδία
ἔχων, ἐπιβάλλων ταῖς θύραις σημεῖ᾽, ὄναρ
πλουτῶν.
<ΧΑ>   τὸ δ᾽ εἴδωλον τί τοὐμόν;

338.   οἶδε Kassel
343.   βοῶμεν Kassel, βοησομεν B
344.   καὶ suppl. Austin
347.   οὐ suppl. Austin; οὐδ᾽ ἐγώ assigned to Chairestratos by Austin, B continues with Chaireas
356.   οἰμώξετ᾽ ἄρα τῷ δοκεῖν· given to Chairestratos by B, Sandbach, τῷ δοκεῖν given to Daos by Kassel, Austin, Arnott, Jacques; after δοκεῖν dicolon in B
357.   διοικήσει many, διοικησαι B, διοικήσας Page, Jacques
359.   changes of speaker suggested by Kassel

from grief – pretty much. I'm well aware that you've got a gloomy
side to you, one prone to depression. Then a doctor [340] will be called
in, someone who weighs up all the symptoms and says the trouble's
pleurisy or phrenitis or one of those ailments that carry people off
quickly.

CH.   And then?

DAOS   Suddenly you're dead. We cry 'Chairestratos is gone', and we beat
our breasts outside the door. [345] You're locked up inside while your
dummy corpse, all shrouded up, will lie in view.

CH.   Do you understand what he's saying?

CHAIREAS   By Dionysus, no.

CH.   Neither do I.

DAOS   Your daughter becomes an heiress, just like the girl currently being
claimed. [350] Your estate, though, is in the region of sixty talents, hers
four, and the old moneygrubber is the same relation to both.

CH.   Now I understand.

DAOS   You're dense if you don't. Straight away he'll be happy to hand her
over before umpteen witnesses [355] to the first man who asks for her
hand, and then he'll take your daughter –

CH.   He'll be sorry!

DAOS   – or so he thinks. He'll organise the whole house, go round with the
keys, put seals on the doors, a rich man in his dreams.

CH.   What about my dummy?

<ΔΑ>   κείσεται,
ἡμεῖς τε πάντες ἐν κύκλῳ καθεδούμε[θα,   360
τηροῦν]τες αὐτὸν μὴ προσέλθῃ· πολλ[α

(one or two lines missing)

[   ]ν τοὺς φί[λους
[   ]ου πεῖραν ἔσται τιν[
[   ]πως ἦλθεν ἐπὶ τὴν οἰκίαν   365
[   ]τις γέγον' ὀφείλων· εἴ τινι
[   ] διπλάσιον εἰσπράττει πάνυ.
<ΧΑ> εὖ γ' ἐσ]τὶν ὃ λέγεις, Δᾶε, τοῦ τ' ἐμοῦ τρόπου.
<ΔΑ> τιμωρί]αν δὲ τοῦ πονηροῦ τίν' ἂν ἔχοις
λαβεῖν] σφοδροτέραν;
(ΧΑ)   λήψομαι, νὴ τὸν Δία,   370
ὧν] μ' ὠδύνηκε πώποτ' ἀξίαν δίκην·
τὸ γ]ὰρ λεγόμενον ταῖς ἀληθείαις "λύκος
χ]ανὼν ἄπεισι διὰ κενῆς".
(ΔΑ)   πράττειν <δὲ> δεῖ
ἤ]δη. ξενικόν τιν' οἶσθ' ἰατρόν, Χαιρέα,
ἀστεῖον, ὑπαλαζόνα;
(ΧΑΙΡΕΑΣ)   μὰ τὸν Δί', οὐ πάνυ.   375
(ΔΑ) καὶ μὴν ἔδει.
(ΧΑΙΡΕΑΣ)   τί δὲ τοῦ<το>; τῶν ἐμῶν τινα
ἥξω συνηθῶν παραλαβὼν καὶ προκόμιον
αἰτήσομαι καὶ χλανίδα καὶ βακτηρίαν
αὐτῷ, ξενιεῖ δ' ὅσ' ἂν δύνηται.
ΔΑ.   ταχὺ μὲν οὖν.
(ΧΑ) ἐγὼ δὲ τί ποῶ;
(ΔΑ)   ταῦτα <τὰ> βεβουλευμένα·   380

---

361.   suppl. Handley, Borgogno; πολλ[ὰ μὲν Gaiser, πολλ[άκις many
367–70.   division of speakers uncertain
368.   suppl. Austin
369.   suppl. Kassel
370.   λαβεῖν suppl. Austin; εἰπεῖν Handley, εὑρεῖν Borgogno

DAOS It'll lie there [360] and we'll all sit around it [on watch to make sure] he doesn't come close. Many [*one or two lines missing*] the fr[iends] there'll be [a chance] of testing [ ] [365] came to the house [ ] someone who owes a debt [ ]. If something [ ] you exact fully twice the amount.

CH. [It's good], what you say, Daos, and just after my own heart.

DAOS What better [vengeance] could you [exact] from the scoundrel?

CH. [370] By Zeus, I'll exact a fitting penalty for all the trouble he's ever caused me. It's true, as the saying goes, 'The wolf's jaws are open, but he'll go off hungry'.

DAOS So, we need to act now. (*Turning to address Chaireas*) Do you know a foreign doctor, Chaireas, [375] a smooth operator, something of a charlatan?

CHAIREAS No by Zeus, not at all.

DAOS Well, you should.

CHAIREAS What about this? I'll get one of my friends and come back. I'll beg a wig and a fancy cloak and stick for him. He'll do his best to put on a foreign accent.

DAOS OK, but be quick about it. (*Chaireas exits to the right*)

CH. [380] But what am *I* to do?

DAOS What we planned. Die and good luck to you.

54   Menander

ἀπόθνησκ᾽ ἀγαθῇ τύχῃ.
(ΧΑ)   ποήσω· μηδένα
ἔξω γ᾽ ἀφίετ᾽, ἀλλὰ τηρεῖτ᾽ ἀνδρικῶς
τὸ πρᾶγμα.
(ΔΑ)   τίς δ᾽ ἡμῖν συνείσεται;
(ΧΑ)   μόνῃ
δεῖ τῇ γυναικὶ ταῖς τε παιδίσκαις φράσαι
αὐταῖς ἵνα μὴ κλάωσι, τοὺς δ᾽ ἄλλους ἐᾶν   385
ἔνδον παροινεῖν εἴς με νομίσαντας νεκρόν.
(ΔΑ) ὀρθῶς λέγεις. εἴσω τις ἀγέτω τουτονί.
ἕξει τιν᾽ ἀμέλει διατριβὴν οὐκ ἄρ<ρ>υθμον
ἀγωνίαν τε τὸ πάθος, ἂν ἐνστῇ μόνον,
ὅ τ᾽ ἰατρὸς ἡμῖν πιθανότητα σχῇ τινα.   390

ΧΟΡΟΥ

(ΣΜ) ταχύ γ᾽ ἦλθ᾽ ὁ Δᾶος πρός με τὴν τῶν χρημάτων
φέρων ἀπογραφήν, πολύ τ᾽ ἐμοῦ πεφρόντικε.
Δᾶος μετὰ τούτων ἐστίν. εὖ γε, νὴ Δία·
καλῶς ἐπόησε. πρόφασιν εἴληφ᾽ ἄσμενος
πρὸς αὐτὸν ὥστε μὴ φιλανθρώπως ἔτι   395
ταῦτ᾽ ἐξετάζειν, ἀλλ᾽ ἐμαυτῷ συμφόρως·
τὰ γὰρ οὐ φανερὰ δήπουθέν ἐστι διπλάσια·
ἐγᾦδα τούτου τὰς τέχνας τοῦ δραπέτου.
(ΔΑ) ὦ δαίμονες, φοβερόν γε, νὴ τὸν Ἥλιον,
τὸ συμβεβ[ηκός· ο]ὐκ ἂν ᾠήθην ποτὲ   400
ἄνθρωπο[ν εἰς] τοσοῦτον οὑτωσὶ ταχὺ
πάθος ἐμ[π]εσεῖν. σκηπτός τις εἰς τὴν οἰκίαν
ῥαγδαῖος ἐμπέπτωκε.

381–6.   attribution of parts disputed. *Paragraphi* in 381, 383, 386. *Dicola* after τύχῃ (381),
πρᾶγμα and συνείσεται (383), νεκρόν (386). μηδένα...πρᾶγμα assigned to Daos by Kassel,
μηδένα...συνείσεται assigned to Daos by Jacques. B has the marginal note χαιρεας at 383,
suggesting assignment of τίς ... συνείσεται to Chaireas (Austin), corrected by many
382.   ἔξω γ᾽ Sandbach, ἔξω δ᾽ Austin, Sisti, εξωτ᾽ B
387–90.   assigned to Daos by Gaiser, to Chaireas by Austin
400–6.   either missing from B or severely mutilated
400–2.   suppl. Vitelli

CH.   I'll do just that. Don't let anyone outside. Be resolute in guarding the scheme.

DAOS   Who'll be in on it with us?

CH.   Only my wife and the girls themselves need be told, [385] so they don't get upset. Let the rest vent their spleen against me indoors thinking me dead.

DAOS   Quite right. Someone take him inside. (*Slaves help the old man back inside his house*) This disaster will provide some fine entertainment and sport, that's for sure – once it gets going [390] and our doctor puts on a reasonably persuasive act. (*He disappears into Chairestratos' house*)

CHORUS

Act III

(*Smikrines appears from his house*)

SMI.   My, Daos really has been speedy in coming to me and bringing the inventory of goods. A fat lot of thought he's given me! Daos is in with them. Well, fine, by Zeus! He's done well. I'm glad he's given me an excuse [395] to check this stuff over without any further 'by your leave', but looking to my own interests. There's doubtless twice as much that he's not declaring. I know this runaway's tricks.

(*Daos bursts out of Chairestratos' house rushing about the stage in a state of high emotion*)

DAOS   Oh ye powers that be! It's dreadful, by Helios, [400] what's happened. I would never have thought a man could succumb so quickly to such a calamity. A furious storm has descended on the house.

56   *Menander*

(ΣΜ)   τί ποτε βούλεται;

(two lines missing)

[. . . .]μονον βα[. . .]ν[
[. . .] . . [. .]αρα[405
ἄνθρωπος· ὐπ[
(ΔΑ) "οὐκ ἔστιν ὅστις π[άντ' ἀνὴρ εὐδαιμονεῖ".
πάλιν εὖ διαφόρως. ὦ πολ[υτίμητοι θεοί,
ἀπροσδοκήτου πράγμα[τος] καὶ ἀ[
(ΣΜ) Δᾶε κακόδαιμον, ποῖ τρέχ[εις;]
[ΔΑ]   καὶ το[ῦτό που.   410
"τύχη τὰ θνητῶν πράγματ', οὐκ εὐβουλία."
ὑπέρευγε. "θεὸς μὲν αἰτίαν φύει βροτοῖς,
ὅταν κακῶσαι δῶμα παμπήδην θέλῃ."
Αἰσχύλος ὁ σεμνά –
(ΣΜ)   γνωμολογεῖς, τρισάθλιε;
(ΔΑ) "ἄπιστον, ἄλογον, δεινόν."
(ΣΜ)   οὐδὲ παύσεται;   415
(ΔΑ) "τί δ' ἐστ' ἄπιστον τῶν ἐν ἀνθρώποις κακῶν;"
ὁ Καρκίνος φήσ'· "ἐν μιᾷ γὰρ ἡμέρᾳ
τὸν εὐτυχῆ τίθησι δυστυχῆ θεός."
εὖ πάντα ταῦτα, Σμικρίνη.
(ΣΜ)   λέγεις δὲ τί;
(ΔΑ) ἀδελφός – ὦ Ζεῦ, πῶς φράσω; – σχεδόν τί σου   420
τέθνηκεν.
(ΣΜ)   ὁ λαλῶν ἀρτίως ἐνταῦθ' ἐμοί;
τί παθών;
(ΔΑ)   χολή, λύπη τις, ἔκστασις φρενῶν,
πνιγμός.
(ΣΜ)   Πόσειδον καὶ θεοί, δεινοῦ πάθους.
(ΔΑ) "οὐκ ἔστιν οὐδὲν δεινὸν ὧδ' εἰπεῖν ἔπος
οὐδὲ πάθος –"

406. ἄνθρωπος many
408. suppl. many
409. καια[B interpreted by Austin
410. καὶ το[ῦτό που Austin, καί π[ου τόδε Jacques
416. τί δ' van Leeuwen, τισδ B
421–31. line endings missing from B

SMI. What on earth does he mean?
      [*two lines are missing, three badly damaged*]
      406 [ ] the man [ ].
DAOS 'There is no man who is completely fortunate'. Again, wonderfully put. Oh ye much [honoured gods], what an unexpected and [ ] event.
SMI. 410 Daos, you wretch, where are you rushing off to?
DAOS (*'Failing' to hear Smikrines' question*) Then there's this one: 'Chance, not Prudence, (rules) the affairs of men'. Marvellous. 'God plants guilt in mortal men when a house he wishes utterly to destroy'. Aeschylus of the noble sentiments –
SMI. Spouting mottos, you wretched creature?
DAOS 415 (*Still failing to acknowledge Smikrines's presence*) 'Incredible, illogical, dreadful!'
SMI. Will he never stop?
DAOS 'What of mortals' woes is past belief?' That's what Carcinus says. 'For in a single day God brings the fortunate to misery'. (*Finally turning to Smikrines*) All these are well said, Smikrines.
SMI. What are you talking about?
DAOS 420 Your brother – oh Zeus, how can I tell you? – he's at death's door.
SMI. When he was here talking to me just now? What happened?
DAOS Bile, grief, a fit of madness, choking.
SMI. Poseidon and the gods, what a terrible affliction!
DAOS 'There is nought so terrible to relate, 425 no affliction...'

(ΣΜ)　　　　ἀποκναίεις σύ.
(ΔΑ)　　　　　　　　"τὰς γὰρ συμφορὰς　　　　　　425
ἀπροσδοκήτους δαίμον[ες δι]ώρισαν."
Εὐριπίδου τοῦτ' ἐστί, τὸ δὲ Χαιρήμονος,
οὐ τῶν τυχόντων.
(ΣΜ)　　　　　　εἰσελήλυθ[εν] δέ τις
ἰατρός;
(ΔΑ)　οἴχεται μὲν οὖν ὁ Χαιρέας
ἄξων.
(ΣΜ)　τίν' ἆρα;
(ΔΑ)　　　　　τουτονί, νὴ τ[ὸν Δία,　　　　　430
ὡς φαίνεται. βέλτιστ', ἐπίσπ[ε]υ[δ'.
[ΙΑΤΡΟΣ]　　　　　　　　　　[
(ΔΑ) "δυσάρεστον οἱ νοσοῦντες ἀπορίας ὕπο."
ΣΜ. ἐμὲ μὲν, ἐὰν ἴδωσιν, εὐθὺς ἄσμενον
φήσουσιν ἥκειν, τοῦτ' ἀκριβῶς οἶδ' ἐγώ,
αὐτός τ' ἐκεῖνος οὐκ ἂν ἡδέως μ' ἴδοι　　　　435
[. . . . .]ιδ' ἄτοπον οὐδ' ἐπηρόμην

(about sixteen lines missing)

[　　　　　　　　　　] . ν·

(one line missing)

<ΙΑ.>　　　　　　　　]αὑτῷ τὰν χολὰν
[　　　　　　　　　　]ιμε[. .]. δη φερομένῳ　　　　440
[　　　　　　　]διὰ τὰ[ν] παρεῦσαν ἀπορίαν.
(ΣΜ)　　　　] . ω· τοῦτο [δ]ήπου μανθάνω.
(ΙΑ)　　　　　]σαν.
(ΣΜ)　　　　　　ταῦτα δήπου μανθάνω.

426.　suppl. Vitelli, δαιμονων[B, δαιμον[....]ωρισαν F, δαιμόνων [τις] ὥρισεν Austin
hesitantly
427.　τοδεχα[B, το[....]υρημενον F, restored by Handley
429.　ουθεις B, ουδεις F inserted before οἴχεται; οὐθείς deleted by Vitelli, οὐθείς· οἴχετ' οὖν
ὁ Χαιρέας Koerte, Austin
430.　νὴ τ[οὺς θεούς Austin
439.　αὑτῷ Austin

SMI.   You're wearing me out.

DAOS   'For tragedies unforeseen the gods ordained.' One's from Euripides, the other Chairemon, not run-of-the-mill writers.

SMI.   Has a doctor come?

DAOS   Chaireas has gone [430] to fetch one.

SMI.   Who?

(*Chaireas enters from the right bringing with him the 'doctor' and his 'assistant'*)

DAOS   This one, by [Zeus], so it seems. (*He addresses the 'doctor'*) Hurry along, sir.

DOCTOR   [ ]. (*Chaireas, the 'doctor' and his 'assistant' disappear into Chairestratos' house*)

DAOS   'By their helplessness are sick men hard to please'. (*He exits into Chairestratos' house*)

SMI.   (*To himself*) If they see *me*, they'll say I've come at once because I'm glad. I know that for a fact. [435] He himself wouldn't be pleased to see me. [ ] odd, and I didn't make any enquiries.

[*c. eighteen lines missing*].

DOCTOR   (*Having emerged from Chairestratos' house, the 'doctor' outlines to Smikrines the patient's state of health*) [ ] His bile [ ] [440] carrying [ ] on account of his current helplessness.

SMI.   [ ] I quite understand.

DOCTOR   [ ]

SMI.   I quite understand.

(ΙΑ)   α]ὐτὰς τὰς φρένας δή μοι δοκῶ
[   ] ὀνυμάζειν μὲν ὧν εἰώθαμες   445
ἀμὲς φ]ρενῖτιν τοῦτο.
<ΣΜ>   μανθάνω. τί οὖν;
οὐκ ἔστ]ιν ἐλπὶς οὐδεμία σωτηρίας;
<ΙΑ> καίρια] γάρ, αἱ μὴ δεῖ σε θάλπεν διὰ κενᾶς,
τὰ τοια]ῦτα.
(ΣΜ)   μὴ θάλπ᾽, ἀλλὰ τἀληθῆ λέγε.
(ΙΑ) οὐ πάμπαν οὗτός ἐστί τοι βιώσιμος.   450
ἀνερεύγεταί τι τᾶς χολᾶς· ἐπισκοτεῖ
[   ]εντ . [. .] καὶ τοῖς ὄμμασι
[π]υκνὸν ἀναφρίζει τε καὶ
[   ] . ας ἐκφορὰν βλέπει.
(ΣΜ)   ].
[ΙΑ]   προάγωμες, παῖ.
(ΣΜ)   σέ, σὲ   455
[   ].
[ΙΑ]   μετακαλῇς;
(ΣΜ)   πάνυ μὲν οὖν.
[δ]εῦρ᾽ ἀπὸ τῆς θύρας ἔτι.
(ΙΑ)   οὐ]κ ἂν βιῴης τὼς τέως.
(ΣΜ)   ] αὐτὸν εὔχου τρόπον ἔχειν
[   ] . πολλὰ γίνεται.
(ΙΑ)   γέλα   460
[   ] φαμὶ τᾶς ἐμᾶς τέχνας
[σ]ὺ δ᾽ αὐτός μοι δοκῇς
[. .] . [.] . [.] κεαλην ἀλλ᾽ ὑπέρχεταί τι τοι
φθιτικὸν νόσαμα· σὺ μὲν ὅλως θανάτους βλέπεις.

446. ἀμὲς suppl. Kassel; change of speaker after τοῦτο indicated by Austin
447. hesitantly assigned to Smikrines as a question by Austin. B implies the doctor spoke
447–9a
448. suppl. Kassel
449. suppl. Austin
453. π]υκνὸν Austin
458. τεως B, θεώς (*i.e.* θεούς) Gronewald, Jacques, deriving βιῴης from βιάω not βιόω
463. κε<φ>αλὴν Austin

DOCTOR   His very mind, I'm thinking ⁴⁴⁵ [ ]. The normal name we give it
      is phrenitis.
SMI.   I see. And then? Is there *no* hope of recovery?
DOCTOR   If I'm not to give you false hopes, [such] things are [fatal].
SMI.   No false hopes, just tell the truth.
DOCTOR   ⁴⁵⁰ He isn't at all likely to live. He's bringing up bile; his sight
      is failing; [ ] his eyes as well [ ]; he's foaming a lot at the mouth and
      [ ] he looks fit for burial.
SMI.   ⁴⁵⁵ [ ].
DOCTOR   (*The 'doctor' and his 'assistant' begin to leave*) Let's be on our
      way, boy.
SMI.   Hey, you. [ ].
DOCTOR   [ ] You calling me?
SMI.   Yes indeed [ ] over here, a bit further away from the door.
DOCTOR   (*Peering at Smikrines*) [ ] You may [not] live as hitherto.
SMI.   [ ] You pray to have the same constitution. ⁴⁶⁰ [ ] Many things
      happen.
DOCTOR   You can laugh [ ]. I say that my skill [ ]. You yourself seem to
      me [ ], but there's a consumptive condition creeping over you. You
      really look like death. (*The 'doctor' and his 'assistant' exit right*)

(ΣΜ) ἦ που φέρουσιν αἱ γυναῖκες ὡσπερεὶ   465
ἐκ πολεμίων· ἐπιτάττεται τοῖς γείτοσι
διὰ τῶν ὑδορροῶν.
ΔΑ.   θορυβήσω τουτονί,
ἀλλ' ὅπερ ἔπραττον πρατ[

(about two hundred and five lines missing)

[ΧΟΡΟΥ]

(?) β<u>οῶ</u>σι<ν> "οἴχεθ['
(?) <u>Χαιρ</u>εστρατ[470
ΣΜ. <u>δεδρ</u>ακιχ'. [
<u>τέθ</u>νηκε. :
(?)   [
<u>ἀνὴ</u>ρ ἀπόλ[ωλε
(?) τὸ μηδὲ ἕ[ν
ὑπόλοιπο[ν   475
<u>ἤδη</u> δικαι[
(?) <u>ἐνθ</u>άδ[
(?) <u>μὴ</u> δια[
(?) <u>γραμμ</u>[
(?) ον . [480
ου. [
<u>υ</u> . . . . [
(?) <u>λαμ</u>βαν[
(ΣΜ?) τὸ μὲν ἐγγυᾶν[
ἴσως τοιούτου π[485
ὑμῖν γενομεν[
πολλῶν σεπ[. . .]υρο[
ἕτοιμος ἀποφαίνει[ν

465–8.   assigned to Daos by Jacques, who believes that δαος, written above θορυβησω in B
is misplaced, despite the paragraphus at the line beginning and the dicolon after ὑδορροῶν
in 467; 465–8 given to Daos by Gaiser
466.   ἐπιτάττεται Austin, ἔπειτ' ἄγεται Gaiser, επιταττετε B
467.   ησυχη written above θορυβήσω as a stage direction
471.   δεδρακιχ' B, δέδρακεν, οἴχετ' Austin
487.   σεπ[. . .]υρο B, σ' ἐποδύρομαι Gronewald

SMI. 465 (*To himself*) Well, I expect the women are looting the estate as if it were enemy territory. Instructions are being passed to the neighbours via the water channels.

DAOS (*Daos emerges from Chairestratos' house speaking to himself*) I'll throw him into confusion, [I'll carry on doing] what I was doing [*c. 205 lines missing*].

[CHORUS]

Act IV

(*Smikrines is on stage; he hears cries off stage announcing the death of Chairestratos and is joined by another character is in a state of high emotion who confirms the news*)

SMI.? They're shouting, 'He's gone' [ ].
       – – 470 Chairestratos,

SMI.   He has done [ ]
       – – He's dead [ ]
       – –The man has perished [ ]
       – – Nothing [ ]
       475 remaining [ ]
       now right [ ]
       – – here [ ]
       – – no [ ]
       – – written [ ]
       480 [ ]
       [ ]
       [ ]
       – –Take [ ]

SMI.? The question of betrothal [ ]
       485 perhaps of such (a person) [ ]
       happening to you people [ ]
       of many [I bewail?]
       ready to produce [ ]

ὅσ' ἂν κελεύῃς πρα[
ἐναντίον σου ταῦτα . [490

ΚΛΕΟΣΤΡΑΤΟΣ
ὦ φιλτάτη γῆ, χαῖρ[ε
προσεύχομαί σοι μ[
πολλῶν σεσωκὼς· εἰ[
πάρειμι τὴν σωτηρ[ίαν
ὁρῶ δεομένην τὴν[495
εἰ δ' αὖ διαπέφευγε[ν
ὁ Δᾶος εὐτυχῶς ἀπ[
νομίσαιμ' ἐμαυτό[ν.
παιητέα δ' ἐσθ' ἡ θύρ[α.
(ΔΑ)   [τίς τὴν θύραν;
(ΚΛ) ἐγώ.
(ΔΑ)   τίνα ζητεῖς; ὁ μ[ὲν γὰρ δεσπότης   500
τῆς οἰκίας τέθνηκ[ε
(ΚΛ) τέθνηκεν; οἴμοι δυ[στυχής
[ΔΑ]   [
καὶ μὴ 'νόχλει πενθ[οῦσι
(ΚΛ) οἴμοι τάλας· ὦ θεῖ'. ἀν[
ἄνθρωπέ μοι κακόδ[αιμον   505
(ΔΑ)   [
μειράκιον. ὦ Ζεῦ,[
(ΚΛ) Δᾶε, τί λέγεις;
(ΔΑ)   . [
ἔχω σε;
(ΚΛ)   κατ[

(about five or six lines missing)

489. οσαν B
492. μ[όλις ἐμαυτὸν ἐκ πόνων suppl. Gronewald
493. πολλῶν Willis, Gronewald, πολλον B; εἰ [δὲ καὶ σῶς οἴκαδε suppl. Gronewald
499. θύρ[α suppl. Austin, who also suggested ending the line [παῖδες. Δα. τίς εἶ;
500. suppl. Austin
502. suppl. Austin
505. suppl. Austin

whatever you order [ ]
490 these things before you [ ].

(*The stage is cleared of characters. After a moment Cleostratos enters right, from the harbour*)

CLEOSTRATOS   Greetings, oh dearest land [ ] I pray to/for you [ ] I, saved
from many [dangers?]. If [ ] I am here, [having found?] safety, [ ]
495 I see [my sister not?] in need [ ] and/but if by good fortune Daos
has escaped [ ] I'd think myself [blessed?]. I must knock at the door.
(*He approaches Chairestratos' door and tries to attract attention. A voice answers from inside*)

DAOS   [Who knocked?]
CLEO.   500 I did.
DAOS   Who are you looking for? [The master] of the house is dead.
CLEO.   Dead? Oh no! Poor [man/me]
DAOS   [ ] and don't bother us in our mourning. [ ]
CLEO.   Oh, good grief! Uncle! [Open the door] 505 for me, you wretched
fellow.
DAOS   (*Daos appears at the door*) [ ] young man. Oh Zeus! [ ]
CLEO.   Daos, what are you saying?
DAOS   (*Embracing his young master*) [ ] Is it you I hold?
CLEO.   [ ] [*some eight or nine lines missing or badly damaged*].

[	]θαν<ε>ι	
[	]τι :	510
[	]μηδὲ σύ	
[	ἀ]νοίγετε	
[	] . ι	
[	ἐγρ]ηγορώς	
[	] . ομεν.:	515

[ΧΟΡΟΥ]

[ΔΑ?]	] . ὁμολογῶ	
[	] . ς ἴσος	
[	γυ]ναῖκες ἄσμεναι	
[	]ι τἄνδοθεν	
[	]ν παρείλκυσεν	520
[	γί]νεται διπλοῦς γάμος	
[	τὴν] ἑαυτοῦ θυγατέρα	
[	] τὴν ἀδελφ<ιδ>ῆν πάλιν	
[	] . . [. .]τὴν δὲ πᾶσαν οὐσίαν	
[	]ν τ[αῦ]τα πάνθ᾽ ἕξει πέρας. :	525
[	]αν που περιπατεῖ τὸν γείτονα	
[	]ηρον οὑτοσί γε, νὴ Δία	
[	]Χαιρέα, πρόσελθέ μοι	
(ΧΑΙΡΕΑΣ)	]πάντα, νὴ τὸν Ἥλιον. :	
(ΔΑ?)	πάρεσ]τιν ἀρτίως Κλεόστρατος. :	530
(ΧΑΙΡΕΑΣ)	]ν μὲν οὖν ᾤμην ἐγώ	
[	]ψεις εἶτα ποῦ ᾽στιν; :	
(ΔΑ?)	ἐνθαδί	
[	]τ᾽ ἀσπάσαι φίλον λαβών	
[	]ανεις προσέρχεται	
[	παρ]αλαλῶν εὐωχίαν	535
[	παρ]έξων δῆλός ἐστιν οὑτοσί·	

523. αδελφην B, ἀδελφ<ιδ>ῆν Lloyd-Jones
530. suppl. Austin, Gronewald
535. παρ]αλαλῶν Willis, Jacques
536. suppl. Gaiser

⁵¹⁰ [ ] don't you
[ ] (you folk) open
[ ]
[ ] having woken,
⁵¹⁵ [ ]. (*Cleostratos and Daos exit into Chairestratos' house*)

[CHORUS]

Act V

(*A character (Daos?) emerges from Chairestratos' house announcing the implications of Cleostratos' return – Chairestratos' return from the dead and a double wedding being prepared*)

DAOS?   I agree [ ] equal [ ] glad women [ ] the things from inside [ ] ⁵²⁰ he spun things out [ ] a double wedding is under way [ ] his own daughter [ ] his niece again [ ] the whole estate [ ] ⁵²⁵ in the end he'll have all this. [ ]

(?)   I suppose he's walking about, the neighbour [ ] this man here, by Zeus [ ].

DAOS Chaireas, come here to me. (*Chaireas enters*)

CHAIREAS?   [ ] everything, by Helios.

DAOS ⁵³⁰ [ ] Cleostratos has just arrived.

CHAIREAS   [ ] I thought [ ]. Then where is he?

DAOS Here [ ] take and greet him as a friend [ ]. (*Chaireas is sent indoors. Daos sees Smikrines about to enter the stage*) He's approaching ⁵³⁵ [ ] chatting, festivity [ ]. *He's* clearly about to cause [trouble] and if

[   ]ᾶν τε κόπτῃ πολλάκις
[   ]υτῳ κοσμιώτερον ποῶ
[   ]ηρ ἐστί μοι τρόπον τινά. :
(ΣΜ?)   ]ον τοῦτ' ἔχειν τὴν ἐγγύην   540
[   ]ειναι μαρτύρων δ' ἐναντίον
[   ] Χαιρέᾳ δ' ἃ βούλεται
[   ] γὰρ τήνδ' ἐγὼ τὴν οὐσίαν
[   ]μοι παρενοχλοῦντος < > :

Fragment of Pap. B not located within the established text:

recto   verso

]ερφνη[   ] . [. .] . [
] . νταπ[   ] νυμφιον [
]ενην[[δη μαλ[

Fragment assigned to the end of Act III by Gaiser (ZPE 51, 1983, 37–43)

[ΔΑ]   ]ιν ἔκδικος [
ὁ λ]όγος τυράννου καὶ νόμος φυ[
[ΣΜ] ἔα·] τί ἤγεσθ'; ἡ κόρη δὲ καὶ προσ[ῆν;
[ΔΑ] ὀδ]υρομένη δὲ πρὸς μόρον τ[
ἔμυ]ξεν "αῖ πάτερ, πάτερ", καὶ οὐ[5
"ὦ π]εριπλάκηθί μοι, πάτερ, τὸ τ[
[ΣΜ] πρ]ὸς τὴν παροῦσάν μοι τύχη[ν
[ΔΑ] κο]ὺκ ἐν καλῷ καλὸς κρίτη[ς

Gaiser fragment
1. εἰ καὶ] πᾶ[σ]ιν ἔκδικος [δοκεῖ Gaiser
2. φυ[λακτέος Gaiser φυ[λάττεται Kannicht
3. suppl. Gaiser, προσ[ίζανε Jacques
4. τ[ὸν ἄθλιον Kannicht
5. ἔμυ]ξεν Gaiser, ᾤμω]ξεν Kannicht; καὶ οὐ[κ Gaiser

he knocks a lot [ ] I make (him) better behaved [ ] I have to in some way. (*Daos withdraws to one side*)

SMI.? (*To himself*) [ ] [540] for me the betrothal involves this [ ] before witnesses [ ] to Chaireas what he wants [ ] for I, this estate [ ] of someone causing me annoyance.

Fragment of Pap. B not located within the established text:

> [ ] bridegroom [ ]
> [ ] very [ ]

Fragment assigned to the end of Act III and supplemented by Gaiser:

[DAOS?] unjust [ ] the word and law of a tyrant [must be obeyed]

[SMI.?] [Ha!] What have you put on one side? Was the girl there as well?

[DAOS?] Grieving at death [ ] [5] she [sobbed], 'Oh, father, father,' and [ ]. 'Oh, take me in your arms, father,' [ ].

[SMI.?] To my present fortune [ ].

[DAOS?] And not a good judge in a good situation...

Book fragments assigned to Menander's Aspis
Stobaeus *Eclogue* IV, 8, 7

ὦ τρισάθλιοι
<ὅσοι> τι πλέον ἔχουσι τῶν ἄλλων· βίον
ὡς οἰκτρὸν ἐξαντλοῦσιν οἱ τὰ φρούρια
τηροῦντες, οἱ τὰς ἀκροπόλεις κεκτημένοι·
εἰ πάντας ὑπονοοῦσιν οὕτω ῥᾳδίως   5
ἐγχειρίδιον ἔχοντας αὐτοῖς προσιέναι,
οἵαν δίκην διδόασιν.

Stephanus Byzantinus, p. 324 Meineke

Ἑλληνίς, οὐκ Ἰβηρίς

Erotian, *Voc. Hippocr.*, e 17

ἔμυξεν

Pollux, *Onomasticon* 10, 137

κανδύτανες

Stobaeus Eclogue *4, 8, 7*
2.   <ὅσοι> τι Borgogno, <οὗτοι> τί Kaibel

Book fragments assigned to Menander's Aspis

Stobaeus *Eclogue* IV, 8, 7

> Wretched men who have more than the others. What a pitiable existence they endure, those who guard the forts and hold the citadels. [5] If they suspect that everyone can approach them so easily, dagger in hand, what a price they pay.

Stephanus Byzantinus, p. 324 Meineke

> A Greek girl not Iberian

Erotian, *Voc. Hippocr.*, e 17

> He/she sobbed.

Pollux, *Onomasticon* 10, 137

> box

COMMENTARY

1–18. Daos' monologue: Though the text is marred by the loss of its initial words (the general sense is readily restored from the context, hence [sorry]), it is clear that what survives represents the play's actual beginning, and as the foundation upon which subsequent action is based Daos' monologue shows clear evidence of careful planning by Menander in terms of theme, structure and style. The sombre tone, evident from the outset, adherence to the stricter (tragic) forms of metre in the first nine lines (discussed in detail by Cusset p. 129–32) and the heavy implications of death (Katsouris 1975a, p. 106–8 compares Euripides' *Hecuba* and *Troades*, cf. Lombard p. 124) all present a highly charged and unexpected opening for what purports to be a comedy. This was clearly designed to arrest the audience's attention with a tantalising amount of information: the speaker is a slave, a former tutor; his master is young and went on campaign for the sake of his sister; the future expectations of all three have been frustrated; the young man's shield has returned but its owner has not. Underpinning the expository importance of the speech is its structural form: following the opening address (lines 1–3) Menander introduces an outer framework formed by the failure to return home ('I thought you'd come back...this shield which failed to save you'). Within this comes first, concern for the sister, and only then Daos' thoughts for his own future, the order of presentation aptly mirroring his priorities of concern: seven lines for his master's family (4–10), a mere two (11–12) for himself (Blundell p. 72, cf. Krieter-Spiro p. 121). Stylistically too the greater length and grammatical complexity of sentences in the speech – the fact that 'I thought ... services' constitutes a single structure in the Greek – introduce an economy of form, allowing the maximum of information to be injected within a small compass (Ireland 1981, cf. Katsouris 1975b, p. 111), which in turn reveals the speech as an initial prologue in its own right. On a smaller scale too Menander mirrors techniques often found in the plays of Euripides: placing significant words and phrases at the two important positions within lines, their beginnings and ends, as in the case of *master* (2), *your sister* (8), *in my own case* (11), *while I* (14), which mark the shift of attention from one character to another, or *shield* at the beginning of line 16. In addition, there is the exploitation of linguistic balance in 'you're gone...while I' (13–14) and (lit.) 'the shield that *did not save you*, but often *by you was saved*' (15–16) (see further Feneron p. 92).

2. young master: Daos' use of the term immediately identifies his servile status within the household, expanded upon at 14 by his description as 'tutor' lit. *paidagogos*, given the task of attending a son while outside, in particular on his way to school. His close association with Cleostratos thus forms a natural basis for the subsequent display of loyalty and intervention to thwart Smikrines' plan, just as his role within the family underpins his depiction as intelligent (cf. Krieter-Spiro p. 14).

7. General or Counsellor: Since it was specifically for his sister's sake that Cleostratos went on campaign, the reference here serves to bolster thoughts of the young man's success ('covered in glory') and to contrast with the theme of disappointed hopes, rather than to represent any real aim for personal advancement.

8–9. for whose sake…: The reference to military service here and in line 5 strongly suggests that Cleostratos' role was that of mercenary, but with the added poignancy:

1) that his motivation was altruistic, aimed at securing a dowry that would ensure an advantageous marriage for his sister,
2) that the provision of such a dowry was not a legal duty for a brother (Harrison 1968 p. 48, Groton p. 46),
3) that the young man has fallen, as we later learn, when his task was substantially complete. Such factors are to form an important point of contrast with the greed that is soon to be revealed as the central characteristic of Smikrines.

12. rest from my long labours: Like Habrotonon's hopes for freedom at *Epitrepontes* 548f. as reward for discovering the true parents of the foundling, the element of self-interest serves to make Daos a more rounded figure rather than an unblemished paragon of virtue. At the same time we find here a distinct theme of the slave's future dependent upon the fortune of his owner, resurrected at 213–15, though in totally different terms, and marking a strong contrast between Cleostratos and his elder uncle (cf. Krieter-Spiro p. 120, Cox).

13. But as it is: With this simple phrase, emphatically placed at the beginning of its line Daos marks the stark transition from expectation to reality, from past to present.

14. Cleostratos: As in the prologue later delivered by Chance Cleostratos is the only human character specifically named in Daos' speech, thus emphasising his centrality to the plot despite his total absence from the stage until the end of Act IV. Analogies elsewhere (*Dyskolos, Samia, Perikeiromene*) indicate that it was Menander's practice to identify other characters in these contexts simply by the roles they play and their relationship to one another, understandable in a genre heavily reliant on stock figures, but, more importantly, designed not to overload such speeches with details that only become relevant when we see their owners and view their interaction (hence the mutual naming of Daos and Smikrines at 19–20).

15f. this shield…back safe: The mutual dependence of a warrior and his arms was a frequent theme: from the Spartan 'Come back with your shield or on it' to references in such tragedies as Euripides' *Troades* 1194f. ('O shield that kept fair Hector's arm safe, you have lost your best guardian') and *Heracles Mainomenos* 1098–1100 ('Winged arrows and bow are strewn upon the ground, my companions in arms, that once kept safe my side and were kept safe by me'). In the present case, by means of what is little more than a passing reference, Daos draws the audience's attention to an item later revealed as the crucial factor in producing the misapprehension upon which the play is built.

17. Yours was a gallant soul: Lit. 'You were a man great of soul', with connotations not only of physical bravery but also of generosity, honour, virtue and chivalry, as Aristotle makes clear at *Nicomachean Ethics* 1123b–1125a.

18. Smikrines: In the absence of any indication in the text commentators are divided as to when Smikrines enters the scene and from where. The abruptness of his intervention here, unless designed to illustrate at this early stage the inhumanity that is later to become all too evident, and the presumption that he has heard Daos' speech strongly suggest that he accompanied the slave on stage and has been present from the beginning, unnoticed among the other silent figures on the stage (G.-S. p. 63, Frost p. 21f., Blume p. 148 n. 58). An alternative scenario would have the old man emerge from his house in response to the noise outside in order to overhear Daos' monologue either from the outset (Jacques 1998a, p. XXVIII, Beroutsos p. 22) or, even less likely, during the course of its delivery (Groton p. 38). The main weakness of these, however, is the danger they pose in diverting attention away from Daos, the focal point Menander clearly intended, to a figure lurking to one side.

turn of events: Lit. 'chance'. It can hardly be accidental that in his very first statement Smikrines uses a word (*tyche*) that is to form so important a feature of the play, reflected not only in the name of the prologue-speaker, who is 'in control of directing and managing' the action (147f.), but reinforced through later verbal echoes at 25 and 27 ('successful'), 58 ('fortunately'), 248 ('chance'), 287 (lit. 'suffered bad luck'), 381 ('good luck'), 411 ('Chance'), 418 ('fortunate / misery'), 497 ('good fortune') (Konet, Omitowoju p.150f.). Though Smikrines' later questions and comments will begin the process of exposing him as the villain of the piece, his initial role is rather to prompt the disclosure of information (19f., 22, 39), fulfilling a *quasi-protatic* role that in other plays is given to purely *protatic* characters, like Chaireas in *Dyskolos*, whose main purpose is to elicit information and who thereafter disappear for ever from the action, an indication of their purely technical function (Ireland 1981 p. 180, 1992 p. 99f.).

20f. For a soldier…is easy: Sententious lines and highly apposite in the context of a character who will use literary quotes to devastating effect in Act III (cf. Apollodorus Comicus fr. 2 K-A, 'It's a job to find a soldier who's successful through to old age, unless he's a coward', Feneron p. 121 n. 8, who cites numerous additional examples in the play, including 27f., 191, 248f.). As Lombard p. 125 points out, the present instance has something of a retarding effect, forcing Smikrines to intervene again at 22 before anything of substance is forthcoming.

23. There's a river: Daos' description of events is redolent of the tragic messenger speech (cf. Aeschylus' *Persae* 447ff., 'There's an island in front of Salamis…'; see further Lombard p. 130f.), but disguised by Smikrines' interventions. These, like the comments inserted by Chaireas into Pyrrhias' description of his encounter with Knemon at *Dyskolos* 102ff., serve the additional purpose of breaking into manageable sections what would otherwise have been a lengthy monologue, something to be avoided in view of the deferred prologue to come:

1) the initial success of the Greek forces in both military and financial terms;
2) Cleostratos' personal share in this and his plans for its safe disposal;
3) Daos' departure with much of the booty, followed by enemy preparations and slack discipline in the Greek camp;
4) the enemy attack and its aftermath – the arrival of the first survivors;
5) the measures taken by Daos and his party for their own protection resulting in a three-day delay before further movement;
6) the location of Cleostratos' body;
7) its identification, the mass-cremation and departure for Athens.

Lycia: An area of south-west Asia Minor, only partially Hellenised and much contested by the successors to Alexander. The fact that there is no reference to such disputed control in the text and that the campaign was ostensibly directed against the native population suggests that this was a freebooting expedition taking advantage of a power-vacuum (G.-S. p. 65, Jacques 1998a, p. LXXXIf.).

28. Someone who's taken a knock…: The dangers inherent in success leading to slack discipline are graphically illustrated by historical events: Xenophon *Hellenica* 4,1,17 (a Persian attack on Greek foragers scattered over a plain with little thought for defence); Diodorus Siculus 19, 95, 3–5 (the disastrous results of over-confidence – a night attack by Nabateans on the army of Athenaeus).

30f. the protection of the camp: Lit. 'the palisade' as in 63, designed to provide safety for an army's living quarters or give temporary protection.

31–3. looting…money: The lack of connection between details given here (asyndeton) adds a matter-of-fact tone to the description – as if the events constituted a natural chain of events. Similarly, in stark contrast to modern sensibilities there is no hint of disapproval over the act of looting, rather a presumption of normality, especially in the context of Greek actions against barbarians.

32. selling their booty: Presumably to merchants who accompanied the expedition, thus allowing the troops to convert their bulky spoils into more portable cash. Cleostratos clearly adopted a different approach, taking advantage of Daos' presence to arrange for the booty's initial transport to Rhodes.

33. Splendid!: Smikrines' reaction to the mention of booty here is in stark contrast to the sombre tone of Daos' account, just as later he shows little sign of sympathy in response to the description of Cleostratos' death (Katsouris 1975b, p. 112f., cf. Paduano p. 15, who describes the old man's interventions as banal). Goldberg p. 33, in contrast, regards Smikrines' comments as lightening the atmosphere, confirming the image expected of the comic miser, 'a tragic-comic counterpoint that tempers the tragedy of Daos' talk with the promise of comedy to come'.

34f. [six hundred] gold coins: The text is readily restored by reference to the figure at 83. The coins themselves will have been either Persian darics which circulated widely in Asia Minor before the advent of Alexander, or Macedonian staters. If, on the other hand, the Greek term (lit. 'golds') is being used without any reference to actual coins, interpretation as a value-marker, each worth twenty drachmas, is possible. At all events their total value was probably close to 12,000 drachmas or two talents, the sum Chairestratos mentions at 268f. as the size of dowry he proposed to give his niece out of his own pocket, and repeated in the fragmentary text at 321. The other items detailed here: (silver) cups and slaves, when added to the 'very modest' family resources mentioned at 132, thus easily account for the four talents (24,000 drachmas) specified in 351.

40. I set out at dawn: Commentators have indicated a number of apparent illogicalities in Daos' account of the attack and its aftermath (cf. Blume p. 149 n. 59):

1) How did the survivors of the attack learn that the enemy had avoided notice by the Greek lookouts and had discovered Greek troop positions from deserters?
2) How was Daos able to hear the uproar that resulted from the enemy attack when by then he was presumably a day's journey away?

Attempts to create a logical explanation for the latter by imaginative reconstruction of the lacuna after 49 suggesting adverse weather conditions that held up Daos' progress are unconvincing. It may be that what Daos heard was not the attack itself but the noise of the survivors as they approached (Groton p. 75), but more likely, since the scrupulous application of logic has never been a feature of drama, these are factors that more readily occur to a reader than to the theatre audience, swept along by the action and willing to accept the situation offered (cf. Ireland 1995, 358–9n.).

47. the inevitable happened: Daos points out that over-confidence, exacerbated by successful plundering, led the troops in the camp to throw precaution to the wind, and instead to engage in celebrations without thought for possible danger. A degree of uncertainty surrounds interpretation of the Greek at this point (οἷον εἰκὸς γίνεται). Some see it as retrospective, suggesting 'such as usually happens' *i.e.* it was natural for the army to disperse to its tents on return from the looting. Others more rightly see it as prospective – the inevitability of the army carousing after successful looting, with no thought for maintaining a guard. Jacques (1998a, p. 5 n. 2) aptly points out that the words here echo Smikrines' question in 39.

49. Yes…: Lit. 'For there must have been…I think'. The dichotomy between Daos' detailed knowledge of events up to this point and his hesitation here has led some editors (Sisti 1971, Jacques 1998a) to suggest assigning the line to Smikrines – against the evidence of the manuscript, which signals a change of speaker after 'Disgraceful!', and against the fact that nowhere else in the scene does Smikrines add detail to the narrative. Again, attempts to inject such explanatory factors as Daos not being actually present at the attack or an appeal to faulty recollection, are otiose. More likely, the line represents a wistful expression of regret at the degree of devastation caused as a result of the troops' revelries and a reaction to Smikrines' clear disapproval of the troops' celebrations.

56f. men crying out…names: The lack of grammatical connection between phrases here is clearly designed to heighten the tension of the account, just as Daos' specifying the type of troops who arrive in 61 seems to represent their relative mobility. Such asyndeton for dramatic effect was already evident in the description of plundering (30–33), and frequently figures in Daos' descriptions (*e.g.* 199f. 'the place, circumstances, the witness', 356–9 'He'll organise…dreams', 422f. 'Bile, grief, a fit of madness, choking'; see further Feneron p. 93).

59. a rallying point: Lit. 'strong', describing the small hill that offered a point of concentration and protection.

61f. the wounded: The position of the words at the very end of the description (lit. 'There came streaming in cavalry, guardsmen, infantry (sc. all) bearing wounds') adds an element of poignancy to the description: there were survivors, but not unscathed.

62. How lucky…: Smikrines' bathetic failure to demonstrate any shred of sympathy for the fate of the troops here is a telling indictment of the stereotype he belongs to, something underlined by the fact that his attempt at congratulation produces no reaction from Daos.

[**65. αἷς**: The relative pronoun has been attracted from its grammatical accusative form (ἅς) into that of the preceding dative noun, a not infrequent occurrence in Greek cf. 134 τῆς γυναικὸς ἧς ἔχει.]

67–8. the Lycians…prisoners: The mention of prisoners, like the fact that the shield was the only means of identification and the need for a speedy cremation, thus making further enquiries impossible, has been taken by some as a covert hint to the audience as to how the plot will ultimately develop (Goldberg p. 33f., Holzberg p. 29). Whether the audience would be sufficiently receptive to such factors as to appreciate them in advance, however, must remain uncertain, especially in the case of an author like Menander, who on occasion inserts possible lines of plot development only to reject them. See, for instance, the apparent removal of obstacles in the way of Moschion's marriage to Plangon at the end of *Samia* Act IV, only to have another problem intervene at the beginning of Act V, or the fleeting prospect of an obstacle to Sostratos' marriage at the beginning of *Dyskolos* Act V, superseded as it is by quite a different line of development (Ireland 1995, 784–5n.).

[**67. we'd learned**: While the Greek verb πυνθάνομαι normally takes a participle construction in indirect discourse, the infinitive construction is frequently found as an alternative with little or no difference in meaning.]

69–72. It wasn't possible…all bloated: As Beroutsos p.11 observes, this brutal image of the corpses after three days in the sun is unparalleled in extant comedy, but as a fact of war is well recorded (*Iliad* VII, 424, Xenophon *Anabasis* VI, 4, 9 'They buried most of the dead where they fell, for they had already been lying out for five days and it wasn't possible to move them', Ammianus Marcellinus XIX, 9, 9 'Soon after they are killed the bodies of our men disintegrate and fall to pieces, so much so that after four days the face of no dead man can be recognised'). Thus the natural reluctance of the survivors to leave the protection of their position until the danger had passed neatly introduces the circumstances surrounding what we later learn was misidentification (cf. *Misoumenos*, where a similar misinterpretation of evidence surrounding a supposed death results in Krateia's sudden antipathy for Thrasonides, Cusset p. 25f.).

72. his shield: Reference to the shield returns to significance an object that, for all its visible prominence, was only one among many objects brought onto the stage in the opening scene (cf. the mother's sacrifice in *Dyskolos*, introduced at 259ff. merely as the factor that robbed Sostratos of Getas' help, but which develops into a major element in bringing about the dénouement, Ireland 1995, p. 131). Its description as being buckled, and thus not worth removing by the enemy, serves to heighten the pathos of events – it has suffered like its owner.

75–7. That fine commander...delay: Though speedy cremation and a mass burial of the ashes were logical in the circumstances, they were also, in hindsight, the factor that prevented a closer examination of the corpse that might have revealed the truth. At the same time the implicit criticism in Daos' words serves to underline his sense of duty towards his master in the thwarted provision of a proper burial of his ashes at home.

[**77f.** συναγαγὼν πάντας δ᾽ ἀθρόους ἔκαυσε: While the particle δέ is normally found as second word in its clause or phrase, the instance here is deferred in order 1) to contrast with καθ᾽ ἕνα μὲν in 75 and 2) to emphasise the two stages involved here: first the commander gathered all the casualties together, and then he cremated them *en masse*, cf. Handley (1965) 10n.]

82. That's the whole story: Lit. 'You've heard everything from me'. Such ostensibly blatant and rhetorical statements of completed description are often inserted to mark the end of expository material or a specific topic in both tragedy and comedy, cf. Chance's 'That's enough information on that for you' (113f.); *Epitrepontes* 292, 'I've finished my account'; fr. adesp.1093.86 K-A, 'That's the sum total, Strobilus'; Aeschylus *Agamemnon* 582, 'You have the whole story'; Sophocles *Ajax* 480 'You've heard the whole story'.

82–9. Despite Smikrines' denials at 85f. and 89f. it is clear that the whole passage is designed to reveal the old man's acquisitive avarice as he turns once again not to thoughts of sympathy but the booty and its value. Nowhere is this better shown than in the sudden and blatant reversion to type at 85f. 'Do you think that's why I'm asking? Apollo! Was the rest taken?' as he vainly attempts to rebut Daos' barbed recognition of his true interests in 85, 'your "inheritance"', given added force not only by this being the last word in its sentence and the first word in the line but also by its wholly inappropriate use. For, as soon becomes evident, Smikrines is not heir to his nephew's estate, but by placing the term in Daos' mouth Menander highlights the implications of the old man's questions, something echoed at 89 by the matching response 'family property', likewise last word in its sentence and carrying with it overtones of inheritance (Arnott 1975, p. 145). Such references gain added force in the Greek with 'your "inheritance"' represented by the single-word address to Smikrines as 'inheritor', and 'family property' carrying strong implications of ownership by Smikrines himself (hence G.-S. ad loc. who translate as 'This crowd that you see *belongs to you*', cf. Arnott ad loc. 'all *yours* ').

84. forty minae.: The mina could be either a measure of coin, equal to a hundred drachmas, or a weight used of bullion, as is the case here, forty minae being *c.* 24 kg.

no more: Against the evidence of the manuscript Kassel suggested assigning this to Smikrines as a question, cf. Jacques (1998a). The result removes Daos' use of the phrase to suggest further the old man's appetite for wealth.

89. this crowd: The crowd of prisoners that entered with Daos.

90. If only *he*'d survived**: Smikrines' belated expression of regret at the death of his nephew is undercut by the very wording he uses: his failure to use Cleostratos' name, referring to him instead as 'that man' (lit. 'If only that man had survived').

93. As a rare instance of 'stage direction' the manuscript inserts the word ἡσυχη (quietly) into the right-hand margin at this point suggesting an aside spoken by the old man (cf. 467n.). Opinion is divided, however, as to its interpretation: whether it is to be applied to the whole speech here (Beroutsos ad loc.), which might suggest sinister intention on Smikrines' part, whether it has been slightly misplaced and refers only to 'But now...these people – most gently' (Del Corno 1970b, p. 214, Arnott 1979a, Jacques 1998a), or whether it is an unwarranted insertion of the copyist, who misinterpreted what was intended simply as self-address after Daos' departure (Bain p. 132f., Taplin p. 125f., Frost p. 22).

96. most gently: The last word spoken by Smikrines in the Greek text as he departs into his house, deliberately so positioned to contrast with the reality we have already seen and which is soon to be confirmed by the deferred prologue. The aura of deliberate calculation that permeates his intentions – his wish to appear concerned rather than be concerned – strengthens the impression of cynical hypocrisy that will soon become only too clear.

97ff. Chance's prologue: Following the decidedly uncomic atmosphere of the play's opening, the appearance of a divine prologue-speaker immediately sets the play onto a more congenial track by reference in 97f. to the convention that gods avoided contact with death (cf. Euripides' *Hippolytus* 1437f., *Alcestis* 22f.). Straight away this provides a vital clue to the play's eventual outcome, reinforced by references to misinterpretation at 99 and 110, and patently specified at 112f. ('He's alive...'), the culmination of what some would argue is a series of such indications in the opening scene (see above 67–8n.), and logically the only route possible to the obligatory happy ending. Assured now that the death of Cleostratos is not a reality the audience is able to enjoy the continued misapprehension of the stage-characters as they stumble their way through a situation that is their own making.

Structurally, as in the case of *Dyskolos* (Ireland 1995, p. 109f.), the prologue displays considerable care exercised by the playwright in constructing the complex framework that encompasses the two characters at its heart: Cleostratos and

Smikrines (Holzberg pp. 29, 83, cf. Dworacki 1973a, p. 37f., Jacques 1998a, p. XXIV):

1) An outer frame centred on Chance, revealing herself as a goddess at the beginning (97f.), and her function and name at the end (147f.)
2) Details of the attack and its aftermath, introduced and concluded by (a) the theme of mistaken interpretation: 'they're labouring under a misapprehension' (99), 'this fellow came to completely the wrong conclusion' (110), and by (b) the echo of μαθήσεται ('will realise this') in 100 by μεμαθήκατε (lit. 'you've learned that') at 113.
3) Information on Cleostratos' wider family, itself built upon an outer framework detailing Smikrines' character (114–21) and his plans to secure his nephew's estate by exploiting his niece's new status as an heiress (137–43). Within this Menander provides details of the younger uncle which have their own internal structure:
   (a) Chairestratos' contrasting character and financial status (122–6),
   (b) his responsibility for the girl following Cleostratos' departure abroad (127–9),
   (c) his good character repeated (130),
   (d) the manifestation of that responsibility in arranging a marriage for the girl and the financial aspect of providing a dowry (131–6).

Further balance is injected as both the Cleostratos and Smikrines sections are concluded by assurances as to future developments: the young man is not dead (112); his uncle's schemes will come to nothing and his true nature will be revealed (143–6).

97f. If something...come on next: The 'metatheatrical' opening of the prologue, breaching any semblance of dramatic illusion with direct address to the audience, reference to stage action, and undisguised self-identification by the speaker can be traced back to fifth century tragedy and the opening of plays like Euripides' *Hippolytus* and *Bacchae* (see further Ireland 1995, p. 110f.).

these people: Chance's reference here neatly echoes that of Smikrines in 96 (cf. *Dyskolos* 521f.), not only forming a mild verbal link between the two scenes but also emphasising that Cleostratos' family lies at the centre of both human and divine thoughts.

100–4. Supplements to restore some of Chance's account, lost through damage to the text, have been variously suggested by editors. Those in the translation are *exempli gratia* only, though 'Anyone who pays attention' as a form of encouragement to the audience echoes the sentiment of Pan's appeal at *Dyskolos* 45f., 'the details [you'll see] if you so wish – and do make it your wish'.

103. mercenary: The Greek term used here, ξένος, is capable of a wide spectrum of interpretation: from 'guest' to 'foreigner'. The fact, however, that it is here used in a context inviting identification with Cleostratos' comrade killed in the attack, suggests that 'mercenary', attested elsewhere, is appropriate.

[105. ὁπλιζόμενοι [τὸ] παρὸν ἕκαστος πλησίον: While one might expect to find ὁπλίζομαι taking a dative of instrument, the use of an accusative is also found (cf. Sophocles' *Electra* 995f.).]

106. this fellow: Despite his prominence in the play Daos receives little attention in the prologue, being mentioned again only at 110 – in the same non-specific terms – and at 122, where his entry into Chairestratos' house is simply used to introduce the younger uncle (Dworacki 1973a, p. 39). This may be because his appearance in the opening scene makes further specific reference here unnecessary, or, more likely, Menander wished to concentrate for the moment upon the central characters involved in the situation.

112f. By revealing the actual outcome of the play for Cleostratos here and Smikrines at 143–6 Menander forgoes the opportunity for injecting wide-ranging surprise into the play, just as he does at *Perikeiromene* 165–7 where the goddess reveals her purpose. Instead the audience is invited to concentrate not upon the end-result but upon the obstacles that will be placed in its path. Such a technique does not exclude the possibility of surprise altogether, but limits it to individual episodes (see below 455n.).

but not just yet: The emphatic insertion of this limiting proviso (ὅσον οὐδέπω) at the end of the sentence and the beginning of its line in the Greek text is a device Menander used elsewhere in contexts where he wished to tantalise his audience, cf. *Dyskolos* 667–9, 'I've never in all my life seen a man more conveniently drowned – or near enough' (see further Ireland 1995, 666n.).

114–21. The description of Smikrines' character is achieved with considerable economy and stylistic effect, employing both balance and antithesis: balance in (lit.) '*in terms of family* he's his uncle on his father's side; *in terms of villainy* he's the last word' (lit. 'in villainy he has completely surpassed everyone'), with 'family' and 'villainy' occupying the significant first-word position in their respective lines (cf. '*neither* family *nor* friend' in 117f.). Antithesis occurs in (lit.) 'has considered *none* of the wickedness… he wants *everything*', both words coming at the end of their respective clauses (see further Cusset pp. 57–66).

121. He lives like a hermit with an old serving woman: Such isolation, upon which the existence of an old servant clearly does not impinge, was a conventional trait of the unsympathetic character-type, cf. the description of Knemon at *Dyskolos* 30, 'The old man himself lives *on his own* with his daughter and an old serving woman' (Ireland 1995, p. 14f.). Smikrines in *Epitrepontes* and Euclio in Plautus' *Aulularia* similarly have only an old woman as servant. The very description 'like a hermit', *monotropos*, in fact provided the title for plays by Ophelion and Anaxilas centred on hermit-like characters, and is graphically illustrated in Phrynichus' play *Monotropos* produced in 414 (fr. 19 K-A), 'My name is Monotropos… I live the life of Timon, unwed, by slave unattended, quick to anger, unapproachable, devoid of laughter and conversation, self-willed'.

[122. Next door: Lit. 'in the neighbourhood'. The ostensibly ungrammatical phrase ἐν γειτόνων is created by ellipse of a word like οἰκίᾳ, and, with related forms, is a frequent colloquialism in comedy (cf. *Dyskolos* 25, *Perikeiromene*147).]

123–5. Since the complications developed in the play are in large part founded upon family relationships, Menander here signals their importance by placing the significant words 'younger', 'brother' and 'young man' at the beginning of each line, just as 'money-grubber' occupies the important position at the end of 123. Later, it is the age differential between Smikrines and Chairestratos that allows the old man to dismiss out-of-hand his brother's wedding arrangements, as Chance herself points out at 142f., just as 'money-grubber', *philargyros*, is pointedly echoed at 149 in Smikrines' first statement when he returns to the stage: 'So that no one can say that I'm totally *fixated with money*'.

127–8. It's in his charge: For the legal implications of Cleostratos' leaving his sister with his uncle when he left for service overseas see *Introduction: The Legal Background*. The description of Chairestratos in this section of the prologue is clearly designed not only to provide details essential for understanding the plot but also to point a specific and graphic contrast to Smikrines: Chairestratos is good, not the last word in villainy; he is rich and generous, not a money-grubber; he has an extended family with wife, daughter, step-son and niece, not someone who recognises neither family nor friend and whose hermit-like existence is mitigated only by the presence of an old servant woman.

132. his resources very modest: The calculation is doubtless based upon both the reality of Cleostratos' estate before his departure and comparison with what we learn at 350 to be the value of Chairestratos' wealth: fifteen times as much as that of his now-heiress niece.

134–6. he planned...was intending: The same verb and tense are used in Greek, 'he was intending' both serving to emphasise the interruption and frustration of Chairestratos' plans (G.-S. 130–6n.)

his wife's son by her previous husband: While Chaireas' status as Chairestratos' step-son is introduced here as little more than a passing reference, it later becomes an essential factor in thwarting Smikrines' scheme (cf. the theme of sacrifice at *Dyskolos* 260, initially introduced as no more than the subject of a peevish complaint from Sostratos, but soon to become the event that alters the whole course of the play). Had Chaireas been Chairestratos' own son, he would be the one to inherit his father's estate. The fact that the old man only has a daughter allows the girl to become an heiress no less than Cleostratos' sister and thus a prey to Smikrines' unwanted attention (Harrison 1968, pp. 108–15).

[**146f.** λοιπὸν τοὔνομα [το]ὑμὸν φράσαι: The idiom, in full <τὸ> λοιπόν <ἐστι>…, occurs frequently in Menander: cf. *Dyskolos* 583, 759, 841, *Perikeiromene* 498f., *Samia* 729. Punctuation in the lines varies between editors, mainly depending upon whether τίς εἰμι is to be taken as dependent upon φράσαι (Borgogno, Arnott) or an independent question as here.]

147f. in control...Chance: Though Dworacki (1973a, p. 37) suggests that delaying revelation of the prologue speaker's name to the very last word was designed to minimise Chance's role in the action and that the information provided could easily have been delivered by a different deity, the positioning of her name is clearly significant in a play based on a chance misidentification (see above 18n. and *Introduction*). By its position it creates a greater impact than the naming of Agnoia (Misapprehansion) at *Perikeiromene* 141, or of Pan at *Dyskolos* 12.

149–54. So that no one…about me: By the very act of disclaiming an interest in the booty brought back the moment he re-enters Smikrines neatly confirms his obsession with it. This links the present scene not only with the earlier one with Daos, where he had similarly tried to deny what was all too obvious ('do you think that's why I'm asking?' 85), but also with the details given in the prologue, through the repetition of *philargyros* ('money-grubber' at 123, 'fixated with money' here). Similarly, his claim that he didn't check how much gold Daos had brought is undercut by the fact that he had already established the amount at 82f. ('You say you've got six hundred gold coins?') and by his self-congratulatory assurance at 154f. that such information can easily be obtained. The very fact that in law Smikrines has no claim on the booty is itself a telling indictment, his presumption of such a right introducing an early, as yet unspoken, hint of his emerging plans. This leads easily into an additional theme that begins to surface, hypocrisy: his concern with appearance rather than reality (already evident in the calculation behind his final words before the prologue), and his belief that he is the victim of his family's neglect and ill-will, a belief that surfaces again at 172–3 and will serve as justification for his claim on Cleostratos' sister.

155. slaves: Smikrines' confidence is based on the routine extraction of evidence from slaves through torture (Harrison 1971, p. 147f.) and the assumption that they would have no vested interest in keeping any details secret. In referring to slaves here Smikrines means specifically those brought back as part of Cleostratos' booty, though the word he uses (οἰκέται), identical to that in 140, contains connotations of their being part of the family property, echoing in turn Daos' use of family property in 89 and his description of himself at 192.

156f. abide by the law and justice: While the reference remains as yet unspecific, the context is undoubtedly Chairestratos and his family and provides another early hint of what is to come: Smikrines' invoking of the law on heiresses.

157. no one will let them get away with it: A neat piece of dramatic irony in that the audience knows that it is Smikrines who will not succeed.

158–61. This wedding…weddings: The abrupt insertion of the topic seems designed to emphasise something that is soon to become of crucial importance. Once again Smikrines confirms by denial; for while he deems thoughts of a wedding inappropriate in the context of a death (lit. 'people are not concerned with / busy with weddings'), it is exactly this that lies at the forefront of his own mind.

164. Daos: As Frost notes p. 24 (cf. Jacques 1978, p. 45f.), there is a curious disconnection between Smikrines' intention to call Daos out and the slave's actual appearance, while Daos' puzzled question at 167 ('Me?') injects a no less incongruous failure to remember that the old man specifically mentioned such a future meeting at 93. On one level it might be argued that Menander's decision to forgo the conventional scene of knocking at the door was intended specifically to avoid what was primarily a comic routine (cf. *Dyskolos* 458f., 498, 911ff., *Epitrepontes* 1075, Frost p. 9), though this effectively then robs Daos' entry of any obvious motivation. True, the playwright mitigates the effect by having Daos continue to address the women inside with evident concern for their plight (cf. Frost p. 7f.), thus forming a thematic link with his exit indoors at 90–2, but commentators have recognised that this, of itself, does not motivate the appearance. As a result, G.-S. suggest hesitantly that in exiting Daos may wish to escape the women's grief, while Jacques (1978, p. 45) hazards the slave's intention to inform Chairestratos of recent developments. The absence of any reference to either in the text, however, suggests either a more recondite reason, or, more likely, that the playwright simply invited the audience to accept the situation. Is it that Daos' appearance before Smikrines can summon him is designed to point the distinction between the altruism of one and the other's self-obsession (Frost p. 25, Jacques 1998a, p. 12 n. 2), and to suggest further that the old man's control of the situation is not as firm as he would like to believe – Daos appears, but not at Smikrines' behest? And does the evident failure to remember Smikrines' earlier reference to a meeting, signalled in 167, form a cue for those feelings of neglect to which Smikrines will soon given voice?

166. humanly: *I.e.* like rational human beings, aware that disasters like sudden death are part of the human condition.

[**168.** ὃν δίκαιον ἦν: Lit. 'who it was right' (*i.e.* to live and deal with these things).]

170–1. in charge of my whole estate...: Commentators have long recognised the discrepancy between the claim here that Cleostratos would become heir to Smikrines' property on his death and the actual law of inheritance, which would have divided the estate between Cleostratos (in place of his father, presumed dead) and Chairestratos (Harrison 1968, pp. 143–6). MacDowell's suggestion (1982, p. 44f.), that Smikrines intended to adopt his nephew, who would thus become his automatic heir (cf. G.-S. p. 76f. who speculate on the possibility of a will), founders largely on the absence of any specific reference in the text. Brown, in turn, (1983, p. 415) argues that the audience may not have been expected to grasp the legal implications of Smikrines' statement in its entirety, though the fact that the old man raises the issue of his estate again at 183 suggests that Menander did expect them to be aware of the general principles of inheritance. Indeed, Smikrines' insertion of 'in accordance with the law' may have been expressly intended by the playwright to alert the audience to the specious nature of the old man's argument, intimation of a deliberate lie from him. More likely, therefore, Smikrines' words represent a cynical and hypocritical sigh of regret at the very point when he is about to initiate the process of securing Cleostratos' estate for himself (see further *Introduction: The Characters*, Karabelias p. 369f., Beroutsos p. 63, Traill p. 58).

174. Quite: The Greek can be interpreted in a number of ways: either as a surprised question (lit. 'Have you any sense?', hence Arnott's 'Are you serious?') or as an ironic statement (Austin, Jacques 1998a), *i.e.* 'There's sense in what you say'. However, since it is unlikely that a slave would overtly question Smikrines' complaint in such a delicate situation, the words should perhaps be taken in a more neutral, non-committal way.

177. goodness knows who: The statement may be taken either literally, the result of Smikrines' lack of contact with Chairestratos' household and his exclusion from family decisions (G.-S. ad loc.), or as an example of Menander's economy, here used to deepen characterisation. For while in terms of logic Smikrines may, in fact, not know the identity of the intended groom, the audience does, and by transferring that knowledge (by implication) to the old man the playwright converts the statement into one of unfeeling harshness, allowing Smikrines to downgrade the wedding and thus justify in his own mind the disruption of it. For other instances of such transferred knowledge, employed this time to facilitate plot-development, cf. *Samia* 695ff., where on his entry Demeas is aware of his son's anger without any indication that he witnessed Moschion's earlier outburst which gave rise to it, or *Dyskolos* 358f., where knowledge of Knemon's return home, witnessed by the audience but not by his stepson Gorgias, is transferred from one to the other.

183–7. I'll not leave…law states: Smikrines here encapsulates the two basic factors that lie at the heart of his plans: greed and those paranoid feelings of neglect described at some length in the preceding lines and used to justify the manifestation of his greed. Implicitly acknowledging the girl's new status as *epikleros*, an heiress, Smikrines' intention to marry her will thus both give him control of the wealth she carries with her and, in the event of male offspring from her, will prevent his own estate from passing into the hands of those he sees as working against him. To justify his actions he invokes the law of inheritance, which, as at 170–1, he misrepresents, claiming that it virtually compels him to take the course he proposes (see further *Introduction: The Legal Background*), despite the attempted camouflage with the phrase 'more or less' (187) and the reference to advice from others (184f.). These latter are clearly no more than an invention, another instance of Smikrines' attempted depersonalisation of his plans, shifting onto others what is really a self-centred and self-absorbed decision (cf. Hunter p. 159 n. 28), just as his use of 'one' at 96 was intended to disguise his calculated approach to those inside.

187–9. You yourself…uninvolved: A further instance of Smikrines' double standards. At 175–8 he had complained of neglect from his family: the fact that he was excluded from decisions as though an outsider, like some illegitimate offspring or even a slave. Here he reverses the argument, claiming that Daos, a slave, should be actively involving himself in advancing Smikrines' plans, presumably on the grounds that he has influence with Cleostratos' wider family (cf. G.-S. at 188), another instance of his parasitic use of others, whether real or fictitious, to advance his schemes.

189. it…seems to me: The echo of Smikrines' words in 186, even occupying the same position within the line, cannot be accidental, as Daos implicitly begins to distance himself from the old man's planned course of action, something that becomes even clearer later in the scene.

191. Know yourself: Inscribed over the entrance to the temple of Apollo at Delphi and frequently quoted, if for other purposes (Jacques 1998a, p. 14 n. 3, Menander *Koneazomenai* fr.1, 'This saying "Know yourself" means if you know your own affairs and know what you ought to do.'). The words invited those who stood before the temple not to indulge in self-analysis (as the modern reader might understand them), but to avoid claiming privileges beyond those proper to mortals. On this basis Daos justifies his decidedly eclectic approach to those topics he is prepared to involve himself with, using his slave status and the deference he owes to the freeborn, his ostensible superiors (200–4, 208–9), to avoid being drawn into complicity with the old man. Thus, purely factual matters centred on the booty or any contracts entered into by his master he can detail; family law or property he pointedly eschews (Cox p. 30f.). By way of contrast, in Act II there is no such reluctance on Daos' part to engage in frustrating Smikrines' plans, demonstrating there his clear superiority over the freeborn in terms of both intellect and determination (Gaiser 1973, p. 127f.). Similarly, at 206 Daos uses his origins in Phrygia, the inhabitants of which were conventionally regarded in literature as both cowardly and effeminate (hence the Waiter's reaction at 242, cf. Euripides' *Orestes* 1369ff., 1528, Tertullian *De Anima* 20, 'Comic writers mock the Phrygians as being timid') in order to distance himself from the implications of Smikrines' interpretation of Attic law. As G.-S. p. 80 observe, that a Phrygian should implicitly criticise Athenian customs yet clearly have right on his side is 'a pleasant paradox' (cf. Jacques 1996, p. 329–31).

193a. How [remarkably] restrained: A fragment of the line (missing from B) is preserved in papyrus O (see *Introduction: The Text*), which has a *paragraphus* at the beginning and the last letter of Daos' name in the margin of 194, suggesting a brief interruption by Smikrines before Daos resumes his speech.

194–7. Restoration of the text based on the evidence of MSS B and O must remain largely problematical, especially in the case of 194–5, for how does interrogation of the other slaves referred to in 195–6 accord with Daos' mention of an account from himself in 194?

[**195.** There is a major textual problem here. Restoration of the reading in B produces πάντας θερά[ποντ]ας, 'all the (male) slaves'; O, on the other hand, reading π[.] . τασθεραπαινα . [, provides an unequivocal reference to female slaves, but if restoration of the line opening based on the reading of B is inserted, there is then the problem of how the masculine πάντας is to be interpreted. Handley posited reading πᾶν τὰς, accepted by Jacques, but while τὰς is easily accepted in the context of *the* female slaves, what are we to make of the neuter πᾶν? Does it refer back to something in the lacuna of 194, in which case it would represent a striking enjambement, or does it look forward to the rest of the line as *e.g.* 'you can [interrogate] the serving girls...*about everything*'?]

[**200**. τοῦ παρόντος: an alternative for τίνος παρόντος : 'in whose presence' *i.e.* 'the witness'.]

211. I understand: Despite the claim it seems clear that Smikrines has actually learned little from Daos' implicit disapproval of his plans and has no answer to the refusal to become involved. His comment, though, may in retrospect underline his interpretation of what he sees at 391ff. as Daos' reluctance to present an inventory of the booty.

211–13. one of these people...if there's no one inside – No, no one: Smikrines here refers obliquely to his brother Chairestratos, the only figure legally competent to discuss what is being planned. Logically there is nothing in the text to indicate why he should assume his brother's absence from the house, but the incongruity is well disguised by Daos' immediate confirmation, and it neatly serves to motivate the old man's exit to look for him in the market.

213–5. Like the reference to Pan in the context of the mother's dream at *Dyskolos* 407ff., the appeal to Chance here acts as a reminder of the force the audience knows from the prologue is directing the action of the play. Ironically, though, the negative overtone that Daos injects into the situation – the fact that as a slave he will become subject to Smikrines' power if the old man succeeds in his plan to marry Cleostratos' sister – provides an element of humour in its contrast with the revelations of the goddess herself (cf. Zagagi 1994, p. 146–7, Ireland 1992, p. 104).

216. Cook: The entry of the cook, followed at 233 by that of the Waiter, with their inconsequential complaints and banter, neither advances the plot nor forms the bridge between Acts that Menander often employs to minimise the impact of choral interludes (*e.g. Dyskolos*, where Daos forms a bridge between Act I and II, Kallippides between Acts IV and V, *Epitrepontes*, where Onesimos bridges Acts II and III, *Samia*, where Demeas bridges Acts I and II). Indeed, rather than being prospective the cook's entry harks back to the play's beginning and Cleostratos' death, now viewed from a totally different perspective, a reverse mirror of the opening scene (cf. the mirror scenes of Sikon and Daos at *Dyskolos* 456ff., 885ff.). Thus, an Act that began with solemn news of tragedy ends with the re-entry of that same news, but now converted into black humour, what Goldberg (p. 29ff.) terms the 'mixture of modes', the alternation of dark and light that is a prominent feature of the play as a whole (cf. Jacques 1998a, p. XXX–II, Handley 1969, p. 14f. = Segal p. 34). In the opening scene Cleostratos' death was to a large extent seen through its disastrous effect upon the expectations of his household; here it is converted into the bathetic theme of its effect upon the cook's employment (Hurst 1990, p. 100).

216–20. If ever...off and away: The cook's whinging complaint here is nicely reflected in the balanced structure of his language, in 'either...or', and the repetition of 'then' strategically placed at the beginnings of their respective lines.

218. hush-hush pregnancy: Bain p. 221 observes that though there is no hint of such a development in the play, the reference here serves as a reminder to the audience of a standard theme of New Comedy: the impact of an extra-marital pregnancy upon families (cf. Menander's *Epitrepontes*, *Samia*, Plautus' *Aulularia*, Terence's *Hecyra*. In *Dyskolos* Gorgias' oblique reference to rape at 289–93 likewise introduces a standard theme, but one that, as here, plays no role in the action).

219. the party's cancelled: Lit. 'they're no longer making sacrifices' *i.e.* as part of a celebration.

224–6. money in the bank...them away: Lit. 'these (drachmas)...these'. Editors have been at times concerned with the repetition of the same word (ταύτας) within two lines and have suggested changing one or the other to 'them'. However, as Beroutsos ad loc. observes, the repetition highlights the cook's anxiety over payment.

224f. some corpse: Black humour adding emphasis to the cook's aggrieved sense of disappointment through its absurd exaggeration, but at the same time underlining the fact that Cleostratos' death has been announced the very day of the intended wedding, as Chance made clear at 136f.

227. You useless article: Lit. 'you temple robber', a crime that could result in the death penalty, but often, as here, at *Dyskolos* 640, *Epitrepontes* 952, *Perikeiromene* 366 and *Samia* 678, the term was used as a generic insult.

230. Aristeides: A prominent Athenian politician ostracised in 482, whose incorruptibility made him a proverbial figure and gained him the name of 'the Just' (Diodorus Siculus XI, 47, 2, 'He acquired a very high reputation for justice and because he excelled in it he was called "the Just"', Beroutsos ad loc.).

232f. As for the waiter...funeral tea: The cook's final grumble before departure returns to the theme of a lost contract, comparing this with the possibility that the waiter will recoup something from the situation by serving at the meal that normally ended the three-day fast between death and funeral.

233. probably: Emphatic in the Greek by being placed at the very end of the cook's speech, and made more so by the strengthening of 'perhaps' (ἴσως) through the addition of τυχόν, as at *Dyskolos* 125, *Epitrepontes* 504, *Perikeiromene* 337, 491, *Samia* 543.

Waiter: Though less frequently represented on the stage than the cook – this is in fact the only extant example of an actual appearance on the stage (see, however, passing references in *Dyskolos* 647, *Samia* 290, Diphilus fr. 42.2f. K-A, Philemon fr. 64 K-A, Alexander fr. 3 K-A) – the introduction of the waiter allows further development of the theme of disappointment, this time along cruder lines. But who does he address on entry? It is the usual assumption that the cook and his entourage leave at 233 and that the waiter directs his opening complaint to the women inside, with his use of 'cut up' at 234 echoing the same verb in 228, where it signified 'beating their breasts'. At the same time, coming immediately after the cook-scene, it also provides a variation on the 'chopping' pun often associated with the character (*e.g. Dyskolos* 398f. 'It's me, the cook, who's being chopped up', *Samia* 283–5 'Really, cook, I don't know why you carry knives with you. Your chattering's enough to chop everything up', Alexis fr. 177.12 K-A 'Don't cut me up; cut up the meat instead', Anaxippus fr. 1.23 K-A 'It's me you'll cut to pieces, not what we're supposed to sacrifice'). An alternative scenario, hesitantly suggested by G.-S., would have the waiter direct his words instead to the departing cook, allowing both the double aspect of the pun and making the statement less brutal in its effect than if it were meant for the grieving women. Or should we assume that the waiter's opening statement is no more than a whinge, like that of the cook, addressed to no one in particular?

234f. I'll be...are: Lit. 'In being cut up (*i.e.* distressed) I'll not be a jot different from you people'.

235f. Daos' rejoinder to the waiter's entry is cut short by damage to the text. It may be that the news the waiter expects is centred on the payment he hopes for, but certainty is elusive. Clearly, though, his hopes are dashed, hence the irritated reference to the funds Daos brought back and the lost opportunity to abscond with them, a further passing indication of the slave's loyalty to Cleostratos' family (Krieter-Spiro p. 88).

239. you idiot: Lit. 'struck senseless' or 'paralysed', the term often being converted into an general insult.

242. Useless: Lit. 'nothing holy' a proverbial expression describing something as worthless and explained by the scholiast to Theocritus V 21f. by referring to the story of Heracles' reaction upon seeing a statue of Adonis, *i.e.* 'nothing special'.

A queer: Lit. 'a man-woman' *i.e.* an effeminate male. Menander inserts a neat contrast between Daos' earlier use of his origins as a means to avoid being drawn into Smikrines' plans at 206 (cf. 191–3) and the reaction it evokes here: a low-level comic jibe from a figure who sets the traditional prejudice against Phrygians beside his own macho image as a rough-and-ready Thracian and their subgroup the Getae, their implied criminal tendencies then allowing reference to the conventional theme of consignment to work in the mills as punishment (Menander *Heros* 2f. 'So you're on tenterhooks, expecting the mill and leg-irons', Plautus' *Epidicus* 121 'I'll have the fellow irrigated with whips and sent to the mill'. See further, Krieter-Spiro p. 191–3, Goldberg p. 128 n. 8).

244f. That's why...of us: Assignment of the line to Daos, either as it stands (Jacques) or emended to read 'full of you' (Reeve) contradicts the evidence of the manuscript and is unnecessary. As Beroutsos observes ad loc., such boasting, even when directed against himself, is not out of character for this brutish figure.

246–9. There's another crowd...: The reference presupposes an initial crowd – either the slaves mentioned at 89 or, less likely, an oblique criticism of the disturbance caused by the departure of the cook and his retinue. Daos' words now mark the formal introduction of the chorus, whose drunken arrival (serving as the motive for clearing the stage) was traditionally signalled only at the end of Act I cf. *Dyskolos* 230–2, *Epitrepontes* 169–71, *Perikeiromene* 261–2 (Gaiser's suggestion of an entrance announcement for the chorus existing at the end of a later Act in a fragment attributed to Menander's *Hydria* cannot be substantiated:

Handley 1990, p. 131). Subsequent interventions by the chorus seem to emerge directly from the departure of the actors, and this may provide some evidence for the chorus' continued presence in the orchestra during later Acts. While, however, choral introductions such as this, in addition to insertion of the Greek word XOPOY (lit. 'of the chorus') in the manuscripts, show their presence, the activity they engaged in – whether song and dance or merely dance – cannot be determined. As Hunter (1979, p. 23f.) observes, however, an introductory announcement would be pointless if some form of performance did not take place. What does seem certain is that such songs as there may have been were non-organic, *i.e.* unconnected with the action and inserted simply because they were part of the genre's tradition and allowed the illusion of time passing. It is a process already visible in the last two extant plays of Aristophanes, *Ecclesiazusae* and *Plutus*, where the signal XOPOY is used but no text appears, and was a feature of later tragedy as Aristotle notes at *Poetics* 1456a27–9 (see further, G.-S. p. 12, Sifakis 1971, Webster 1974, p. 72, Handley 1987, Hunter 1985, p. 9f.). Csapo and Slater p. 351 indeed suggest that the essentially 'amateur' nature of the chorus, drawn as it was from the general population, made it an embarrassment in the context of a theatre that was becoming increasingly professionalised in terms of actors.

Equally contentious is the point at which the chorus finally departed, whether immediately prior to Act V or at the very end of the play. Again, direct evidence is lacking, but the fact that the final appeal for the audience's favour is now given to an actor does not of itself indicate the chorus' absence (*pace* Pöhlmann p. 356; see further Zagagi 1994, p. 72–6, Sifakis 1967, p. 113–15, Lape 2006, who suggests that by Menander's time the chorus had in fact been superseded by a *komos* or revel performance).

In one respect Daos' introduction of the chorus is without parallel: his direct address to it at 248f. (unless Frost p. 27 is correct in seeing another example at Alexis fr. 112 K-A). Such a departure from what appears to be normal practice is perhaps to be explained by the stark dichotomy between the slave's despondency at the transience of life and the 'eat, drink and be merry' message implicit in the chorus' drunkenness. His reference to the ways of chance being uncertain, on the other hand, injects a degree of comic humour through dramatic irony, mirroring that at 213–15, both of them providing a considerable contrast between the gloom of the stage characters and the audience's appreciation of reality (Zagagi p. 147).

249: Enjoy yourselves...can: Lit. ' Enjoy yourselves for as much time as is possible'.

Act II

250ff. Following the interruption created by the intervention of the chorus the re-entry of Smikrines brings with it a return to the one factor that can be said to bind together Acts I and II: the theme of a disrupted wedding. At 213 the old man had left the stage determined to inform his brother of his intentions. Now, his entry with someone evidently from the older generation and immediately identified by name carries with it the presumption that this is the younger brother referred to in the prologue (cf. 172, where Smikrines described himself as the eldest member of the family, something he repeats at 255). The impression that we come upon them in mid-conversation was a conventional means of injecting both an air of naturalness into their appearance on stage (cf. *Dyskolos* 50, 'What's that you're saying?...', 233ff. 'Do you mean to tell me...?') and a degree of economy, avoiding the need to repeat what the audience already knows and allowing us to see instead the aftermath. The result is an intensification of the shocked reaction heard earlier from Daos, its moral correctness confirmed by being placed into the mouth of a freeborn individual, and one intimately involved in the situation, the very kind of person Daos had specified at 203–4. Augmenting Chairestratos' overt disapproval of Smikrines' intention to marry a girl far younger than himself is the assumption that the original prospective groom is present throughout the exchange: hence the reference to 'Chaireas here' at 262, 'to *him*' (lit. 'to this fellow') at 271, Smikrines' use of a plural verb at 274 'Send Daos to me', the probability that '[I] always [thought] you'd marry the girl' at 279 was directly addressed to Chaireas, and the fact that at 284–6 he clearly knows of Cleostratos' supposed death, which he could only have learned from one or other of the old men. As such, Chaireas becomes a silent witness to the wrecking of his future happiness (Frost p. 28, Beroutsos p. 86, Jacques 1978, p. 41f.) and ignored by Smikrines, who at 177 had referred to him as 'goodness knows who'.

251–2. the funeral: Significantly, Chairestratos' immediate concern for the funeral highlights the gulf between the two brothers: on one side the formal aspects of mourning in the absence of anything to inter, on the other, obsession with the girl, relegating mention of the funeral (252f.) to a mere passing detail. The fact that Smikrines so brusquely begins to take control of the situation, thrusting aside his brother's close involvement with Cleostratos' side of the family and any arrangements the young man may have made, is clearly an extension of both a determination to indulge his greed and his earlier complaint about exclusion from family affairs.

256. I need to get the same: Smikrines' bald statement here that he needs to secure a wife and family like those of Chairestratos begs a number of questions, the answers to which are all too obvious to the audience:

1) Why does Smikrines need a family? – to prevent his estate falling into Chairestratos' hands on his death.
2) Why does he need to marry at this precise moment and to this precise girl? – to gain control of the wealth that goes with her by invoking a law which allows him to inflict himself upon his niece (with the implication that he would stand no chance of marriage in other circumstances). That Chairestratos too is well aware of this latter factor becomes clear from his offer at 264–6 to cede his nephew's estate to Smikrines.

257. no sense of decency: Lit. 'Have you no concern for moderation?', *i.e.*

while Smikrines bases his claim upon strict application of the law on *epikleroi*, Chairestratos emphasises instead both the excessive age differential involved and the fact that the marriage already arranged is the result of long acquaintance. While marriage between a young girl and an older man was not out of the ordinary in either Greek society or New Comedy (*e.g. Misoumenos* and *Sikyonioi*, in both of which the eventual groom is a soldier of some standing, and therefore not a stripling), the implicit difference in ages here seems rarely to have met with success, cf. Menander's *Georgos*, and *Misoumenos* (in the latter the reunion of Demeas and his daughter at 216–21 is misinterpreted as unwanted attention), Plautus' *Aulularia, Mercator, Casina, Asinaria* (contrast Scafuro p. 289f.). Indeed, as Brown argues (1993, p. 193f.), the whole tenor of the scene is slanted towards support of Chairestratos' case.

Ha!: The Greek here can be interpreted either as an interjection, as in the translation, or as 'boy!', used to address a young person or slave. Adopting the latter some have suggested a role here for Chaireas, making him the source of 'Smikrines... decency', 'Do you mean...your age?', 'You strike...too old'. However, since this would diminish not only the strong contrast in the scene between the two old men, but also the pathos of Chaireas' powerlessness and the force of 284ff., when he does eventually break his silence, the idea has met with little approval.

[**264. No need...a thing**: Lit. an imperative, 'Don't lose out' or 'Suffer no loss' (G.-S.).]

269. Melitides: A proverbial simpleton. Eustathius' commentary on *Odyssey* X, 552 explains that he 'is said not to have known how to count beyond five and to have been unaware which of his parents gave birth to him' (cf. Sbordone pp. 41–5). Smikrines' barbed response to his brother's offer reveals not only an astute understanding of the Attic law of inheritance but also a paranoid distrust of any assurances of sincerity Chairestratos makes. As a result, and prompted by Chairestratos' overt, and accurate, association of Smikrines' intention to marry with the inheritance, the old man drops all pretence of ulterior motive and calls for an inventory of the goods.

276. Damage to the text prevents detailed examination of the action at this point, though presumably Smikrines exited to await the arrival of the inventory, leaving Chairestratos and Chaireas to bemoan their respective misfortunes: Chairestratos' centred upon family property, Chaireas' much more personal, hence the likelihood that he is left alone on stage at 283, the centre of attention, in contrast to the peripheral role he has had so far. Suggestions that Chairestratos may instead have remained on stage, slumped in despair (Del Corno 1970a, pp. 216–19, 1971, Sisti, Borgogno, Holzberg p. 32, Katsouris 1975a, p. 108 n. 2, Belardinelli p. 256) would inevitably result in distracting the audience from the monologue to come (Frost p. 29, cf. Jacques 1978, p. 48f.), and it is not, in fact, till 299 that we hear of his collapse. That the old man has no explicit statement signalling his departure is not without precedent elsewhere in Menander (Frost p. 15f.).

280f. both heirs to my [estate]: MacDowell 1982, p. 45f. points out that there is a legal ambiguity here since in law the two young men would not inherit jointly; rather upon marriage Cleostratos would become sole controller of his uncle's estate as husband, and therefore *kyrios*, of Chairestratos' daughter. Chaireas, a stepson, could not inherit, otherwise the plot devised by Daos against Smikrines would be invalidated (see below on 348–55). Whether we are to presume an intention on Chairestratos' part to adopt Chaireas or whether Menander invited his audience simply to accept Chairestratos' words at face value cannot be determined from the text. Omitowoju p. 148, for instance, points out an impediment to any adoption of Chaireas if he is heir to his own natural father's estate, but such a consideration once again lies outside the orbit of the drama we have.

284ff. Chaireas' lament, with its sombre personal tone, its opening address to Cleostratos, its theme of unrealised expectations and the stress placed upon Cleostratos' misfortune before his own, proves in many ways a mirror-image of Daos' monologue with which the play opened (Beroutsos p. 94). As Blundell p.74 observes, however, it differs in the prominence Chaireas places upon his own plight (the constant reference to himself in 286 'my own', 287 'I have', 289 'to me', 291 'to me', 293 'my mother'), making this very much a lover's complaint. Yet for all the pathos of his situation Chaireas' role in the play remains curiously under-developed by modern standards. Elsewhere his intervention in the extant text is limited to three short statements (347, 375, 376–9) and perhaps a role in Act V (further interaction in the highly fragmentary lines at 277f. is signalled by Jacques 1998a). This led Arnott (1979a, p. 6) to suggest a lapse in dramatic skill by Menander, though against this one might argue: 1) There is a natural emphasis in the play upon the older generation at the head of their respective households and thus able to determine the future of others. 2) In consequence, the younger generation inevitably becomes portrayed as the victims of any decisions made by them. 3) Chaireas' role, exemplified in his total silence during the previous scene, suggests that the playwright emphasises rather what the young man represents, the personification not only of his own plight but also that of his fiancée, whom we never see.

288. I didn't choose to fall in love: Brown (1993, p. 198f.) points to the varying perspectives through which marriage is viewed in the play: 1) an arrangement typically involving the payment of a dowry (130–7), 2) the natural result of close association (262f.), 3) a love match (284–98). Within the present context Chaireas emphasises the propriety of both his emotions and his conduct: 1) his love for the girl is genuine, not the result of calculation (cf. *Dyskolos* 53 where the theme of a calculated love-affair is introduced specifically in order to discount it as a possible factor in the plot); 2) he has not resorted to improper action, a standard oblique reference to the theme of rape (cf. Gorgias' equally oblique reference at *Dyskolos* 290–3, again inserted only to dismiss it); 3) instead, he sought not only the permission of Chairestratos, in whose charge the girl was left, but also that of his mother, who had no legal authority in the matter, but whose inclusion places additional stress upon the rightness of his actions. The result of this were feelings of utter joy as he envisaged himself on the very brink of marriage (294f.), followed by despair that he will be denied all contact with her in future, a possible exaggeration in the context of a family circle, but its insertion serves to underline both the depths of the young man's grief and Smikrines' lack of human feeling.

294. blessed: Chaireas here uses a word (μακάριος) frequently found in the context of a young man on the brink of marriage, *e.g. Dyskolos* 389, *Misoumenos* 260, *Sikyonios* 381, 400.

295. my very goal: *I.e.* 'the very pinnacle' (of happiness).

299. Daos: The lack of any indication of stage action at this point in the text has produced a number of suggested scenarios. From available evidence the most likely is either that Daos exits from Chairestratos' house addressing the old man slumped inside before turning to appeal to Chaireas for help (Frost p. 29, Blume p. 152f., Jacques 1978, p. 48f., 1998a ad loc.) or that his first words are spoken off-stage, followed by his appearance (G.-S. p. 88, Halliwell). Alternatives based upon the continued presence of Chairestratos on stage are dramatically unsatisfactory, as Goldberg p. 129 n. 10 points out. Similarly problematic are the means by which Chairestratos emerges at 305, as appear he must despite his state of collapse. Jacques (1978, pp. 51–5, 1998a ad loc., 2000, p. 92f.) suggests use of the *ekkyklema*, a movable platform, often, though not exclusively, associated with tragedy, used to bring on stage scenes and tableaux that would logically be set indoors (*e.g.* the display of bodies as suggested in Aeschylus' *Oresteia*) and given support here by the instruction to open the doors found elsewhere in association with possible uses of the *ekkyklema* (Halliwell). Frost p. 30, however, observes that an address to reveal himself directed to someone actually on the *ekkyklema* is without parallel (cf. Hunter p. 171 n. 24), and the emergence of the old man either without the help of others, having got to his feet as instructed at 299, or assisted by Daos and Chaireas (Blume p. 58f.) or by supplementary slaves (Arnott 1979a ad loc.) whose continued presence may be given some support from Daos' words at 387 that Chairestratos be taken back inside, has many obvious attractions (see further, G.-S. pp. 239–41).

306. depression: Lit. 'I'm suffering from black bile' (cf. 339, where the same basic word is translated as 'prone to depression', 422n., Jacques 1998b, 229ff.). Chairestratos' ability to describe his state at some length in terms of shock and depression injects an element of comic exaggeration that prevents the audience from taking his condition too seriously and, like his wish for death at 314, echoing 282, introduces that very factor upon which Daos is to build his scheme to thwart Smikrines' plans.

[307. I can't control myself: Lit. 'I'm not within myself'. The grammar, found again at *Samia* 340, is irregular and probably to be accounted for by assimilation into that found with prepositions such as ἐκτός and ἐντός, which do require a genitive or the ellipse of a noun.]

310. Did you say married?: A somewhat incongruous and illogical question from someone who at 185f. heard Smikrines voicing this very intention. However, it serves to draw Daos into the situation in readiness for what is to come. This in turn requires a reversal of his earlier non-committal approach towards Smikrines' intentions and a role prefiguring the cunning slave so prominent in Roman comedy (Krieter-Spiro pp. 96–101). The significant difference from the later Roman model, though, is that while in Roman comedy the slave frequently masterminds the plot's resolution (*e.g.* Tranio in *Mostellaria*), here there is scope for effort from others (Goldberg p. 38 compares the roles of Pleusicles and Periplectomenos in Plautus' *Miles Gloriosus*), and the dénoument in *Aspis* stems not from Daos' efforts but simply from Cleostratos' return.

[**314. I'll die**: The construction here, a double negative + subjunctive reproduces the effect of a strongly negatived future indicative.]

315–8. Assignment of parts here is problematic. A *paragraphus* and *dicolon* occur in 315, indicating a change of speaker after 'I see it happen'. A further *paragraphus* occurs in 317 with *dicola* after 'It won't be easy' and 'nevertheless', suggesting, as Borgogno prints:

Daos	So how could one out-manoeuvre the vile scoundrel? It won't be at all easy.
Chairestratos	No not easy, but possible, nevertheless?
Daos	Possible, and the task well worth the effort, by Athena…

More recent editors, believing that a *dicolon* has been omitted or misplaced suggest a variety of solutions, *e.g.* Sandbach:

Daos	So how could one out-manoeuvre the vile scoundrel? It won't be at all easy, no not easy, but possible, nevertheless.
Chairestratos	Possible? And the task well worth the effort , by Athena…

Cf. Jacques:

Daos	So how could one out-manoeuvre the vile scoundrel? It won't be at all easy, no not easy, but possible, nevertheless; yes, possible.
Chairestratos	And the task well worth the effort , by Athena…

The present text follows that of Arnott, with the objection once made to assigning an oath by Athena to a slave now diminished by fr. adesp.1063.8 K-A., spoken by a slave, and Philemon fr. 82.3 K-A., where it is used by a cook.

321ff. Despite damage to the text it is clear that Daos begins to formulate his plot, and, as at 23ff., Menander inserts comments by others in order to divide up into more manageable sections, each with its own topic, what would otherwise have been a lengthy monologue: 1) temptation (321–7), 2) illness (329–42), 3) death (343–6), 4) inheritance (348–52). The overall result is reminiscent, in fact, of ring-composition, where a passage begins and ends on the same theme. Thus, Daos opens with a reference to 'two talents', which probably harks back to the value of Cleostratos' booty, but is equally relevant to the dowry Chairestratos mentioned at 268f. From this he progresses to the as yet unspecified alternative and the effect this will have on Smikrines. In response to Chairestratos' request for clarification (328) we hear details of the deception to be carried out, but it is clear from the reaction of father and son that they have failed to link the pretended death with the financial factor. Only by returning to the mention of the talents in the context of Chairestratos' vastly superior estate do the pieces fall into place. In this way Menander not only allows a natural process of explanation to be played out on stage, but also ensures that the audience is given every opportunity to grasp what is being proposed. As Zagagi points out p. 83 (cf. Munteanu p. 125f.), the play now involves two reported deaths, one a patent fiction, the other believed to be real, but itself a fiction (as the audience is well aware), and two heiresses threatened in turn by unscrupulous weddings – two plays, in fact, one inside the other.

327. a very poor judge of reality: Lit. 'a very foolish judge of the truth'. This is an essential requirement if Daos' scheme is to succeed cf. Diphilus fr. 99 K-A, 'The sordid love of gain is a most stupid thing. For concentrating on gain the mind sees nothing else'. The basis for that success, however, needs to be established since up to this point Smikrines has not lacked an astute appreciation of his own interests. Now, though, Daos plans to turn that very astuteness against him by offering a prize so lucrative (350) that the old man becomes blind to the blatant trickery directed against him in Act III. Significantly too Daos himself now displays a not inconsiderable degree of understanding as regards the laws of inheritance, though in the present instance directed towards good. As Nünlist 2002, p. 240 n. 70 observes, in what follows Daos provides a vivid 'rehearsal scene' of what is later to happen, bringing before the eyes of the audience a narrative of subsequent action, cf. *Epitrepontes* 513–35.

329f. a different tragic act: *I.e.* different (ἀλλοῖον) from that caused by the report of Cleostratos' death. Others interpret the word as a euphemism for 'bad', hence Arnott's 'a sombre tragedy', a sense attested elsewhere. In view of the manuscript's textual problem here, reading 'You folk must put on a tragic act *affecting the family*' (Ferrari, Jacques) also has some appeal, though it requires 'family' to be understood in the more restricted sense of Chairestratos' immediate family.

336f. Most ailments...from grief: Cf. Philemon fr. 106,1–3 K-A, 'For everyone by its very nature grief is the cause of many problems. It's through grief that madness and incurable illnesses come to many people'.

338f. gloomy side...prone to depression: G.-S. ad loc. point out the incongruity that someone here described as having a gloomy side should be portrayed elsewhere in much more positive terms. However, insertion of the description is used to explain the depression Chairestratos is now to feign, depression which the old man had himself introduced at 306 as a passing reference.

340. weighs up all the symptoms: Lit. 'philosophises', but with connotations of conducting an examination accompanied by pretentious verbiage.

346f. Do you understand...?: Just as Daos was earlier portrayed as being more morally correct than Smikrines in his attitude to the old man's schemes (despite deferring to his supposedly greater understanding of Attic law), so here Daos is pointedly shown to be more intelligent than either Chairestratos or Chaireas.

348–55. Your daughter becomes an heiress…: In detailing the plan Daos forecasts that Smikrines will forgo his claim to Cleostratos' sister, tempted by an even greater profit, and will marry her off to the first suitor who asks for her, presumably Chaireas. Commentators, however, have pointed out the flaw in this – the fact that Chairestratos cannot remain dead for ever, and once he resurfaces there may be nothing to prevent Smikrines from reverting to his former plan (Ireland 1992, p. 107, Scafuro pp. 340–50). Whether Daos recognises the flaw, or whether it ever becomes a factor in the action may be masked by textual loss in later Acts. Equally, as Brown (1983, p. 419) points out, the whole situation becomes irrelevant the moment Cleostratos returns, and he questions whether Menander ever gave thought to such hypothetical developments and, in consequence, if we should. Further textual loss after 361 also removes the means by which it is suggested Chairestratos will turn the tables on his brother. Mention of exacting twice the amount at 367 suggests the standard penalty for theft (Demosthenes XXIV, 105 'If a man has recovered property he lost, the penalty will be twice the amount; if he has not recovered it, the penalty will be twice (or ten times) the amount in addition to the penalties set down by law', Lloyd-Jones p. 184f., cf. Jacques 1998a, p. 26 n. 1), but it is unclear how the fragmentary references here can be reconciled with fixing seals on Chairestratos' property mentioned at 357f. Presumably they are to prevent items from being removed from rooms, or at least to indicate attempted removal if the seals are found broken. Or is the fact that Smikrines may be found appropriating property before the necessary court decision awarding him ownership the issue here? (See further Harrison 1968, p. 207 n. 2, Scafuro pp. 342–4).

351. hers four: Presumably the total value of Cleostratos' estate: what he inherited from his father and the value of the booty.

353. You're dense if you don't: Lit. 'Unless you're made of rock'. It is uncertain whether such an overtly risqué comment from a slave is to be taken as an aside (Lloyd-Jones p. 184, Gaiser 1973, p. 127), as a jocular interjection within the conspiratorial atmosphere, or whether it forms a momentary lapse of patience by Daos (Bain p. 127).

356. or so he thinks: The manuscript gives the words as part of Chairestratos' rejoinder to the idea that Smikrines will attempt to impose himself upon his daughter: 'He'll be sorry for imagining that' (G.-S.). Kassel, however, suggested that the assignment of parts at this point is at fault, and that the words in fact belong to Daos: Smikrines will claim Chairestratos' daughter – or so he thinks, as in the translation.

[**358f. in his dreams**: ὄναρ here is an accusative of respect.]

368–75. The assignment of parts in the papyrus would suggest:

Chairestratos   …after my own heart…scoundrel?
Daos   By Zeus…hungry.
Chairestratos   So we need…charlatan.

Editors, however, have generally supposed the loss of a *dicolon* after 'my own heart', thus allowing the desire for vengeance to come from Chairestratos, who has more clearly suffered from Smikrines' machinations.

[**372. It's true...goes**: Lit. 'Truly the saying (goes)...'. ταῖς ἀληθείαις has basically the same meaning as the singular form τῇ ἀληθείᾳ used adverbially, *i.e.* 'in truth'. In what follows διὰ κενῆς is perhaps to be interpreted as indicating the condition in which the wolf goes off: lit. 'in emptiness' or 'to no purpose' *i.e.* hungry (see *LSJ* I, 2).]

373. The wolf's jaws are open: A proverbial expression of frustrated hopes that appears in various forms elsewhere in literature: 'like a ravenous wolf' (Aristophanes' *Lysistrata* 629), 'the man's after your estate, mouth agape like a ravenous wolf' (Plautus' *Stichus* 605), 'like a gaping wolf' (Euboulos fr. 14.11 K-A), 'you alone have found the technique of the wolf not gaping to no effect' (Euphron fr. 1.30f. K-A).

374f. a foreign doctor...charlatan: Since the main medical schools of antiquity (Cos, Cnidus, Sicily) were in Doric-speaking areas, those doctors who were portrayed on the comic stage were usually given the appropriate dialect. Like cooks and soldiers they formed part of the stock assemblage of professional types, and were characterised in general as self-important and bombastic figures ripe for derision, hence the description here (cf. Alexis' *Mandragorizomenos* fr. 146 K-A, where a character complains that instructions given by a local doctor are ignored, while one giving the same instructions in a foreign dialect is regarded with admiration). By introducing a friend of Chaireas suitably disguised instead of a real doctor Menander is not only able to account for the character's ready participation in the deception but also to exaggerate even further all those traits that contained comic potential, and through that exaggeration to point out even more clearly Smikrines' gullibility.

377f. a wig and a fancy cloak and a stick: The first and last are required in order to age the character, to suggest the wisdom of experience, the cloak to suggest the affluence that comes with success.

381–90. Assignment of parts here is disputed, with some early editors (Austin, Borgogno) giving a continuing role to Chaireas on the basis of his name being included as a marginal note at 383. Daos' instruction to hurry at 379, however, would suggest an exit for the young man at this point. Others have over-ridden the evidence of *dicola* in the text to produce, *e.g.* Jacques:

Chairestratos	I'll do just that.
Daos	Don't let anyone outside. Be resolute in guarding the scheme. Who'll be in on it with us?
Chairestratos	Only my wife...dead.
Daos	Quite right...persuasive act.

The text adopted here follows the assignment suggested by the manuscript's *dicola* and accepted by Sandbach and Arnott.

383f. Only my wife...: A parting quip designed to illustrate once again Chairestratos' humanity in sparing his immediate family the grief associated with death, but also allowing the introduction of comedy in the pointed contrast with what the old man envisages will be the reaction of his wider household to the news.

386. vent their spleen: Lit. 'behave loutishly as the result of drink', cf. *Dyskolos* 93. Chairestratos paints a comic contrast between the 'normal' behaviour of his slaves and what he envisages will be their reaction to news of his death – an outpouring of their true feelings.

388–90: fine entertainment…persuasive act: The final words of the Act serve as foreshadowing, preparing the audience for what is to come in Act III: the creation of a comedy within an ostensible tragedy and the exaggerated antics of the false doctor.

Act III

391. Smikrines: The opening of the Act, with the entry of the old man, brings back into dramatic focus Smikrines' designs on his nephew's estate, signalled by his determination to secure the inventory he demanded at 274–5, just before his last exit. But as his efforts in this direction reach their climax, the counter-measures devised by Daos likewise come into play, with the charade promised in the previous Act now brought on stage. Behind the logic of Smikrines' barbed and sarcastic opening statement lie multiple levels of irony:

1) the old man is correct in assuming a conspiracy against him and that Daos is a participant in it, but it is a conspiracy based on factors far removed from the deliberate delay in providing information that he envisages;

2) while his interpretation of events allows him to indulge in self-congratulation over his astuteness, this comes at the very point his greed will make him blind to the deception prepared against him;

3) though he is on his guard against any attempt at deception by Daos, he shows himself fundamentally gullible when faced by the slave's blatant histrionics. For the audience the entry of Daos apparently in the depths of despair signals the 'play within a play' they have been led to expect, a display of high emotion apt for the situation but in a form that roots it firmly in farce: parodies of tragic norms through the combination of quotation and banal reference to their sources (Blänsdorf pp. 137–41, Hunter p. 121, Zagagi p. 54, Hurst 1990, p. 96), and quotations that seize the old man's attention but also irritate him by the delay their profusion injects into his attempts to attract attention. The scene becomes all the more effective theatrically as Daos' outpourings are matched by his evident frantic rushing about the stage (hence Smikrines' question at 410 'where are you rushing off to?', Anderson p. 232f.), a stark contrast to the introduction of Cleostratos' supposed death with which the play opened.

395. by your leave: Lit. 'with humane feelings'. Smikrines is clearly now determined upon exploitation of his own advantage without any reference to its effect upon others.

398. runaway: The last word in the line and a pointed contrast to the Waiter's criticism at 241, that absconding with the booty is specifically what Daos did not do. Though the word is a common form of abuse against a slave, it may represent yet another, if gentle, pointer to the dichotomy between Smikrines' thinking and reality.

399. Daos: As at 164 the entry of the slave is self-motivated, this time, though, with the deliberate intention of 'interaction' with the old man, clear from the overtly 'tragic' opening words which set the tone of what is to follow. Commentators have questioned the rationale of the slave's entry: how he comes to be aware of Smikrines' presence on stage as the cue to begin his 'performance'. Suggestions that he entered by chance during the old man's opening statements, noticed him and then launched upon his tragic display (Anderson p. 233) are unnecessary. As often, the audience is simply invited to accept the situation as presented (Bain 175f.).

408. Again, wonderfully put: The words indicate that we have lost at least one quotation in the preceding lines; of those that remain a number were popular tags:

407, ('There is no man...') the opening line from Eupripides' lost play *Stheneboea* (fr. 661 Kannicht) and frequently quoted, *e.g.* by Aristophanes' *Frogs* 1217, Aristotle *Rhetoric* 1394b2, and by the fragmentary comic writers Nicostratus (fr. 29.1K-A) and Philippides (fr. 18.3 K-A).

411, ('Chance not prudence...') from the 4th century tragedian Chaeremon's *Achilles Thersitoktonos* (fr. 2 Snell), cited elsewhere by Plutarch *Moralia* 97c.

412f., ('God plants..') Aeschylus' *Niobe* (fr. 154a 15–16 Radt), cited elsewhere by Plato in *Republic* 380a and Plutarch's *Moralia* 17b, 1065b.

415, ('Incredible....') an unknown tragedy, though some commentators (*e.g.* Jacques) interpret the words as merely a comment from Daos rather than a citation from literature (cf. Carcinus II fr. 5a Snell).

416, ('What of mortals'...') from an unknown play of Carcinus II (fr. 5a Snell).

417f., ('For in a single day...') either from an unknown play, or continuing the attribution to Carcinus II (fr. 5a Snell).

424f. ('There is nought...') the opening lines of Euripides' *Orestes*.

425f. ('For tragedies...') a line attributed to both Chaeremon (fr. 42 Snell) and Euripides (fr. 944a Kannicht). The quotations and their use are discussed in detail by Cusset p. 144–58.

419. All these...Smikrines: Having extracted the desired degree of comedy from the incongruity of the situation on both visual and aural levels, Menander effortlessly converts what was essentially a highly managed form of disguised dialogue into a real exchange, and with an abruptness that fully exposes for the audience the sham of Daos' earlier 'failure' to register Smikrines' presence. Similarly, the quotations that emerge at 424–6 continue the theme of mockery with the pedantic scholarship of their referencing and the contrast between true emotion and its parody (Omitowoju p. 157f.).

420f.: Your brother...death's door: In delivering the supposed reality behind the series of tragic quotations Menander ensures maximum impact by placing the significant words first and last in their sentence and as the first words in their respective lines.

422. bile: Referred to also at 439, 451, often found in the form 'black bile' (hence the English 'melancholy', cf. 306n. above) and regarded as a cause and symptom of mental disturbance (cf. Menander *Dyskolos* 89, *Samia* 416). Grief is likewise found associated with insanity in Antiphanes fr. 287 K-A 'Grief seems to me to be akin to madness', and Alexis fr. 298 K-A 'Grief has something in common with madness', while madness itself is here described lit. as 'being out of his mind' The list of symptoms, like so much else here, is clearly designed to emphasise the gravity of the situation.

428f. Has a doctor come?: Only at this point does Smikrines manage to seize the initiative in the dialogue and steer the exchange (necessarily) onto a new track. There may be an additional level of irony here if Poole (p. 56f.) is correct in seeing Daos' earlier tragic quotations as a desperate series of cues for the false doctor to make his entrance.

430. This one: G.-S. (*Dyskolos* 78ff.n.) criticise resort to such coincidental arrivals, but the appearance of the 'doctor' at the precise moment he is mentioned uses a convention without which drama could not function (cf. Sophocles *Oedipus Tyrannos* 73–9, a reference to Creon's delay in reporting back followed immediately by his entry). Here it is disguised by the instruction to hurry along, itself a potential source of humour in the contrast between the urgent need for attention and what is probably the doctor's self-important and stately progress onto the stage. (cf. Plautus' *Menaechmi* 888, 'Just look at him (*i.e.* the doctor) coming along – quicken your ant's pace.'). If, as suggested, the doctor responded to the plea for haste in 431, this would account for the total silence of Chaireas, who probably accompanied him, since all three speaking actors would already be accounted for (Frost p. 32).

433. If they see *me*: Smikrines' reluctance to follow the doctor into Chairestratos' house is necessary on a technical level in order to allow for offstage action (cf. *Dyskolos* 639ff.), but like Terence's *Hecyra* 348ff. it 1) chimes in with the old man's suspicious nature, picking up the hint at 432 ('By their helplessness...' itself a line from Euripides' *Orestes* 232), 2) harks back to the rift between himself and the rest of the family, and 3) in his use of 'I didn't make any enquiries' echoes the old man's calculating thought processes at 149 'So that no one can say...'.

439. At some stage in the intervening gap the 'doctor' re-entered the stage and began a description of Chairestratos' symptoms, employing comic Doric word-forms suited to the charlatan mentioned at 374f. (G.-S. p. 99, Jacques 1998a, p. XL). These are often translated into an equally comic form of Scots; readers, however, are invited to insert their own prejudices. More importantly, as Hurst (2000, p. 104) observes, since the scene underpins much of the play's dramatic action and Daos' plan in particular, the 'doctor' must not only engage in burlesque for the amusement of the audience, ultimately no less a parody than Daos' tragic histrionics, but he must also initially display a level of realism sufficiently plausible to fulfil the credibility specified by Daos at the very end of Act II (cf. Hurst 2004, p. 66).

444–6. mind…phrenitis: The mind was popularly regarded as associated with the diaphragm *(phrenes)*, not the brain, hence the variation in possible translation here, *e.g.* Arnott ad loc., 'the diaphragm itself'.

446–7. The manuscript places a *dicolon* at the end of 446 (after 'And then?'), suggesting that what follows is spoken by the doctor as a statement ('There is no hope of recovery'). However, many editors prefer to regard the *dicolon* as misplaced from the end of 447 on the grounds that a categorical pronouncement here would pre-empt that at 450 ('He isn't at all likely to live'), whereas interpretation as a question from Smikrines leads naturally into what follows.

455. Hey you: Textual difficulties make interpretation of this final part of the doctor's role problematic. Why does Smikrines call him back when he has already received the news of Chairestratos' impending death, and why does he insist upon drawing the doctor away from the door (presumably his brother's)? Various possible reconstructions of the text are discussed by Hurst (2000), who suggests that 'You calling me?' (456) might be taken in the technical sense of being called upon to give a medical consultation and that Smikrines is here hoping for an opinion on his own health, though why he should want this when at 459 he boasts of his robust constitution remains elusive. Alternatively, there is much to recommend the idea that the dialogue here serves to illustrate on stage, in the case of Smikrines, the doctor's supposed skill at diagnosis that he hypothetically displayed earlier while off stage (cf. Hurst 2004, p. 67f.), and thus to demonstrate further Smikrines' blindness in the face of evident mockery. This gains added support if Menander intended to tantalise his audience by introducing the possibility of a last-minute impediment to the deception, as happens at the beginning of *Dyskolos* Act V, where a fleeting reference to an objection from Kallippides raises the spectre of an obstacle to Sostratos' marriage to Knemon's daughter before its deflection onto quite a different track. Thus, here too Smikrines' interruption of the doctor's departure may raise the possibility that he has seen through the ruse and that the whole scheme is on the brink of collapse, before it is skilfully steered back into further burlesque as he becomes the victim of palpable ridicule. But why does Smikrines insist upon drawing the doctor from what Jacques (1998a, p. 33 n. 1) argues must be Chairestratos' door? Is it to demonstrate further the old man's secretive tendencies so that no one can learn the result of any supposed consultation (Hurst 2004, p. 68), or is it simply the theatrical necessity of setting the burlesque scene that follows centre-stage (cf. the cajoling of Knemon by Sikon and Getas in *Dyskolos* Act V) rather than stage-right, near the city-exit?

458. You may [not] live as hitherto: Interpretation of the Greek and the doctor's dialect here is problematic. Jacques, for instance, derives the verb not from 'live' but from 'force' and emends τέως 'as hitherto' to θεώς 'the gods', *i.e.* 'you should not force the hand of the gods' though this produces a strained effect.

464. look like death: The doctor's final verdict on Chairestratos at 454 is here mirrored in the phrasing used about Smikrines himself, with the evident implication of a similar outcome: death.

465–7. Well, I expect…water channels: Interpretation of the text as far as the supposition that the servants inside Chairestratos' house are taking advantage of his 'death' to engage in looting is clear enough (cf. 385–6). However, reference to communication via the water channels is altogether obscure, and Gaiser's view of them, based on his emendation of the Greek to produce 'then (things) *are being taken* to the neighbours through the water channels' (1973, p. 136) is unconvincing. An added complication is the suggested attribution of the lines to Daos by Gaiser (1971) and Jacques (1998a). This, though, requires the audience immediately to realise that the statements are bogus and made principally to cause Smikrines anxiety, and over-rides the evidence of the manuscript, which indicates a change of speaker to Daos after 'water-channels'.

467. I'll throw him into confusion: Insertion of the word ησυχη (quietly) between lines in the manuscript (cf. 93n.) suggests it was interpreted by the copyist as an aside, though whether it marks Daos' response to overhearing Smikrines' previous comment or the slave's re-entry following his presumed departure from the stage with the doctor at 432 must remain uncertain (Bain p. 107). In what followed Daos doubtless put his intended ragging of Smikrines into effect, but the loss of the final ten or so lines of the current page and the next two whole sheets of the manuscript removes the end of Act III and virtually the whole of Act IV. Gone too is all direct information on how the situation progressed in the intervening scenes, though as Jacques argues (1998a, p. XLII) it would be strange if these did not include a return to Smikrines' interest in an inventory of Cleostratos' estate. When the mutilated remains of the last extant sheet resume, these consist of no more than line beginnings from the last two scenes of Act IV, followed by line endings from the opening scene of Act V. A general outline, however, is partially recoverable from what does remain, from the demands of the plot, and from the foreshadowing given by Chance in the prologue.

Act IV

If the action now follows Menander's usual technique as seen in other plays where the text is more securely based, the situation developed so far reaches its climax before the resolution marked by the return of Cleostratos at 491. Before that comes a scene in which Chairestratos' death is announced (469–90). The manuscript identifies one of the speakers as Smikrines, but opinion is divided as to the other: either Chaireas (Borgogno, Jacques 1998a), or Daos (Gaiser), or an entirely different character. Following the rapid exchange that marks the actual announcement of death comes a speech (484–90) with mention of a betrothal, which may signal Smikrines' speedy diversion of attention from one heiress to another and his readiness to come to an agreement with Chaireas about Cleostratos' sister, as envisaged at 354f. and mentioned subsequently at 540–4. Jacques (1998a, p. XLIIf., p. 35 n.1), supposing Chaireas to be the character interacting with Smikrines at 469ff., has the two exit towards town at 490 in order to arrange the financial aspects of transferring Cleostratos' sister to the young man. Certainty, however, is elusive.

Following 490 the stage must momentarily have been cleared of characters in readiness for the arrival of Cleostratos and what Goldberg p. 26 rightly refers to as a 'gatekeeper scene', in which a character returning after an absence finds his entry blocked (cf. Euripides' *Helen* 435ff., Aristophanes' *Clouds* 131ff., Plautus' *Amphitryo* 292ff., *Mostellaria* 445ff.). Cleostratos' return follows the traditional pattern of an address to his homeland (which serves to identify him) and a statement reminding the audience of his situation and state of knowledge, followed by interaction with Daos (named in 507), who fails to recognise him and announces the death of Chairestratos as the reason for refused entry, then Cleostratos' shocked response to this and the inevitable recognition of master and servant. Stage action at this point, in particular Daos' failure to recognise his master, is readily explained by supposing either an initial refusal to open the door, with Cleostratos addressed from off-stage (Arnott, Jacques), or that the door is only partially opened (G.-S. ad loc.).

[**469–83**: Following the evidence of the manuscript *paragraphi* have been inserted under the initial letters of lines to indicate changes of speaker.]

469. He's gone: The Greek here carries the same connotations of death as in English.

488–9. ready to produce…whatever you order: It is tempting to see here an indication of Smikrines' willingness to accede to any demands so long as he is able to free himself of what he earlier represented as the legal necessity to marry Cleostratos' sister.

491ff. Despite the tantalising remains of the text there remain many uncertainties for any restoration of Cleostratos' speech here. So for instance, how do we interpret the feminine entity represented by the words 'in need' in 495? Is it a continuing reference to the young man's homeland or his home, or has he shifted his attention to his sister? And do his extant words betoken fears on his part that he may find her in need, or does the subsequent mention of Daos' possible safe return suggest his hope that he does *not* find her in need?

506. Oh Zeus!: The process of mutual identification, which probably began with Cleostratos' reference to his uncle in 504 and perhaps a demand that those inside open the door, here reaches its climax with Daos' appearance attempting to get rid of this troublesome young man, then an exclamation of disbelief and delight.

[**510–44.** Following the manuscript evidence *dicola* (:) are inserted into the Greek text to indicate a potential change of speaker, even if the identity of the speaker cannot be ascertained from the context.]

512. open: The instruction, addressed to more than one person, may indicate that with the need for a show of mourning at an end Chairestratos' house can now be opened up (Arnott 1979a ad loc.).

Act V

Though only the endings of the Act's first 29 lines are preserved, the evident change of metre from iambic trimeters to longer trochaic tetrameters signals a shift in atmosphere to one of greater liveliness more suited to both the wedding celebrations mentioned at 521 and, on the analogy of *Dyskolos* 880ff. where there is a change to iambic tetrameters, the probable punishment of Smikrines. (For possible reconstructions of the Act see Arnott 1979a, pp. 89–93, Holzberg p. 149, Blume pp. 156–8, Jacques 1998a, pp. XLIII–V). Identification of speakers continues to be problematic and must be determined by internal factors such as context, the insertion of names, like that of Chaireas at 528, and the presence of *dicola* at the end of 525, 529, 530, 539, 544, and after 'Where is he?' in 532, as marked in the Greek text (Jacques 1998a ad loc. suggests another before 'everything by Helios' in 529). That said, it seems certain that the opening lines are spoken by Daos, the character most suited to announce the 'resurrection' of Chairestratos, implicit in the references to 'his own daughter' and 'his niece' (522–3), and to reveal to Chaireas, who must have arrived on stage by 528–9, the fact that Cleostratos has returned. Thereafter, Chaireas is probably directed indoors to join his step-cousin while Daos awaits the appearance of Smikrines, perhaps the character said to be approaching at 534. Certainly the reference to knocking in 537 and the need to 'make him better behaved' in 538 (cf. Getas' determination to tame Knemon at *Dyskolos* 902–3) suggest the slave himself withdrew inside, while Smikrines entered at 540, still ruminating on the transfer of Cleostratos' sister to Chaireas. If this is correct, there may well have been a further gatekeeper scene leading into one revealing the truth of the situation to him (cf. *Epitrepontes* 1111ff.) and the old man's discomfiture.

524. the whole estate: The reference may link up with 280–1 where Chairestratos had expressed the hope that he might leave Cleostratos and Chaireas as heirs to his property.

526. I suppose…neighbour: The insertion of a *dicolon* at the end of 525 may indicate the arrival of Chaireas musing on offstage action before noticing Daos, 'this man here'. However, this would require an unsignalled change of speaker either at the end of 527 ('by Zeus'), or immediately before 'Chaireas' in 528, since by the end of the line the young man is clearly being addressed. As a result, Gronewald's suggestion (accepted by Jacques) that the *dicolon* in 525 marks not a change of speaker but of topic – from Daos' thoughts about the wedding to the whereabouts of Chaireas (thereby continuing with Daos as speaker till 528/9) – has much to recommend it.

537. he knocks: Possible foreshadowing of Smikrines' attempt to gain entry to Chairestratos' house in the belief that he now has rights over its contents. If so, it invites a confrontation with Daos, mirroring that at the end of Act IV, but with totally different results.

540ff. The references to what Chaireas wants and to witnesses echo 354f. Similarly, the mention of annoyance in 544 may refer to the complications caused by

Cleostratos' sister which have been impeding the transfer of the old man's interest to Chairestratos' daughter.

Fragment of Papyrus B

A scrap of papyrus which provides no more than a series of letters from a total of five lines from which only two words belonging to the second column can be confidently established. Editors have traditionally and hesitantly assigned the text to the breaks at 404–6 and 436–9.

Fragment assigned to Act III

The fragment, which lacks any external indication of either author or play, was assigned to the end of Act III of *Aspis* by Gaiser (1983) based on a number of coincidences of theme between it and Menander's play:

1) A girl is reported to be grieving over the approaching death of her father. This would fit a situation in which, following his determination at 467 to throw Smikrines into confusion, Daos reports events taking place inside the house as Chairestratos dies, with emphasis upon the daughter's reaction (fictional in view of 384f.) as a cue for Smikrines' change of plan.
2) The fragment contains a strong reference to law, and suggested restoration has been used to expand the dichotomy between obedience to the law and the appropriateness of that obedience (cf. Sophocles' *Antigone*). This would seem to fit with Smikrines' emphasis of the legal claim he has on his niece at 186f., and further references to law in the play at 156–8, 170, 291, 298.
3) The fragment mentions a 'good judge'. This seems to echo, and invert, the reference to Smikrines at 326f. as 'a very poor judge of reality'.
4) The reference to 'put on one side' (lit. 'carry away for oneself – *LSJ* ἄγω B 1) in line 3 may echo Smikrines' fear at 465 that part of Chairestratos' estate, which he intends to inherit, is being removed by others (cf. Daos' earlier forecast at 356–8 that the old man would go round the house with seals in order to secure the property). Gaiser links this to his emendation (1973, p. 136) of ἐπιτάττεται ('instructions are being passed', lit. 'orders are being given') at 466 to ἔπειτ' ἄγεται ('then (things) *are being taken*').

However, at the same time there are a number of factors which make attribution to the play hazardous:

1) In view of the total number of New Comedy poets active and the number of plays produced by Menander himself, the statistical probability of the fragment belonging to *Aspis* is small in the extreme, even in the context of a girl sobbing.
2) As Gaiser himself recognises, the loss of line beginnings and ends means that the

passage lacks any identification of speaker or even at what points the speakers change. Hence the at times radical variation of Jacques' assignment of parts (and text):

Smikrines	…unjust [ ] the word and law of a tyrant [must be obeyed]…
Daos	The girl was there as well. Grieving at death [ ] she sobbed, 'Oh, father, father,' and [ ]. 'Oh, take me in your arms, father, [ ].
Smikrines	To my present fortune [ ]
Daos	And not a good judge in a good situation…

3) The themes of law and reported grieving are not unique to the play.
4) Association of the fragment with Menander's play is based on arguments that in many respects are circular. Thus, there is a distinct possibility that suggested restoration, and the interpretation that comes from this, has been formulated on the premise that the connection exists, which automatically influences the choice of restoration. This is best seen in the supplement [ἔμυ]ξεν in line 5. Certainly, Erotian attributes the word to *Aspis*, but the existence of possible alternatives, makes any categorical acceptance here unsafe (see further Jacques 1998a, p. 40f.).

Stobaeus Eclogue 4, 8, 7
Any attempt either to locate the quotation within the action or to assign a speaker must remain highly conjectural. Its contents, with the allusion to the hazards of desiring more than others, suggest an analogy with Smikrines' greed. The tone of regret created by 'wretched' and 'pitiable existence', likewise, may suggest a comment on the old man's state following his discomfiture in Act V, but there can be no certainty. Similarly, Arnott 1979a, p. 92 n. 1 signals the series of assassinations that took place in the Greek world towards the end of the fourth century as perhaps providing some inspiration for the reference, but counsels against using this as evidence of dating (cf. Jacques 1998a, pp. LXXXI–III, 41 n. 1).

THE ARBITRATION: INTRODUCTION

The Plot and its Construction

Though direct information on the details of the plot is frequently hampered by the defective state of the text, combining what is known (if only by inference) with the generic characteristics of New Comedy allows a reasonably accurate outline to be established.

(Act I): On his return home (presumably from a business trip abroad) the young man Charisios has been informed by his slave Onesimos that during his absence his wife Pamphile has given birth to a baby and has had it exposed. Realising that after a mere five months of marriage the child cannot possibly have been conceived in wedlock and that his wife must have come to him as 'damaged goods', he has fled his home, moved in with his friend next door, Chairestratos, and has hired a music girl in what seems to his father-in-law Smikrines to be a non-stop round of parties that threatens to squander the dowry Pamphile brought to the marriage. As we later learn, however, Charisios' behaviour is, in fact, a vain attempt to blot out the pain of his discovery, pain that is clear not only from subsequent evidence[1] but also from the very course of action he has taken. Under other circumstances social convention and the law would require Charisios to repudiate his wife and send her back to her father in disgrace;[2] instead, it is he who has left home and has revealed nothing of the true cause of his distress. It is not that he has ceased to love his wife, but rather that something has arisen to disrupt the young couple's mutual affection – the pregnancy. However, as the original audience will have learned from the lost deferred prologue, presumably spoken by an omniscient divinity or personified abstraction, the cause of the pregnancy, Pamphile's rape nine months earlier, was perpetrated by the very man who has subsequently become her husband, with neither recognising the other because of the darkness at the time. During the rape,

---

1   *E.g.* his hostile reaction to Onesimos and the music girl Habrotonon reported at the beginning of Act III.
2   Harrison (1968) p. 35f., G.-S. p. 292. It should, however, be noted that analogies for such action in real life involve defilement of an already existing marriage. Whether the extension to rape before marriage is valid must remain a moot point, cf. the situation in Terence's *Hecyra.*

however, Pamphile was able to seize a ring from her assailant and this forms part of the birth-tokens that have been left with the child.

(Act II): In the meantime, the infant has been discovered by the shepherd Daos, but following second thoughts on the prospect of its upbringing he has been induced to hand it over to the charcoal-maker, Syriskos, whose wife is pining because of the recent loss of her own baby. Syriskos subsequently learns that Daos retained the items found with the child and demands that they be restored to their true owner. In the ensuing wrangle they refer the matter for arbitration (the title-scene of the play) to the old man Smikrines, unknowingly the child's own grandfather, who determines that the trinkets be restored to the baby. The subsequent intervention of Onesimos, while Syriskos and his wife are examining the trinkets, leads to recognition of the ring as belonging to Charisios, and Onesimos' determination to show it to his master.

(Act III): Faced with his master's continuing enmity as the cause of his misery Onesimos hesitates to carry out his plan despite the efforts of Syriskos to bring this about. At this point the appearance of the music-girl Habrotonon, her evident sympathy for the child and her memory of a rape that took place nine-months earlier at a festival she attended, lead to her take over control of the plot by using the ring to pose as the child's mother in order to confirm Charisios as father – a ring, after all, might be lost in any number of circumstances. Only then does she feel it right to begin the process of establishing the identity of the mother. In the event, Habrotonon's claims reach the ears not only of Charisios and his party-friends but also of Smikrines, who is scandalised by the news that the young man is the father of an illegitimate child, and he determines to remove his daughter from her marital home.

(Act IV): In the ensuing confrontation between father and daughter Smikrines attempts to persuade his daughter to leave her husband, emphasising the ruination of Charisios' finances if he establishes Habrotonon as his mistress, the neglect that Pamphile will inevitably suffer from Charisios' fixation with his mistress, and the eventual usurpation of her very role as wife. For her part Pamphile counters with a spirited display of loyalty to her husband, but this is evidently not enough to dampen the old man's determination. As Pamphile is left alone bewailing her misfortune, she comes face to face with Habrotonon carrying the child. On one side Habrotonon recognises Pamphile as the girl who was raped at the festival; on the other Pamphile

evidently recognises something the baby is wearing, and from this comes the realisation that with rapist and victim now married the one factor that threatened to tear them irrevocably apart has evaporated. In the meantime Pamphile's defence of her marriage, overheard by Charisios, has resulted in a radical reappraisal of his own behaviour, part of which is reported by Onesimos, the rest coming from the young man himself in a bout of savage self-criticism. Soon, however, he too is rescued from his plight as Habrotonon reveals the truth of the child's origins.

(Act V): With the underlying problem that formed the basis of the plot now resolved the final Act conventionally exists to tie up loose ends, reward those who have helped in overcoming obstacles, and to show others the error of their ways. The first two may be partially inferred from the evidence of the Act's fragmentary opening (major losses of text affecting over 70 lines) and a reference in the ancient writer Choricius to a character called Chairestratos somewhere in a Menandrian play who is in love with a harp-girl.[3] All this suggests a scene revealing 1) Chairestratos' unhappiness at the news that Charisios has fathered offspring on Habrotonon, 2) Chairestratos' own attraction to the woman, yet readiness to suppress his feelings out of loyalty to his friend, and 3) the happy resolution of his anguish by revelation of the truth, which may lead to a new lover for Habrotonon and perhaps the freedom she had hoped for in Act III. Much of this, however, must remain speculation. With virtue presumably rewarded, the ogre of the play, Smikrines, who left the stage shortly after 835, now returns bringing with him Pamphile's old nurse Sophrone, ostensibly to add weight to the case for divorce he made at the beginning of Act IV. Before he can act on his planned removal of his daughter from her husband, however, he is accosted by Onesimos, who berates the old man for his foolishness and reveals the truth through allusion to a parallel situation in tragedy, the relevance of which Sophrone grasps far more quickly than her master, demonstrating the essential folly of his thinking. Though subsequent action is largely lost, the intervention of Chairestratos and analogies elsewhere suggest that with Smikrines suitably chastened he is nevertheless led inside to join the festivities that resolution of the play's problems has brought about.

---

3   The fact that Chairestratos figures also as a character in Menander's *Aspis* and *Eunouchos* suggests caution against too ready acceptance of Choricius' comment here, though the association of the name with a harp-girl lends weight to the argument.

The Characters

The characters of Menander have been aptly described as the undistinguished rich and the undistinguished poor, together with those lesser individuals with whom they might come into contact: slaves, cooks, soldiers, prostitutes, essentially a tiny assemblage of figures centred on one or two family units. Such description, giving rise to their depiction as stock character-types, has the disadvantage that it suggests an overarching uniformity of presentation which is far from the reality. For while in general it is true that totally distinct individuals such as Knemon in *Dyskolos* are rare, each character within a group nevertheless contains elements that sets him or her apart from the others. True, the same names are often found from play to play, but not only are these at times found connected to figures who fall within different categories (*e.g.* old man/young man, prostitute/wife) but also, since character is adjusted to the prime function of plot, they display a variety of nuance to fit the role they play within the individual play. In this way Menander produces a veneer of uniformity while injecting into it a degree of individuality.

Smikrines: A name traditionally attached to old men within Menander's comedies, as evidenced by *Aspis* and *Sikyonios*, and often bearing connotations of small-mindedness, but in each case with a distinct variation.[4] Thus, while the Smikrines of *Aspis* is a truly acquisitive miser and a definite ogre-figure, the Sikyonian version, for all that he is described in Act IV as having oligarchic tendencies, must ultimately be shown in a much more favourable light as father of the play's 'hero', the soldier Stratophanes. Smikrines in *Epitrepontes*, on the other hand, while closer to the *Aspis* version in the emphasis he places upon finance as opposed to the emotional trauma caused to his daughter, is seen in a more positive light by writers like MacCary (1971 p. 307), who emphasises the old man's role in the arbitration scene – how he unknowingly determines the fate of his own grandson, how his interference, if wrong-headed and misdirected, is seriously motivated and founded on a sense of justice, and how, though he acts as barrier to the obligatory happy ending, he is also the catalyst to its achievement through the reunion of baby and trinkets.[5]

---

4   Cf. Brown (1987) p. 196f. A Smikrines was evidently also the 'miserly' character in the Greek original of Plautus' Roman version, *Aulularia*, if the evidence of Choricius *Apol. Mim.* XXXII, 73 is correct: 'Smikrines the miser type, who 'is afraid that smoke gets out and takes with it something inside his house', cf. *Aulularia* 299–301, 'He immediately calls on God and man to witness that he's lost everything and been wiped out the moment any smoke from his fire gets out'.

5   Cf. Martina II.1, pp. 246–8.

Charisios: For all the restriction of Charisios' appearance on stage to a single episode in Act IV,[6] his role in the play is of pivotal importance. The fact that he also forms the focus of attention for others means that we are presented with a whole range of characterisation: the Charisios of Onesimos, a master whose resentment inspires apprehension and fear; the Charisios of Smikrines, a son-in-law living a profligate life; the Charisios of Chairestratos, a friend who deserves loyalty; the Charisios of Habrotonon, an employer whose neglect of amatory opportunities inspires sympathy; and the Charisios of Pamphile, a husband whom she will support despite the troubles in their marriage. The reality of Charisios is more difficult to gauge, his stage appearance dominated as it is by biting self-recrimination in a situation far removed from normality. Yet within the self-loathing to which he gives expression there is the unmistakable demonstration of his true feelings of love for a wife he has unwillingly abandoned, a love that places into their proper perspective those other aspects of his behaviour we see: his resentment towards Onesimos for revealing Pamphile's disgrace and his neglect of a hedonistic lifestyle he had evidently hoped would blot out his feelings of misery at the breakdown of his marriage.

Pamphile: Abandoned by her husband, assailed by her father's attempts to remove her from her marital home, a casualty of pre-marital rape, Pamphile is personified as the victim of the males who surround her, her very name, 'Dear to all',[7] a seeming contradiction of the situation in which she finds herself. Doubtless, revelation of the true situation in the prologue would provide surface mitigation of her plight, but it is a feature of ancient drama that despite such information the audience is nevertheless caught up in the pathos of her situation, be this real,[8] or imaginary – Onesimos' forecast of possible divorce at 566–71.[9] The sympathy that this automatically evokes from an audience is further heightened by Pamphile's actual appearance on stage in Act IV and the spirited and firm defence she makes of the husband who has deserted her, the more so in view of the cost that this exacts, as

---

6   Because of the often fragmentary nature of the text certainty here is impossible; hence some would posit a role for him also in Act V (*e.g.* Arnott (1979a) pp. 505–8).

7   As G.-S. observe p. 291, the name was found attached to both respectable women and *hetairai* in Athenian society, while elsewhere it occurs only in the Roman adaptations.

8   The audience would, for instance, have known that the young girl whose rape is described by Habrotonon at 486ff. is actually Pamphile.

9   The slave hypothesises Charisios' reaction if the mother of the child is ultimately discovered to be freeborn – divorce for Pamphile to make way for the new girl and her baby. A variation on this is later presented to Pamphile by Smikrines in Act IV based on the supposition that Charisios has fathered a child on a prostitute.

revealed in fr. 8, traditionally located before 853 and coming immediately before the process of ending her misery.

Chairestratos: A name shared in New Comedy by both the older generation (*Aspis*) and the younger, as here.[10] Within the extant text his function is highly restricted, providing 1) a sounding board by which Smikrines' fulminations at the end of Act I can be gauged, 2) possible interaction with the old man in the highly fragmentary sections at the end of Act III, 3) the means by which Habrotonon is rewarded, if interpretation of the beginning of Act V is correct, and 4) the means perhaps of both confirming the information given to Smikrines by Onesimos towards the end of the final Act, and of reintegrating the old man into the family so that the play can end on a note of general reconciliation. As such he may represent a lighter version of Charisios himself, the as yet unmarried boon companion and stand-in for situations in which Charisios himself cannot become involved.

Habrotonon: As a *hetaira*,[11] and the property of a pimp Habrotonon might have been expected to present a one-dimensional image within the context of a minor role in the play. Instead Menander has chosen to create in her arguably the most complex figure of the action, one indeed that illustrates well the playwright's ability to inject new and surprising facets into what might be regarded as a stereotype.[12] It is with this standard picture, in fact, that Menander begins, if her wish at 166 that many houses be turned upside-

---

10   Chairestratos was also the young man in Menander's *Eunouchos*, Phaedria in Terence's adaptation.

11   Lit. 'female companion', but English has no word to cover the full spectrum of typology represented in antiquity. At the lowest level are those like Habrotonon who are slaves to a pimp and hired out to a variety of clients, their highest aspiration to attract the affection of a lover willing to buy them and either keep them for their personal gratification, or free them and maintain them as mistresses like Philematium in Plautus' *Mostellaria*. Others, though free-born, came from the lower strata of society or were non-Athenian, and if they had no relative to act as legal guardian and to provide for them, might be forced into prostitution simply by poverty and the restrictions society placed upon their economic prospects. The best that they could hope for was to become the long-tem mistress of a citizen, like Chrysis in *Samia*. In either case the personal qualities of such women, allied with the artistic skills they possessed, might attract a lover whose status would in turn allow them to rise in society; in other cases those same qualities could attract a range of wealthy lovers, offering the prospect of amassing sufficient funds to support them after their beauty had faded, often through setting up a brothel of their own (cf. Scapha's advice to Philematium in *Mostellaria* 199–217; see further Fantham pp. 49–52, Krieter-Spiro pp. 43–54, Brown (1990) p. 247–50).

12   Arnott (1979a) pp. xxxii–v, cf. Ireland (1992) p. 74.

down is built upon the thought that domestic upset creates more clients for herself. If so, it marks what Arnott 1979a p. xxxiv calls 'an opportunism' that later recurs at 541–9 in the hope that involvement in discovering the origins of the baby will win her freedom, but already by then the 'standard' picture has begun to change radically if not exactly been replaced.[13] So for instance, at the beginning of Act III the neglect, even hostility, she receives from Charisios, rather than causing resentment, results in sympathy, albeit set within what for her are the realistic terms of finance (437). So too the feelings she expresses for the child at 466 have their limits, as rejection of any desire for children of her own at 547 makes clear: altruism in not wanting to see Charisios' son brought up a slave, but with no strings attached. Mention of the ring lost at the Tauropolia leads to thoughts of the girl raped and the damage to her clothes, mingling emotional trauma with material loss, but here mingled too with empathy produced by thoughts of her own lost virginity. Where one might have expected a plot solved by the ingenuity of a male slave (*e.g.* Daos in *Aspis*), it is Habrotonon's intelligence that takes over the task of resolution, leaving Onesimos bemoaning his own ponderous lack of initiative, attributing to Habrotonon a self-centred motivation clearly at variance with reality,[14] yet hoping to gain from it some advantage for himself. Confronted with Pamphile in Act IV her behaviour brings to a climax the altruism seen so far, combined with her acute awareness of the delicate situation that social propriety imposes upon her. Faced with Charisios, a more matter-of-fact attitude comes through, though one still suffused with sympathy, despite damage to the text.

In view of his decision to engineer a resolution such as we see Menander might well have produced a figure overwhelmingly good, like Bacchis in Terence's *Hecyra*; the result would have been cloying, something Terence (or the creator of the Greek original, Apollodorus of Carystus) avoided by introducing the woman herself only in the final scenes of the play. Rather, Menander creates a balanced depiction: someone whose hopes for personal advantage stem not from her own thoughts but from the insinuations of another (539f.), whose fiction about her relationship to the child is balanced by her honesty elsewhere, who expresses qualms about what she undertakes (555f.) but who has the courage to carry it through.[15]

---

13 For the variety of opinion that the depiction of Habrotonon has produced from commentators see G.-S. p. 334, Krieter-Spiro p. 115f.
14 As Brown (1990) p. 258 points out, there is a strong contrast between how characters describe Habrotonon and what we see of her, cf. Martina II.1 p. 289, Traill pp. 196–203, pp. 223–35.
15 See further Henry pp. 51–60.

Onesimos: For a character who is so closely bound up with the difficulties faced by Charisios and Pamphile, Onesimos proves a curiously inept character, his very name, 'Helpful' being an ironic reversal of his role in the play. Rather, his tendency to inquisitiveness (fr. 2a, 387), and to reveal unwelcome information (424f.), severely reduces his usefulness to any resolution of the plot. Instead his function swings dramatically from forwarding plot development, as for instance in recognising ownership of the ring in Act II, to its retardation in Act III by his pusillanimous unwillingness to follow through the implications of that recognition for fear of exciting even greater enmity from his master. The result is a fixation with discovering the child's mother rather than confronting Charisios with the evidence of rape (451–7), and Onesimos' replacement in terms of effective management of the situation by Habrotonon. True, he is concerned for the future of Pamphile (568–71) but this only really emerges in our extant text after the planning of a solution has been taken over by the harp-girl, and the part he plays here seems geared as much to revelation of her character as his own: someone well aware of his limitations (560–2) and distrustful of others (563–5). A more conventionally comic aspect may well have interposed itself in the highly fragmentary text at the beginning of Act II (see Commentary on 180–216), where he seemingly diverts Smikrines from entering Chairestratos' house in order to confront his son-in-law, and is certainly present in Act V where, with a display of impertinence, he brings the old man to a realisation of the truth. That there is a considerable discrepancy between his behaviour in earlier Acts and here is perhaps to be accounted for by 1) the removal of the apprehension that was earlier a major feature of his approach to the situation, 2) the more festive atmosphere often found in final Acts (cf. *Dyskolos*) in the context of 'punishing' the character who has been the main retarding factor, and 3) the loss at times of whole scenes, especially in Act I.

Daos: As often in New Comedy slave names indicate an ethnic origin – Phrygian if analogy with Daos in *Aspis* (206) is fully applicable, though a derivation from Dacia has also been suggested.[16] Essentially Daos' character is built upon the premise of providing a strong contrast with that of Syriskos, personifying the rough-and-ready countryman, an impediment to progress within the plot by his self-centred insistence on retaining for himself the trinkets found with the child. His speech claiming ownership of them shows a simplicity and directness of style, but mingled with a tendency 1) to regret

---

16   Krieter-Spiro p. 55.

initial decisions, 2) to emphasise his own interests, the inessential and the illogical, 3) to 'prove' by assertion and to assume validity for his arguments by simple narration.[17] As such he condemns himself out of his own mouth in considering the child no more than another piece of property, and is surprisingly (and comically) aggrieved when the verdict goes against him as a result.

Syriskos: The slave represents an important stage in the journey towards the play's happy ending – the character through whose efforts an abandoned infant is reunited with its birth tokens, leading ultimately not only to identification of its parents but also to the restoration of a marriage that for a while seems destined to disintegrate.[18] Endowed with a pronounced sense of natural justice, a character capable of complex thought and its articulation through a well reasoned thread of argument, Syriskos is clearly designed to form the antithesis of Daos. Yet this very astuteness, like his knowledge of tragic plots, makes him a problematic character, one who displays an element of refinement at variance with what might be expected from someone with a servile background. It is clearly an incongruity intended by the playwright, and in many respects it is subsumed beneath the general impression of intelligence that Syriskos evinces. Similarly, his ability to construct a case devastatingly destructive to his opponent's through its acuity indicates a rhetorical skill designed to resonate with the Athenian audience and to impress Smikrines, all the more so in view of the old man's initial hostility. It comes as a surprise, therefore, that despite his earlier skill he becomes powerless to reverse Onesimos' intervention into the situation at the end of Act II, able only, in Act III, to initiate the process whereby Onesimos too is sidelined from the major thread of action. And it is probably in the context of this developing gradation of character-effectiveness that Syriskos' character is ultimately to be seen – a figure who is designed to

---

17 See further, Commentary 240ff. For detailed analysis of speech-style in the play see Feneron pp. 107–12, Krieter-Spiro pp. 239–44.

18 For all Syriskos' importance to the drama, much of commentators' interest has centred rather on the disputed form of his name: Syros on a panel depicting the arbitration scene in a mosaic found in the so-called House of Menander in Mytilene (see Kahil pl. 1b, Walton-Arnott pl. 11), Syriskos at 270 in manuscript C. The situation is complicated by the fact that the Mytilene mosaic, while correctly identifying the central figure as Smikrines, labels the slave to the left Syrus, the one to the right a charcoal-burner, rather than Daos, who is a shepherd. The error casts suspicion on the validity of the mosaic's evidence, and this suspicion has been given further substance by Pap. Oxy. 4641, where the form Syriskos is written as an inter-linear gloss between lines 212–13.

make an overwhelming impression in what is surely the central scene of the play, but whose dramatic role, limited by his station in life, must be superseded by that of others.

Karion: By tradition the cook was a conventional comic character, instantly recognisable by his appearance and the equipment he brought with him, and typified by a tendency to boast about his culinary skills (see *Aspis* Commentary 216) and by his loquaciousness (*ibid.* 233). Often in Menander, however, there are additional factors brought into play: in *Aspis* his complaints about being robbed of an engagement, in *Dyskolos* complaints about the uncontrollable sacrificial victim (393–9) and boasts about his skill in borrowing equipment (489–97). Within the action of *Epitrepontes*, unfortunately, the potential for development of Karion is masked by damage to the text both in the opening scene with Onesimos (which merely discloses his inquisitiveness) and at 603ff., where he ostensibly reveals the consternation that Habrotonon's claimed motherhood of the baby has caused within Chairestratos' house, details overheard by Smikrines. Some additional indication may be provided by Themistius' comment in the context of fr. 2b, that the cook irritated guests by his boastfulness, but this does little to broaden knowledge.

The Text of Epitrepontes

P: Membrana Petropolitana 388: Lines 127–48, 159–77
Two pages (out of three) of a fragmentary parchment codex dating to the 4th century AD discovered by Tischendorf in 1844 in the monastery of St. Catherine on Sinai. In form it is a *palimpsest*; that is, the original Menandrian document was partially erased and overwritten by an eighth century Syriac script. The third page contains lines of Menander's *Phasma*.

C: Papyrus Cairensis 43227: Lines 218–667, 680–701, 714–25, 749–59, 853–922, 934–58, 969–89, 1000–14, 1018–23, 1035–49, 1052–7, 1060–1131
Part of a 5th century papyrus codex discovered at Aphroditopolis in Egypt by Gustav Lefèbvre in 1905 and the main source for our knowledge of the play. Originally a much larger volume, it was the property of the lawyer Flavius Dioscurus and was discovered on top of, and around, a jar filled with papyri. As well as the *Epitrepontes* the codex also has parts of *Perikeiromene*, *Samia* and shorter fragments of *Heros* and an unidentified play.[19]

19   A detailed analysis of the manuscript's form and contents is given by Martina II.1, pp. 326–36, where details of subsequent minor finds of the papyrus are also provided cf. Furley pp. 31–5.

O4: Papyrus Oxyrhynchica 1236: Lines 880–901, 923–43
A vellum leaf dating probably from the 4th century AD written on both sides
and providing sections of text not found in other sources. This is certainly
the case with the verso (923–33), though general damage and the loss of
many line-beginnings complicate interpretation.

O14: Papyrus Oxyrhynchica 2829: Lines 218–56, 310–22, 347–61 and fr. V–X
The remains of a 3rd or 4th century AD manuscript much used in antiquity.
The three larger sections of text overlap with material found in C, and apart
from a textual variant in 227 add nothing new. The smaller fragments, often
little more than parts of words, cannot be positioned within the text and add
nothing to our understanding of the play.

O23: Papyrus Oxyrhynchica 3532 fr. 1–3 (= Sandbach O19): Lines 788–835
O24: Papyrus Oxyrhynchica 3533 (= Sandbach O20): Lines 789–809
Two 2nd century AD papyrus fragments containing overlapping text of 3532
fr. 3 and 3533 (both of which are highly fragmentary). 3532 fr. 1, however,
is better preserved and gives the beginnings of most of 812–35.

O25: Papyrus Oxyrhynchica 4021: Lines 150–164 and Martina fr. 8, placed
after 177
Three fragmentary texts of a 3rd century AD manuscript (the literary text
shares its space with other documents, one of which specifies a date in the first
half of the 3rd century). Fragments 1 and 2 provide lines 150–64, securely
located because of overlap with P 159–64. Fr. 3 has the line-beginnings of a
monologue which Martina locates after 177.

O26: Papyrus Oxyrhynchica 4022: Lines 290–301, 338–45, 376–400, 421–47
Fragments from two consecutive leaves originally in a 2nd century AD
papyrus codex, of which the first leaf provides little more than occasional
letters, supplementing C. The text of the second leaf is much better preserved,
but again overlaps with C.

O27: Papyrus Oxyrhynchica 4023: Lines 657–67 (= Sandbach 655–65) and
Martina fr. 14
A fragment of a parchment codex dated to the third or fourth centuries
AD. The flesh side adds little to the already established text. The hair side
contains scattered letters that cannot be linked to a known section and is
included by Martina as fr. 14.

O28: Papyrus Oxyrhynchica 4020: Hypothesis
A scrap of reused papyrus providing the initial letters of what must have
been the *hypothesis* or summary of the play, a feature often added to post-
production manuscripts.[20] The fact that the *hypothesis* incorporates parts of
fr. 1 (Menander fr. 600K) indicates that these must have been, in fact, the
play's opening lines. Also included is a list of the contrasting characters
within the action.

Onov: Papyrus Oxyrhynchica 4641: Lines: 195–216
A fragment of 2nd–3rd century AD papyrus containing parts of 22 lines
identifiable as coming from *Epitrepontes* by an overlap in lines 13–14 with
two lines of a fragment attributed to the play by Stobaeus (*Eclogae* III, 30,
7).[21] In addition, the appearance of the name Syriskos between lines 18 and
19 of the papyrus (= lines 212–13 of this edition) both guarantees that this
is the true form of the slave's name and strongly suggests that the fragment
comes early in Act II, shortly before the beginning of the Cairo manuscript
at 218.

Papyrus Oxyrhynchica 4936
The remains of two columns of text containing the ends of some 35 lines
followed by the beginnings of 35 lines including changes of speaker: Karion,
Onesimos and Chairestratos, suggesting a position within the play between
the opening fragments and line 127ff.

Papyrus Berol. 21142 = Martina fr. 5
A 2nd century scrap of papyrus which may belong to the opening scene
between Onesimos and Karion.

Papyrus Laurentiana (PL III 310 A): Lines 664–8, 690–3 (= Sandbach 662–
666, 688–691)
A fragment of a 5th century AD codex containing overlaps with C in terms
of 664–8 and with C and Michigan fragments in terms of 690–3, allowing
some improvement of text.

---

20   See, for instance the hypothesis attached to the Bodmer papyrus of Menander's *Dyskolos*,
where it is wrongly ascribed to Aristophanes of Byzantium, one of the foremost scholars of
Alexandria.
21   The Stobaeus material, numbered fr. 6 in Sandbach's *OCT* and Arnott 1979a, is now
located at 207–9 in the present edition.

M: Michigan Papyri

A collection of 2nd century AD papyrus fragments which at times overlap and extend text known from other sources, or provide snatches of text that cannot be interpreted or placed with certainty:[22]

P. Mich. 4733 fr. 1 and 2:

fr. 1 (lines 676–701) overlaps with C 680–701 (= Sandbach 680–99) and marks the end of Act III; fr. 1 is further extended to 710 by P. Mich. 4807 g.1–3, and 4801 j.

fr. 2 (lines 786–823) overlaps with P. Oxy. 3532–3, which continue to 835, and is further augmented by 4801 a.

Other Michigan fragments include:

P. Mich. 4733 4 Koenen-Gagos, which Martina locates after 759

P. Mich. 4733 1, 6 Koenen-Gagos

P. Mich. 4800 B.26/B 17.F Koenen-Gagos

P. Mich. 4801 g.1–3 supplies 1127–44 and an unplaced fragment

P. Mich. 4807 c Koenen-Gagos

The large number of manuscripts involved in reconstruction of the play, combined with the facts that, 1) they were all individually produced by hand and thus open to the introduction of error either by commission or omission, and 2) many have suffered severe damage, presents editors with the task not only of understanding and interpreting what text there is, but also of interpreting those insertions made by scribes. It was the practice of antiquity, for instance, not to separate words and to be sparing in the addition of such diacritical marks as breathings and accents, which can at times lead to uncertainty of meaning. More serious is the reluctance to indicate clearly the speaker involved at any particular moment, with actual names inserted in the margin, or more rarely between lines, at the beginning of Acts, where a character enters a scene, and sporadically elsewhere.[23] More usually a change of speaker is indicated by a *paragraphus*, a line drawn under the first letters of a line to indicate that a change will take place somewhere within it or at its end, and a *dicolon* (:) at the actual point of change. However, just as there are times when the scribe has introduced or transmitted textual corruptions, so there are occasions where *paragraphi* and *dicola* are omitted, misplaced, confounded with neighbouring

---

22   Pap. Mich. 4733 fr. 1 and 2 published by M. Gronewald, *ZPE* 66 (1986), 1–13; others made available by L. Koenen and T. Gagos and published by Martina (1997).

23   Even where actual names are given, there is the possibility of error in their positioning. So, for instance, at 369 we find Syriskos' name inserted, though he does not speak till 370.

letters, confused with punctuation and other marks, or simply removed by damage. In addition to marking a change of speaker there are also times when the dicolon indicates a change of addressee, *i.e.* when a speaker turns from one character to another, or simply a pause.

Textual marks: *see* Aspis *Introduction*

Specifically in Epitrepontes

1. Text:

α̣ε̣ί̣   *Paragraphus* (line under the initial letters of a line), to show evidence of a change of speaker in highly damaged sections

:   *Dicolon* inserted to indicate the precise position of change of speaker or person being addressed in fragmentary text

2. Translation: ( ) Material added to facilitate sense

3. Metre: See *Aspis* Introduction.
The metre of *Epitrepontes'* extant text is exclusively iambic trimeters.

MENANDER

THE ARBITRATION

ΕΠΙΤΡΕΠΟΝΤΕΣ

ΕΠΙΤΡΕΠΟΝΤΕΣ

Dramatis Personae
ΚΑΡΙΩΝ
ΟΝΗΣΙΜΟΣ
ΘΕΟΣ
ΣΜΙΚΡΙΝΗΣ
ΧΑΙΡΕΣΤΡΑΤΟΣ
ΑΒΡΟΤΟΝΟΝ
ΔΑΟΣ
ΣΥΡΙΣΚΟΣ
ΠΑΜΦΙΛΗ
ΧΑΡΙΣΙΟΣ

ΧΟΡΟΣ

Hypothesis (P. Oxy. 4020)
Ε . . [
Ἐπιτρέ[ποντες
οὐχ ὁ τ[ρόφι-
μός σο[υ, πρὸς
θεῶν [5

τὸ δρᾶμα τῶν ἀ[ρίστων
περιγέγονεν γὰ[ρ
ἠθῶν ἁπάντων [
δύο, τὸν μὲν σωφ[ρόνως
δ' αἰσχυνομένω[ς   10
γ]αμετὴν κοσμίω[ς
ἑταίραν ἀφελῶς . [
φιλάργυρον λογισμ[
θ]εράποντα δικαι[

Hypothesis
2–4.   suppl. Parsons
6.   suppl. Parsons
9.   suppl. Parsons

THE ARBITRATION

Characters *(reconstructed from the text in order of appearance):*

KARION	Cook
ONESIMOS	Slave of Charisios
[DIVINITY	Prologue speaker]
SMIKRINES	Father of Pamphile
CHAIRESTRATOS	Friend of Charisios
HABROTONON	Harp-girl
DAOS	Shepherd
SYRISKOS	Charcoal-burner
PAMPHILE	Wife of Charisios
CHARISIOS	Young man

CHORUS

Non-speaking parts

Wife of Syriskos
Simias	Assistant to Karion
Sophrone	Slave of Smikrines

Hypothesis

    …

Arbitra[tion …
[Did]n't your m[aster, Onesimos
by [the] [5] gods [who's now got …

the play (one) of the b[est]
is superior, for [ ]
of all characters [ ]
two, the one sensib[ly]
[10] the other disgracefully [ ]
a wife decently [ ]
a girl-friend brazenly [ ]
money-grubbing (in his) calculation [ ]
servant just [ ]

126 Menander

Fragments of Act I

1. (Fr. 1 K-T, 600 K = Commentator on Aristotle's De Interpretatione IV, 5, p. xxii)
(ΚΑΡΙΩΝ)
οὐχ ὁ τρόφιμός σου πρὸς θεῶν, Ὀνήσιμε,
ὁ νῦν ἔχων <τὴν> Ἁβρότονον τὴν ψάλτριαν
ἔγημ' ἔναγχος;
(ΟΝΗΣΙΜΟΣ) πάνυ μὲν οὖν.

2a. (Fr. 2 K-T, 849 K = Elias on Aristotle's Categories XVIII, 1, 27)
(ΚΑΡΙΩΝ)
                        φιλῶ σ', Ὀνήσιμε·
καὶ σὺ περίεργος εἶ.

2b. (Fr. 2 K-T, 850 K = Elias on Aristotle's Categories XVIII, 1, 27)
(ΚΑΡΙΩΝ)
                        οὐδέν <ἐστι> γὰρ
γλυκύτερον ἢ πάντ' εἰδέναι.

3. (Fr. 3 K-T, = Photius, Berlin MS 83.2)
(ΟΝΗΣΙΜΟΣ)
τί δ' οὐ ποεῖς ἄριστον; ὁ δ' ἀλύει πάλαι
κατακείμενος.

4. (Fr. 4 K-T, 185 K = Erotian 14.81, Nachmanson)
ἐχῖνος

5. (Fr. 5 K-T, 178 K = Athenaeus III, 119e)
                        ἐπέπασα
ἐπὶ τὸ τάριχος ἅλας, ἐὰν οὕτω τύχῃ.

Fragments
5. ἂν MSS

Act I

(A country road not far from Athens. To the rear stand two houses, that to the right belonging to Charisios, that to the left to Chairestratos. Onesimos enters from the right accompanied by a cook and his assistants, hired for the day.)

Fr. 1.

KARION   By the gods, Onesimos, didn't your master, who's now got the
          company of the harp-girl, Habrotonon, recently get married?
ONESIMOS   Quite so.

Fr. 2a.
KAR.   I like you, Onesimos – you're nosy too.

Fr. 2b.
KAR.   There's nothing nicer than knowing all the facts.

Fr. 3.
ON.   Why aren't you making lunch? He's been at the table for ages,
       fretting away.

Fr. 4.   Jar.

Fr. 5.   I've sprinkled salt onto the salt-fish if this should happen.

128 Menander

P. Oxy. 4936: 34 lines of fragmentary words including (column 1):

13.]γενομεν[
15.]..... ις ὅλην
16. κ]αλη[.] κόρη
17.] σφόδρ᾽ οἶσθ᾽ ὅτι
18.] . τι
19.] .... μεις ἴσα

20. οὐδέπω
21. κ]ρεάδιον
22.] Χαρισιο[
25. ὀν]όματ[ο]ς
26.] . εις φρε[ν]ῶν

(column 2):

7. ΚΑΡ. εἴρηκ᾽ ἐγώ[
8. ΧΑΙ. πέφυκα[
14. ταύτην
15. ἐν γειτόν[ων
16. αὐτην δι[
17. ἅ γ᾽ ἂν τύ[χῃ
18. ἔσθ᾽, ὡς ἔο[ικε
19. ἀλλὰ πατ[
20. αὐτὸν
23. σοὶ δεῦρο
24. τηρῶν γὰρ

25. κλείσω
26. περιμει[ν
27. τὴν μία[ν
28. (ΚΑΡ) αὐτὸς καλ[
29. ΟΝ. καὶ Θασι[
30. ΧΑΙ. σοὶ πειθ[
31. (ΚΑΡ) οἶνον Θά[σιον
32. ἀλλ᾽ οὔ τι χ[αίρων
33. ΟΝ. ἂν ἔτι λα[λ
34. ποῖ νῦν

(paragraphi __ inserted to indicate change of speaker within or at the end of the line)

P. Oxy. 3946: continuing dialogue between Onesimos and Karion followed by the intervention of Chairestratos
Column 1:

13. happening
15. whole
16. pretty girl
17. you know perfectly well that
18. something
19. equal things

20. no way
21. a piece of meat
22. Charisios
25. name
26. mind

Column 2:

7. KAR. *I* said
8. CH. (I was / you were) born
14. this girl
15. next door
16. her
17. if this happens
18. it is, so it seems
19. but
20. him
23. to you here
24. on the look-out for

25. I shall close
26. wait for
27. one
28. (KAR) he himself
29. ON. and Thasian (wine)
30. CH. persuade / agree with you
31. (KAR) Thasian wine
32. it won't do any good
33. if you go on talking
34. where to now

[ΣΜΙΚΡΙΝΗΣ]

[   ]
ἄνθρωπος οἶνον. αὐτὸ τοῦτ' ἐκπλήτ[τομαι   127
ἔγωγ'. ὑπὲρ <δὲ> τοῦ μεθύσκε<σ>θ' οὐ λέγω.
ἀπιστίᾳ γάρ ἐσθ' ὅμοιον τοῦτό γε,
εἰ καὶ βιάζεται κοτύλην τις τοὐβολ[οῦ   130
ὠνούμενος πίνειν ἑαυτόν.
(ΧΑΙΡΕΣΤΡΑΤΟΣ)   τοῦτ' ἐγ[ὼ
προσέμενον· οὗτος ἐμπεσὼν διασκ[εδᾷ
τὸν ἔρωτα.
ΣΜ.   τί δέ μοι τοῦτο; πάλιν οἰμω[ζέτω.
προῖκα δὲ λαβὼν τάλαντα τέτταρ' ἀργύρ[ου
οὐ τῆς γυναικὸς νενόμιχ' αὐτὸν οἰκέτ[ην·   135
ἀπόκοιτός ἐστι· πορνοβοσκῷ δώδεκα
τῆς ἡμέρας δραχμὰς δίδωσι.
(ΧΑΙ)   δώδεκα·
πέπυσ]τ' ἀκριβῶς οὑτοσὶ τὰ πράγματα.
(ΣΜ) μηνὸ]ς δια[τ]ροφὴν ἀνδρὶ καὶ πρὸς ἡμερῶν
ἕξ.
(ΧΑΙ) εὖ] λελ[όγ]ισται. δύ' ὀβολοὺς τῆς ἡμέρας,   140
ἱκανό]ν τι τῷ πεινῶντι <πρὸς> πτισ[άνη]ν ποτέ.

(ἈΒΡΟΤΟΝΟΝ)
Χαρίσι]ός σ[ε] προσμένει, Χαιρέ[στρατε.
τίς ὅδ' ἐσ]τι δ[ή], γλυκύτατε;
(ΧΑΙ)   ὁ τῆς [νύμφης πα]τήρ.
(ἈΒΡ) ἀλλὰ τί παθ]ὼν ὡς ἄθλιός τις[
[ὁ] τρισκακοδ[αίμων;
<ΣΜ>   ψάλ]τριαν   145
[   ]σαν γυναῖκα [. . . . .] ι

128. <δὲ> suppl. Cobet, ὑπὲρ τοῦ <μὴ>, Sisti, Martina
133. after ἔρωτα a single point and space, interpreted by Koerte as change of speaker, many
continue with Chairestratos; οἰμω[ζέτω Koerte, οἰμω[ξέται Wilamowitz, Martina
139. μηνὸ]ς Sudhaus
140. ἕξ. – εὖ] Sudhaus. At end of line *dicolon* added by second hand; 141 given to
Chairestratos by some, to Smikrines by others
141. ἱκανό]ν Wilamowitz; <πρὸς> suppl. Sudhaus; πτισ[άνη]ν suppl. Gomperz
142–3a. given to Simias by many
143. beginning suppl. Jernstedt; end suppl. Kock
145. change of speaker after τρισκακοδ[αίμων Sudhaus, Arnott

(*Smikrines enters from the right grumbling to himself and overheard by Chairestratos, who stands outside his house commenting on what he hears*)

SMIKRINES   The fellow('s drinking the most expensive) wine. *This* is what I'm utterly amazed at – never mind his drunkenness – what is nigh-on incredible is this, [130] how anyone can even bring himself to drink stuff he buys for an obol a half-pint.

CHAIRESTRATOS   This is just what I expected. He'll rush in and break up the love affair.

SMI.   But what's that to me. To Hell with him again! Yet he's got four talents' worth of silver as dowry, [135] but he doesn't see fit to live with his wife, doesn't share her bed. No, he pays a pimp twelve drachmas a day.

CH.   Twelve - this fellow's [learned] the terms precisely.

SMI.   Enough to keep a man for [a month] and [six] days on top.

CH.   [140] His arithmetic's [spot on]. At one time two obols a day were [enough] for barley-cake for a starving man.

(*Habrotonon emerges from Chairestratos' house*)

HABROTONON   Chairestratos, [Charisios] is waiting for you. (*Noticing Smikrines*) [Who's this], darling?

CH.   His [wife's] father.

HAB.   [But what's up with him…] like some miserable [ ], [145] [the] wretched man.

SMI.   [harp]-girl [ ] [146] woman/wife [ ].

(The final letters of 147–8, followed by a gap at the junction of two manuscripts)

προσε[151
. . . . . [
<u>ἀπο</u>δοὺ[ς] δ[
ἈΒΡ. τη . . ρ . ικ . . [   ] . . [
<u>ὁ γέρω</u>[ν] ε . . τω[.] . . [155
α . . ο . [.] . κα . ον[.] . . [ ] . . [
<u>της</u> ν . [.] . ος· ε . [. .] . . [Ἀ]βρο[τον
ἈΒΡ. <u>ἀλλ</u>’ οὐκ ἐκαλ . [   ] . ων[. .] . [
(?) οὕτως ἀγαθόν τί σοι γένοιτο, μὴ λέγε
<u>ἀεί</u> πο[τε.]
ΧΑΙ.   οὐκ ἐς κόρακας; οἰμώξει μακρά.   160
(ΣΜ) εἴσ<ε>ιμι δ’ οὖν εἴσω, σαφῶς τε πυθόμενος
ἅ]παντα τ[αῦ]τα τῆς θυγατρός, βουλεύσομαι
ὅντινα τ]ρόπον πρὸς τοῦτον ἤδη προσβαλῶ.
(?ἈΒΡ) φράσω[μ]εν αὐτῷ τοῦτον ἥκοντ’ ἐνθάδε;
(ΧΑΙ) φράσ[ω]μεν. οἷον κίναδος· οἰκίαν ποεῖ   165
ἀνάστα]τον.
(ἈΒΡ)   πολλὰς ἐβουλόμην ἅμα.
(ΧΑΙ) πολλάς;]
(ἈΒΡ)   μίαν μὲν τὴν ἐφεξῆς.
(ΧΑΙ)   τὴν ἐμήν;
(ἈΒΡ) τὴν σ]ήν γ’. ἴωμεν δεῦρο πρὸς Χαρίσιον.
(ΧΑΙ) ἴωμ]εν· ὡς καὶ μειρακυλλίων ὄχλος
εἰς τ]ὸν τόπον τις ἔρχεθ’ ὑποβεβρεγμέν[ων   170
οἷς] μ[ὴ] ’νοχλεῖν εὔκαιρον εἶν[α]ί μο[ι δοκεῖ .

154.   τὴ[ν π]ρ[ο]ῖκ[α Parsons
154–7.   interlinear traces suggesting changes of speaker: σ[μικ] between 154–5, χ[αιρ] between 156–7
155.   ὁ γέρω[ν] Parsons, ὅ γ’ ἐρῶ Furley
160.   over οὐκ, χα(ιρ) in O25; οὐκ ἐς... given to Smikrines by Hutloff, Arnott
163.   suppl. van Leeuwen
165.   suppl. Jernstedt; space before οἷον in P, 164 and οἷον... ἀνάστα]τον given to Chairestratos by Martina
166.   suppl. Kock; διάστα]τον Sudhaus
167–70.   suppl. Jernstedt
171.   οἷς Kock; line end suppl. Jernstedt

[*lines of fragmentary text*]

SMI.? [ ] [153] giving back [ ].

HAB. [the dowry] [155] the old man.

SMI. [ ].

CH. [157] [ ] Habrotonon.

HAB. [158] But [he] didn't call [ ] [159] Why, bless you, don't say [160] for ever.

CH. (*Aside directed against Smikrines*) Damn you, you'll regret this good and proper.

SMI. Well, I'll go in, and when I've got a clear picture of how everything is with my daughter, I'll plan [how] to tackle *him* then. (*Smikrines goes into Charisios' house*)

HAB. Should we tell him this fellow's arrived on the scene?

CH. [165] Yes, let's. What a fox he is. He turns a house [upside down].

HAB. I wish a lot were like that.

CH. [A lot?]

HAB. One, at least – next door.

CH. Mine?

HAB. Yes, yours. Let's go in to Charisios.

CH. Yes, let's be off since there's a crowd of young men [170] coming this way somewhat the worse for drink. I don't [think] this is the right moment to tangle [with them]. (*They depart into Chairestratos' house*)

ΧΟ]Ρ[ΟΥ

(?ΟΝΗΣΙΜΟΣ)
ἐπι[σφαλῆ μὲν] πάντα τἀνθ[ρώπων
οἰόμ[ενος εἶναι
καὶ τοπ[
ὁ δεσπό[της   175
ὁ γέρω[ν
οὐδὲ λο[

(a few lines missing)

P. Oxy. 4021 (O25.3) = Martina fr. 8: (which he inserts after 177), cf.
Nünlist ZPE 2003 p. 59–61, Menandro Cent' Anni 2004, p. 95–106

(180a–c: three lines of scattered letters)
π]αρατριβομ[
[.]ωρασανα . [
τ]ὸ γὰρ π[έ]ρας [180e
ἀ]παλλάγηθι .
ἀ]γαθὰ γένοι[το
κ]άθευδ' ἀνασ . [
κλίνην ἐμο . [
ἀπώλεσεν . [180j
ἀγαθὸν γένο[ι
ἐλάλει δέ μοι . [
αὐτὸν ἐθέλε . [
ὑμᾶς ἐνοχλε[
οὐθὲν δεομ . [180o
οὐ] τῷ τυχόντ[ι

(Four lines of broken text including]γυναικ[followed by a gap of a few lines)

172–7.   given to Onesimos by many
172.   suppl. Jernstedt
173.   suppl. Sudhaus

P. Oxy. 4021.3 = O25.3
180j.   suppl. Nünlist; ἴσασιν ἢν ἔχω Parsons
180q.   suppl. Parsons

CHORUS

Act II

(*Onesimos enters from Chairestratos' house reporting on events inside*)

ON.   Thinking that all human affairs [are precarious ...] and [ ] [175] the
         master [ ] the old man [ ] nor [ ].
[*a few lines missing*]

P. Oxy. 4021.3 (= Martina fr. 8):
[*three fragmentary lines*]
         I'm exhausted [ ]
         [180e]_ _

         To cut a long story short [ ]
         off with you [ ]
         so help [me]
         go and sleep it off [ ]
         [180j] bed [ ]
         he lost [ ]
         so help [me/you]
         he told me [ ]
         he wanted him [ ]
         [180o] trouble you [ ]
         need[ing] nothing
         not any old [ ]
         _ _

         [ ] woman/wife [ ]

(*A few lines missing during which Smikrines evidently enters and interacts
with Onesimos, who then leaves. Smikrines reviews his interview with his
daughter*)

136 Menander

P. Oxy. 4641 = Nünlist: Onov (Menandro Cent' Anni 2004, p. ·95–106),
which he places a few lines before the beginning of the Cairo papyrus at
218. The fact that Syriskos is indicated as a speaker shows that it must
come from near the beginning of Act II

(ΣΜ) . . . . .] ουτ . ν θυγατέρ[α   195
[. . . τὸ] δὴ λεγόμενον η[
[. . . . .] . ε πείσῃ καρτερησ[
[. . . .] . ν τὸ μὴ παρὰ τοῦ τοι[ούτου
[. . . . .]ν πεπόηκε μυρίου[ς
[. . .]ον γε τὸ κακόν, εἰ δεῆσ[ει   200
αὐτὸ]ν λέγοντ᾽ "ἄσωτός εἰμ᾽, ου[
[. . . .]στα, μεθύω, κραιπαλῶ ["
[. .] . [. .] . δουν αὐτῷ φράσω ν[
π]εῖραν προσάγειν, ὡς νῦν α[
ο]ὐθεὶς λέγει τούτῳ γάρ· "ε[205
ἐ]ργάζετ᾽". ἐρρῶσθαι γάρ ἐστ . [
ἀργὸς δ᾽ ὑγιαίνων τοῦ πυρέττοντος πολύ
ἐστ᾽ ἀθλιώτερος· διπλάσιά γ᾽ ἐσθίει
μάτην· ἰδεῖν βουλήσομ᾽ αὐ[τὸν

[ΔΑΟΣ]
π]ροσμείνατ᾽, ὦ δείλης μετα[210
[ΣΥΡΙΣΚΟΣ]
ἔρ]ρωσο καὶ τὸ κατὰ σὲ πρόσμ[εινον μόνον.
π]αρ᾽ ἕνα γάρ ἐσθ᾽ ἕκαστον ἡ σω[τηρία.
[ΔΑ] ο]ὐθὲν λέγεις δίκαιον.
ΣΥ.   οὐ μα[
[. . . .]ε πρὸς τὸν δεσπότην [
[. . . . .]ον. κατοικεῖ δ᾽ ἐνθα[δ   215
[. . . . . . .] . [.]μεν οἰκε . . ου[
(a few lines missing)

207–9. Stobaeus III, 30, 7, variously emended: μάτην γοῦν ἐσθίει / διπλάσια Wilamowitz

P. Oxy. 4641 (Onov) which Nünlist locates here

SMI.?   [ ] 195 daughter [ ] as the saying goes [ ] he persuades, stand your
ground [ ] not from such a [man] [ ] he has made countless [ ] 200
the trouble, if necessary [ ] him saying 'I'm a profligate man' [ ]
'I'm drunk; I've got a skin-full' [ ]. Should I tell him to have a go,
as now [ ] 205 for no one tells him '[ ] is working' [ ] to be healthy
is [ ] An idler in good health is far worse than one with a fever – he
eats twice as much but with no good coming from it. I'll want to see
him.

(*Smikrines slowly begins to leave the stage. Syriskos and his wife enter from
the left followed by Daos*)

DAOS   210 Hang on; oh what an afternoon [ ].
SYRISKOS   Off with you, and as far as you are concerned, [you just wait].
     Each man is responsible for his own sa[lvation].
DAOS   There's no justice in what you say.
SYR.   No [ ] to the master [ ] 215 he lives here [ ].
[*a few lines missing*]

138   *Menander*

(ΣΥ) φεύγεις τὸ δίκαιον.
(ΔΑ)   συκοφαντεῖς δυστυχής.
οὐ δεῖ σ' ἔχειν τὰ μὴ σά.
(ΣΥ)   ἐπιτρεπτέον τινί
ἔστι περὶ τούτων.
(ΔΑ)   βούλομαι· κρινώμεθα.   220
(ΣΥ) τίς οὖν;
(ΔΑ)   ἐμοὶ μὲν πᾶς ἱκανός. δίκαια δὲ
πάσχω· τί γάρ σοι μετεδίδουν;
(ΣΥ)   τοῦτον λαβεῖν
βούλει κριτήν;
(ΔΑ)   ἀγαθῇ τύχῃ.
(ΣΥ)   πρὸς τῶν θεῶν,
βέλτιστε, μικρὸν ἂν σχολάσαις ἡμῖν χρόνον;
(ΣΜ) ὑμῖν; περὶ τίνος;
(ΣΥ)   ἀντιλέγομεν πρᾶγμά τι.   225
(ΣΜ) τί οὖν ἐμοὶ μέλει;
(ΣΥ)   κριτὴν τούτου τινὰ
ζητοῦμεν ἴσον· εἰ δή σε μηδὲν κωλύει,
διάλυσον ἡμᾶς.
(ΣΜ)   ὦ κάκιστ' ἀπολούμενοι,
δίκας λέγο[ν]τες περιπατεῖτε, διφθέρας
ἔχοντες;
(ΣΥ)   ἀλλ' ὅμως· τὸ πρᾶγμ' ἐστὶν βραχύ,   230
καὶ ῥᾴδιον μαθεῖν. πάτερ, δὸς τὴν χάριν·
μὴ καταφρονήσῃς, πρὸς θεῶν. ἐν παντὶ δεῖ
καιρῷ τὸ δίκαιον ἐπικρατεῖν ἁπανταχοῦ,
καὶ τὸν παρατυγχάνοντα τούτου τοῦ μέρους
ἔχειν πρόνοιαν· κοινόν ἐστι τῷ βίῳ   235
πάντων.
ΔΑ.   μετρίῳ γε συμπέπλεγμαι ῥήτορι.
τί γὰρ μετεδίδουν;
(ΣΜ)   ἐμμενεῖτ' οὖν, εἰπέ μοι,
οἷς ἂν δικάσω;
ΣΥ.   πάντως.

218–19.   *dicolon* after δυστυχής; οὐ δεῖ σ' ἔχειν τὰ μὴ σά continued to Daos by Sandbach, Arnott, Nünlist, given to Syriskos by Sudhaus, Wilamowitz, Martina
219.   *dicolon* after σά in C and O14, disregarded by Wilamowitz, Martina
220.   after κρινώμεθα *dicolon* in C, disregarded by Sisti

SYR. [218] You're trying to wriggle out of what's right and proper.
DAOS You're blackmailing me, you wretch. You've no right to what's not yours.
SYR. We need to hand the matter over to someone [220] for judgement.
DAOS That's all right by me. Let's have arbitration.
SYR. Who then?
DAOS Anyone suits me. It's just what I deserve. Why did I go shares with you?
SYR. Are you willing to have this guy as arbitrator?
DAOS All right.
SYR. (*Interrupting Smikrines' departure*) Please sir, could you spare us a little time?
SMI. [225] You? What for?
SYR. We're in dispute over something.
SMI. What's that got to do with me?
SYR. We're looking for an impartial judge for it. If there's nothing stopping you, settle our quarrel.
SMI. Blast you! You traipse around in working clothes indulging in lawsuits.
SYR. [230] All the same, it's a little matter – easy to grasp. Do us a favour, sir. Don't give us the brush-off, please. In all circumstances justice should prevail the whole world over; anybody on the spot should [235] be concerned for it – it's a universal factor of life.
DAOS (*Aside*) It's a right speechifier I've got tangled up with. Why did I go shares with him?
SMI. Well, tell me, will you abide by my decision?
SYR. By all means.

(ΣΜ)   ἀκούσομαι· τί γὰρ
τό με κωλύον; σὺ πρότερος ὁ σιωπῶν λέγε.
ΔΑ. μικρόν γ᾽ ἄνωθεν, οὐ τὰ πρὸς τοῦτον μόνον   240
πραχθένθ᾽, ἵν᾽ ᾖ σοι καὶ σαφῆ τὰ πράγματα.
ἐν τῷ δασεῖ τῷ πλησίον τῶν χωρίων
τούτων ἐποίμαινον τριακοστὴν ἴσως,
βέλτιστε, ταύτην ἡμέραν αὐτὸς μόνος
κἀκκείμενον παιδάριον εὗρον νήπιον   245
ἔχον δέραια καὶ τοιουτονί τινα
κόσμον.
(ΣΥ)   περὶ τούτων ἐστίν.
ΔΑ.   οὐκ ἐᾷ λέγειν.
(ΣΜ) ἐὰν λαλῇς μεταξύ, τῇ βακτηρίᾳ
καθίξομαί σου.
(ΣΥ)   καὶ δικαίως.
(ΣΜ)   λέγε.
(ΔΑ)   λέγω.
ἀνειλόμην, ἀπῆλθον οἴκαδ᾽ αὔτ᾽ ἔχων,   250
τρέφειν ἔμελλον. ταῦτ᾽ ἔδοξέ μοι τότε·
ἐν νυκτὶ βουλὴν δ᾽, ὅπερ ἅπασι γίνεται,
διδοὺς ἐμαυτῷ διελογιζόμην· ἐμοὶ
τί παιδοτροφίας καὶ κακῶν; πόθεν δ᾽ ἐγὼ
τοσαῦτ᾽ ἀναλώσω; τί φροντίδων ἐμοί;   255
τοιουτοσί τις ἦν. ἐποίμαινον πάλιν
ἕωθεν. ἦλθεν οὗτος – ἐστὶ δ᾽ ἀνθρακεύς –
εἰς τὸν τόπον τὸν αὐτὸν ἐκπρίσων ἐκεῖ
στελέχη· πρότερον δέ μοι συνήθης ἐγεγόνει.
ἐλαλοῦμεν ἀλλήλοις. σκυθρωπὸν ὄντα με   260
ἰδών, "τί σύννους" φησὶ "Δᾶος;" "τί γάρ;" ἐγώ,
"περίεργός εἰμι," καὶ τὸ πρᾶγμ᾽ αὐτῷ λέγω,
ὡς εὗρον, ὡς ἀνειλόμην. ὁ δὲ τότε μὲν
εὐθὺς πρὶν εἰπεῖν πάντ᾽ ἐδεῖθ᾽, "οὕτω τί σοι
ἀγαθὸν γένοιτο, Δᾶε" παρ᾽ ἕκαστον λέγων,   265
"ἐμοὶ τὸ παιδίον δός. οὕτως εὐτυχής,
οὕτως ἐλεύθερος. γυναῖκά" φησι "γὰρ
ἔχω, τεκούσῃ δ᾽ ἀπέθανεν τὸ παιδίον",

239. τοκωλυονμε C, corr. Eitrem, τοκω[.]υον[O14
249. καὶ δικαίως given to Syriskos by Sandbach

SMI. Then I'll hear you. What's to stop me? You speak first – the quiet one.

DAOS [240] I'll start a little way back – not just my dealings with him – so that you have the facts absolutely clear. About thirty days ago now I was looking after my flock all on my own in the woods near here, sir, [245] and I found a little new-born baby that had been abandoned, along with a necklace and some other such trinkets.

SYR. That's what this is all about.

DAOS He's not letting me speak.

SMI. I'll hit you with my stick if you interrupt.

SYR. And quite right too.

SMI. Carry on.

DAOS Very well. [250] I picked it up; I went off home with it; my intention was to bring it up. That seemed a good idea to me at the time, but that night I took stock of the situation, as everyone does, and I thought to myself: What do I want with raising children and suchlike troubles? Where will I [255] get all the money for such expenses? Why take on such worries? That's how it was with me. Come morning, I went out with my sheep again. Then *he* came along to the same place – he's a charcoal-burner – to saw up some logs there. I'd got to know him earlier. [260] We began chatting together. He saw I was down-in-the-mouth and said, 'Why the gloomy look, Daos?' 'Why?' I said. 'I will stick my nose in', and I told him the story – how I found the baby, how I'd picked it up. Then, before I could tell the whole tale, he straight away started pleading, adding [265] 'A blessing upon you, Daos' to everything. 'Give me the child, and may fortune and freedom be yours. I've a wife' he said. 'Her child died at birth.' He

ταύτην λέγων, ἣ νῦν ἔχει τὸ παιδίον.
ἐδέου, Συρίσκε;
<ΣΥ>　　　　　<ἔγωγε.>
(ΔΑ)　　　　　　　ὅλην τὴν ἡμέραν　　　　　　270
κατέτριψε. λιπαροῦντι καὶ πείθοντί με
ὑπεσχόμην. ἔδωκ', ἀπῆλθεν μυρία
εὐχόμενος ἀγαθά· λαμβάνων μου κατεφίλει
τὰς χεῖρας. ἐπόεις ταῦτα;
(ΣΥ)　　　　　　　　ἐπόουν.
(ΔΑ)　　　　　　　　　ἀπηλλάγη.
μετὰ τῆς γυναικὸς περιτυχών μοι νῦν ἄφνω　　　275
τὰ τότε συνεκτεθέντα τούτῳ – μικρὰ δὲ
ἦν ταῦτα καὶ λῆρός τις, οὐθέν – ἀξιοῖ
ἀπολαμβάνειν καὶ δεινὰ πάσχειν φήσ', ὅτι
οὐκ ἀποδίδωμ', αὐτὸς δ' ἔχειν ταῦτ' ἀξιῶ.
ἐγὼ δέ γ' αὐτόν φημι δεῖν ἔχειν χάριν　　　　280
οὗ μετέλαβεν δεόμενος· εἰ μὴ πάντα δὲ
τούτῳ δίδωμ', οὐκ ἐξετασθῆναί με δεῖ.
εἰ καὶ βαδίζων εὗρεν ἅμ' ἐμοὶ ταῦτα κ[αὶ
ἦν κοινὸς Ἑρμῆς, τὸ μὲν ἂν οὗτος ἔλαβ[εν ἄν,
τὸ δ' ἐγώ· μόνου δ' εὑρόντος, οὐ παρὼν τ[ότε　285
ἅπαντ' ἔχειν οἴει σε δεῖν, ἐμὲ δ' οὐδὲ ἕ[ν;
τὸ πέρας· δέδωκά σοί τι τῶν ἐμῶν ἐ[γώ·
εἰ τοῦτ' ἀρεστόν ἐστί σοι, καὶ νῦν ἔχε·
εἰ δ' οὐκ ἀρέσκει, μετανοεῖς δ', ἀπόδος πά[λιν
καὶ μηδὲν ἀδίκε[ι] μηδ' ἐλαττοῦ. πάντα δέ,　　290
τὰ μὲν παρ' ἑκόντος, τὰ δὲ κατισχύσαντά με,
οὐ δεῖ σ' ἔχειν. εἴρηκα τόν γ' ἐμὸν λόγον.

269.　*paragraphus* at line beginning, *dicolon* at end in C
270.　ΣΜΙΚ in margin of C; line beginning continued with Daos de Stefani, assigned to
Smikrines by Arnott; εδεουσυρισκ': C; <ἔγωγε> Hense, van Leeuwen, Sandbach; (Σμ) ἐδέου
σὺ <ταῦτα; (Συ) φήμι> Sudhaus; <εὖ ἴσθ'> Capps; (Σμ) ἐδέου σὺ γ'; (Συ) <ἱκετεύων> ὅλην
Arnott
274.　*dicola* before and after ἐπόεις ταῦτα, given to Smikrines by Sudhaus, Koerte, Arnott;
de Stephani continues with Daos
284.　suppl. Sudhaus
285.　suppl. van Leeuwen
287.　suppl. Ellis, ἑκών Lefèbvre

meant the woman here who's now holding the child. [270] Was this what you asked, Syriskos?

SYR. Yes.

DAOS He spent the whole day, begging me, persuading me till I promised. I handed it over. He went off calling down countless blessings on me. He took hold of my hands and kept kissing them. Did you do this?

SYR. I did.

DAOS Off he went; [275] now he's turned up with his wife, suddenly presumes to get his hands on the stuff left with the baby then – they were small bits and pieces, junk – worthless. He says he's being done down because I don't hand them over and presume to hang on to them myself. [280] For my part I say he should be grateful for the share he got with his pleading. I shouldn't be answerable to him if I don't give him everything. If he'd found this stuff while out on a walk with me and it was a shared windfall, he['d] have taken one half and [285] I the other. But I made the find on my own; you weren't there [at the time]; do you think you should have the lot and I nothing? And finally: I've given you something that was mine. If you like it, keep it. If you don't, and you've changed your mind, give it back [290] and don't do me down or pose as the victim. You shouldn't get the lot – one part a gift from me, the rest by cajoling me. I've finished my account.

144   *Menander*

ΣΥ. εἴρηκεν;
ΣΜ.   οὐκ ἤκουσας; εἴρηκεν.
ΣΥ.   καλῶς.
οὐκοῦν ἐγὼ μετὰ ταῦτα. μόνος εὖρ᾽ οὑτοσὶ
τὸ παιδίον, καὶ πάντα ταῦθ᾽ ἃ ν[ῦ]ν λέγει   295
ὀρθῶς λέγει, καὶ γέγονεν οὕτως, ὦ πάτερ.
οὐκ ἀντιλέγω. δεόμενος, ἱκετεύων ἐγὼ
ἔλαβον παρ᾽ αὐτοῦ τοῦτ᾽· [ἀ]λη[θ]ῆ γὰρ λέγει.
ποιμήν τις ἐξήγγειλέ μοι, πρὸς ὃν οὑτοσὶ
ἐλάλησε, τῶν τούτῳ συνέργων, ἅμα τινὰ   300
κόσμον συνευρεῖν αὐτό[ν· ἐ]πὶ τοῦτον, πάτερ,
αὐτὸς πάρεστιν οὑτοσί. – [τὸ] πα[ιδί]ον
δός μοι, γύναι. – τὰ δέραια καὶ γνωρίσματα
οὗτός σ᾽ ἀπαιτεῖ, Δᾶ᾽· ἑαυτῷ φησι γὰρ
ταῦτ᾽ ἐπιτεθῆναι κόσμον, οὐ σοὶ διατροφήν.   305
κἀγὼ συναπαιτῶ κύριος γεγενημένος
τούτου· σὺ δ᾽ ἐπόησάς με δούς. νῦν γνωστέον,
βέλτιστε, σοί ταῦτ᾽ ἐστίν, ὡς ἐμοὶ δοκεῖ,
τὰ χρυσί᾽ ἢ ταῦθ᾽ ὅ τί ποτ᾽ ἐστὶ πότερα δεῖ
κατὰ τὴν δόσιν τῆς μητρός, ἥτις ἦν ποτε,   310
τῷ παιδίῳ τηρεῖσθ᾽, ἕως ἂν ἐκτραφῇ,
ἢ τὸν λελωποδυτηκότ᾽ αὐτὸν ταῦτ᾽ ἔχειν,
εἰ πρῶτος εὗρε τἀλλότρια. τί οὖν τότε,
ὅτ᾽ ἐλάμβανον τοῦτ᾽, οὐκ ἀπῇτουν ταῦτά σε;
οὔπω παρ᾽ ἐμοὶ τότ᾽ ἦν ὑπὲρ τούτου λέγειν.   315
ἥκω δὲ καὶ νῦν οὐκ ἐμαυτοῦ σ᾽ οὐδὲ ἓν
ἴδιον ἀπαιτῶν. κοινὸς Ἑρμῆς; μηδὲ ἓν
εὕ]ρισχ᾽, ὅπου πρόσεστι σῶμ᾽ ἀδικούμενον·
οὐχ] εὕρεσις τοῦτ᾽ ἔστιν ἀλλ᾽ ἀφαίρεσις.
βλέ]ψον δὲ κἀκεῖ, πάτερ· ἴσως ἔσθ᾽ ο[ὗτο]σὶ   320
ὁ πα]ῖς ὑπὲρ ἡμᾶς καὶ τραφεὶς ἐν ἐργάταις
ὑπ]ερόψεται ταῦτ᾽, εἰς δὲ τὴν αὐτοῦ φύσιν
ᾄξα]ς ἐλεύθερόν τι τολμήσει πονεῖν,

293.   ΣΥΡ in margin of C; [ΣΜ]ΙΚΙΔΙ in margin of O26
302.   suppl. Bodin
315.   λεγων C, O14
321.   suppl. Jensen, van Leeuwen
323.   suppl. Leo from Clem. Alex. *Stromateis* 1, 153, 5

SYR. Has he finished?

SMI. Didn't you hear? He's finished.

SYR. Good. So, my turn next. This guy found [295] the baby on his own, and everything he's now saying is correct; that's how it happened, sir. I don't deny it. I got this child from him by begging and pleading. What he says is true. A shepherd he'd [300] talked to – one of those who work with him – told me: the fact that he'd found some trinkets along with it. It's these, sir, he's here for in person. (*Syriskos turns to his wife*) Give me the child, wife. (*With the baby in his arms he turns to Daos*) This child, Daos, is claiming back from you the necklace and (other) recognition-tokens. He says that they were put there [305] for *his* adornment, not for your benefit. And I join in that claim since I've become his guardian. You made me that when you handed him over. (*Syriskos hands the child back to his wife and turns to address Smikrines*) So now, dear sir, to my mind the point you need to decide is this: whether these bits of gold or whatever they are should be kept safe for the child until he grows up [310] in accordance with his mother's gift – whoever she was – or whether the man who has robbed him should keep them on the grounds of having found somebody else's property first. Why then did I not demand them from you then, when I got the child? [315] At the time I wasn't as yet in a position to speak on his behalf. But now I'm here and I'm not demanding anything from you that's mine. 'A shared windfall'? Don't claim a find when it involves someone being wronged. That's not finding; it's robbing. [320] Then again, sir, consider this. Suppose this child's of higher birth than us. Brought up among workmen, he'll look down on his lifestyle, [turn] to his

146 *Menander*

θηρᾶν λέοντας, ὅπλα βαστάζειν, τρέχειν
ἐν ἀ]γῶσι. τεθέασαι τραγῳδούς, οἶδ' ὅτι,   325
κ]αὶ ταῦτα κατέχεις πάντα. Νηλέα τινὰ
Π]ελίαν τ' ἐκείνους εὖρε πρεσβύτης ἀνὴρ
αἰπόλος, ἔχων οἵαν ἐγὼ νῦν διφθέραν,
ὡς δ' ᾔσθετ' αὐτοὺς ὄντας αὐτοῦ κρείττονας,
λέγει τὸ πρᾶγμ', ὡς εὗρεν, ὡς ἀνείλετο.   330
ἔδωκε δ' αὐτοῖς πηρίδιον γνωρισμάτων,
ἐξ οὗ μαθόντες πάντα τὰ καθ' αὑτοὺς σαφῶς
ἐγένοντο βασιλεῖς οἱ τότ' ὄντες αἰπόλοι.
εἰ δ' ἐκλαβὼν ἐκεῖνα Δᾶος ἀπέδοτο,
αὐτὸς ἵνα κερδάνε[ι]ε δραχμὰς δώδεκα,   335
ἀγνῶτες ἂν τὸν πάντα διετέλουν χρόνον
οἱ τηλικοῦτοι καὶ τοιοῦτοι τῷ γένει.
οὐ δὴ καλῶ[ς ἔχ]ει τ[ὸ] μὲν σῶμ' ἐκτρέφειν
ἐμὲ τοῦτο, [τὴ]ν [δὲ] τοῦδε τῆς σωτηρίας
ἐλπίδα λαβόντα Δᾶον ἀφανίσαι, πάτερ.   340
γαμῶν ἀδελφήν τις διὰ γνωρίσματα
ἐπέσχε, μητέρ' ἐντυχὼν ἐρρύσατο,
ἔσωσ' ἀδελφόν. ὄντ' ἐπισφαλῆ φύσει
τὸν βίον ἁπάντων τῇ προνοίᾳ δεῖ, πάτερ,
τηρεῖν, πρὸ πολλοῦ ταῦθ' ὁρῶντ' ἐξ ὧν ἔνι.   345
ἀλλ' "ἀπόδος, εἰ μή" φης' "ἀρέσκει." τοῦτο γὰρ
ἰσχυρὸν οἴεταί τι πρὸς τὸ πρᾶγμ' ἔχειν.
οὐκ ἔστι δίκαιον· εἴ τι τῶν τούτου σε δεῖ
ἀποδιδόναι, καὶ τοῦτο πρὸς ζητεῖς λαβεῖν,
ἵν' ἀσφαλέστερον πονηρεύσῃ πάλιν,   350
εἰ νῦν τι τῶν τούτου σέσωκεν ἡ Τύχη;
εἴρηκα. κρῖνον ὅ τι δίκαιον νενόμικας.
(ΣΜ) ἀλλ' εὔκριτ' ἐστί· πάντα τὰ συνεκκείμενα
τοῦ παιδίου 'στί. τοῦτο γινώσκω.

334. ειδεκελαβων C, corr. Bodin-Mazon
335. αυτω C, corr. Croenert
339. suppl. von Arnim
348. ουκεστι C, οὐκέτι Sudhaus, Arnott

true nature and strive after noble endeavour – hunt lions, bear arms, run [325] in the games. You've seen the tragedies, I'm sure, and know all this. Take someone like Neleus and Pelias - an old goatherd with a jerkin just like mine found them. And since he saw that they were a cut above himself, [330] he told them what had happened – how he found them, how he picked them up. He gave them the little bag of birth-tokens. From this the boys, who till then had been goatherds, learned everything for certain about themselves and became kings. But if Daos had taken those tokens out and had sold them, [335] so that *he* could profit to the tune of a dozen drachmas, men of such stature and nobility would have lived out their lives unknown. It's not fair that I should rear this child's body while Daos [340] takes and does away with its hope of deliverance, sir. Through birth-tokens one man avoided marrying his sister; another met and rescued his mother; another saved his brother. By its very nature life for all men is precarious; [345] we must protect it with foresight, sir, keeping a special eye on what makes this possible. But he says 'Give it back if you're not satisfied'. He thinks this argument carries some weight in the matter. That's not right. In case you're required to give up one of his possessions, are you trying to get your hands on him as well [350] so that you can indulge your wickedness again, with less risk, seeing that Chance has preserved some of his things? I've finished. Give your judgment as you think right.

SMI.   It's a clear-cut case. Everything left with the child is his. That's my verdict.

(ΔΑ)   καλῶς·
τὸ παιδίον δέ;
(ΣΜ)   οὐ γνώσομ' εἶναι μὰ Δ[ία σοῦ   355
τοῦ νῦν ἀδικοῦντος, τοῦ βοηθοῦντος δ[ὲ καὶ
ἐπεξιόντος τἀδικεῖν μέλλοντί σο[ι.
(ΣΥ) πόλλ' ἀγαθά σοι γένοιτο.
(ΔΑ)   δεινή γ' ἡ [κρίσις
νὴ τὸν Δία τὸν Σωτῆρ'· ἅπανθ' εὑρὼν [ἐγὼ
ἅπαντα περιέσπασμ'. ὁ δ' οὐχ εὑρὼν ἔχ[ει.   360
οὐκοῦν ἀποδιδῶ;
(ΣΜ)   φημί.
(ΔΑ)   δεινή γ' ἡ κρ[ίσις,
ἢ μηθὲν ἀγαθόν μοι γένοιτο.
(ΣΥ)   φέρε τ[αχύ.
(ΔΑ) ὦ Ἡράκλεις, ἃ πέπονθα.
(ΣΥ)   τὴν πήραν χ[άλα
καὶ δεῖξον· ἐν ταύτῃ περιφέρεις γάρ. βρα[χὺ
πρόσμεινον, ἱκετεύω σ', ἵν' ἀποδῷ.
(ΔΑ)   τί γὰρ ἐγὼ   365
ἐπέτρεψα τούτῳ;
(ΣΜ)   δός ποτ', ἐργαστήριον.
<ΔΑ> αἰ]σχρά γ' ἃ πέπονθα.
(ΣΜ)   πάντ' ἔχεις;
(ΣΥ)   οἶμαί γε δή,
εἰ] μή τι καταπέπωκε τὴν δίκην ἐμοῦ
λέγοντος, ὡς ἡλίσκετο.
(ΔΑ)   οὐκ ἂ[ν ᾠ]όμην.

356. suppl. Croenert
357. ταδικειν C, τἀδικεῖν Sandbach, Arnott = τῷ ἀδικεῖν printed by many; <τοῦ>τ' ἀδικεῖν
Sudhaus
358. suppl. Lefèbvre
362. suppl. Leo, Mazon
363. suppl. Koerte
364. *dicolon* after γάρ in C
366. δός ποτ', ἐργαστήριον given to Syros by many, to Smikrines by Sandbach, Arnott
369. ΣΥΡ in margin of C

DAOS   Fair enough. [355] And the child?

SMI.   I'll not decide it goes [to you], by Zeus, since you're trying to defraud it, but to the man who's coming to its rescue [and] opposing your intended criminality.

SYR.   A thousand blessings on you.

DAOS   That's a terrible [verdict], by Zeus the Saviour. I found everything [360] and I'm stripped of everything, while he found nothing and gets the lot. Do I have to hand them over?

SMI.   That's what I say.

DAOS   That's a terrible [verdict] or I'll be damned.

SYR.   Come on, [hurry].

DAOS   Heracles, what an outcome for me!

SYR.   [Open] the bag and show me. That's where you've got the stuff. (*He turns to address Smikrines*) Just wait [365] a moment, please, till he hands them over.

DAOS   Why did I give the case to *him*?

SMI.   (*Rounding on Daos*) Hand them over, you gaolbird.

DAOS   It's scandalous what I've suffered.

SMI.   (*Turning to Syriskos*) Have you got everything?

SYR.   I think so, unless he's swallowed something while I was making my case, when he found that he was losing.

DAOS   I would never have believed it.

(ΣΥ) ἀλλ᾽ εὐτύχει, βέλτιστε. τοιούτ[ου]ς ἔδ[ει   370
θᾶττ[ο]ν δικάζειν πάντας.
(ΔΑ)   [ἀδί]κ[ου π]ρ[άγμ]ατος.
ὦ Ἡράκλεις, οὐ γέγονε δειν[οτέρα] κρίσ[ι]ς.
ΣΥ. πονηρὸς ἦσθας.
<ΔΑ>   ὦ πό[ν]ηρ᾽, ὅ[π]ω[ς σ]ὺ νῦν
τούτῳ φυλάξεις αὐτ[α   ]η
εὖ ἴσθι, τηρήσω σε π[ά]ντα [τὸ]ν [χρό]νον.   375
(ΣΥ) οἴμωζε καὶ βάδιζε. σὺ δὲ ταυτί, γύναι,
λαβοῦσα πρὸς τὸν τρόφιμον ἐνθάδ᾽ εἴσφερε
Χαιρέστρατον. νῦν γὰρ μενοῦμεν ἐνθάδε,
εἰς αὔριον δ᾽ ἐπ᾽ ἔργον ἐξορμήσομεν
τὴν ἀποφορὰν ἀποδόντες. ἀλλὰ ταῦτά μοι   380
πρῶτ᾽ ἀπαρίθμησαι καθ᾽ ἕν. ἔχεις κοιτίδα τινά;
βάλλ᾽ εἰς τὸ προκόλπιον.
ΟΝ.   μάγειρον βραδύτερον
οὐδεὶς ἑόρακε· τηνικαῦτ᾽ ἐχθὲς πάλαι
ἔπινον.
ΣΥ.   οὑτοσὶ μὲν εἶναι φαίνεται
ἀλεκτρύων τις καὶ μάλα στριφνός· λαβέ.   385
τουτὶ δὲ διάλιθόν τι. πέλεκυς οὑτοσί.
ΟΝ. τί ταῦτα;
(ΣΥ)   ὑπόχρυσος δακτύλ[ι]ός τις οὑτοσί,
αὐτὸς σιδηροῦς· γλύμμα τ[αῦ]ρος ἢ τράγος·
οὐκ ἂν διαγνοίην· Κλεόστρατος δέ τίς
ἔσ]τιν ὁ ποήσας, ὡς λέγει τὰ γράμματα.   390
(ΟΝ) ἐπί]δειξον.
(ΣΥ)   ἤν. σὺ δ᾽ εἶ τίς;
(ΟΝ)   οὗτός ἐστι.
(ΣΥ)   τίς;
(ΟΝ) ὁ δα]κτύλιος.

---

372. suppl. Sudhaus
373. *paragraphus* but no *dicolon* in C; ὦ πό[ν]ηρ᾽ given to Daos by von Arnim; end suppl.
by Croiset
385. στριφνός C, στιφνός O26
389. διαγνοιη C, διαγνοιης O26
391. suppl. Sudhaus

SYR.   [370] Goodbye, sir. (*Smikrines exits towards the city*) All judges should be like that, and no mistake.

DAOS It's [unfair]! Heracles, a worse verdict there's never been!

SYR.   You were the villain.

DAOS Villain yourself. Just make sure you keep them safe for him [till he grows up]. [375] I'll keep my eye on you the whole time, rest assured.

SYR.   On your way and be damned! (*Daos trudges off towards the country. Syriskos turns to his wife*) You take these things, dear, and carry them inside to young master Chairestratos here. We'll stay here for now, but in the morning we'll set out back to work, [380] once we've paid our dues. But first, go through them one at a time for me. Have you got a box? (*She shakes her head*) Well, put them in your pocket.

ON.   (*Entering from Chairestratos' house*) No one's ever seen a slower cook. By this time yesterday they were well into the wine.

SYR.   This looks like [385] a cock, and a very solid one at that. Here, take it. This one's set with stones. Here's an axe.

ON.   (*Noticing the other two*) What's going on here?

SYR.   Here's a ring – gold plate on iron. There's an engraving – a bull or goat. I couldn't say which. [390] Made by some Cleostratos, so the inscription says.

ON.   Show me.

SYR.   (*Handing over the ring*) There, but who are you?

ON.   That's it.

SYR.   What?

ON.   The ring.

(ΣΥ)   ὁ ποῖος; οὐ γὰρ μανθάνω.
(ΟΝ) τοῦ] δεσπότου τοὐμοῦ Χαρ[ι]σίου.
(ΣΥ)   χολᾷς.
(ΟΝ) ὃν ἀ]πώλεσεν.
(ΣΥ)   τὸν δακτύλιον θές, ἄθλιε.
(ΟΝ) τὸ]ν ἡμέτερόν σοι θῶ; πόθεν δ᾽ αὐτὸν λαβὼν   395
ἔχ]εις;
(ΣΥ)   Ἄπολλον καὶ θεοί, δεινοῦ κακοῦ.
οἷον ἀ]π[ο]σῶσαι χρήματ᾽ ἐστὶν ὀρφανοῦ
παι]δός. ὁ προσελθὼν εὐθὺς ἁρπάζειν βλέπει.
τ]ὸν δακτύλιον θές, φημί.
(ΟΝ)   προσπαίζεις ἐμοί;
τοῦ δεσπ[ό]του ᾽στι, νὴ τὸν Ἀπόλλω καὶ θεούς.   400
(ΣΥ) ἀποσφαγείην [π]ρότερον ἂν δήπουθεν ἢ
τούτῳ τι κ[α]θυφείμην. ἄραρε, δικάσομαι
ἅπασι κ[α]θ᾽ ἕνα. π[αι]δίου ᾽στιν, οὐκ ἐμά. –
στρεπτόν τι τουτί· λαβὲ σύ. πορφυρᾶ πτέρυξ.
εἴσω δὲ πάρ[αγ]ε. – σὺ δὲ τί μοι λέγεις;
(ΟΝ)   ἐγώ;   405
Χαρισίου ᾽στιν οὑτοσί· τοῦτόν ποτε
μεθύω[ν ἀπώλ]εσ᾽, ὡς ἔφη.
(ΣΥ)   Χαιρεστράτου
εἴμ᾽ οἰκέτης. ἢ σῷζε τοῦτον ἀσφαλῶς,
ἤ μοι δ[ός, ἵν᾽ ἐγ]ώ σ[ο]ι παρέχω σῶν.
(ΟΝ)   βούλομαι
αὐτ[ὸ]ς φ[υλάττειν.]
(ΣΥ)   [ο]ὐδὲ ἕν μοι διαφέρει·   410
εἰς ταὐτὸ [γ]ὰρ παράγομεν, ὡς ἐμοὶ δοκεῖ ,
δεῦρ᾽ ἀμφότεροι.
(ΟΝ)   νυνὶ μὲν οὖν συνάγουσι καὶ
οὐκ ἔστιν εὔκαιρον τὸ μηνύειν ἴσως
αὐτῷ περὶ τούτων, αὔριον δέ.

395.   colon after ἡμέτερον in O26; does τὸ]ν ἡμέτερον continue Syriskos' order in 394?
398.   *dicolon* at end of line
409.   suppl. Jensen
410.   suppl. Croiset

SYR.   What ring? I don't understand.

ON.   My master Charisios'.

SYR.   You're mad.

ON.   [The one] he lost.

SYR.   Put the ring back, you wretch.

ON.   395 Put back what's ours, to please you? Where did you get it from?

SYR.   Apollo and the gods, this is terrible! What a job it is to defend an abandoned child's belongings. The moment he turns up he's looking to grab it. Put the ring back I say.

ON.   Are you having me on? 400 It's my master's, by Apollo and the gods.

SYR.   I'd sooner have my throat cut than give in to *him*; that's for sure. My mind's made up – I'll take everyone to court, one at a time. These are baby's things, not mine. (*Turning back to his wife*) Here's a torque; take it. And a bit of crimson shawl. 405 In you go. (*Syriskos' wife disappears into Chairestratos' house. Syriskos turns back to Onesimos*) What's this you're telling me?

ON.   What, me? This belongs to Charisios. He lost it once – when he was drunk, so he said.

SYR.   My master's Chairestratos. You either keep it safe or [give] me it [so] I can take good care of it for you.

ON.   I prefer 410 to [keep] it myself.

SYR.   That makes no odds to me. We're both heading in the same direction, I think.

ON.   They've got company right now, and it's not perhaps the best time to tell him about it. Tomorrow.

(ΣΥ)   καταμενῶ·
αὔριον ὅτῳ βούλεσθ' ἐπιτρέπειν ἑνὶ λόγῳ   415
ἕτοιμος. οὐδὲ νῦν κακῶς ἀπήλλαχα.
πάντων δ' ἀμελήσανθ', ὡς ἔοικε, δεῖ δίκας
μελετᾶν· διὰ τουτὶ πάντα νυνὶ σῴζεται.

ΧΟΡΟΥ

ΟΝ. τὸν δακτύλιον ὥρμηκα πλεῖν ἢ πεντάκις
τῷ δεσπότ[ῃ] δεῖξαι προσελθών, καὶ σφόδρα   420
ὢν ἐγγὺς ἤ[δ]η καὶ πρὸς αὐτῷ παντελῶς
ἀναδύομαι. καὶ τῶν πρότερόν μοι μεταμέλει
μηνυμάτων· λέγει γὰρ ἐπιεικῶς πυκνά
"ὡς τὸν φράσαντα ταῦτά μοι κακὸν κακ[ῶς
ὁ Ζεὺς ἀπολέσαι." μή με δὴ διαλλαγ[εὶς   425
πρὸς τὴν γυναῖκα τὸν φράσαντα ταῦ[τα καὶ
συνειδότ' ἀφανίσῃ λαβών. καλῶς [ποῶ,
ἕτερόν τι πρὸς τούτοις κυκᾶν ὃς [βούλομαι.
κἀνταῦθα κακὸν ἔνεστιν ἐπιεικῶς [μέγα.
ΑΒΡ. ἐᾶτέ μ', ἱκετεύω σε, καὶ μή μοι κακὰ   430
παρέχετ'. ἐμαυτήν, ὡς ἔοικεν, ἀθλ[ία
λέληθα χλευάζουσ'· ἐρᾶσθαι προσ[εδ]όκω[ν,
θεῖον δὲ μισεῖ μῖσος ἄνθρωπός με τι.
οὐκέτι μ' ἐᾷ γὰρ οὐδὲ κατακεῖσθαι, τάλαν,
παρ' αὐτόν, ἀλλὰ χωρίς.
(ΟΝ)   ἀλλ' ἀποδῶ πάλιν   435
παρ' οὗ παρέλαβον ἀρτίως; ἄτοπον.
ΑΒΡ.   τάλας
οὗτος. τί τοσοῦτον ἀργύριον ἀπολλύει;
ἐπεὶ τό γ' ἐπὶ τούτῳ τὸ τῆς θε[ο]ῦ φέρειν
κανοῦν ἔμοιγ' οἷόν τε νῦν ἐστ', ὦ τάλαν·
ἁγνὴ γάμων γάρ, φασίν, ἡμέραν τρίτην   440
ἤδη κάθημαι.

425. suppl. Wilamowitz
427. ποῶ Arnott, ποῶν Wilamowitz, ποεῖ Parsons
428. suppl. Arnott; οὐ βούλομαι Leo, ὃς ἂ[ν θέλῃ Parsons, ἀπεσχόμην Jensen, Sudhaus
431. suppl. van Leeuwen
432. suppl. Capps

SYR.   I'll wait. [415] Tomorrow I'm ready to hand the matter over to whoever you like, without any further ado. (*Onesimos goes inside*) I didn't come so badly out of it this time either. It looks like I've got to drop everything and practise the law. That's how you keep anything safe these days. (*He disappears into Chairestratos' house*)

CHORUS

Act III

(*Onesimos enters talking to himself, followed shortly by Habrotonon, similarly wrapped up in her situation; initially neither sees the other*)

ON.   Five times or more I've set out [420] to go and show the ring to master, but the moment I get close to it and I'm on the very point of doing so, I back out. I'm sorry I told him anything before. Time and again he says 'Zeus damn and blast that tell-tale'. [425] (I'm afraid) that if he gets back together with his wife, he'll get hold of the tell-tale who knows too much and get rid of him. A fine thing I'm doing – [wanting] to stir another factor into the present situation! The present mess is quite bad enough.

HAB.   [430] (*Emerging from Chairestratos' house and talking back to those inside*) Let go of me, please; don't pester me. (*She moves away from the door*) Oh dear, without realising it I've made a fool of myself, it seems. I expected he'd make love to me, but the man hates me with a passion. Poor me, now he doesn't even let me sit [435] beside him; instead I'm moved away.

ON.   Should I give it back to the man I got it from just now? That would be stupid.

HAB.   Poor man! Why is he throwing away so much money? As far as he's concerned, as of this moment I'm qualified to carry the goddess' basket. Oh poor me! [440] I've already been sitting around for two days, a *virgo intacta*, as they say.

(ΟΝ)   πῶς ἂν οὖν, πρὸς τῶν θεῶν,
πῶς ἄν, ἱκετεύω –
ΣΥ.   ποῦ 'στ[ιν, ὃν ζη]τῶν ἐγὼ
περιέρχομ' ἔνδον; οὗτος [ἀπόδος], ὦγαθέ,
τὸν δακτύλιον, ἢ δεῖξον ᾧ μέ[λ]λεις ποτέ.
κρινώμεθ'· ἐλθεῖν δεῖ μέ ποι.
ΟΝ.   τοιουτονί   445
ἔστιν τὸ πρᾶγμ', ἄνθρωπε· τοῦ μὲν δεσπότου
ἔστ', οἶδ' ἀκριβῶς, οὑτοσὶ Χαρισίου,
ὀκνῶ δὲ δεῖξαι· πατέρα γὰρ τοῦ παιδίου
αὐτὸν ποῶ σχεδόν τι τοῦτον προσφέρων
μεθ' οὗ συνεξέκειτο.
(ΣΥ)   πῶς;
(ΟΝ)   ἀβέλτερε,   450
Ταυροπολίοις ἀπώλεσεν τοῦτόν ποτε
παννυχίδος οὔσης καὶ γυναικῶν. κατὰ λόγον
ἔστιν βιασμὸν τοῦτον εἶναι παρθένου·
ἣ δ' ἔτεκε τοῦτο κἀξέθηκε δηλαδή.
εἰ μέν τις οὖν εὑρὼν ἐκείνην προσφέροι   455
τοῦτον, σαφὲς ἄν τι δεικνύ[οι] τεκμήριον·
νυνὶ δ' ὑπόνοιαν καὶ ταραχὴν ἔχει.
(ΣΥ)   σκόπει
αὐτὸς περὶ τούτων. εἰ δ' ἀνασείεις, ἀπολαβεῖν
τὸ]ν δακτύλιόν με βουλόμενος δοῦναί τέ σοι
μι]κρόν τι, ληρεῖς. οὐκ ἔνεστιν οὐδὲ ε[ἷ]ς   460
πα]ρ' ἐμοὶ μερισμός.
(ΟΝ)   οὐδὲ δέομαι.
ΣΥ.   [τα]ῦτα δή.
ἥξ]ω διαδραμών – εἰς πόλιν γὰρ ἔρχομαι
νυ]νί – περὶ τούτων εἰσόμενος τί δε[ῖ] ποεῖν.
(ΑΒΡ) τὸ] παιδάριον, ὃ νῦν τιθηνεῖθ' ἡ [γ]υνή,
Ὀν]ήσιμ', ἔνδον, οὗτος εὗρεν ἀν[θ]ρακεύς;   465
(ΟΝ) ναί,] φησίν.

442.   suppl. von Arnim, Leo, Wilamowitz
443.   suppl. Wilamowitz
450.   (Συ) πῶς; (Ον) ἀβέλτερε Arnott, (Συ) πῶς, ἀβέλτερε others
462–3.   suppl. Wilamowitz

ON.   How could I, by the gods? I ask you, how could I?

SYR. (*Bursting out of Chairestratos' house*) Where is he, the guy I'm going all round the house looking for? See here, chum, [give] the ring [back], or show it to the guy you intend. ⁴⁴⁵ Let's have arbitration. I've got to leave.

ON.   It's like this, mate. This belongs to my master – I know that for certain – Charisios here, but I'm reluctant to show him it. If I take it to him, I'm pretty well making him the father of the child ⁴⁵⁰ it was left with.

SYR. How come?

ON.   You dimwit – he lost it some time ago at the Tauropolia, when the all-night festival was being held and there were women around. It's a sound bet that a girl got raped; she had this baby and, obviously, abandoned it. ⁴⁵⁵ So, if one were to find her and present her with it, that would constitute clear proof. But the current situation just causes suspicion and confusion.

SYR. That's your problem. If you're trying something on, wanting me to take the ring back and to give you a little something, ⁴⁶⁰ you're off your head. As far as I'm concerned there's no question of going shares.

ON.   That's not what I want.

SYR. Very well then. I've an errand to run, but I[' ll be back]. I'm off to town right now – to see what needs to be done about this. (*Syriskos leaves and Habrotonon, whose attention was caught by the altercation and the mention of the Tauropolia, intervenes*)

HAB. The child the woman's nursing ⁴⁶⁵ indoors at the moment, Onesimos, did the charcoal-burner here find it?

ON.   [Yes], so he says.

(ΑΒΡ) ὡς κομψόν, τάλαν.
(ΟΝ) καὶ τουτονὶ
τὸ]ν δακτύλιον ἐπόντα τοὐμοῦ δεσπότου.
(ΑΒΡ) αἴ, δύσμορ'· εἶτ' εἰ τρόφιμος ὄντως ἐστί σου,
τρεφόμενον ὄψει τοῦτον ἐν δούλου μέρει,
κοὐκ ἂν δικαίως ἀποθάνοις;
(ΟΝ) ὅπερ λέγω,   470
τὴν μητέρ' οὐδεὶς οἶδεν.
(ΑΒΡ) ἀπέβαλεν δέ, φής,
Ταυροπολίοις αὐτόν;
(ΟΝ) παροινῶν γ', ὡς ἐμοὶ
τὸ παιδάρι[ο]ν εἶφ' ἀκόλουθος.
`ΑΒΡ δηλαδὴ
εἰς τὰς [γ]υναῖκας παννυχιζούσας μόνος
ἐνέ[πεσε· κἀμο]ῦ γὰρ παρούσης ἐγένετο   475
τοιοῦτον ἕτερον.
(ΟΝ) σοῦ παρούσης;
(ΑΒΡ) πέρυσι, ναί,
Ταυροπο[λίοις· π]αισὶν γὰρ ἔψαλλον κόραις,
αὐτ[ή] θ' [ὁμοῦ συ]νέπαιζον. οὐδ' ἐγὼ τότε,
οὔπω γάρ, ἄνδρ' ᾔδειν τί ἐστι.
<ΟΝ> καὶ μάλα.
<ΑΒΡ> μὰ τὴν Ἀφροδίτην.
(ΟΝ) τὴν δὲ παῖδ<ά γ'> ἥτις ἦν   480
οἶσθας;
(ΑΒΡ) πυθοίμην ἄν· παρ' αἷς γὰρ ἦν ἐγὼ
γυναιξί, τούτων ἦν φίλη.
(ΟΝ) πατρὸς τίνος
ἤκουσας;
(ΑΒΡ) οὐδὲν οἶδα· πλὴν ἰδοῦσά γε
γνοίην ἂν αὐτήν. εὐπρεπής τις, ὦ θεοί·
καὶ πλουσίαν ἔφασάν τινα.
ΟΝ. αὕτη 'στὶν τυχόν.   485

474. μονος C, μόνας van Herwerden, Wilamowitz
475. suppl. many
478. αὐτή...συνέπαιζον van Leeuwen, αὕτη...συνέπαιζεν Capps
479. καὶ μάλα given to Onesimos by Wilamowitz
480. suppl. many, τὴν δὲ δὴ παῖδ' Arnott
485. αὕτη...τυχόν; Sudhaus, Jensen

HAB.   Dear me, what a lovely baby.

ON.   And this ring along with it that belongs to my master.

HAB.   Oh, poor you! Then if it's really your master's son, could you see it being brought up as a slave? [470] Wouldn't you deserve to die if you did?

ON.   As I say, no one knows the mother.

HAB.   He lost it at the Tauropolia, you say?

ON.   While he was drunk and looking for trouble, so the lad who was with him told me.

HAB.   Well, obviously he [stumbled upon] the women as they were celebrating the festival and he was on his own. [475] Something like that happened when [I] was there.

ON.   When you were there?

HAB.   Yes, last year at the Tauropolia. I was playing for some young girls, and I was taking part in their revels myself. At the time I too didn't as yet have any experience of what men are like.

ON.   Oh yeh?

HAB.   [480] No, by Aphrodite.

ON.   Do you know who the girl was?

HAB.   I could find out. She was a friend of the ladies I was with.

ON.   Did you hear who her father is?

HAB.   I don't know anything, except I'd recognise her if I saw her. Goodness, she was pretty [485] – and rich, they said.

ON.   Perhaps it's her.

160 Menander

(ΑΒΡ) οὐκ οἶδ'· ἐπλανήθη γὰρ μεθ' ἡμῶν οὖσ' ἐκεῖ,
εἶτ' ἐξαπίνης κλάουσα προστρέχει μόνη,
τίλλουσ' ἑαυτῆς τὰς τρίχας, καλὸν πάνυ
καὶ λεπτόν, ὦ θεοί, ταραντῖνον σφόδρα
ἀπολωλεκ[υ]ῖ'· ὅλον γὰρ ἐγεγόνει ῥάκος. 490
(ΟΝ) καὶ τοῦτον ε[ἶχ]εν;
(ΑΒΡ)   εἶχ' ἴσως, ἀλλ' οὐκ ἐμοὶ
ἔδειξεν· οὐ γὰρ ψεύσομαι.
(ΟΝ)   τί χρὴ ποεῖν
ἐμὲ νῦν;
(ΑΒΡ)   ὅρα σὺ τοῦτ'· ἐὰν δὲ ν<ο>ῦν ἔχῃς
ἐμοί τε πείθῃ, τοῦτο πρὸς τὸν δεσπότ[ην
φανερὸν ποήσεις· εἰ γάρ ἐστ' ἐλευθέρα[ς 495
παιδός, τί τοῦτον λανθάνειν δεῖ τὸ γε[γονός;
(ΟΝ) πρότερον ἐκείνην ἥτις ἐστίν, Ἀβρότονο[ν,
εὕρωμεν. ἐπὶ τούτῳ δ' ἐμοὶ νῦν συ[γγενοῦ.
(ΑΒΡ) οὐκ ἂν δυναίμην, τὸν ἀδικοῦντα πρὶν [σαφῶς
τίς ἐστιν εἰδέναι. φοβοῦμαι τοῦτ' ἐγ[ώ, 500
μάτην τι μηνύειν πρὸς ἐκείνας ἃς λ[έγω.
τίς οἶδεν εἰ καὶ τοῦτον ἐνέχυρον λαβ[ὼν
τότε τις παρ' αὐτοῦ τῶν παρόντων ἀπέβαλεν
ἕτερος; κυβεύων τυχὸν ἴσως εἰς συμβολὰς
ὑπόθημ' ἔδωκ', ἢ συντιθέμενος περί τινος 505
περιείχετ', εἶτ' ἔδωκεν· ἕτερα μυρία
ἐν τοῖς πότοις τοιαῦτα γίνεσθαι φιλεῖ.
πρὶν εἰδέναι δὲ τὸν ἀδικοῦντ' οὐ βούλομαι
ζητεῖν ἐκείνην οὐδὲ μηνύειν ἐγὼ
τοιοῦτον οὐδέν.
ΟΝ.   οὐ κακῶ[ς] μέντοι λέγεις. 510
τί οὖν ποήσῃ τις;
ΑΒΡ.   θέασ', Ὀνήσιμε,
ἂν συναρέσῃ σοι τοὐμὸν ἐνθύμημ' ἄρα.
ἐμὸν ποήσομαι τὸ πρᾶ[γμ]α τ[ο]ῦτ' ἐγώ,
τὸν δακτύλιον λαβο[ῦσ]ά τ' εἴσω τουτονὶ
εἴσειμι πρὸς ἐκεῖνον.

496. suppl. many
498. suppl. Headlam, σὺ νῦν γενοῦ Sudhaus
506. περιειλετ' C, περιείχετ' Wilamowitz, Koerte, Arnott
514. λαβοῦσα τ'οἴσω Nicole

HAB.   I don't know. She was there with us but wandered off. Then, all of a
       sudden she came running up on her own, crying and tearing her hair
       and, goodness, her beautiful fine dress quite [490] ruined. It was torn to
       shreds.

ON.   And did she have this (ring)?

HAB.   She may have, but she didn't show it to me. I'll not tell lies.

ON.   What should I do now?

HAB.   That's for you to decide. If you've any sense and follow my advice,
       you'll tell all this [495] to your master. If it belongs to a free-born girl,
       why should he keep [what's happened] in the dark?

ON.   First, let's find out who *she* is, Habrotonon. [Help] me now with it.

HAB.   I couldn't, not before knowing [for certain] [500] who the culprit is. I'm
       reluctant to reveal anything to the ladies [I mentioned] if it doesn't
       get us anywhere. Who knows if someone got the ring from him as a
       surety – someone who was there – and then lost it – someone else.
       He might perhaps have handed it over as pledge for a stake while
       gambling, [505] or got involved in some business deal, found himself
       in difficulties and handed it over. Thousands of things like that can
       happen when men are drinking. I don't want to look for the girl or
       breathe a word of anything like this till I know the culprit.

ON.   [510] Good advice. So what should one do?

HAB.   I've an idea, Onesimos; see what you think of it. I'll make the event
       something that happened to me. I'll take this ring inside [515] and
       approach him.

(ΟΝ)   λέγ' ὃ λέγεις· ἄρτι γὰρ   515
νοῶ.
(ΑΒΡ) κατιδών μ' ἔχουσαν ἀνακρινεῖ πόθεν
εἴληφα. φήσω "Ταυροπολίοις παρθένος
ἔτ' οὖσα", τά τ' ἐκείνη γενόμενα πάντ' ἐμὰ
ποουμένη· τὰ πλεῖστα δ' αὐτῶν οἶδ' ἐγώ.
(ΟΝ) ἄριστά γ' ἀνθρώπων.
(ΑΒΡ)   ἐὰν οἰκεῖον ᾖ   520
αὐτῷ τὸ πρᾶγμ<α δ'>, εὐθὺς ἥξει φερόμενος
ἐπὶ τὸν ἔλεγχον καὶ μεθύων γε νῦν ἐρεῖ
πρότερος ἅπαντα καὶ προπετῶς· ἃ δ' ἂν λέγῃ
προσομολογήσω τοῦ διαμαρτεῖν μηδὲ ἓν
προτέρα λέγουσα.
(ΟΝ)   ὑπέρευγε νὴ τὸν Ἥλιον.   525
(ΑΒΡ) τὰ κοινὰ ταυτὶ δ' ἀκκιοῦμαι τῷ λόγῳ
τοῦ μὴ διαμαρτεῖν· "ὡς ἀναιδὴς ἦσθα καὶ
ἰταμός τις".
(ΟΝ)   εὖγε.
(ΑΒΡ)   "κατέβαλες δέ μ' ὡς σφόδρα·
ἱμ]άτια δ' οἷ' ἀπώλεσ' ἡ τάλαιν' ἐγώ"
φή]σω. πρὸ τούτου δ' ἔνδον αὐτὸ βούλομαι   530
λα]βοῦσα κλαῦσαι καὶ φιλῆσαι καὶ πόθεν
ἔλα]βεν ἐρωτᾶν τὴν ἔχουσαν.
ΟΝ.   Ἡράκλεις.
(ΑΒΡ) τὸ] πέρας δὲ πάντων, "παιδίον τοίνυν" ἐρῶ
"ἐσ]τὶ γεγονός σοι", καὶ τὸ νῦν εὑρημένον
δε]ίξω.
(ΟΝ)   πανούργως καὶ κακοήθως, Ἀβρότονον.   535
(ΑΒΡ) ἂ]ν δ' ἐξετασθῇ ταῦτα καὶ φανῇ πατὴρ
ὢν οὗτος αὐτοῦ, τὴν κόρην ζητήσομεν
κατὰ σχολήν.
(ΟΝ)   ἐκεῖνο δ' οὐ λέγεις, ὅτι
ἐλευθέρα γίνῃ σύ· τοῦ γὰρ παιδίου
μητέρα σε νομίσας λύσετ' εὐθὺς δηλαδή.   540

520–1.   εανδ' C, δ' placed after πρᾶγμα by Arnott, alii alia

ON.   Go on. I'm beginning to understand.

HAB.   When he sees me with it, he'll ask where I got it. I'll say 'At the Tauropolia, while I was still a virgin', and I'll pass off everything that happened to the girl as my own experience. I know most of it.

ON.   520 Great!

HAB.   If this hits home with him, he'll rush straight in and give himself away. He's having a drink at the moment, and he'll blurt out the whole thing ahead of me. I'll agree with whatever he says so as not to make any mistakes 525 by speaking first.

ON.   Brilliant, by the sun!

HAB.   To avoid any mistakes, I'll sweet-talk him with platitudes like, 'How brutal and reckless a person you were'.

ON.   Good.

HAB.   'How roughly you threw me to the ground. Poor me – what a dress I lost', 530 I'll say. Before this, though, when I'm inside, I want to take the baby, cry over it, kiss it and ask the woman who has it where she got it from.

ON.   Heracles!

HAB.   And finally, I'll say, 'So you've got yourself a baby', and I'll show what's just been found.

ON.   535 There's cunning and double-dealing, Habrotonon!

HAB.   If the case is proven and it's clear he's its father, then we can look for the girl without any distractions.

ON.   One thing you haven't mentioned. You'll get your freedom. 540 If he thinks you're the child's mother, he'll set you free straight away, that much is certain.

(ΆΒΡ) οὐκ οἶδα· βουλοίμην δ᾽ ἄν.
(ΟΝ)   οὐ γὰρ οἶσθα σύ;
ἀλλ᾽ [ἢ] χάρις τις, Ἁβρότονον, τούτων ἐμοί;
(ΆΒΡ) νὴ τὼ θεώ, πάντων γ᾽ ἐμαυτῇ σ᾽ αἴτιον
ἡγήσομαι τούτων.
(ΟΝ)   ἐὰν δὲ μηκέτι
ζητῇς ἐκείνην ἐξεπίτηδες, ἀλλ᾽ ἐᾷς   545
παρακρουσαμένη με, πῶς τὸ τοιοῦθ᾽ ἕξει;
(ΆΒΡ)   τάλαν,
τίνος ἕνεκεν; παίδων ἐπιθυμεῖν σοι δοκῶ;
ἐλευθέρα μόνον γενοίμην, ὦ θεοί.
τοῦτον λάβοι[μ]ι [μ]ισθὸν ἐκ τούτων.
ΟΝ.   λάβοις.
(ΆΒΡ) οὐκοῦν συν[αρ]έ[σκ]ει σοι;
(ΟΝ)   συναρέσκει διαφόρως·   550
ἂν γὰρ κακοηθεύσῃ, μαχοῦμαί σοι τότε·
δυνήσομαι γάρ. ἐν δὲ τῷ παρόντι νῦν
ἴδωμεν εἰ τοῦτ᾽ ἐστίν.
(ΆΒΡ)   οὐκοῦν συνδοκεῖ;
(ΟΝ) μάλιστα.
(ΆΒΡ)   τὸν δακτύλιον ἀποδίδου ταχύ.
(ΟΝ) λάμβανε.
(ΆΒΡ)   φίλη Πειθοῖ, παροῦσα σύμμαχος   555
πόει κατορθοῦν τοὺς λόγους οὓς ἂν λέγω.
(ΟΝ) τοπαστικὸν τὸ γύναιον. ὡς ἤσθηθ᾽ ὅτι
κατὰ τὸν ἔρωτ᾽ οὐκ ἔστ᾽ ἐλευθερίας τυχεῖν
ἄλλως δ᾽ ἀλύει, τὴν ἑτέραν πορεύεται
ὁδόν. ἀλλ᾽ ἐγὼ τὸν πάντα δουλεύσω χρόνον,   560
λέμφος, ἀπόπληκτος, οὐδαμῶς προνοητικὸς
τὰ τοιαῦτα. παρὰ ταύτης δ᾽ ἴσως τι λήψομαι,
ἂν ἐπιτύχῃ· καὶ γὰρ δίκαιον. ὡς κενὰ
καὶ διαλογίζομ᾽ ὁ κακοδαίμων, προσδοκῶν
χάριν κομιεῖσθαι παρὰ γυναικός· μὴ μόνον   565
κακόν τι προσλάβοιμι. νῦν ἐπισφαλῆ

542. suppl. Wilamowitz, ἀλλ᾽ [ἡ] χάρις τίς Gronewald, Martina
543. παντων C, πάντως Vollgraft
550. suppl. van Leeuwen

HAB.   I don't know. It's what I'd like.

ON.   You don't know? Well, do I get any thanks out of this, Habrotonon?

HAB.   By the two goddesses, I'll regard you as the cause of all my good luck.

ON.   And what if you abandon [545] the enquiries about her – on purpose – and instead let it drop and leave me in the lurch, what then?

HAB.   Goodness, what for? Do you think I actually want children? Just let me get my freedom, by God. Let that be the reward I get from this situation.

ON.   I hope you do get it.

HAB.   [550] So, do you like my plan?

ON.   I like it very much indeed. But if you double-cross me, then I'll fight you. I'll be able to do so, but for the moment let's see if this is the situation.

HAB.   So it's agreed?

ON.   Yes.

HAB.   Give me the ring – quick.

ON.   [555] There it is.

HAB.   Dear Persuasion, be my ally and make whatever I say hit home. (*She disappears into Chairestratos' house*)

ON.   She's a clever one, that girl. When she saw that she can't win her freedom through love and is wasting her effort this way, she's trying another [560] tack. But as for me, I'll be a slave for ever, drivelling and gaga, totally incapable of thinking up schemes like that. But perhaps I'll get something from her if she's successful. It would be only right. But what idle dreams these are, you poor fool, expecting [565] to earn gratitude from a woman! Just let me steer clear of further trouble.

166   Menander

τὰ πράγματ' ἐστὶ τὰ περὶ τὴν κεκτημέ[νην·
ταχέως ἐὰν γὰρ εὑρεθῇ πατρὸς κόρ[η
ἐλευθέρου μήτηρ τε τοῦ νῦν παιδί[ου
γεγονυῖ', ἐκείνην λήψεται ταύτην [δ' ἀφεὶς   570
[...]υξε[.....] .. ν .. ν ἀπολείπειν ο[
καὶ νῦν χαριέντως ἐκνενευκέναι δο[κῶ
τῷ μὴ δι' ἐμοῦ ταυτὶ κυκᾶσθαι. χαιρέ[τω
τὸ πολλὰ πράττειν· ἂν δέ τις λάβῃ μ[έ] τ[ι
περιεργασάμενον ἢ λαλήσαντ' ἐκτεμεῖν   575
δίδωμ' ἐμαυτοῦ – τοὺς ὀδ[ό]ντας· οὑτοσὶ
τίς ἐσθ' ὁ προσιών; Σμ[ι]κρίνης ἀναστρέφει
ἐξ ἄστεως πάλιν ταρ[ακτι]κῶς ἔχων
αὗτις· πέπ[υσ]ται τὰς ἀλ[ηθείας ἴσ]ως
παρά τινος οὗτος. ἐκπ[οδὼν δὲ β]ούλομαι   580
ποιεῖν ἐ[μαυτόν   ]λα[λ]ειν·
προ[   ]ν με δεῖ.
(ΣΜ) εξηι[
ἄσωτ[[ἡ πόλις
ὅλη γὰ[ρ ᾄδει τὸ κακόν   585
εὐθὺς[   ]δη
σαφῶς[
πίνειν[   ]ιων
τοὔνομ[α   ] ψαλτρίας
ζῆν αὐτὸ[ν   ]ης ἔφη   590
πλέον ἡμ[ερῶν
αὐτὸν διαλλ[   ]ενον.

570. [δ' ἀφεὶς Sudhaus, [ἀφεὶς von Arnim, Koerte, [δ' ἐγὼ Jensen, δ' [ἴσως Sudhaus
571. [ἐπε]ίξε[ται τὴ]ν ἔνδον ἀπολείπειν Sudhaus, [ἐπε]ύξε[ται τὸ]ν ἔνδον ἀπολείπειν
ὄ[χλον Arnott
572. suppl. Koerte, van Leeuwen
573. suppl. Lefèbvre
574. suppl. Wilamowitz,
576. τους οδ[ο]ντας αλλ' C, ἀλλ' deleted by von Arnim, τὰς γονάς· ἀλλ' Arnott
578. suppl. van Herwerden, Koerte
579. ἀλ[ηθείας ἴσ]ως suppl. Jensen
580–1. suppl. von Arnim
584–5. suppl. from Orion Etym. 23, 1
591. suppl. Robert

Right now mistress' position is precarious. If a girl is found who's a
freeman's daughter and the mother of the baby in question, 570 he'll
promptly marry her [and by divorcing] mistress here, [will rush?] to
escape [the mess inside?]. So I think I've neatly side-stepped things,
since this affair is none of *my* stirring. Good riddance to meddling.
If anyone finds I've been 575 sticking my nose in or gossiping, I give
him permission to cut off my – teeth. (*Smikrines begins to appear
from the right*) Who's this coming along? It's Smikrines coming
back from town – creating trouble again. Perhaps he's found out the
truth 580 from someone. I want to make myself scarce. [ ] to speak [
] I'd better [ ]. (*Onesimos hurries into Chairestratos' house*)

SMI.   583 [ ] 585 [The] whole [city is talking about the disgrace] 586 at once [
] 587 clearly [ ] 588 to drink [ ] 589 the name [ ] of the harp-girl 590 that
he was living [ ] he said [ ] 591 more than days [ ] 592 that he [ ] 593 oh

οἴμοι τάλ[ας   ] . η
κοινωνὸ[   ]λη
προσῆλθ[   ]εγω   595
ὅτε τὴν[   ]υ τοῦτό γε
πυνθαν[ομεν   ]τησέ με
φιλο[τ]ῷ τρόπῳ
ἐναντ[ι   ]τα τὴν ἁπλοῦν
[   ]καὶ ψάλτριαν   600
[   ]κύβοι τυχόν
[ἀ]λλὰ χαιρέτω.

(?ΚΑΡ)   ] πολλῶν ἐγὼ
[   ]ων ἐκτησάμην
[   ] . φ . ινο   605
[   ]η μοι μόνη
[   ] ν εἶναι στά[σιν
[   ] . λογ . . . . [
οὐδεὶς . [. . . . . . .] ἕτερος ὑμῖν.
(ΣΜ)   ποικίλον
ἄριστον ἀρι[σ]τῶσ[ι]ν.
(ΚΑΡ)   ὦ τρισάθλιος   610
ἐγὼ κατὰ πολλά. νῦν μὲν οὖν οὐκ οἶδ' ὅπως
δ[ια]σκεδάν[νυντ'] ἐκτός· ἀλλ' ἐὰν πάλιν
π . . . [   ] μαγείρου [τι]ς τύχῃ
. . . ν[   ] . ε βαλεῖτ' ἐς μακαρίαν.
ΣΜ. [   ]ις τινος   615
[   ]ν . . [
[   ]κει
τα[   ]ιν
πα[ἄ[π]αξ
κα[μ]ενον   620
ΣΜ. Χαρ[ίσιος   ψαλ]τρίας
ΚΑΡ. νῦ[ν   ]ωσι καὶ

602.   ἀ]λλὰ χαιρέτω Robert; οὐκ ἔστ' ἐμὸν τὸ πρᾶγμα· πολλὰ χαιρέτω suggested by Jensen from Diogenianus VII, 9
612.   suppl. Jensen
621.   suppl. Sudhaus, Robert
622.   ἀριστ]ῶσι καὶ Arnott

dear [ ] ⁵⁹⁴ sharing [ ] ⁵⁹⁵ came to [ ] I ⁵⁹⁶ when the [ ] this at least ⁵⁹⁷
finding out [ ] ⁵⁹⁸ dear [ ] in character ⁵⁹⁹ opposite [ ] simple ⁶⁰⁰ [ ] and
a harp-girl [ ] ⁶⁰¹ gambling perhaps [ ] ⁶⁰² but good riddance.

KAR. (*Emerging from Chairestratos' house*) ⁶⁰³ [ ] of many I [ ] ⁶⁰⁴ I
       obtained ⁶⁰⁵ [ ] ⁶⁰⁶ for/to me, she alone [ ] ⁶⁰⁷ to be strife [ ] ⁶⁰⁹ no one
       [ ] other for you people.
SMI.   (*Sarcastically*) They're having ⁶¹⁰ a very varied lunch!
KAR. What rotten luck in many ways I've got. Now, they're somehow
       spilling out in all directions. If anyone should happen [to need] a
       cook in the future, [ ] you can go to blazes.
SMI.   ⁶¹⁵ [ ] of someone/something [ ] ⁶¹⁹ once [ ] ⁶²¹ Ch[arisios] [ ] of [the]
       harp-girl.
KAR. Now [ ] and [ ].

με[
(ΣΜ) [   ] ἆρά γε
. ε [
(?ΚΑΡ) . .   ἔ]χουσι δή
(?ΣΜ) ο[
(?ΚΑΡ) [πέ]μπειν ἵνα   625
 [   ] τὰ χρήματα
αι[   ]ν ἡλίκη
ει[βού]λομαι
εἶν[αι   δ]έσποιν᾽ οἰκίας.
ὦ Ἡρ[άκλεις   ] Σιμίας   630
ἀπίωμ[εν
[?ΧΑΙ]   νὴ τὸ]ν Ἥλιον
μικροῦ γ[   ] ταύτην ἐγώ.
πρώην ἀρ[   ] τὰς ὀφρῦς
ἐπάνωθ[εν
ἔγωγ᾽ ἀπολ[οίμην   635
ὀκνηρο[
ΣΜ. ἔπειτα δ[
θυγατέρα [
τέτοκε κ[
(?ΧΑΙ) λαβόντ᾽ α[640
παρακαλ[
διακονε[
(ΣΜ) Χαρ[ισι
τὸ φ[
ὑμῶν ἑταῖρος οὗτος οὐ[δ]᾽ ἠσ[χύ]νετο 645
παιδάρ[ιο]ν ἐκ πόρνης [
προσω[
εἴληφ[
παρ . . [
ενη[   ]τις   650

625. suppl. Robert
628. suppl. Robert
630. suppl. Lefèbvre, ιμμίας C, Σιμίας Wilamowitz
635. suppl. Kuiper, ἀπόλ[ωλα Lefèbvre
642. διάκρινε Jensen
645. suppl. Sudhaus

SMI.   [ ] Then [ ].
KAR.?   [ ] they do indeed have
SMI.?   625 [*half a line missing*]
KAR.   [ ] to send so that [ ] the money [ ] how great [ ] I wish [ ] to be [ ]
        mistress of the house. 630 Heracles! [ ] Simias, let's go. (*They exit
        right towards the city*)
CH.?   (*Emerging from his house*) [ ] by the sun, I almost [ ] her. The other
        day [ ] eyebrows up [ ] 635 I'd rather die [ ] hesitant.
SMI.   Then [ ] daughter [ ] has given birth [ ].
CH.?   640 Taking [ ] summon [ ] serve.
SMI.   643 Cha[risios...] 645 this companion of you folk, and he wasn't
        ashamed [to father] a child on a whore [ ] 647 has taken [ ]

```
[                              ]θας
[                              μ]άλα
[                              ]τεται
[                              το]υ βίου
[                              το]ῦ δυστυχοῦς                          655
<?ΧΑΙ>                         ]ν δυστυχῇ;
```

(ΣΜ) τοῦτο[ν μὰ τ]ὸν Διό[νυσο]ν· ἀλλ᾽ ἴσως ἐγὼ   (655S)
πολυπραγμονῶ [πλεί]ω τε πράττω τῶν ἐμῶν,
κατὰ λόγον ἐξὸν ἀ[πιέν]αι τὴν θυγατέρα
λαβόντα. τοῦτο μὲ[ν π]οήσω καὶ σχεδὸν   660
δεδογμένον μ[οι τυγ]χάνει. μαρτύρομαι
ὑμᾶς δ᾽ ὀμό[σας, Χ]αιρέστρατ᾽ [(660S)
μεθ᾽ ὧν σ[. . . . . ἔ]πεμψα . [
<?ΧΑΙ> θυγατέρα τὴ[ν σὴν λ]αμβάν . [
ἀνάξι᾽ ἡμῶν[   ]
(ΣΜ)   [665
μηδὲ λέγε τ[. . . . . λ]έγων . [
καὶ περιβόητον πᾶσιν ἀνθρώποις <ποῶν>   (665S)
αὑτόν, ἀκρατὴς καὶ τοῦτο δὴ τὸ λεγόμενον
ἥττων ἑαυτοῦ πορνιδίῳ τρισαθλίῳ
ἑαυτὸν οὕτω παραδέδωκεν [670

(c. seven lines missing followed by four of scattered letters)

[ΣΜ] μισεῖ τὸν ἡδὺν λεγόμενον τοῦτον βίον;   680
ἔ[π]ινε μετὰ τ[ῆ]ς δεῖνος, εἶχεν ἑσπέρας

657.   suppl. Turner-Parsons
658.   suppl. Wilamowitz
659.   suppl. Sudhaus
661.   suppl. Sudhaus, Parsons
662.   ὀμό[σας Kassel, ὀμό[σαι Parsons, ὁμο[λογεῖν Sudhaus
664.   change of speaker indicated by Nünlist; λ]αμβάν . [Parsons, Nünlist
665.   paragraphus at line beginning; ΣΜ? in margin of 666
666.   μηδὲ λέγε τ[Nünlist; μηδὲ λέγετ[αι Pintaude-López Garcia; λ]έγων Parsons
667–80.   = *Com. Adesp.* fr. 78 K-A (Nünlist 1999)
667.   suppl. Kassel
680.   assigned to Smikrines by Sandbach, Martina, to Chairestratos by Wilamowitz, Koerte,
Arnott (2004a)
682.   suppl. Sudhaus

652 [ ] very [ ] 654 of life 655 [ ] of the wretched man [ ].

CH.?   [ ] wretched man?

SMI.   657 *Him*, by Dionysus. But perhaps I'm meddling and overstepping my rights, though I have every reason for taking my daughter away. 660 That's what I'll do; my mind's pretty well made up. I call on you folk to witness, having sworn, Chairestrat[os…] with whom/which [ ] I sent [ ].

CH.?   Take [your] daughter [ ] 665 unworthy of us [ ].

SMI.   And don't say [ ] saying [ ] and making himself the subject of scandal on everyone's lips, devoid of self-control and, as the saying goes, cheapening himself, 670 he has handed himself over to a wretched little whore like this[ ].

[*about eleven lines either missing or highly damaged*]

SMI.   680 Does he hate this so-called 'dolce vita'? He was drinking with some woman; spent the evening with some woman; was planning

τ]ὴν δεῖν’, [ἔ]μελλ[ε] δ’ αὔριο[ν τὴν] δεῖν’ ἔχει[ν.
π]ολλὰς πεπό[η]κεν [οἰ]κ[ίας ἀναστάτ]ους
οὗ]τος ὁ βίος [καὶ] λέκ[τρα πόλλ’ ἀπολώλ]εκεν.
ἔχ]θρας, νοσο[. .]ειου [. . . . .] . ει   685
αὑτῷ [κ]αθ’ ἑκ[άσ]την εὖ φ[ρ]ονή[σας ἡμέραν,
ἀλλ’ οὐκ ἔπειθεν. τοιγαροῦν, ὅπερ [πρέπ]ει,
ἀπ]οδιδότω τ[ὴ]ν προῖκα.
ΧΑΙ.   μήπω, Σμ[ικρίνη.
ΣΜ. οὐδ’ ἄν, μὰ τὴν Δήμητρα, δέκατον ἡμέ[ρας
μέρος καταμε[ίνε]ι’ ἡ θυγάτηρ ἐνταῦθ’ ἔτι.   690
ἦ μὴν μετοικήσα[σ]ι παραγεγραμμένοις
ἡμῖν κεκήδευκε.
ΧΑΙ.   οὐδ’ ἐκεῖνος οἴεται.   (690S)
ΣΜ. ὑψηλὸς ὤν τις αὐτὸς οὐκ οἰμώξεται;
καταφθαρείς τ’ ἐν ματρυλείῳ τὸν βίον
μετὰ τῆς καλῆς γυναικὸς ἣν ἐπεισ[άγει   695
βιώσεθ’, ἡμᾶς δ[’ ο]ὐδὲ γινώσκειν δοκῶν.
<ΧΑΙ> αὐτ[ὴν] μὲν ἕξε[ι], τὴν δ’ ἐπ[ει]σάξει λαβών   (695S)
. . . . [. .]ς εὐθὺς π[ρὸς] αὐτὸν; δηλαδή.
πᾶν δ’ ἀν]ατέτραπτ[αι] τοὐμόν, [ὡ]ς ἐμοὶ δοκεῖ.
ὅμως μελ]ητέον δ[ὲ κ]αὶ πορευ[τέο]ν   700
πρὸς ἣν] ἐτάχθη[ν] ἐπ[ι]μελ[ειάν] ἐστί μοι.

ΧΟΡ[ΟΥ]

683. suppl. Koenen
684. suppl. Koenen-Gagos
686. [κ]αθ’ ἑκ[άσ]την Koenen-Gagos; φ[ρ]ονή[σας ἡμέραν Gronewald
687. ἔπειθεν Koenen-Gagos, ἔπειθον Rife; [πρέπ]ει Arnott
690. καταμε[ίνε]ι’ Gronewald
691. ημη C, ειμη M, ἦ μὴν Arnott, εἰ μὴ Martina
692. οιεται L, οἴο[μαι Koenen seminar, Arnott
693. αυτος M, ουτος C
697. assigned to Chairestratos by Arnott; Chairestratos’ name in margin of M at 698
699. suppl. Koenen
700–1. suppl. Koenen-Gagos

to have some woman tomorrow. This kind of life has turned many a [household upside down] and has [wrecked many a] marriage. [685] Hostility, disease [ ] [enjoying himself] every single [day], but he/she wasn't convincing; so let him give the dowry back as [is right].

CH.   No, Sm[ikrines], not yet.

SMI.   No, by Demeter, [690] my daughter won't stay there an hour longer. Good gracious, he's been treating us like illegal immigrants.

CH.   Not even he thinks that.

SMI.   Isn't he to pay for being so high-and-mighty? Having ruined his life in a brothel, he's going to live [695] with this fine woman he's bringing into the house! He thinks we don't know. (*He departs into Charisios' house to persuade Pamphile to leave*)

CH.   Will Charisios keep Pamphile and take and introduce the other woman [ ] straightaway to him? Sure he will. All my expectations are turned upside down, so it seems. [700] [Still,] I [have to] go and [see to] the task I've been given. (*He leaves by one of the side exits*)

CHORUS

ΣΜ. οὐκ οἶδα τούτων [τῶν κακῶν ἀπαλλαγήν·
ἀλλ᾽ ἀπιέναι δε[ῖ δ᾽ ὡς τάχιστ᾽ ἐνθένδ᾽ ἐπεὶ
μί᾽ ἐστὶν ἀρετή, τὸν ἄτοπον φεύγειν ἀεί.
ΠΑΜΦΙΛΗ
πάπ<π>α, τί <δὲ> τοῦτ᾽ ἐστ[ιν   705
ἀεὶ σὺ γίνῃ κύριό[ς μου;
ΣΜ.   [ταῦτ᾽ ὄνου
σκιά. σχολὴ γάρ ἐ[στί μοι νῦν οὐδαμῶς.
ΠΑ. τἀμφίβ[ο]λα δεῖ[ται
ΣΜ. πάλαι προτεί[νω σοι
ΠΑ. ὑπὲρ ἐμ<ὲ> τοῦθ᾽ [710

(three lines missing)

[ΠΑ] ἀλλ᾽ εἴ με σῴζων τοῦτο μὴ πείσαις ἐμέ,
οὐκέτι πατὴρ κρίνοι᾽ ἂν ἀλλὰ δεσπότης.   715
(ΣΜ) λόγου δὲ δεῖται ταῦτα καὶ συμπείσεως;
οὐκ ἐπ[ιπ]ό[λαιον; α]ὺ[τό, Π]αμφίλη, βοᾷ
φωνὴν ἀφιέν· εἰ δὲ κἀμὲ δεῖ λέγειν,
ἕτοι]μ[ό]ς εἰμι, τρία δέ σοι προθήσομαι.
οὔτ᾽] ἂν ἔτι σωθείη ποθ᾽ οὗτος [οὔ]τε σύ.   720
[. . . . .]ν ἀμε[λ]ῶς ἡδέως, [σὺ] δ[᾽ οὐ] σφόδρα
[   ]κουσ᾽ ἐαθείης ἔτ᾽ ἂν
[δια]κόνῳ τούτων τι[
[   ]ν ἔχουσ᾽· ἅπαν[
[   ] . [.]ται δ᾽ ο[725

(c. twenty three lines missing)

702.   τῶν κακῶν ἀπαλλαγήν / τῶν κακῶν ἄλλην λύσιν Gronewald
703.   suppl. Koenen-Gagos, δ[εῖ σ᾽ ὡς τάχιστα, Παμφίλη Arnott
704.   cf. Men. fr. 157n. K-A (*Heniochos*) = Orion VII, 6
705.   suppl. Koenen-Gagos; παπα M, παπαὶ Koenen, Arnott
706.   (Σμ) [ταῦτ᾽ ὄνου] Gronewald, cf. Menander fr. 141 K-T (ὄνου σκιά), Aristophanes
Wasps 191, fr. 199 K-A (περὶ ὄνου σκιᾶς)
707.   σκιά Gronewald, σκιαι M; ἐ[στί *etc.* Gronewald, ἐστιν οὐ πολλή γε μοι Arnott
708–9.   suppl. Gronewald
710.   suppl. Gronewald, Martina; ὑπὲρ <δ᾽> ἐμ[α]υτοῦ θ[Stoevesandt, van Minnen
717.   ἐπ[ιπ]ό[λαιον suppl. Jensen; α]ὺ[τό Wilamowitz, Π]αμφίλη suppl. Sudhaus
719–21, 723.   suppl. Sudhaus

Act IV

(*Smikrines and Pamphile appear from Charisios' house in mid-conversation*)

SMI.   I can see no [escape] from these [troubles]. But [you] must leave [here as quickly as possible since] there is only one good course: always to avoid an untenable position.

PAMPHILE   [705] Father, what's this [ ] Are you to be [my] guardian always?

SMI.   [It's a donkey's] shadow. [I've no] time [ ].

PAM.   Doubtful matters need [ ].

SMI.   [I've] long been advising [you...].

PAM.   [710] This for me [ ]. [*3 lines missing*] [714] But if in trying to save me you weren't to persuade me of this, [715] you'd no longer seem my father but my owner.

SMI.   But does this need talk and persuasion? Isn't it quite [obvious]? The situation itself shouts it out loud. But if I do have to speak, I'm [ready], and I'll put three points to you. [720] *He* can't be saved now; neither can you [ ] carefree, in pleasure, you [ ] very [ ] you would be still be allowed [ ] for a servant of these [ ] having all [ ].

[*about 23 lines missing*]

178   *Menander*

τὴν πολυτέλειαν. Θεσμοφόρια δὶς τίθει,
Σκίρα δίς· τὸν ὄλεθρον τοῦ βίου καταμάνθανε.   750
οὔκουν ἀπόλωλεν οὗτος ὁμολογουμένως;
σκόπει τὸ σὸν δή· φησὶ δεῖν εἰς Πειραιᾶ
αὐτὸν βαδίσαι· καθεδεῖτ' ἐκεῖσ' ἐλθ[ών· σὺ δὲ
τού[τοις] ὀδυνήσει, περιμενεῖς παννυχίδα
ἄδει[πν]ος· ὁ δὲ πίνει με[τ' ἐκε]ίνης δη[λαδή   755
[. . .] ευ[.] . . . . ς ἐξῆλθε. [
[. . . .]κ . . ρευο[.] παντ[
[. . . . .] . . . σοι βούλο[μ
[. . . .] . . . [. .] . . . λοι[

*P. Mich. 4733 fr. 4 = Martina fr. 9, cf. Arnott 2004a p. 281: eleven lines of
often fragmentary words including.*

2.   ψάλτριαν τ . [6.   ]μαίνε[ται
3.   ἀργύριον . [10.   ]εαυ[τ
4.   μ]αθήσε[ται

[ΣΜ] γυναῖ]κ' ἐπίβο[υλον   786
ἢ δια]βαλεῖ σε λυ[μανεῖταί τε
. . το]ῦτ' ἐνέγκα[ι . . . .]σὰ δὲ
καλ]ῶς βιώσετα[ι   , σὺ δὲ κ]ακ[ῶς.
ἔσται δὲ] τοῦτ' αὐτῇ παραμύθιον τότε,   790
ἀεὶ σ]κυθρωπάζουσα, νουθετοῦσ' ἀεί,
γαμε]τῆς ἔχουσα σχήματ' ἐξίσακε καθ' [ἕν.
ἐνταῦ]θα παραλύσει σε. χαλεπόν, Παμφίλη,
ἐλευθέρᾳ γυναικὶ πρὸς πόρνην μάχη.

753. ἐλθ[ών suppl. Sudhaus, σὺ δὲ Wilamowitz
754. τού[τοις] Guéraud, τοῦτ', οἶ[δ' Wilamowitz; παννυχίδα Koenen-Gagos, πάλιν [τρέχειν
Arnott
755. ἄδει[πν]ος Sudhaus; με[τ' ἐκε]ίνης Jensen; δη[λαδή Koerte
786. [γυναῖ]κ'Gronewald; ἐπίβο[υλον Koenen-Gagos
787. suppl. Gronewald, Koenen-Gagos
788–9. Koenen-Gagos
790. ἔσται δὲ suppl. Merkelbach, ἕξει δὲ Koenen-Gagos
791. ἀεὶ] suppl. Lloyd-Jones,
792. γαμε]τῆς suppl. Gronewald; [ἕν Turner
793. suppl. Gronewald

749 the expense. The Thesmophoria – double expenses. 750 The Skira
– double expenses. Envisage the ruin of his finances. Isn't *he* clearly
ruined? And just look at your own position. He says he has to go to
the Peiraeus. He'll go there and lounge about. You on the other hand
will be upset by this. You'll wait around for him all night 755 without
dinner, while, of course, he's drinking with her [ ] he came out [ ]
all [ ] for you I want [ ].

[gap of about 26 lines into which is inserted P. Mich 4733.4 = Martina fr. 9]

      [ ]
2.   harp-girl [ ]
3.   money [ ]
4.   he'll learn [ ]
6.   he's raving mad [ ]
10.   himself/herself
[five lines of very fragmentary scraps]

      786 treacherous [woman…] [who] will slander and [offend you;
you'll have] to bear it [ ]. She'll live [well and you] badly. 790 [ ]
She['ll have] this encouragement then: [always] scowling, always
giving advice, in all appearances [a wife], she gradually becomes
your equal. [Then] she'll edge you out. It's difficult, Pamphile, for a

180   Menander

πλείονα πανουργεῖ, πλείον᾽ οἶδ᾽, αἰσχύνεται   795
οὐδέν, κολακεύει μᾶλλον, αἰσχρῶν [ἅπτεται.
μάλ᾽ ἀσφ]αλῶς νῦν ταῦτά σοι τὴν Πυθ[ίαν
εἰρηκέ]ναι νόμιζ᾽ ἀκριβῶς ἐσόμενα.
ὅθεν π]ροθεμένη τοῦτο παντὶ τῷ [λόγῳ
τοῦδ᾽ οὐ]δὲν ἄκοντος ποήσαις οὔποτ᾽ ἄν.   800
[ΠΑ] ὦ πάτε]ρ, ἐμὴν γνώμην λέγειν πεπλασ[μένην
δεῖ περὶ ἁ]πάντων, ὅ τι ποθ᾽ ἡγεῖ συμφέρε[ιν,
ἢ κἀφ]ελῆ; καὶ γὰρ φρονεῖν εἰ[μι
βέλτ]ιον, ἡ δ᾽ εὔνοια παρισταμένη [
[. . . . .]ς σε, πείθεσθα[ί θ᾽] ὃ μᾶλλον ἐπ[άγεται   805
[. . . . .]ε τοῦτο, πάπ<π>᾽· [ἐμοὶ] δυνατὸν δοκεῖ
[. . . . . .] μηδὲν ἠδικηκυῖαν Τύχην
[. . . . . .] ἁμαρτούσας ἐῶμεν. δεύτερο[ν
τῶν μοι] παρὰ τούτου γ᾽ αἴτιον τοῦτο[ν λέγεις.
ἀλλ᾽ οὐ]δὲν αἰσχρόν ἐ[στ᾽ ἐ]ν ὀλίγοις εὐ[παθεῖν.   810
ἀκρι]βὲς οἱ πολλοὶ [
ἴσ]ασι καὶ λέγουσιν ὡς [χρηστὸς φίλος
ἀτυχῶν ἐπίπροσθε π[λουσίου τίθεται κακοῦ.
φ[υ]γεῖν δὲ δεῖ τοῦτον [με;
ὃ μὲν γὰρ εἶπας ἀρτίω[ς, ἤδη γάμους   815
ἀφ[ῆ]κας, ἀπολεῖθ᾽ οὗ[τος· αὐτὸν γ᾽ ἀπολίπω

796. suppl. Turner, [ἄρχεται Gronewald
797. μάλ᾽ ἀσφ]αλῶς suppl. Gronewald; Πυθ[ίαν Turner
798. suppl. Gronewald
799. ὅθεν π]ροθεμένη Koenen-Gagos, καιρῷ π]ροθεμένη Gronewald; τῷ [λόγῳ Koenen-Gagos
800–1. suppl. Gronewald
802. δεῖ περὶ ἁ]πάντων suppl. Arnott, ἔχω περὶ] πάντων Gronewald
803. line beginning suppl. Gronewald
804. βέλτ]ιον Arnott; τὸ βέλτ]ιον or τὸ καίρ]ιον Koenen-Gagos; παρισταμένη O24, ὑπερισταμένη Arnott
805. suppl. Koenen-Gagos
806. πάπ<π>᾽· [ἐμοὶ] Koenen-Gagos
809. τῶν μοι] Gronewald; τούτο[υ δὲ τί Gronewald
810. εὐ[παθεῖν Arnott, εὐ[φρονεῖν Koenen-Gagos
811. ἀκρι]βὲς Koenen-Gagos
812. suppl. Gronewald
813. suppl. Koenen-Gagos
814. [με; Koenen-Gagos
815–16. suppl. Koenen-Gagos, νῦν τοὺς γάμους Arnott in 815

freeborn woman to fight against a whore. [795] She's better schooled in mischief, knows more, feels no shame, is better at flattery, [engages] in shameful actions. You should certainly imagine that the Pythia has just [told] you exactly how this will be. If you keep this in mind in every [way?], [800] you'll never do anything against [my] will.

PAM. [Oh father, should I] speak my mind on everything – whatever you think relevant – with dissemblance or straight? For I am [ready and willing] to consider [what is for the best], but the affection that exists [ ] [805] you [and] to be convinced [as to what matters] more [ ] and that this [ ], Father. It seems possible [to me] [ ] Chance when it's done no wrong; let's drop [all talk of] fallen women. Secondly, [you say] that he's responsible for [the results] of this [for me] [810]) [but it's] not disgraceful to [enjoy oneself] with a few people. Many people [ ] know [precisely] and say that [a good friend] who's down on his luck [is] preferable [to one who's rich but bad]. Must [I] leave him? [ ] [815] As you said just now, you've [already] broken off [my marriage]; he'll come to a bad end. [Should I leave him]

διὰ τοῦτο; πότερον ἦ[λ]θ[ον ὡς τούτῳ
συνευτυχήσουσ', ἂν δ[' ἀτυχήσῃ, μὴ τότε
αὐτοῦ προΐδω; μὰ τὸν [Δί', αὐτῷ γάρ, πάτερ,
κοινωνὸς ἦλθον το[ῦ βίου   820
ἔπταικεν; οἴσω τοῦτ[ο
δύ' οἰκίας οἰκοῦνθ' ὑπ[
προσέχοντ' ἐκείνῃ λα[
ἀλλ' εἰ μὲν ἕτερον μ' εἰ[ς
μηδὲν ὀδυνηρὸν μη[825
καλῶς ἔχει μοι τοῦτ[ο
εἰ δ' ἐστ' ἄδηλον τοῦτ[ο
ταῦτ', εἰς τοιαῦθ' ἥξου[σα
ἀλλ' ἐκβαλεῖ με; τῷ Χα[ρισίῳ
αἰ<σ>θήσετ' εὔνουν οὖσ[αν ἐμὲ   830
τιμῶν ἐκείνην, ἐν[
ἔχ]ων. ὅταν γὰρ πρὸς [
ὁ]ρᾷ τὸ χεῖρον ῥᾳδίως [
ἡ]μᾶς ἐκείνη διαβ[αλεῖ;
ἄ]ν θ' ἐν δ[ι]αβ[ά]λλῃ [835

(c. seventeen lines missing)

817–19.   suppl. Koenen-Gagos
818.   ἀτυχῇ Arnott
820.   suppl. Turner
823.   εκεινη O23 εκειναι[ς] M
824.   εἰ[ς γάμον δώσεις, ἐφ' ᾧ Gronewald, Martina; εἰ[ς γάμον δοῦναι θέλεις Arnott
828.   suppl. Turner, Handley
829.   suppl. Turner
830.   οὖσ[αν ἐμὲ Koenen-Gagos
832.   ἔχ]ων Koenen-Gagos, ὀρ]ῶν Gronewald
833.   suppl. Gronewald
834.   suppl. Turner

because of it? Did I come [ ] to share his good fortune, but if [he falls on hard times] am I to give no thought for him? No, by [God]. 820 I came to share his [life, father]. [ ] Has he stumbled? I shall bear this [ ] though he lives in two houses [ ] clinging to *her*. But if [ ] me to another [ ] 825 [there's] no pain [ ], no thank you [ ]. But if this is unclear [ ] these things, when [I] have come to such a state [ ]. But will she displace me? 830 She'll realise that [I'm] loyal to Ch[arisios]. Though he honours her [ ], for whenever to [ ], he easily sees what is worse [ ]. Will *she* slander us? [ ] 835 If she talks slander on one thing [ ].

(*about 17 lines missing during which Smikrines leaves, presumably to secure the help of Sophrone*)

Scholion to Eupripides Phoenissae *1154 (fr. 8 K–T, 184 K) = Martina fr. 10*

[ΠΑ]   ἐξετύφην μὲν οὖν
κλαίουσ᾽ ὅλως.

(ΑΒΡ) ἔξειμ᾽ ἔχουσα· κλαυμυρίζεται, τάλαν,
πάλαι γάρ· οὐκ οἶδ᾽ ὅ τι κακὸν πέπονθέ μοι.
(ΠΑ) τίς ἂν θεῶν τάλαιναν ἐλεήσειέ με;   855
ΑΒΡ. ὦ φίλτατον [τέκνον, πότ᾽] ὄψει μη[τέ]ρα;
καὶ [   ]
(ΠΑ)   πορεύσομαι.
(ΑΒΡ) μικρόν, γύναι, πρόσμεινον.
(ΠΑ)   ἐμὲ καλ[εῖ]ς;
(ΑΒΡ)   ἐγώ.
ἐναν]τίον [βλέ]πε.
[ΠΑ]   [ἦ μ]ε γινώσκεις, γύναι;
(ΑΒΡ) αὐτή ᾽στιν [ἣν] ἑό[ρ]ακα· χαῖρε, φιλτάτη.   860
(ΠΑ) τί[ς δ᾽ εἶ] σύ;
(ΑΒΡ)   [χε]ῖρα δ[εῦ]ρό μοι τὴν σὴν δίδου.
λέγε μοι, [γλυκ]εῖ[α], πέρυσιν ἦ[λθ]ες ἐπὶ θ[έαν
τοῖς Ταυροπολίοις ε[
(ΠΑ) γύναι, πόθεν ἔχεις, εἰπέ μοι, τὸ παιδί[ον
λ]αβοῦσα;
(ΑΒΡ)   ὁρᾷς τι, φιλτάτη, σοι γνώριμον   865
ὧν] τοῦτ᾽ ἔχει; μηδέν με δείσῃς, ὦ γύναι.
(ΠΑ) οὐκ [ἔ]τεκες αὐτὴ τοῦτο;
(ΑΒΡ)   προσεποιησάμην,
οὐχ ἵν᾽ ἀδικήσω τὴν τεκοῦσαν, ἀλλ᾽ ἵνα
κατὰ σχολὴν εὕροιμι. νῦν δ᾽ εὕρηκα σέ·
ὁρῶ γάρ, ἣν καὶ τότε.

852.   [τὸ παιδίον] suggested by Sudhaus for the end of the line
856.   τέκνον Jensen, πότ᾽ Fraenkel
859–60.   many continue with Habrotonon but there is a *paragraphus*, and *dicolon* after
γύναι
859.   ἐναν]τίον [βλέ]πε Sudhaus; [ἦ μ]ε Merkelbach
860.   αὐτή Capps, αὕτη Sudhaus
861.   [χε]ῖρα Jensen; the rest suppl. Sudhaus
862.   [γλυκ]εῖ[α] Jensen; θ[έαν Wilamowitz

PAM.   *(fr. 8 K-T)*: I was completely burned up with weeping.

HAB.   ⁸⁵³ (*Entering from Chairestratos' house carrying the baby but failing to see Pamphile*) I'll go out with (it). Poor thing, it's been crying for ages. I don't know what's the matter with it – something I've done.

PAM.   ⁸⁵⁵ What god will take pity on me in my wretchedness?

HAB.   Dear [child, when] will you see your mother? And [ ]

PAM.   I'll go. (*She turns towards Charisios' house but is interrupted by Habrotonon*)

HAB.   One moment, madam.

PAM.   Are you addressing me?

HAB.   Yes, look at me.

PAM.   Do you know me, madam?

HAB.   ⁸⁶⁰ (*To herself*) It's the girl I saw. (*To Pamphile*) Hello, dear.

PAM.   And who [are] you?

HAB.   Here, give me your hand. Tell me, sweetheart, last year did you go [to watch] the Tauropolia [ ]?

PAM.   Madam, where did you get the baby you're holding? Tell me.

HAB.   ⁸⁶⁵ Is there something you see it wearing that you recognise, dear? Don't be afraid of me, madam.

PAM.   Aren't *you* its mother?

HAB.   I pretended to be – not to do the mother any wrong, but to gain time to find her. And now I've found her – you! ⁸⁷⁰ I'm looking at the girl I saw before.

(ΠΑ)   τίνος δ' ἐστὶν πατρός;   870
(ἈΒΡ) Χαρισίου.
(ΠΑ)   τοῦτ' οἶσθ' ἀκριβῶς, φιλτάτη;
(ἈΒΡ) εὖ ο]ἶδ' ἔ[γωγ'· ἀλλ'] οὐ σε τὴν νύμφην ὁρῶ
τὴν ἔνδον οὖσαν;
(ΠΑ)   ναιχί.
(ἈΒΡ)   μακαρία γύναι,
θεῶν τις ὑμᾶς ἠλέησε. τὴν θύραν
τῶν γειτόνων τις ἐψόφηκεν ἐξιών.   875
εἴσω λαβοῦσά μ' ὡς σεαυτὴν εἴσαγε,
ἵνα καὶ τὰ λοιπὰ πάντα μου πύθῃ σαφῶς.

ΟΝ. ὑπομαίνεθ' οὗτος, νὴ τὸν Ἀπόλλω, μαίνεται·
μεμάνητ' ἀλ[η]θῶς· μαίνεται νὴ τοῖς θεούς.
τὸν δεσπότην λέγω Χαρίσιον. χολὴ   880
μέλαινα προσπέπτωκεν ἢ τοιοῦτό [τι.
τί γὰρ ἄν τις ε[ἰκ]άσειεν ἄλλο γεγον[έναι;
πρὸς ταῖς θύραις γὰρ ἔνδον ἀρτί[ως πολὺν
χρόνον διακύπτων ἐνδ[ιέτριψεν ἄθλιος.
ὁ πατὴρ δὲ τῆς νύμφης τι περὶ [το]ῦ [π]ρ[άγματος   885
ἐλάλει πρὸς ἐκείνην, ὡς ἔοιχ', ὁ δ' οἷα μὲν
ἤλλαττε χρώματ', ἄνδρες, οὐδ' εἰπεῖν καλόν.
"ὦ γλυκυτάτη" δὲ "τῶν λόγων οἵους λέγεις"
ἀνέκραγε, τὴν κεφαλήν τ' ἀνεπάταξε σφόδρα
αὑτοῦ. πάλιν δὲ διαλιπών, "οἵαν λαβὼν   890
γυναῖχ' ὁ μέλεος ἠτύχηκα." τὸ δὲ πέρας,
ὡς πάντα διακ[ο]ύσας ἀπῆλθ' εἴσω ποτέ,
βρ[υ]χηθμὸς ἔνδον, τιλμός, ἔκστασις συχνή.
"ἐγὼ" γὰρ "ἀλιτήριος" πυκνὸν πάνυ
ἔλεγεν "τοιοῦτον ἔργον ἐξειργασμένος   895
αὐτὸς γεγονώς τε παιδίου νόθου πατὴρ

872.   εὖ ο]ἶδ' ἔ[γωγ' Wilamowitz; ἀλλ'] Sudhaus
881.   suppl. Robert
882.   ε[ἰκ]άσειεν Croiset; γεγον[έναι Sudhaus
883.   suppl. Leo
884.   suppl. Robert
885.   suppl. Croiset
890.   δε C, τε Ο4

PAM.   But who's the father?

HAB.   Charisios.

PAM.   Do you know this for certain, dear?

HAB.   [Yes, but] aren't I looking at his wife who lives here?

PAM.   Yes.

HAB.   Happy lady! Some god has taken pity on you. [875] (*A noise comes from Chairestratos' door*) There's the neighbour's door – someone's coming out. Take me inside to your place so you can learn all the rest from me clearly. (*The two withdraw into Charisios' house as Onesimos emerges from that of Chairestratos*)

ON.   The guy's crazy, by Apollo, deranged, really out of his mind. He's deranged, by the gods. [880] I mean my master, Charisios. Black depression's fallen on him, or [some] such affliction. How else could anyone explain what has happened? Just now, inside you see, he [spent] ages eavesdropping at the door, [poor man]. [885] His wife's father was going on about [the situation] to her, so it seems, while Charisios – I couldn't rightly describe the colours he went, gentlemen. 'Oh my darling, to utter such words' he cried, and punched himself hard on the head. [890] Then, after a while, 'What a wife I've got, only to be in this wretched mess.' Finally, when he'd heard everything, he went inside and there he howled the place down, tore at his hair, totally beside himself. 'I'm all to blame' he kept saying [895] 'I commit an act like that – me – and I'm the father

οὐκ ἔσχον οὐδ' ἔδωκα συγγνώμης μέρος
οὐθὲν ἀτυχούσῃ ταῦτ' ἐκείνῃ, βάρβαρος
ἀνηλεής τε." λοιδορεῖτ' ἐρρωμένως
αὐ]τῷ βλέπει θ' ὕφαιμον ἠρεθισμένος.　　　　　900
πέφρικ' ἐγὼ μέν, αὖός εἰμι τῷ δέει.
οὕτως ἔχων γὰρ αὐτὸν ἂν ἴδῃ μέ που
τὸν διαβαλόντα, τυχὸν ἀποκτείνει[ε]ν ἄν.
διόπερ ὑπεκδέδυκα δεῦρ' ἔξω λάθρᾳ.
καὶ ποῖ τράπωμαί γ'; εἰς τί βουλῆς; οἴχομαι.　　905
ἀπόλωλα· τὴν θύραν πέπληχεν ἐξιών·
Ζεῦ σῶτερ, εἴπερ ἐστὶ δυνατόν, σῷζέ με.

ΧΑΡΙΣΙΟΣ
ἐγώ τις ἀναμάρτητος, εἰς δόξαν βλέπων
καὶ τὸ καλὸν ὅ τι πότ' ἐστι καὶ ταἰσχρὸν σκοπῶν,
ἀκέραιος, ἀνεπίπληκτος αὐτὸς τῷ βίῳ –　　　910
εὖ μοι κέχρηται καὶ προσηκόντως πάνυ
τὸ δαιμόνιον – ἐνταῦθ' ἔδειξ' ἄνθρωπος ὤν.
"ὦ τρισκακόδαιμον, μεγάλα φυσᾷς καὶ λαλεῖς,
ἀκούσιον γυναικὸς ἀτύχημ' οὐ φέρεις,
αὐτὸν δὲ δείξω σ' εἰς ὅμοι' ἐπταικότα,　　　915
καὶ χρήσετ' αὐτή σοι τότ' ἠπίως, σὺ δὲ
ταύτην ἀτιμάζεις· ἐπιδειχθήσει θ' ἅμα
ἀ]τυχὴς γεγονὼς καὶ σκαιὸς ἀγνώμων τ' ἀνήρ."
ὅμο]ιά γ' εἶπεν οἷς σὺ διενόου τότε
πρὸς] τὸν πατέρα· κοινωνὸς ἥκειν τοῦ βίου　　920
　　　κ]οὐ δεῖν τἀτύχημ' αὐτὴν φυγεῖν
τὸ συμβ]εβηκός. σὺ δέ τις ὑψηλὸς σφόδρα
[　　　　　　　　　]ν
[　　　　　　　　　]βάρβαρο[ς
[　　　　　　　　　]υν ταύτῃ σοφῶς　　　　925
[　　　　　　　　]ε μέτεισι διὰ τέλους
[　　　　　τῶν δαιμ]όνων τις· ὁ δὲ πατὴρ

900.　suppl. von Arnim, Wilamowitz
913.　καιμεγαλα C
919.　suppl. many
922.　suppl. von Arnim
927.　τῶν Hunt, δαιμ]όνων Wilamowitz

of an illegitimate child; yet I didn't feel or show an ounce of mercy to that woman when she fell into the same misfortune, heartless brute that I am.' He railed against himself unsparingly, [900] his eyes all bloodshot, and frenzied. I'm terrified, dry-mouthed with fear. While he's in this state, if he sees me, the guy who spilled the beans, he might just kill me. That's why I've slipped out here unseen. [905] But where can I turn? What plan is there? I'm done for. I've had it. (*A noise at Chairestratos' door*) There's the door; he's coming out. Zeus saviour, save me, if that's possible. (*He dashes into Charisios' house as the young man emerges from that of Chairestratos*)

CHARISIOS   A faultless individual, that's me, one who had his eye fixed on reputation, a judge of what is right and wrong, [910] pure and beyond reproach in his own life – well some power above has dealt with me good and proper. In this I've shown myself human. 'You wretch! You give yourself airs, your talk's all moralistic; you won't tolerate your wife's misfortune, though she's not to blame for it, [915] but I'll show that *you*'ve stumbled into the same predicament. Then *she*'ll treat you with kindness, but *you* insult her. Well, you'll be shown up as wretched, boorish, unfeeling, all at the same time.' She doubtless spoke to her father in the terms that used to go through your mind: [920] she came to share your life [ ] and shouldn't turn her back on the misfortune that's happened. You're too high-and-mighty [ ] barbarous [ ] [925] to her wisely [ ] some [god] will pursue [me] through to the end. Her father will treat her very [badly]. But what's

χαλε]πώτατ' αὐτῇ χρήσεται. τί δέ μοι πατρός;
ἐρ]ῶ διαρρήδην "ἐμοὶ σύ, Σμικρίνη,
μὴ] πάρεχε πράγματ'· οὐκ ἀπολείπει μ' ἡ γυνή.　　　　930
τ]ί συνταράττεις καὶ βιάζῃ Παμφίλην; "
τ]ί σ' αὖ βλέπω 'γώ;
ΟΝ.　　　　　　　πάνυ κακῶς ἔχω σφόδρα,
ο]ἴμοι τάλας. καὶ σο[ῦ δ]έομαι τούτοις [γύναι,
μή μ' ἐγκαταλίπῃς.
<ΧΑΡ>　　　　　　οὗτος ἐπακροώμε[νος
ἔστηκας ἱερόσυλέ μου;
[ΟΝ]　　　　　　　[μ]ὰ τοὺς θεούς,　　　　935
ἀλλ' ἀρτίως ἐξῆλθον. ἀ[λλὰ πῶς] λαθεῖν
ἔσται σ'; ἔπρα[ξ'] ὑμῖν το[σαῦτα], νὴ Δ[ία·
πάντ' ἐπακροάσει.
(ΧΑΡ)　　　　　ποτ[. . . . .]ουθ[
ἐγώ σε λανθάνειν πον[ηρὸν ὄντα καὶ
βροντῶντα.
(ΟΝ)　　　δια . ε[　　　　　　　　　940
(ΑΒΡ) ἀλλ' οὐθὲν ὀφθήσε[ι
(ΧΑΡ) τίς εἶ σ[ύ; . .] . αυ . εισ . [
(ΑΒΡ) οὐκ αἰσ[. .] ν [
(ΧΑΡ)　　　　　　[
(ΑΒΡ) οὐκ ἦν ἐ[μὸν τὸ π]α[ιδίον
(ΧΑΡ) οὐκ ἦν σό[ν;　　　　　　　945
(ΑΒΡ) βούλει μ' ἀπ[
(ΧΑΡ) ἀλλ' ἐξαπί[νης
(?ΑΒΡ) ἔμ' ἔπρ[επε
(?ΟΝ) ἔ[δ]ει σε[

928. χαλε]πώτατ' Arnott, ἀφρον]έστατ' Sandbach; αυτης Ο4
929. suppl. Koerte, Wilamowitz
933. ο]ἴμοι...σο[ῦ δ]έομαι Hunt, [γύναι Wilamowitz; τοῦτ', ὦ γύ[ναι Arnott
934. change of speaker suggested by Hunt
936. ἀ[λλὰ πῶς] Arnott, (Χαρ) ἀ[δύνατον] Jensen, ἀ[λλὰ]...ἐπακροάσει given to Charisios by Sandbach
937. suppl. Arnott
939. suppl. Arnott
944. ἐ[μὸν Koerte; το π]α[ιδίον Arnott
947. ἐξαπί[νης Arnott, εξαπει C
948. ἔπρ[επε Sudhaus
949. ἔ[δ]ει σε[Sandbach

her father to me? I['ll tell] him bluntly: 'Don't give me [930] any grief, Smikrines. My wife's not leaving me. Why are you upsetting and bullying Pamphile?' (*To Onesimos as he emerges sheepishly from Charisios' house*) Why are you here again?'

ON. Oh dear, I'm in the most awful fix. (*Addressing Habrotonon, still inside*) And don't you go and leave me in the lurch, la[dy], I beg you.

CHARISIOS Oi you, have you been [935] standing there listening to me, you villain?

ON. No, by God. I've just come out. [But how can] I keep you in the dark? I've done [such things] for you folk, by God. You'll hear it all.

CHARISIOS [And when could] I not be aware of your villainy and [940] loud mouth?

ON. [ ].

HAB. (*Emerging from the house and perhaps addressing someone inside*) [ ] You'll not be seen at all [ ].

CHARISIOS Who are you? [ ].

HAB. Not [ ].

CHARISIOS [ ].

HAB. The [child] wasn't m[ine].

CHARISIOS [945] It wasn't yours? [ ].

HAB. Do you want me [ ].

CHARISIOS At once [ ].

HAB.? I ought [ ].

ON.? You should [ ].

(ΧΑΡ) τ]ί φής, Ὀν[ήσιμ’], ἐξεπειράθη[ς ἐμοῦ;   950
(ΟΝ) αὕ]τη μ’ ἔ[πε]ισε, νὴ τὸν Ἀπόλλω [καὶ θε]ού[ς.
(ΧΑΡ) καὶ σύ μ]ε περισπᾷς, ἱερόσυλε;
(ΑΒΡ)   μὴ μάχου,
γλυκύτ]ατε· τῆς γαμετῆς γυναικός ἐστί σου
τέκνον] γ[ά]ρ, οὐκ ἀλλότριον.
(ΧΑΡ)   εἰ γὰρ ὤφελεν.
(ΑΒΡ) νὴ τὴν] φίλην Δήμητρα.
(ΧΑΡ)   τίνα λόγον λέγεις;   955
(ΑΒΡ) τίνα; τὸν] ἀληθῆ.
(ΧΑΡ)   Παμφίλης τὸ παιδίον;
ἀλλ’ ἦν ἐμ]όν;
(ΑΒΡ)   καὶ σόν γ’ ὁμοίως.
(ΧΑΡ)   Παμφίλης;
Ἁβρότο]νον ἱκετεύω σε, μ[ή] μ’ ἀναπτεροῦ

(c. ten lines missing)

(ΧΑΡ)   ]αι γὰρ[
(ΑΒΡ)   ] πῶς ἐγώ, τάλαν,   970
[πρ]ὶν πάντ’ εἰδέναι
(ΧΑΡ)   ] ὀρθῶς λέγεις
[   ]ο μοι·
[   ]τερε
[   ]ὅμως   975
[το]ῦτο δή
[   ]βούλομαι
[   ]ματα.

[ΧΟΡΟΥ]

950. τ]ί φής, Ὀν[ήσιμ’], ἐξεπειράθη[ς ἐμοῦ Sudhaus, ἐξεπειράθ[ητέ μου Jensen,
Sandbach
951. αὕ]τη μ’ [ἔ]π[ε]ισε Sudhaus, [καὶ θε]ού[ς Jensen
952. καὶ σύ μ]ε Sudhaus, τί σύ μ]ε Jensen, πῶς σύ μ]ε van Herwerden
953. suppl. Wilamowitz
954. τέκνον] Sudhaus, Koerte, ἴδιον] Arnott, τουτὶ] Wilamowitz, δῆλον] Croiset, αὑτῆς] Capps
955. suppl. Headlam, Hense
956. suppl. Coppola; ἐγὼ; τὸν] Jensen, Wilamowitz, Koerte
957. suppl. Sandbach
971. suppl. Koerte
973–8. speaker uncertain

CHARISIOS ⁹⁵⁰ What's that you're saying, On[esimos]? You were testing
    [me?]
ON.   *She* persuaded me, by Apollo [and] the gods.
CHARISIOS Are you leading me up the garden path [as well], you
    villain?
HAB.   Don't quarrel, [dear]. It's your own wife's [baby], no one else's.
CHARISIOS If only it were.
HAB.   ⁹⁵⁵ By dear Demeter it is.
CHARISIOS What are you saying?
HAB.   [What? The] truth.
CHARISIOS The baby's Pamphile's? [But it's also mine]?
HAB.   Yes, yours too.
CHARISIOS Pamphile's? [Habroto]non, please don't raise my hopes [ ].

[*about ten lines missing*]

CHARISIOS [ ] for [ ].
HAB.   ⁹⁷⁰ How could I, dear me [ ] before knowing everything?
CHARISIOS [ ] What you say is right. [ ] to me [ ] ⁹⁷⁵ nevertheless [ ] this
    indeed [ ] I want [ ].

(*Charisios rushes into his house to be reunited with Pamphile, followed
perhaps by Habrotonon and Onesimos*)

[CHORUS]

[?ΧΑΙ]   ]ειμενον
[τα]ύτη[ν] ἐπ[εὶ   980
[   ]λω ...... [..] . [...] ἐναντίο[ν,
Χ[α]ι[ρέστρ]ατ᾿, ἤδη τὸ μετὰ τα[ῦ]τα σκεπτέ[ον,
ὅπως [δια]μενεῖς ὢν Χαρισίῳ [φ]ί[λος
οἷός ποτ᾿ ἦσθα πιστός. οὐ γάρ ἐσ[τί που
ἑταιρίδιον τοῦτ᾿ οὐδὲ τὸ τυχὸν[985
σπουδῇ δέ· καὶ παιδάριον ἤδ᾿[
ἐλεύθερος. πάξ. μὴ βλέπ᾿ εἰς τ[
καὶ πρῶτον αὐτὴν κατὰ μόνα[ς
τὸν φίλτα[το]ν καὶ τὸν γλυκύτατ[ον

(c. eleven lines missing followed by the beginnings or near-beginnings of fifteen others)

1000   [....] . οτρ[1010   ὅσα μ . [
        [.....]καλ[ην μο[ι
        εἰ τὸ καλὸν .[ἔνδον πο. [
        ὥσπερ λύκ[ος   ἔοικεν: οὐ [
        ἀπελήλυ[θ   [....]οσπ . [
1005   ἀποστ[
        φιλο[
        δια . [
        οὐ κρι[
        καιν[

(an uncertain number of lines missing)

ἐπ᾿ αὐτὸν
ὄντως . β[
ἀλλ᾿ ἐξαπατ[1020

979ff.   assigned to Chairestratos by Webster
980.   suppl. Koerte
982.   Χ[α]ι[ρέστρ]ατ᾿ Sudhaus; τα[ῦ]τα σκεπτέ[ον van Leeuwen, Jensen
983.   [δια]μενεῖς Sudhaus, Ellis; [φ]ί[λος many
984.   οισθα C, corr. von Arnim; ἐσ[τί που Wilamowitz, ἐσ[τι νῦν Arnott
987.   βλέπ᾿ εἰς Schwartz, βλέπεις Sandbach

Act V

(Chairestratos enters from the city unaware of recent developments)

CH.   [ ] ⁹⁸⁰ her since [ ] the other way round, Chairestratos, you need to consider what comes next, how you can remain a loyal [friend] to Charisios, as you were before; for she's no mere ⁹⁸⁵ bit of fluff, and this isn't a casual [affair; it's] serious. And then she['s had] a child [ ] free. But enough of that. Don't keep casting glances at [the girl]. First, on their own [ ] her and her darling sweetheart.

[scraps of lines or lacunae to 1059, paragraphi marked _]

     ¹⁰⁰¹ good [ ] ¹⁰⁰² if the good [ ] ¹⁰⁰³ like a wolf [ ] ¹⁰⁰⁴ <u>has</u>/have gone away [ ] ¹⁰⁰⁵ [_]

(Onesimos enters from Charisios' house perhaps accompanied by Charisios)

     ¹⁰⁰⁶ <u>friend</u>(ly) [ ] ¹⁰⁰⁷ <u>through</u>(?) [ ] ¹⁰⁰⁸ not [ ] ¹⁰¹⁰ such as [ ] ¹⁰¹² in<u>side</u> [ ] <u>it</u> seems. Not [ ] *[lacuna of uncertain length]* ¹⁰¹⁸ to/<u>aga</u>inst him [ ] ¹⁰¹⁹ <u>actually</u> [ ] ¹⁰²⁰ <u>but</u> she? deceived [ ].

196   *Menander*

ON. ἀπέσωσε συ . [
ἐγὼ δὲ προσ[
σ . αν [

(ten to fourteen lines missing followed by remnants of fifteen lines including:)

1035]ελαβ[1036   τ]ουτ[. .]ι   1038   ] . ου κακὰ
1039]οὐχ ὁσ[1040   Ἁ]βρότονον   1047   το]οῦτ' ἀλλὰ σὺ
1048] . ς τουτ[ο]νὶ

(four lines missing)

ἀπα]τωμένου: 1052
τὸ]ν Δία
]αὐτοῦ τῷ σφόδρα
]ως ὁμολογῶ: 1055
εἰ]ς ἐμὲ βλέπει
]αιε[

(c. three lines missing)

[?ΧΑΡ] σώφρονα· τοιαυτησὶ γὰρ οὐκ ἀπέσχετ' ἂν   1060
ἐκεῖνος, εὖ τοῦτ' οἶδ'· ἐγὼ δ' ἀφέξομαι.

ΣΜ. ἂν μὴ κατάξω τὴν κεφαλήν σου, Σωφρόνη,
κάκιστ' ἀπολοίμην. νουθετήσεις καὶ σύ με;
προπετῶς ἀπάγω τὴν θυγατέρ', ἱερόσυλε γραῦ;
ἀλλ' ἢ περιμένω καταφαγεῖν τὴν προῖκά μου   1065
τὸν χρηστὸν αὐτῆς ἄνδρα, καὶ λόγους λέγω
περὶ τῶν ἐμαυτοῦ; ταῦτα συμπείθεις με σύ;
οὐκ ὀξυλαβῆσαι κρεῖττον; οἰμώξει μακρά,
ἂν ἔ[τ]ι λαλῇς τι. κρίνομαι πρὸς Σωφρόνην;
μετάπεισον αὐτήν, ὅταν ἴδῃς. οὕτω τί μοι   1070
ἀγαθὸν γένοιτο, Σωφρόνη, γάρ, οἴκαδε
ἀπιών – τὸ τέλμ' <ε>ἶδες παριοῦσ'; – ἐνταῦθά σε

1056. suppl. Sudhaus
1060–1.   given to Chairestratos or Charisios
1065. αλλαπεριμενω C, corr. Koerte, Wilamowitz
1069. λαλῇς. τί; Arnott

ON.   He/she has saved [ ] ¹⁰²² and/but I [ ] [*lacuna*] ¹⁰³⁵ [ ] took [ ] ¹⁰³⁶ [ ]
this [ ] ¹⁰³⁸ [ ] bad [ ] ¹⁰³⁹ [ ] not [ ] ¹⁰⁴⁰ [ ] Habrotonon [ ] ¹⁰⁴⁷ [ ] this
but you [ ] ¹⁰⁴⁸ [ ] this [ ] [*four lines missing; editors insert*] ¹⁰⁵² [ ]
deceived [ ] ¹⁰⁵³ [ ] Zeus [ ] ¹⁰⁵⁴ [ ] by his vehement [ ] ¹⁰⁵⁵ [ ] I agree
[ ] ¹⁰⁵⁶ [ ] looks at me [ ].

(*about three lines missing, during which Onesimos and Chairestratos exit, leaving Charisios? to muse on the situation*)

CHARISIOS?   ¹⁰⁶⁰ ... self-controlled. *He* wouldn't have been able to keep
his hands off a girl like her, I'm certain. *I* shall, though. (*He exits
into his house as Smikrines enters from the right with Sophrone*)

SMI.   If I don't smash your head in, Sophrone, may I be damned to
perdition. Are you going to tell me off as well? Rushing headlong
to take away my daughter am I, you wicked old woman? ¹⁰⁶⁵ So,
should I wait till her fine upstanding husband has devoured the
dowry I gave and just babble on about what's mine? Is that the
advice you're giving me? Isn't it better to strike quickly? If you say
another word to me, you'll be really sorry. Is Sophrone my judge?
¹⁰⁷⁰ Make her change her mind when you see her. Otherwise, so
Heaven help me, Sophrone, on the way home – did you see that

τὴν νύκτα βαπτίζων ὅλην ἀποκτενῶ,
κ[ἀ]γώ σε ταῦτ᾽ ἐμοὶ φρονεῖν ἀναγκάσω
καὶ [μ]ὴ στασιάζειν. ἡ θύρα παιητέα·   1075
κεκλειμένη γάρ ἐστι. παῖδες, παιδίον·
ἀνοιξάτω τις. παῖδες, οὐχ ὑμῖν λέγω;
ΟΝ. τίς ἐσθ᾽ ὁ κόπτων τὴν θύραν; ὤ, Σμικρίνης
ὁ χαλεπός, ἐπὶ τὴν προῖκα καὶ τὴν θυγατέρα
ἥκων.
(ΣΜ)   ἔγωγε, τρισκατάρατε.
(ΟΝ)   καὶ μάλα   1080
ὀρθῶς· λογιστικοῦ γὰρ ἀνδρὸς καὶ σφόδρα
φρονοῦντος ἡ σπουδή, τό θ᾽ ἅρπασμ᾽, Ἡράκλεις,
θαυμαστὸν οἷον.
<ΣΜ>   πρὸς θεῶν καὶ δαιμόνων –
<ΟΝ> οἴει τοσαύτην τοὺς θεοὺς ἄγειν σχολὴν
ὥστε τὸ κακὸν καὶ τἀγαθὸν καθ᾽ ἡμέραν   1085
νέμειν ἑκάστῳ, Σμικρίνη;
(ΣΜ)   λέγεις δὲ τί;
(ΟΝ) σαφῶς διδάξω σ᾽. εἰσὶν αἱ πᾶσαι πόλεις,
ὅμοιον εἰπεῖν, χίλιαι· τρισμύριοι
οἰκοῦσ᾽ ἑκάστην. καθ᾽ ἕνα τούτων οἱ θεοὶ
ἕκαστον ἐπιτρίβουσιν ἢ σῴζουσι;
(ΣΜ)   πῶς;   1090
λέγεις γὰρ ἐπίπονόν τιν᾽ αὐτοὺς ζῆν [βίον.
(ΟΝ) οὐκ ἄρα φρον[τί]ζουσιν ἡμῶν [ο]ἱ [θεοί;
φήσεις. ἑκάστῳ τὸν τρόπον συν[ῴκισαν
φρούραρχον· οὗτος ἔνδο[ν] ἐπ[ιτεταγμένος
ἐπέτριψεν, ἂν αὐτῷ κακῶς χρη[σώμεθα,   1095
ἕτερον δ᾽ ἔσωσεν. οὗτός ἐσθ᾽ ἡμῖν θεὸς

1074. σε many, σοι C
1080–3. ἔγωγε...δαιμόνων given to Smikrines by Fraenkel; *dicolon* after τρισκατάρατε in C
1083. πρὸς...δαιμόνων given to Smikrines by many
1090–1. πῶς...[βίον given to Onesimos by Richards, Arnott. In C *dicolon* before πῶς,
paragraphus under λέγεις
1092. [ο]ἱ θ[εοί suppl. von Arnim, Richards
1093. suppl. Sudhaus
1094. suppl. Sandbach
1095. suppl. Wilamowitz

pond on your way here? – I'll stick you in it all night long and do for you – I'll make you agree with me [1075] and stop your arguing. *(Tries to open Charisios' door)* The door's locked; I'll have to hammer at it. Slaves, slave. Someone open up. Slaves! Isn't it you I'm shouting to?

ON.   *(Emerging from Charisios' house)* Who's that knocking at the door? Oh, Smikrines, Mr. Trouble, come for his dowry and his daughter.

SMI.   [1080] Yes, it's me, you accursed creature!

ON.   Quite right too. This vehemence is what you'd expect from a man with brains and great discernment; and as for embezzlement, by Heracles, now that is a surprise!

SMI.   By the gods and the powers that be!

ON.   Do you think the gods have so much spare time [1085] that they can dole out good and ill to each man every day, Smikrines?

SMI.   What do you mean?

ON.   I'll spell it out clearly to you. There are in all, roughly speaking, a thousand cities, and thirty thousand inhabitants in each. Do the [gods] [1090] assign each one of these destruction or salvation individually?

SMI.   How could they? You're implying they live [a life] of drudgery.

ON.   'Then, don't [the gods] take any thought for us?', you'll say. In each person [they've placed] his character as guardian. [On duty] inside us, [1095] it brings us down if we treat it badly, but it's the salvation of another. This is our god, responsible for whether each man fares

ὅ τ᾽ αἴτιος καὶ τοῦ καλῶς καὶ τοῦ κακῶς
πράττειν ἑκάστῳ· τοῦτον ἱλάσκου ποῶν
μηδὲν ἄτοπον μηδ᾽ ἀμαθές, ἵνα πράττῃς καλῶς.
(ΣΜ) εἶθ᾽ οὑμός, ἱερόσυλε, νῦν τρόπος ποεῖ   1100
ἀμαθές τι;
(ΟΝ)   συντρίβει σε.
(ΣΜ)   τῆς παρρησίας.
(ΟΝ) ἀλλ᾽ ἀπαγαγεῖν παρ᾽ ἀνδρὸς αὐτοῦ θυγατέρα
ἀγαθὸν σὺ κρίνεις, Σμικρίνη;
(ΣΜ)   λέγει δὲ τίς
τοῦτ᾽ ἀγαθόν; ἀλλὰ νῦν ἀναγκαῖον.
(ΟΝ)   θεᾷ;
τὸ κακὸν ἀναγκαῖον λογίζεθ᾽ οὑ[τ]οσί.   1105
τοῦτον τίς ἄλλος, οὐχ ὁ τρόπος, ἀπολλύει;
καὶ νῦν μὲν ὁρμῶντ᾽ ἐπὶ πονηρὸν πρᾶγμά σε
ταὐτόματον ἀποσέσωκε, καὶ καταλαμβάνεις
διαλλαγὰς λύσεις τ᾽ ἐκείνων τῶν κακ[ῶ]ν.
αὖθις δ᾽ ὅπως μὴ λήψομαί σε, Σμικρίνη,   1110
προπετῆ, λέγω σοι· νῦν δὲ τῶν ἐγκλ[η]μάτων
ἀφεῖσο τούτων, τὸν δὲ θυγατριδοῦν λαβὼν
ἔνδον πρόσειπε.
(ΣΜ)   θυγατριδοῦν, μαστιγία;
(ΟΝ) παχύδερμος ἦσθα καὶ σύ, νοῦν ἔχειν δοκῶν.
οὕτως ἐτήρεις παῖδ᾽ ἐπίγαμον; τοιγαροῦν   1115
τέρασιν ὅμοια πεντάμηνα παιδία
ἐκτρέφομεν.
(ΣΜ)   οὐκ οἶδ᾽ ὅ τι λέγεις.
(ΟΝ)   ἡ γραῦς δέ γε
οἶδ᾽, ὡς ἐγᾦμαι· τότε γὰρ οὑμὸς δεσπότης
τοῖς Ταυροπολίοις, Σωφρόνη, ταύτην λαβὼν
χορῶν ἀποσπασθεῖσαν – αἰσθάνει γε; νή,   1120
νυν<ὶ> δ᾽ ἀναγνωρισμὸς αὐτοῖς γέγονε καὶ
ἅπαντ᾽ ἀγαθά.

1101.   change of speaker after παρρησίας Koerte
1102.   ανδροσσαυτου C, corr. Leo
1113.   change of speaker after μαστιγία Lefèbvre
1119–20.   *dicola* before and after Σωφρόνη, before and after αἰσθάνει γε and after νή in C;
paragraphi under both lines

well or ill. To fare well, treat it well by doing nothing untoward or stupid.

SMI. [1100] So, is my character doing something stupid now, you villain?

ON. It's annihilating you.

SMI. Cheek!

ON. But do you think it's right to take your daughter away from her husband, Smikrines?

SMI. Who says it's right? As things stand, it's unavoidable.

ON. (*To Sophrone*) You see? [1105] This guy reckons wrong is unavoidable. What else is ruining him, if not his character? (*To Smikrines*) Even now, when you're rushing towards an act of wickedness, mere chance has saved you, and you arrive to find those problems resolved and settled. [1110] So don't let me find you rushing headlong into things again, Smikrines – I'm telling you. Drop those complaints right now. In you go; take your daughter's baby and greet it.

SMI. My daughter's baby, you scoundrel?

ON. You were a right thicky, thinking you were so clever. [1115] Was that your way of taking care of a girl of marriageable age? That's how we come to bring up babies four months premature – virtual miracles!

SMI. I don't know what you mean.

ON. But the old woman does, I think. (*He turns to addresss Sophrone*) Before, at the Tauropolia, Sophrone, my master took the girl – [1120] she'd become separated from the dance. Do you understand? (*She nods vigorously*) Yes! And now they've recognised one another, and all is well.

(ΣΜ)   τί φησιν, ἱερόσυλε γραῦ;
(ΟΝ) "ἡ φύσις ἐβούλεθ', ᾗ νόμων οὐδὲν μέλει·
γυνὴ δ' ἐπ' αὐτῷ τῷδ' ἔφυ." τί μῶρος εἶ;
τραγικὴν ἐρῶ σοι ῥῆσιν ἐξ Αὔγης ὅλην   1125
ἂν μή ποτ' αἴσθῃ, Σμικρίνη.
(ΣΜ)   σύ μοι χολὴν
κ]ινεῖς παθαινομένη· σὺ γὰρ σφόδρ' οἶσθ' ὅ τι
οὗτο]ς λέγει νῦν.
(ΟΝ)   οἶδεν, οἶδ', εὖ ἴσθ' ὅτι
ἡ γραῦ]ς προτέρα συνῆκε.
(ΣΜ)   πάνδεινον λέγεις.
(ΟΝ) ο[ὐ] γέγ[ο]ν[εν] εὐτύχημα μεῖζον οὐδὲ ἕν.   1130
<ΣΜ> εἰ το]ῦτ' ἀληθές ἐσθ' ὃ λέγεις, τὸ παιδίον
ἐξ ο[ὐ] γαμετῆς γυν[αικὸς ἢ Χαρισί]ῳ
π[. . . . .]
ΧΑΙ.   ταύτ[η]ν ἢ [. . . . .]νον [
ΣΜ.   ]
ΧΑΙ.   νῦν . . [. . . . .]η
[. . . . . . .] ε[. .]ω[.]ακ . [1135
[. . . . . . ζ]υγομαχεῖς[
[. . . . . . .]ς ἐστ' ἄνθρω[πος
[. . . . . .] ἅπασι Σμικρ[ίνη
[. . . .] . [.] . ε θήσει πα[
[. . . .] . . [.] Σμικρίνη κ[1140

(four lines of scattered letters)

1123–6a.   given to Onesimos by Sandbach. ἡ φύσις...ἔφυ given to Sophrone by many, C has *paragraphus* under 1124 and *dicola* before and after τί μῶρος εἶ, which Koerte gave to Smikrines
1128.   οὗτο]ς von Arnim, αὐτὸ]ς Lefebvre; οι[δ M, omitted from C, thus: (Ον) οἶδεν, οἶ[δ']· εὖ ἴσθ' ὅτι Arnott (2004a, p.280), (Σμ) οἶδεν; (Ον) οἶ[δ']· εὖ ἴσθ' ὅτι Martina
1129.   suppl. Sudhaus
1130–1.   suppl. Wilamowitz; both lines given to Sophrone by many; 1130 given to Onesimos by Sudhaus, 1131 to Smikrines by van Leeuwen
1132.   suppl. Koenen-Gagos

SMI. What's that he's saying, you wicked old woman?

ON. 'Nature willed and nature heeds no laws. Woman was born for this very thing'. Why are you so dim? [1125] I'll quote you the whole tragic speech from the *Auge* if you don't understand, Smikrines.

SMI. (*To Sophrone*) Your antics are making my blood boil. You know very well what [this fellow] means.

ON. Oh she knows, she knows. Rest assured [the old woman] got it before you.

SMI. What you're saying is terrible!

ON. [1130] No greater stroke of luck has ever happened.

SMI. [If] this is true – what you say– the child from the unmarried woman [who is with Charisios]. (*Chairestratos enters from Charisios' house*)

CH. Her who [ ].

SMI. [ ].

CH. [1134] Now [ ] [1136] you're quarrelling needlessly [ ] man is [ ] [1138] to all, Smikrines [ ], will put [ ] [1140] Smikrines [ ].

(*All withdraw into Charisios' house*)

204   *Menander*

Fragments that cannot be precisely located within the play
Fr. 9 K–T, 179 K = Orion *Anth.* VII 8

οὐθὲν πέπονθας δεινὸν ἂν μὴ προσποῇ.

Fr. 10 K–T, 176 K = Stobaeus IV 29, 58

ἐλευθέρῳ τὸ καταγελᾶσθαι <μὲν> πολὺ
αἴσχιόν ἐστι, τὸ δ' ὀδυνᾶσθ' ἀνθρώπινον.

Papyrus fragments
P. Berol. 21142 (= Martina fr. 5, p. 10, Arnott fr. 12)
εἰς ἕτερα ν[
ἤδη 'στι πει[
Χαρισίῳ πρ[
ἀλλὰ λέλυτα[ι
πίνειν μ[5
βινεῖν ε . [
οὐθεις. : – κελ[ευ
προστάξατ . [
ἀγάπα κολα[
ἐπισταλη . [
εἰρη . [

P. Oxy. 2829, fr. V–X (= Martina fr. 13, p. 122; Furley assigns to Act II)
Fr. V: Remnants of four lines including:
4   ] . ει πάλαι[

Fr. VI: Remnants of four lines including:
2   ἀπ]ό[κ]οιτος ἐξ ὅτου[
4   ]ων ἐμοί. : – τί φησι με[

P. Berol 21142
7.   *dicolon* after οὐθεις

P. Oxy 2829, Fr. VI
4.   dicolon after ἐμοί

Unplaced book fragments
Orion *Antholognomici* VII, 8

> You've suffered nothing bad if you pretend it's not so.

Stobaeus *Eclogae* IV, 29, 58

> It's far more shameful when a free man's held up to derision, but
> pain is part of human existence.

Papyrus fragments
P. Berol 21142

> (?) to other things [ ]
> (?) already there is [ ]
> (?) to Charisios [ ]
> (?) but it has been solved/he has been released [ ]
> (?) to drink [ ]
> (?) to have sex [ ]
> (?) no one – order [ ]
> (?) command [ ]
> (?) be content [ ]
> (?) love / be content [ ]
> arranged [ ]
> [ ]

P. Oxy 2829 fr. V–X

Fr. V.3 [ ] long ago [ ]

Fr. VI.2 [ ] sleeping away from home since [ ]
VI.4   [ ] to me – what does he say [ ]

Fr. VII: Remnants of four lines including:
2   εἴλ]ηφ' ὅλως
3   ἐ]βούλετ[ο
4   ] . πεπεισμε . [

Fr. VIII: Remnants of two lines including:
2   ]αναξι[

Fr. IX: Remnants of three lines of which:
2   ]αυτη π[

Fr. X: Fragments of two lines

P. Oxy. 4023 (= Martina fr. 14, p. 124): Remnants of scattered letters in eleven lines.

P. Mich. 4733.1 (= Martina fr. 16, p. 124): Remnants of seven lines including:
1   ] . . . καὶ [
2   ]ον: Καρ[ι(ων)
5   λ]ευκὸ[ν
6   ]ον λία[ν

P. Mich. 4733.6 (= Martina fr. 15 p. 124): Remnants of three lines.

P. Mich. 4801g.1 (= Martina fr. 17, p.126): Remnants of fifteen lines including:
6   ] . [.]λέγε
7   ] . ναι λέγειν
8   μ]άρτυρας
10   π]ρὸς θεῶν
11   ]λως καὶ ταχ[
14   ]γέγονεν [.]α[

P. Mich. 4800 B26/B 17F (= Martina fr. 18, p. 126): Remnants of seven lines.

P. Mich. 4807c (= Martina fr. 19, p. 128): Remnants of four lines.

Fr. VII.2   [ ] has completely taken [ ]
Fr. VII.3   [ ] he/she wanted [ ]
Fr. VII.4   [ ] persuaded [ ]

Fr. VIII.2   [ ] unworthy [ ]

P. Oxy 4023
No discernible words.

P. Mich 4733 fr. 1
1.   [ ] and [ ]
2.   [ ] Karion [ ]
5.   [ ] white [ ]
6.   [ ] excessively [ ]

P. Mich 4733 fr.6
No discernible words.

P. Mich 4801g fr.1
6   [ ] say [ ]
7   [ ] to say [ ]
8   [ ] witnesses [ ]
9   [ ] by the gods [ ]
10   [ ] and quick [ ]
13   [ ] happened [ ]

P. Mich. 4800 B26/B17F
No discernible words.

P. Mich. 4807c
No discernible words.

COMMENTARY

Hypothesis – Summary of the Plot

The highly fragmentary Hypothesis or summary of the play is preserved in P. Oxy. 4020, a scrap of papyrus reused for accounts. In form it divides into two sections: the first, written in a larger script, contains part of the play's name, EPITRE[(cf. ARBITRA[) and the remnants of lines traditionally (and now firmly) assigned to the play's beginning as fr.1 (= fr. 1 K-T = 600K). Preceding this, in the first extant line, is the single letter E, followed by traces of what might be PI, suggesting either 1) that the play's title was written twice (as advocated by Martina II.2, p. 2), or 2) that there existed an alternative title to the play, as was also the case with such extant plays as *Dyskolos* (*Misanthropos*), *Misoumenos* (*Thrasonides*), *Samia* (*Kedeia*), as well as others of which virtually nothing survives (G.-S. p. 130), or 3) that the *hypothesis* opened with a reference to the eponymous archon of that year, thus providing a date (less likely since such information would normally follow not precede any plot summary). If it is in fact an alternative title that the papyrus preserves, the most likely suggested restoration for lines 1 and 2 might be:

Epitrope (*The Act of Arbitration*) *or*
Epitrepontes (*Men at Arbitration*)

The second part of the hypothesis contains what appears to be a critical judgment of the play ('one of the b[est]' and 'superior') fully in accordance with the modern-day verdict, followed by a listing of contrasting pairs of those characters involved:

two (slaves?: Syriskos and Daos), one acting sensibly, the other disgracefully, a wife and *hetaira*, one decent, the other brazen, an old man fixated with financial calculation, a just servant (cf. Webster 1950, p. 190–3).

Text

While most of Act I is lost, restoration of its general features can be achieved with a fair degree of certainty on the basis both of New Comedy's conventions and of later developments in the surviving action. As Arnott (1979a, p. 386–8) points out, the need for exposition, setting out the antecedents of the action, suggests three scenes before the main body of our text begins. For the first of these some of the fragments cited by ancient authors seem particularly relevant, suggesting an entry from town (stage right) by Onesimos, the cook Karion, newly hired to provide lunch (fr. 3) and at least one assistant (Simias, addressed at 630). The numbering of these fragments follows that of Körte-Thierfelder, *Menandri Quae Supersunt* (Leipzig 1959), and Kock, *Comicorum Atticorum Fragmenta* III (Leipzig 1888).

Fr. 1: Cited by (among others) an ancient commentator on Aristotle *De Interpretatione*, attributed to the play by Croiset and specifically to the cook Karion by Wilamowitz p. 49f. on the basis of Themistius' comment on fr. 2b. The fragment is now definitely established as the play's opening lines by reference to the hypothesis, with Karion inviting Onesimos to provide details of a situation, part of which has evidently become common knowledge around town. In this way the convention of introducing characters at the beginning of an Act or scene as though already in mid-conversation (cf. *Aspis* 250ff., *Dyskolos* 50ff., 233ff., 784ff.) provides an easy route for supplying necessary background information, while at the same time tantalising the audience with news of a recently married young man taking up with a harp-girl.

Fr. 2: Given by a number of ancient authorities, including the ancient commentator on Aristotle's *Categoriae*, the fragment is in fact cited as two separate quotations, suggesting different original locations, though a position within the opening scene remains their most likely origin, despite the fact that Themistius (*Oration* 21. 262c, which also gives the cook's name) sets 2b in a context suggestive of an altogether later scene in which the cook irritated the guests by his boasting. It may be, however, that Themistius was applying the quotation to a wider context than its origins would suggest (see further, Primmer p. 125ff.) or that textual losses mask the fragment's relevance to the scene (cf. Handley 2009, p. 27). What is certain, though, is that Menander here neatly motivates the cook's opening gambit with characterisation highly suggestive not only of his own inquisitive nature and love of gossip, but also that this is shared by Onesimos too. It is this shared attribute indeed (cf. 424–7) that we later learn is the cause of the predicament the slave evidently finds himself in, a further piece of potential irony if, as G.-S. suggest ad loc., Karion's words, here meant as congratulatory, underline an altogether different situation for Onesimos.

Fr. 3: While neither context nor speaker is given by the Berlin manuscript of Photius, who nevertheless cites the lines as coming from the play, it has become traditional for commentators to set them within the opening scene, where mention of 'lunch' neatly provides a morning time-frame. Similarly, the implicit need for haste is readily interpreted as the means by which Menander brings the dialogue to an end with the departure of Karion and Onesimos into Chairestratos' house, where Charisios is currently living. As G.-S. (p. 293) and Martina (II.2, p. 23f.) point out, however, variant interpretation remains a possibility in terms of both speaker and person referred to.

Fr. 4: Reference by Erotian to the single word 'jar' in *The Arbitration* provides few clues as to its position within the play, though a scene involving Karion, even if not the opening one, seems justified.

Fr. 5: While the culinary content of the statement, cited by Athenaeus (119e), suggests Karion as the most obvious speaker, its attribution to the first scene cannot be guaranteed. Similarly, a more figurative interpretation, such as heaping coals on coals (Arnott 1979a, p. 395), makes possible attribution to someone like Onesimos and a situation similar to that he finds himself in at the beginning of Act III.

The recent publication of P. Oxy. 4936, which the editor locates in the play's opening scene, suggests the arrival on stage of Chairestratos and his participation in reviewing the situation, something already underway between the cook Karion and Onesimos. The mention of the 'pretty girl', presumably Habrotonon, wine and meat, all point to discussion of the forthcoming party, for which Karion has been hired. Following this all three must have exited into Chairestratos' house since, as already suggested, Fr. 3 might be taken as the cue for this. (See further Furley p.124f.)

Since the major comic effect of New Comedy was derived from dramatic irony, where the audience's superior knowledge enabled it to appreciate the mistaken thought-processes and consequent embarrassment of the stage-characters, the information already given by Onesimos in the opening scene must at some stage have been augmented by details provided by a source aware of the true situation. Reference to *Aspis* and *Perikeiromene* provides a ready analogy: a deferred prologue (since fr. 1 is now seen as the play's actual beginning) delivered by a divinity or some personified abstraction, with suggested speakers including *Tyche*/Chance, *Dike*/Justice, *Agnoia*/Misapprehension, *Peitho*/Persuasion and *Eros*/Love. To allow the audience to appreciate future developments to the full, such a figure must have revealed, 1) that Charisios' abandonment of his wife on the grounds of her pre-marital 'infidelity' is otiose, since he is himself the father of the child, the result of rape, 2) that the exposed child has been rescued by country workers (putting the arbitration scene into a clear dramatic context, G.-S. p. 294), and perhaps 3) that the problems caused by Smikrines throughout the play will come to nothing (cf. the forecast failure of Smikrines' schemes in *Aspis*). In this way the playwright first puzzles his audience with a situation of some seriousness before dissolving the tension by confirmation of a solution that the genre expectations of a happy ending themselves demanded.

The third scene hypothesised for the play's beginning by Arnott explains the presence on stage of Chairestratos (named at 142), ready to overhear and comment upon the monologue of Smikrines (cf. Martina II.1, p. 23). For while the entry of the old man, having heard of Charisios' recent and supposedly riotous lifestyle, is readily motivated by this and his determination to seek clarification from his daughter (161–3), Chairestratos' emergence from his house simply in response to Smikrines' arrival would be dramatically weak. Rather, he most likely appears as a result of events inside and either explains this in a monologue or in dialogue with a character who then departs (Blume p. 104 suggests Habrotonon). The latter, however, would seem unlikely in the context of her appearance at 142, while Primmer's suggestion (p. 134) of an appearance by Charisios has little to recommend it. Rather, one might more readily envisage Chairestratos' entry addressing an unseen character indoors before turning to the situation outside.

127ff. Despite the probable loss of the old man's opening lines it is clear that his tirade against Charisios is designed primarily to outline his own character, confirming that doubtless already given in the absent prologue as someone fixated with the monetary aspect of the situation rather than any marital disloyalty on his son-in-law's part. His shocked outburst that anyone could spend an obol (a sixth of a drachma) for a kotyle (half-pint) of wine, however, extends his depiction still further. For while wine could be bought considerably more cheaply, as G.-S. point out ad loc., more expensive varieties were available. As a result Smikrines' carping criticism here (like his complaint at 136–9. about the money being paid for Habrotonon's hire) seems designed to underline his parsimonious attitude to life, an attitude that judges the present by the monetary values of the past, certainly not one that stems from poverty, as the size of the dowry given to his daughter clearly shows.

131–3. Chairestratos' aside contains problems of both interpretation and assignment. While 'This is…love affair' is readily assigned to Chairestratos, a reference to his expectation that Smikrines will force his way inside and break up the affair between Charisios and Habrotonon, an affair the audience knows is a fiction, editors are divided as to who speaks 'But what's…him again': Smikrines in Sandbach, Verdenius p. 19 and Furley p. 129f., Chairestratos in Wilamowitz, Sisti, Arnott, Martina. The latter seems based largely on the argument that any rejection here of the monetary factor the old man developed in 129–31, only to resume it with thoughts of the dowry in 134, would create an unnatural hiatus in his thinking. In favour of assignment to Smikrines on the other hand one might argue that the very shift of topic – from disapproval of Charisios' carousing involving expensive wine to rejection of concern for his profligate behaviour, then a return to thoughts of where the money is coming from and its implications – is altogether more natural. Unfortunately, interpretation of textual marks at this point and the claimed presence of Smikrines' name in the margin are too uncertain to provide clarity.

134. Four talents…dowry: A large sum (24,000 drachmas), even by New Comedy standards, with three talents in *Dyskolos* (844f.) and *Perikeiromene* (1015), and two talents in *Aspis* (135) and *Misoumenos* (446), though greater figures do occur (*e.g.* fr. 333.11K–T: ten talents). In antiquity the dowry marked the bride's contribution to her husband's household, a contribution which did not become his property (though he had considerable control over its management), but which was held in trust for any offspring, and in the event of divorce had to be returned to the bride's family; see further Harrison 1968, pp. 45–60. Does the discrepancy between the old man's evident parsimony and the size of the dowry imply that Smikrines was trying to impose on Charisios a greater obligation to avoid marital difficulties, or is it inserted simply for the comic value of the contrast? Certainly, the theme of a large dowry reducing a husband to a subservient position was frequently developed in comedy: Anaxandrides fr. 53.4–6 K-A 'A poor man taking a wife who has money gets a mistress – she's no longer his wife – and himself becomes her slave', Antiphanes fr. 270 K-A 'There's no heavier burden than a wife who brings a large dowry', Diodorus Comicus fr. 3.3–4

K-A 'It's better to take a wife who's well brought up but has no dowry than one who's brought up badly with money', Menander fr. 802 K-A 'When someone who is poor chooses to marry and gains wealth as well as a wife, he hands himself over rather than receives her', Plutarch *De Lib. Ed.* 19 'Those who take wives far above themselves unwittingly become not husbands to their wives but slaves to their dowries', Plautus *Aulularia* 478–535 (see further G.-S. pp. 296–8).

137. twelve drachmas a day: It is otiose to explore any potential reality represented here by reference to other sources. Commentators mention restrictions limiting payment for music-girls to two drachmas (Aristotole, *Ath. Pol.*50, 2: 'Of the ten city-controllers five hold office in the Peiraeus, five in the city; they supervise girls who play the pipe, the harp and the lyre to prevent them from being hired for more than two drachmas'), but it is clear from evidence both in literature (Menander *Samia* 392 where the sum mentioned is 10 drachmas, *Kolax* 129: 300 drachmas, Euripides' *Sciron* fr. 675 Kannicht: between 1 and 4 staters) and in real life that variations of status (free or slave) and level of accomplishment could result in enormous disparities. Rather, the sum is once again used to underline Smikrines' money-oriented view of life, his jaundiced view of the expenses Charisios is incurring, and his backward-looking perspective on life. As Chairestratos' comment makes clear, the reference to twelve drachmas being enough to keep a man for more than a month (139f.) harks back to a time when two obols a day was the dole paid out to Athens' poor at the time of the Peloponnesian War a century earlier, making twelve drachmas enough to last thirty six days.

142. The intervention of a new character at this point raises questions of identity and whether lack of any introductory remarks signified that the character had been on stage for some time. At one time most editors were content to accept an entry by Simias, based on the erroneous assumption that the character was a friend of Charisios or Chairestratos rather than Karion's assistant. However, earlier observations that 'darling' at 143 is more suited to a female character like Habrotonon have now been adequately vindicated by P. Oxy. 4021 fr. 1–2, which both serves to reduce the lacuna in the St. Petersburg manuscript (P) (overlapping it when it resumes at 159) and, unlike P, specifically identifies one of the speakers as Habrotonon. Moreover, that she appears from Charisios' house at this very moment, rather than earlier (as the lack of any introduction suggested to some), is strongly implied by her opening words and by her enquiry as to the identity of Smikrines, who has been on stage for some time. At all events, her pivotal role in the play demands her introduction at an early stage in the action. Identification as a *hetaira*, on the other hand, has already been prepared for in the reference to the pimp in 136, but would have needed no verbal signal, with dress and mask enough to make her status clear.

While the scene involves three speaking characters, there is no evidence that Smikrines at any point becomes aware of the other two, whose references to him consist therefore of commenting asides, including the whole of 140–5, the longest aside in Menander (Bain p. 152). This poses a potential problem for stage action, in particular the old man's actions during this period, but may be accounted for by 1) the spatial displacement of the two groups, with Smikrines outside Charisios' house, the other two outside that of Chairestratos, and 2) the ease with which characters can fade out of dramatic focus as attention is diverted elsewhere.

144–59. A number of lines have either fallen out or exist in a very fragmentary state before consistent text resumes at 159. In 145 Smikrines as speaker may be hazarded for 'the wretched man' (thus Webster 1950, p. 37), if the reference is taken to signify Charisios, but editors more generally see it as a comment on the old man himself from one of the other two, especially Habrotonon, in reaction to being told who he is. Similarly, though reference to 'harp-girl' at the end of 145 clearly applies to Habrotonon, there is no certainty as to whether the single word remaining in 146 is to be taken as 'woman' or 'wife', or how this might fit in with what precedes it. When a partial text returns at 151, marginal or interlinear indications of name, for all their fragmentary state, combined with *paragraphi* (lines drawn under the initial letters of a line of text) do supply useful indications of speaker but the contents of the dialogue remain unrecoverable. Further difficulties occur at the junction of P and P. Oxy. 4021 at 158–9; for while Habrotonon as the speaker in 158 and Chairestratos in the second part of 160 are indicated by the papyrus, who it is that delivers 159 and the opening of 160 remains problematical. Certainly, assignment to Smikrines is ruled out by both tone and content, and attempts in the past at restoration of text or of introducing a brief and heated dialogue with the old man have generally fallen foul of subsequent discoveries of papyrus; see further Martina II.2, pp. 85–8.

145. [harp]-girl: Restoration is confirmed by 589.

160. Damn you…proper: Coming immediately before the departure of Smikrines, this is best taken as Chairestratos' irritated reaction to the whole tone of the old man's complaints rather to than any specific statement. That the speaker is Chairestratos and not Smikrines, as suggested by earlier editors, is indicated by the presence of *Cha* above the first word in papyrus O25.

165. What a fox he is: In many contexts the Greek here, κίναδος, said to be Sicilian for fox, was used to indicate the epitome of cunning and shamelessness.

166. upside down: The restoration (or something very similar) seems necessary in view of Habrotonon's wish that the upset Smikrines is likely to cause in Charisios' house should also happen to Chairestratos', among others. Whether her comment is motivated specifically by feelings of neglect she has suffered from Charisios (G.-S. ad loc.) or is more general – that her profession requires upset within households for its success (Arnott 1979a, p. 403 n.1) is difficult to gauge. It may well be that the topic is introduced not to indicate any substantive underlying issue, but as a comic quip echoing the observation in 132f.

169. a crowd of young men: With the departure indoors of Habrotonon and Chairestratos motivated in dramatic terms by the need to inform Charisios about Smikrines' movements and intentions, the arrival on the scene of the chorus and the need to avoid their drunken revels form the technical expedient for departure.

Conventionally within Menander's plays it is only at the end of Act I that the chorus' entry is ever mentioned (cf. *Aspis* 246–9, *Dyskolos* 230–2, *Perikeiromene* 261–2), their inclusion necessitated by the comic tradition, which continued to impose upon dramas a choral element that had always been part of the genre, but which all indications suggest was now an extraneous irrelevance. Certainly, while their drunken state might be explained by the revels taking place indoors, the fact that Chairestratos deliberately avoids them shows that they have no connection with the stage action. Indeed, the introduction of similar groups in *Aspis*, *Dyskolos* and *Perikeiromene* indicates that their description as drunken is no more than a convention. (See further *Aspis*, Commentary 246–9, Martina II.2, pp. 94–109.)

Act II

While most of Act II, including the arbitration scene which gives its name to the play, is well preserved in the Cairo manuscript, its opening is altogether more problematical. The remains of the initial six lines (172–7) are preserved in P, forming a connection with Act I. Thereafter, the gap before C begins at 218 is the suggested location for two lengthy, if unconnected, fragments: P. Oxy. 4021 fr. 3 and 4641 (Nünlist 2003, 2004, cf. Arnott 2004a, p. 281, Martina II.2, pp. 111–19). The fact that their length now exceeds the number of lines that editions have traditionally allotted to the lacuna accounts for the discrepant system of line numbering that presently occurs in texts and the still fluid assessment of the gaps that continue to exist between the fragments. Similarly, the loss of line beginnings and endings in places, together with any dialogue markers there may have been, poses problems for identification of speaker, which must therefore be largely reconstructed from context. Indeed, attribution of P. Oxy. 4021 fr. 3 = lines180a–u to *Epitrepontes* is based solely on its association with fr. 1–2 of 4021, which overlap with the text of P, as Nünlist 2003, p. 59 observes. That the position of fr.3 in the gap somewhere before 150 or 127 is also a possibility is mentioned by ed. pr. p. 34, but cf. Martina II.2, p. 115. Some assistance in reconstructing the dramatic development, though, is perhaps discoverable from what occurs later.

172–7. The absence of *paragraphi* strongly suggests a monologue here, while reference to 'the master' and 'the old man' indicate delivery by the slave Onesimos, detailing the reaction inside the house to the news recently brought by Chairestratos and Habrotonon. That he mentions the precariousness of human existence is, perhaps, indicative of the dismay that has been caused by this.

180–216. The presence on stage of Smikrines when the two slaves, Syriskos and Daos, seek his assistance points to an entry for the old man at some earlier stage in the action, following the interview with his daughter indoors that he mentioned at the end of Act I. That he interacts with Onesimos at this point is again suggested by the slave's reluctance to face him at 579f., in case 'he's found out the truth from someone'. Webster (1950, p. 37) interpreted this as showing that the slave had earlier diverted Smikrines from entering Chairestratos' house and confronting his son-in-law by means of some fabrication. At this point Onesimos would have withdrawn into Chairestratos' house in readiness for his reappearance at 382, leaving Smikrines to review the situation prior to his own intended, but interrupted, departure (cf. Blume p. 105f, Martina II.2, p. 113f.).

180a–u. As Nünlist (2004, p. 99) observes, the fragment probably continues Onesimos' monologue, ostensibly detailing what seems to have been an agitated conversation inside Chairestratos' house (hence, 'To cut a long story short',180f). However, without any points of reference a coherent assessment of detail is fraught with difficulty. So for instance, is it Onesimos who is exhausted at 180d or is he reporting another's words? Who is told to go away at 180g and why? Is this Charisios' rejoinder to someone's attempts to rouse him from his drunken lethargy, and is it followed by an instruction for the young man to sleep off his drink? And who is giving instructions in 180m? While the lack of any discernible *paragraphi* throughout suggests continuity of speaker, the greater damage in 180r–u holds out the possibility either that at this point Smikrines entered and interrupted Onesimos' account or that his entry came in the lacuna that follows and has seemingly removed any dialogue between the two.

195–209. Attribution of the fragment (P. Oxy. 4641) to *Epitrepontes* is guaranteed by overlap with a book fragment (lines 207–9), for the origin of which Stobaeus (III, 30, 7) specifically cites the play, just as an interlinear insertion of Syriskos' name between 212–13 and the contents of the ensuing dialogue ensure its location near the beginning of Act II. Though the speaker of 195–209 is nowhere given, their contents suggest that Smikrines determines to steel himself to a forthcoming confrontation with Charisios ('stand your ground' 197). He envisages potential responses from the young man ('I'm drunk…skin-full' 202, cf. Charisios' own imagined confrontation with the old man at 927ff.), criticises the fact that apparently no one tells him to mend his ways (205), and rounds this off with a proverbial observation on those who are idle and healthy but over-eat, before he determines to go and see his son-in-law (209).

210–16. The final lines of P. Oxy. 4641 clearly represent the opening of a dialogue between characters entering the scene. Identification of one of these by the manuscript as Syriskos makes it certain that the other is Daos, and that the lines mark the beginning of the dispute leading to the great arbitration scene. As Nünlist (2004, p.101f.) observes, however, the lines also present a problem centred on why Daos is there at all, since he has the trinkets we later learn he covets and should have no reason to pursue Syriskos in this way. Nünlist advances an altogether persuasive explanation based on known facts: 1) Syriskos is on his way to see his master (214f., cf. 376–80); 2) Daos is clearly pursuing the other two and accuses Syriskos of blackmail (218), which suggests he is attempting to prevent some action on their part; 3) Syriskos is accompanied by his wife and the baby when his ostensible purpose is simply to pay his dues, which suggests that the child is somehow connected with that action. Is it, therefore, that Syriskos has threatened to refer the disputed ownership of the trinkets to his master Chairestratos, potentially leading to legal action against Daos, and that this is something he is desperate to avoid, hence his willingness to accept private arbitration?

[211f. Off with you...salvation: An attempt at a curt dismissal from Syriskos followed by a veiled threat. In what follows παρ' ἕνα...ἕκαστον, by analogy with instances elsewhere, means 'in each man's hands'.]

219. You've no right to what's not yours: *Dicola* (*i.e.*: indicating a change of speaker) exist in C both before and after the statement, one of which must be superfluous if the flow of dialogue in the lines that follow is to be correctly maintained. Most editors reject the first, giving 'You're blackmailing...not yours' to Daos as the simplest route to clarity, as in the present text. Sisti, however, accepted the evidence of both *dicola* producing:

Daos	You're blackmailing me, you wretch. :
Syriskos	You've no right to what's not yours. :
Daos	We need to hand...
Syriskos	That's all right...

though this assumes the existence of even more textual problems (Nünlist 2004, p. 103), not least that the offer of arbitration comes less logically from Daos (as posited by Weinstein), when it is Syriskos who makes the actual approach to Smikrines. As a variation Martina (with others) rejects the second dicolon and prints:

Daos	You're blackmailing me, you wretch. :
Syriskos	You've no right ...for judgement.
Daos	That's all right...

222. Why did I go shares with you?: Foreshadowing of what is to become a major aspect of Daos' case.

223. arbitrator: Arbitration, first mentioned at 219f., was a not uncommon route for settling private disputes, and the arbitrator's decision was binding so long as those involved agreed to this beforehand (MacDowell 1978, p. 204, Scafuro pp. 117–31, cf. Harrison 1971, p. 65). Some commentators, in fact, see the scene as a valid source of information for the operation of arbitration in late fourth-century Athens (Omitowoju p. 160f.). The present case, however, differs from what we know of the norm in a number of ways: 1) The litigants are slaves, as Smikrines observes with annoyance at 229, and thus formally debarred from normal law-processes (Patterson p. 220f., but cf. Cohen p. 96f.). 2) An arbitrator was generally known to at least one of those involved, whereas here it is evident from that same annoyance that this is not the case (Scafuro p. 160). That Smikrines is unconnected with either Syriskos or Daos may, however, account for why he can be described as 'impartial' at 226f. 3) It was normal for the arbitrator to be already acquainted with the case in question, but as Nünlist observes (2004, p. 104), it is Smikrines' total ignorance of the situation that allows both the old man and the audience to discover the facts simultaneously, a neatly disguised piece of necessary exposition.

[**224. ἂν σχολάσαις**: The optative verb (here in the form of a question) expresses a polite request, equivalent to a mild exhortation or command, but couched in much more conciliatory terms as befits a slave addressing a free man.]

226. What's that got to do with me?: From the audience's viewpoint the statement is full of irony since they will know from the prologue precisely Smikrines' relevance here, even if the baby has yet to be mentioned. Some commentators have seen similarities with, and perhaps the influence of, the situation in Euripides' lost play *Alope*, the plot of which is preserved by Hyginus *Fabulae* 187: Alope, daughter of King Kerkyon, gives birth to an illegitimate child, which is exposed but finds its way into the possession of first one shepherd and then another, who then come into dispute over possession of birth tokens, a dispute referred for arbitration to the child's grandfather (see further Poole p. 58, G.-S. p. 303, Katsouris 1975a, pp. 147–50, Collard-Cropp pp. 115–21).

229. working clothes: Lit. *diphtheras*, leather jerkins typical of rustic dress, hence the significance of *Dyskolos* 415, where the mention of the item symbolically converts the urbane Sostratos into a country worker (cf. Krieter-Spiro p. 20f.). Here, though, Smikrines' reference is designed to emphasise his disdain for the slaves.

231. Do us a favour, sir: The slave's deferential attitude throughout this initial contact is clearly designed both to mitigate the old man's annoyed response, 'Blast you', and to foreshadow Syriskos' rhetorical skills, as Daos observes in his aside at 236, 'It's a right speechifier I've got tangled up with'. Already Syriskos has shown a significant degree of initiative in suggesting arbitration and approaching Smikrines; that he ultimately wins through despite his ostensibly weak position in the face of the old man's clear and continuing hostility is even more impressive (Cohoon p. 158f.).

232–5. In all circumstances...factor of life: Lit. 'It's a common interest for the lives of all men'. The maxim that Syriskos inserts here may be intended both to resonate with the audience's understanding of Smikrines' own sense of injustice suffered at the hands of Charisios, and to serve as a prelude for the much more important decision still to come. Such an appeal to what might be termed 'natural justice' serves to underline what was, in fact, a major feature of Menander's plays: the belief that good must and will ultimately prevail, whether this be the restoration of a baby to its true parents, the reuniting of a disrupted family (*Misoumenos*, *Perikeiromene*), the rewarding of virtue (*Dyskolos*), or the prevention of an old man's mercenary schemes (*Aspis*).

237f. will you abide by my decision?: In terms of logic the question is otiose since Daos' earlier agreement to arbitration presupposed as much, but its emphasis here, at the beginning of the process, underpins its eventual result, when the slave is required to relinquish the trinkets (cf. Martina II.2 ad loc.).

239. You speak first: By reversing the normal order of the legal process and introducing the defendant's speech first (cf. Terence's complaint at *Eunuch* 10–14)

Menander 1) emphasises once again Smikrines' ostensible support for Daos (cf. the implications of 'the quiet one' compared to the old man's hostile reaction to Syriskos' initial approach), thus making the slave's eventual victory all the more striking; 2) ensures that what is clearly the more impressive speech forms the climax of the arbitration process, rather than being simply its opening stage; 3) disguises the technical necessity of presenting the case's history in chronological order, much like a messenger scene, its prime aim being clarity of exposition for the audience's sake. As a point of comparison commentators refer to Plautus' *Rudens* in which a similar dispute between slaves takes place over the contents of a trunk rescued from the sea (Katsouris 1975a, pp. 150–6, Scafuro pp. 154–68, Goldberg p. 67f.).

240ff. As Goldberg observes (p. 66), the speeches of the two slaves are designed as much to characterise the speakers as to set out the details of their dispute. In Daos' case the effect is largely negative, the result of 1) his constant self-absorption and pointed reference to his own viewpoint (especially at 250–6, cf. Katsouris 1975b, p. 121), 2) the damning impression created by his second thoughts (252–5), which suggest a lack of consistency and thus reliability, 3) his description of rearing the child as a source of bothersome trouble and expense for him, 4) his tendency to insert irrelevances ('that night...everyone does', 252; 'he's a charcoal-burner...earlier' 257–60) and illogicalities (the value of the trinkets 276f.), and 5) his use of short staccato statements (as at 249ff.) with little attempt to attach them together, piling one narrative detail on top of another in strict order of occurrence, with no attempt to insert any coherent argument until 280ff. (see further Cohoon p. 169ff., who provides a detailed analysis of the speech, Martina II.2, p. 140ff., Cusset 173ff.). In contrast, Syriskos' speech is marked by careful articulation and structure, his sentences fluent, well argued, and presenting a coherent argument. He never tries to refute the facts that Daos spelled out; rather he begins by confirming them before undermining their validity by addition, suggesting there were salient factors that Daos omitted, *e.g.* the existence of the trinkets (301), rebutting Daos' imputation of greed in claiming them as well as the child with the assertion of being no more than the infant's mouthpiece, refuting the claim of a lucky find by presenting the trinkets' true owner and backing up his case with the analogy of mythology, before finally suggesting a more sinister interpretation of Daos' counter-claim for the return of the child (348–50). (See further Cohoon p. 196ff.)

241. so that...absolutely clear: A signal of what is to come: Daos' reliance upon a bare outline of facts is designed to convince by its persuasive simplicity, but as Cohoon observes (p. 166), 'clearness of narrative may be a fault if not used with judgement', and the honesty and openness of his introduction are soon diminished by his inability to distinguish the important from the incidental. As Cohoon aptly notes, p. 174: 'Daos cannot select what is important, make it prominent, and thrust the unimportant into the background...He retraces the past with a good memory and imagination, reliving it all once more and naming everything in its temporal sequence. Whatever does not fall into this scheme is inserted as a parenthesis wherever it occurs to him'. The effect is to suggest a character whose emphasis upon detail hints at an inherently weak case.

244. all on my own: Ostensibly the words form little more than part of Daos' detailed background to his case – time ('About thirty days ago'), circumstances ('all on my own'), place ('in the woods near here'). Later, however, they assume greater significance, underpinning his claim to sole responsibility for the fate of the child and its trinkets.

245. I found a little new-born baby: The exposure of children for reasons of poverty (*Perikeiromene*) or illegitimacy (as here) or for simply being the wrong sex, in places where they might be found and reared by others, if they survived at all, was a frequent theme in ancient drama both tragic and comic. In the same way the reference to the trinkets was a conventional device in both genres by which a child's identity might later be established (*e.g.* Euripides' *Ion* 1395ff., Menander's *Perikeiromene* 755ff.), despite Aristotle's criticism of it (*Poetics* 1454b19–30). The mention of them here in the context of the dispute would thus be an immediate hint to the audience of future developments, with confirmation of their pivotal role in the plot supplied by Syriskos' intervention, 'That's what this is all about' (247). As elsewhere, though, Menander shows a deft ability to extract a number of effects from a single event. Here for instance, in addition to its dramatic role the slave's interruption allows a brief comic interlude with the threatened beating, confirms Smikrines' continuing prejudice against Syriskos, and on a technical level avoids the creation of two consecutive lengthy speeches by means of intermissions that divide Daos' narrative into discrete, and largely self-contained, elements: 1) preliminaries leading to discovery of the child, 2) Daos' initial intentions and second thoughts, followed by Syriskos' pleas, 3) responsibility transferred, 4) Syriskos' claim to the trinkets (cf. *Aspis*, 23n.).

249. And quite right too: Editors have often assigned the statement to Daos as approval of Smikrines' threat. However, as G.-S. point out, similar reactions from those threatened at *Dyskolos* 602 and *Samia* 389 indicate that delivery by Syriskos is more likely, a means of diminishing the threat's force.

250ff. Just as the insertion of interruptions at 247ff., 270 and 274 serves to divide Daos' speech into manageable parts, so this longest section is itself given variety both by vivid reporting of his second thoughts (253–5) and by quoting the actual words of his subsequent conversation with Syriskos. In this way Daos seeks to give authenticity to his account.

[**254. παιδοτροφίας καὶ κακῶν**: The genitives here are often regarded as partitive, lit. 'What (aspect/part) of raising children and suchlike troubles is to do with me?', cf. τί δέ μοι πατρός; (928): 'what's her father to me?' (G.-S.). Others, however, see them as referential, indicating the point of view from which something is viewed, *i.e.* 'As regards raising children and suchlike troubles what is that to me?' (Verdenius p. 22).]

262. I will stick my nose in: Daos uses the same term, περίεργος ('nosy'), as was used about Onesimos in fr.2a, and in both cases the slaves' tendency to interfere leads to trouble for them.

268. Her child died at birth: This forms both a natural reason for Syriskos to ask for the child and an explanation of his wife's ability to nurse it. Repetition of 'child', three times in 266–9, is seen by Cusset p. 176 as indicative of Syriskos' desperate pleas.

270. The line contains a number of problems for both attribution of speaker and supplementation in order to bring it to its correct metrical length. C places a *paragraphus* at the beginning of 269 and a *dicolon* at its end, *prima facie* evidence of a change of speaker in 270, which it assigns to Smikrines by placing his name in the margin at this point. Though the attribution is accepted by a number of editors (*e.g.* Sisti, Arnott), others question the logic of 1) the old man's reference to Syriskos' name when there is no evidence that he knows it, and 2) why the old man should seize upon such an inconsequential factor for clarification before ever learning the actual point at issue (G.-S. ad loc.). Attempts to retain assignment of the question to Smikrines have usually centred upon 1) either removing Syriskos' name as an element of textual corruption (thereby maintaining the premise that the old man is dealing with total strangers) and replacing it with a variety of formulations (*e.g.* Arnott: Sm.: 'Did you ask?' Da: 'He spent the whole day <pleading>'), or 2) giving Syriskos a role in the line (e.g Sm.: 'Did you ask this?' Sy.: 'I did'. Da.: 'He spent...'), though this would divide the line between three speakers, a rare event in Menander (some would introduce a further instance at 274). A less radical suggestion, positing that the copyist of C has simply transmitted misinterpretation of speaker (that the *dicolon* marks not a change of speaker but of addressee) and that the beginning of 270 actually comes from Daos, removes all difficulties when combined with supplementation of the line's centre as Syriskos' answer. It is logical that Daos would know Syriskos' name, while the request for confirmation of such a peripheral factor is typical of his fixation with detail. Indeed, when taken with the similarly banal question at 274, it serves to emphasise Daos' indignation at the contrast between Syriskos' earlier pleading and gratitude, and the ingratitude and demands now being made. That Syriskos never questions the veracity of the account either here or in his own speech illustrates well its otiose nature.

277. junk: There is a telling dichotomy between the precision and detail that Daos elsewhere injects into his account and the vagueness here, inviting the question why he should be so reluctant to hand over items of such apparently low value. At 309 Syriskos implicitly responds with the suggestion that gold may be involved.

280f. he should be grateful...he got: Daos weakens his case by denying what he has just described so prominently: Syriskos' gratitude on receiving the child. The only thing that has changed is revelation of something Daos earlier omitted to mention – the trinkets.

284. a shared windfall: Lit. 'a shared Hermes', a proverbial reference to the god as patron of profit and lucky finds, cf. Theophrastus *Characters* 30, 9, 'When small change is found in the street by the (mean man's) servants, he's quick to demand a share, saying that it's a shared Hermes'.

293. Has he finished?: The words may be interpreted as motivated by a desire to avoid the hostile response to any unnecessary interruption Smikrines threatened at 248f. More likely, however, is the potential for irony they contain – an unvoiced suggestion that if this is all Daos has to say, it does not amount to much and a criticism (through the echo involved) of the abruptness with which Daos ended his speech, even if this is paralleled at times in oratory (*e.g.* Isocrates XX, 22).

294ff. As mentioned above, rather than denying the truth of Daos' account Syriskos begins by emphasising its accuracy: four times over in 295–8 ('everything he's now saying is correct; that's how it happened, sir. I don't deny it…What he says is true'), at the same time undercutting the stress Daos placed upon his detailed and factual approach by the implicit suggestion that there is more to be said. Instead, Syriskos seeks to refute Daos' claim:

1) that since Daos found the trinkets, the principle of 'finders, keepers' should therefore apply; Syriskos counters that such a principle is only valid if the true owner of such items remains unknown.
2) that since Syriskos had no part in discovering the trinkets he has no claim on them; Syriskos declares that he is acting not for himself but as mouthpiece for the real owner.
3) that the trinkets are worthless; Syriskos suggests that this may not be the case, but more importantly that their importance lies not in their intrinsic value but what they represent, the means by which the infant might discover its true identity and avoid an otherwise inevitable life among slaves.
4) that if dissatisfied with the arrangement Syriskos can return the child to its finder; Syriskos points out the implications that this holds for its future.

Significantly too, unlike Daos' earlier speech, that by Syriskos flows without interruption from start to finish despite its length.

296. sir: Lit. 'father', as at 231, a deferential term of address to an older man, and like the swift confirmation of Daos' factual case perhaps designed to minimise any lingering resentment Smikrines may have for Syriskos; cf. the similar technique of candid honesty employed by Sostratos to deflect Gorgias' hostility at *Dyskolos* 302ff.

302f. Give me the child, wife: By taking the baby into his arms Syriskos underlines through simple stage action both his role as spokesman for the child, who is the true claimant to the trinkets, and the pathos of the situation. The argument is reinforced at 306–7 by the assertion that in handing the child over to Syriskos Daos also transferred to him the role of guardian (*kyrios*). This both gives him the right to act as spokesman and implies that this was also Daos' role while he had custody of it, not the child's owner, as his words at 287 suggested ('I've given you something that was mine').

recognition tokens: Syriskos' use of the term is in telling contrast to Daos' description at 246f. ('necklace and some other such trinkets') and 276f. ('small bits and pieces, junk – worthless'), introducing at an early stage what is to become a major point in his argument. Similarly, at 304f. he contrasts the original purpose of the tokens with what he interprets as Daos' profit-motive. The very reference to the trinkets as 'recognition tokens' serves as a metatheatrical pointer to their later role.

310. whoever she was: The irony within the words would have been immediately evident to the audience, perfectly aware of the mother's identity thanks to the prologue. Martina II.2, p. 196 also points to the balance inserted here between 'bits of gold or whatever they are' and 'his mother's gift – whoever she was'.

312. the man who has robbed him: The verb Syriskos uses here, λωποδυτεῖν, with its connotations of stealing someone's clothes (often in the context of bathing), hints perhaps at the particularly underhand manner of Daos' acquisition of the items.

313f. Why then did I not demand them from you then?: As G.-S. point out, Syriskos attributes to Daos a question he never asked, though it is certainly a pertinent one, and instead of responding with the obvious answer – the fact that he did not know about the trinkets at the time – he uses the question to emphasise again the role he now fulfils as spokesman, thus justifying his more honourable and altruistic role in the dispute.

317. A shared windfall: At 284 Daos had used the phrase as part of his argument to deny any suggestion that Syriskos had a part in finding the baby. Here, though, the slave neatly twists the words to suggest that this was exactly what Daos did imply: that each now has a share in what was found – Daos the trinkets, Syriskos the baby. The theme is further developed by the suggestion that the words were designed to cover up a less pleasant reality, the theft of items from their legal owner (318), emphatically repeated in 319, 'That's not finding, its robbing', the jingle echoing the deliberate effect in the Greek: (οὐχ εὕρεσις τοῦτ' ἔστιν ἀλλ' ἀφαίρεσις).

[**317.** μηδὲ ἓν εὕρισχ']: The negative neatly echoes that occupying the same position in the previous line, οὐδὲ ἓν.]

320–45. From refutation of Daos' original argument Syriskos now turns to the implications of denying the child its birth-tokens, basing his argument on:

1) the loss of social status involved and the threat this poses to the child realising his true potential.
2) the inherent danger of the child falling foul of wrongful actions through ignorance of its origins (341–3).

The first of these has itself two aspects:

a) unfulfilled promise (320–6), drawing on the belief that nature not nurture was the prime determinant of character (cf. Lape 2004, p. 124f.) to suggest that, if nobly born, the child will come to despise his servile surroundings. This then leads to thoughts of what that potential might be – thoughts that by their overtly lofty nature (*e.g.* hunt lions, 324) pass naturally into:
b) the analogy derived from tragedy. In this Syriskos combines flattery of Smikrines, who is presumed to be an expert on such matters, with the more comic presumption that a slave charcoal-burner would also be well versed in such themes.

This inter-theatrical combination of the two dramatic genres of tragedy and comedy is further mirrored in the language and metre used, as G.-S. point out (p. 316): a tendency towards more poetic vocabulary and the stricter rules of metre when dealing with noble endeavours and tragic plays, more relaxed comic rhythms when Syriskos turns to the real world (cf. Hunter p. 135, who sees 'a significant element of theatrical self-consciousness in the speech ... Menander lightly toying with the motifs of his plot', Krieter-Spiro p. 140f., Cusset p. 183–7).

326f. Neleus and Pelias: The myth described was the subject of lost plays by Sophocles (*Tyro*), Astydamas the younger, and Carcinus, its relevance based on the similarity of events: though exposed at birth by their mother, Tyro, the twins were found and reared, before eventually learning their true origins and rescuing their mother. Commentators at times inject unwarranted significance into the variations seen between the account here and what is known of Sophocles' play (*i.e.* discovery by means of a bag of tokens as opposed to a cradle in Sophocles, referred to by Aristotle *Poetics* 1454b 25), or cite other variations in the myth (*e.g.* the replacement of the goatherd by a horse-keeper in Apollodorus I, ix, 8, or Eustathius' commentary on Homer's *Odyssey* XI, 253 describing how the twins were suckled). There is no more reason to demand of Syriskos a consistent version than to expect one from mythology itself.

[**326f.** Νηλέα τινὰ Πελίαν τ' ἐκείνους εὗρε: The Greek contains a nice combination of the tentative (τινά) and the certain (ἐκείνους), as in, 'Take *someone like* Neleus and Pelias; well, *them* it was that an old goatherd found'.]

328. With a jerkin just like mine: By associating himself with the character in the myth in terms of dress (cf. 229), Syriskos implies a similar link between his own championing of the infant and the behaviour of the goatherd (cf. Hurst 1990, p. 112, Cusset p. 86, Cohoon p. 215). And by reverse analogy, his reference to Daos at 334ff. ('But if Daos had taken those tokens...') points the danger Daos represents to the child for the sake of a dozen drachmas, a sum that, while in stark contrast to the possibility of gold mentioned at 309, serves to emphasise the paltriness of the profit Daos might reap compared to the devastating effect on the infant's future.

334. taken those tokens out: G.-S. point to the pathos that would ensue: the twins still in possession of the bag but knowing that the items that could have restored their true identities were gone.

341ff. From description of the positive benefits that would follow from reuniting child and trinkets, as implied by the myth, Syriskos turns to analogies in which such items have averted disaster involving others, this time, though, without any specific reference or narrative detail – the effect is produced by their quantity alone:

1) the unwitting attraction of a brother and sister (a major theme in Menander's own *Perikeiromene*),

2) a mother saved (Sophocles' *Tyro*, Euripides' *Antiope, Melanippe, Hypsipyle,* cf. *Ion,* in which a mother is saved from being attacked by her own son),

3) a brother saved (Euripides' *Iphigeneia in Tauris*), the whole neatly rounded off by a somewhat tortuous and sententious statement on the need to protect against the vagaries of life (343–5: some commentators stress not the means for preserving life here but the need to look ahead to the consequences of any action).

[**343–5.** ὄντ' ἐπισφαλῆ... ἐξ ὧν ἔνι: Difficult lines capable of varying interpretation, *e.g.* whether ἀπάντων is to be taken with τὸν βίον ('all men's lives') or with τῇ προνοίᾳ ('foresight of everything' Verdenius); whether ταῦθ' is the antecedent of ἐξ ὧν or refers back to ἀπάντων (Verdenius). In each case the translation presumes (with most editors) the former. For πρὸ πολλοῦ ('especially') see *LSJ* πρό III.1.]

346. Give it back: A deliberate echo of Daos' words at 289, which clearly contradicted his earlier second thoughts about keeping the baby (254f.). Its very abruptness here suggests there is no reasoning behind it, only self-interest, while the implications of what Daos *might* do if he regains custody of the child – the alternative to relinquishing the trinkets – is given a greater degree of plausibility by the more definite analogy of what Daos would have done in the case of Neleus and Pelias (334f.). And does 'with less risk' (350) in the context of Daos' ensuring he remains in possession of the trinkets suggest that the threat to a child no longer championed by Syriskos and merely peripheral to Daos' real interests is greater than that of simple robbery?

351. Chance: The reference here underlines the considerable impact of chance throughout the play: Smikrines' chance presence on stage when the slaves enter in dispute; the chance death of Syriskos' offspring motivating pleas to Daos; Onesimos' chance arrival when the ring is being described; the chance seizure of the ring during rape; the chance presence of Habrotonon when Onesimos and Syriskos are discussing the ring, at the festival where a rape occurred, and now in Chairestratos' house; the chance marriage of rapist and victim (see further Vogt-Spira pp. 168–83). For the elevation of chance into the goddess Chance see *Aspis*: *Introduction*; Ireland 1995, p. 115).

352ff. The end of Syriskos' case and Smikrines' verdict come remarkably quickly, in marked contrast to the lengthy exposition of their cases by both slaves, an indication perhaps of the clear-cut justice of Syriskos' argument. Interestingly, however, Smikrines' initial decision leaves the situation only partly resolved, for though it reunites the child and its property, it does nothing to determine the child's future. To resolve this Menander skilfully reintroduces Daos at the very point where his hopes seem to be raised ('Fair enough'), only to be dashed, with the stark contrast in his reaction to Smikrines' second decision restoring a more comic atmosphere to the situation.

364f. Just wait a moment: Syriskos' request (prefaced by a *dicolon* in C to mark a change of addressee) signals Smikrines' intention to leave at this point, an unspoken return to his initial plan before being accosted by the pair and his essential lack of interest, ironic insofar as he has just saved his grandson's future.

366. Hand them over, you gaolbird: Editors often assign the riposte to Syriskos as indicative of his impatience, but it may equally suit Smikrines, mirroring in his hostility towards Daos here at the end of the scene that shown to Syriskos at its beginning, just as 'Why did I give the case to *him*?' mirrors Daos' complaints about Syriskos at 222 and 237.

368. unless he's swallowed something: *i.e.* one of the trinkets. Syriskos' quip confirms the comic nature of Daos' disgruntled reaction to the verdict, spread as it is over a number of lines. Goldberg p. 67f. aptly points to the analogy of Plautus' *Rudens*, in which the slave Gripus is similarly 'robbed' of an item he found by having to return it to its rightful owner.

[**371.** ἀδίκου πράγματος: A genitive of exclamation, cf. 396, δεινοῦ κακοῦ.]

375. I'll keep my eye on you: Daos' threat to make sure Syriskos doesn't make off with any of the trinkets himself is later mirrored in Syriskos' own reaction to Onesimos' seizure of the ring.

380. once we've paid our dues: The words return the situation essentially to its starting point at 210, when Syriskos made his entry, but shift the emphasis to a more domestic level. It may well be that the need to make one of their regular payments to Chairestratos was lost in damage to the text at that point. Clearly, Syriskos' work requires him to spend most of his time away from direct supervision by his master, and in consequence gives him a greater degree of independence than might otherwise be expected, hence his ability to assume responsibility for the baby without reference elsewhere. Though an apparently inconsequential interlude preparing for the couple's own departure from the stage, the discussion here is skilfully manipulated by Menander to fulfil both a technical and dramatic function. On a technical level, in a genre that seems to have provided for only three speaking actors, it combines with the final elements of abuse between Syriskos and Daos to allow time for the performer playing Smikrines to change costume and mask in order to emerge as Onesimos (cf. the departure of Gorgias at *Dyskolos* 381 in preparation for his emergence as the slave Getas, Ireland 1995, p. 141). In dramatic terms, once Onesimos is on stage, that same ostensibly unimportant interlude, involving examination of the trinkets, becomes the trigger for further advancement of the plot.

382. pocket: *prokolpion*, lit. a fold created by drawing up part of a garment through the belt. Like Sophrone in *Aspis* Syriskos' wife is played by a mute, her denial here of having a box evidently signalled by gesture.

382–4. Onesimos: The slave's complaints on entry, harking back as they probably do to the play's opening scene, disguise what is essentially an unmotivated entry, not in itself a dramatic fault (G.-S. ad loc., Frost p. 68, Martina II.2, p. 242f.), and well disguised by the rapidity of his incorporation into stage action (cf. *Perikeiromene* 774ff. in which Moschion enters with a brief monologue, unnoticed by others who are in the process of examining trinkets, Blundell p. 16f.). In this way Menander ensures the slave's presence when it becomes dramatically necessary and avoids the distraction of lengthier details.

383. by this time yesterday: As often, Menander keeps his audience informed as to the passage of time (cf. 609f.: lunch interrupted; *Dyskolos* 70: early morning, 555: preparation of lunch, 779: lunch essentially over, 855–7: preparations for a night-time party, Arnott 1979b, pp. 348–50). In the present instance use of the word *ariston*: 'lunch' in fr.3 and the lateness of the meal here suggest early afternoon (*pace* G.-S. ad loc., for whom the reference to wine signifies evening).

385. solid: The significance is obscure. Some argue that Syriskos refers to the hardness or solidity of the material used; Arnott, in contrast, translates as 'scrawny'.

387. What's going on here?: Onesimos' intervention is well motivated by the earlier description of him as inquisitive at fr.2a. On a dramatic level his abrupt interruption of Syriskos' examination of the trinkets just as the mention of a ring and its maker are happening, together with his total neglect of Syriskos' question 'but who are you?' in 391, signal the virtual end of the latter's role in the action. Paradoxically, for all the force of Syriskos' earlier arguments in the arbitration scene and his clear ability to overcome the initial hostility of Smikrines, he progressively loses control of the situation, failing to regain possession of the ring despite 1) his protestations, which become progressively reminiscent of those from Daos after Smikrines' verdict, and 2) the repetition at 403 of the baby's claim (cf. Zagagi 1994, p. 84). Ironically too, it is Syriskos' own further intervention in the situation at 442ff. that attracts the attention of Habrotonon through mention of the Tauropolia festival and allows her in turn to take control. In this way Menander skilfully manoeuvres himself out of a difficulty of his own making: how to ensure the truth of the child's origins comes to light when it is in the possession of characters who are either

1) totally unconnected with the family involved (Daos),
2) merely a transient figure on the stage and connected with the situation only through his own master (Syriskos), or
3) severely limited in his ability to act because of his master's hostility (Onesimos).

Here's a ring: Like the progressive development in personnel connected to the child, the ring assumes ever greater prominence as the play progresses: a piece of passing detail at 387–90, something lost by Charisios at 393ff., possible evidence in a rape-case at 491ff., the item by which Charisios' paternity of the child is established at 514ff. (cf. Cusset p. 26f.).

392–4. I don't understand...Put the ring back: The dialogue at this point underlines the diminution of Syriskos' role as he loses control of the ring itself and clearly has no understanding of its significance.

393. You're mad: Lit. 'You're suffering from bile'. Bile, especially in the form of black bile, was generally regarded as a cause of insanity and depression (cf. *Aspis* 422, *Dyskolos* 89, *Samia* 416, Jacques 1998b).

398f. C places *dicola* before and after 'Put the ring back I say', which, in view of the possible loss of any initial *paragraphi*, has produced varying interpretation from editors. A change of speaker after 'to grab it' seems unlikely, unless assigning 'Put the ring back I say' to Onesimos is interpreted as a sarcastic repetition of Syriskos' own words at 394 (cf. 'Apollo and the gods' at 396, mirrored by Onesimos at 400). However, while 'Are you having me on?' might make sense as Syriskos' response to this, it would then need insertion of a further *dicolon* after it to return the dialogue to Onesimos. All of this is highly convoluted. A more simple solution is to regard the *dicolon* after 'to grab it' as marking a change of addressee, *i.e.* that Syriskos' words up to this point have either been addressed to his wife or are merely exclamatory, and that he then turns to Onesimos with 'Put the ring back I say'.

402f. I'll take everyone to court: Not a declaration of confidence that Syriskos would triumph once again, nor evidence that slaves could initiate legal action (cf. Harrison 1968, p. 167 and n. 6) – hence Smikrines' sarcastic observation at 229 – but an exclamation of frustrated exasperation, as the abrupt change of topic suggests. For the possibility of recourse to law elsewhere in Menander see *Perikeiromene* 503, *Samia* 717f., *Sikyonios* 133f., 138f., 272, *Aspis* 270–3, 365–7; see further, Scafuro p. 424–53.

404. Here's a torque: a collar made of twisted wire. This final review of what trinkets remain, motivated perhaps by the slave's desire to ensure he loses nothing else, and the instruction for his wife to take them inside, neatly remove unnecessary stage characters, allowing concentration upon the two speaking parts as the Act comes to an end.

408. You either keep it safe…: As G.-S. observe (p. 324), in terms of logic Syriskos' agreement to let Onesimos keep the ring is too easily given, since 1) he does not know Onesimos, though he knows he is Charisios's slave (393), 2) he did not see where Onesimos emerged from at 382, and 3) he knows nothing of Charisios' connection to Chairestratos until he notices at 411 that they are apparently heading in the same direction. Frost (p. 68f.) suggests an earlier movement towards Chairestratos' door to explain this last point. More likely, Menander simply transfers to the slave facts known to the audience, just as at *Dyskolos* 358f. Gorgias is aware of Knemon's movements without any indication of how he gained that knowledge, allowing the pace of action to carry the situation along.

416. I didn't come so badly out of it: A rather strange statement for Syriskos to make in the circumstances, but in the context of this summarising exit-monologue perhaps one based on his realisation that securing further arbitration remains an option.

Act III

The playwright's technique of minimising the by-now artificial and otiose intervention of the chorus between Acts through the use of a bridging character or theme is well illustrated here by the re-emergence onto the stage of Onesimos and mention of the ring, the very first word spoken in the Act (cf. *Dyskolos* Acts

I–II). Less naturalistic to modern minds, perhaps, is Habrotonon's subsequent entry from the same place without either noticing the other (cf. Bain p. 138f.). For the ancient theatre, on the other hand, their independent entries allow the delivery of mutually distinct entrance-monologues detailing events inside, the disjuncture disguised by the interweaving of their ensuing statements at 435–42, and by the fact that they have one point of connection in their reason for appearing: escape from an unpleasant situation. Their separation from one another is also necessary in dramatic terms in order to maximise the effect of Syriskos' intervention at 442. The return to temporary prominence of a character who so recently seemed to have exhausted his function makes his role as catalyst for important new developments all the more effective, as Habrotonon now overhears their dialogue, a mirror-image of the way Onesimos became involved in the events of Act II.

Though connection between the two Acts is clear enough in terms of theme, commentators are divided over the time-scale involved, and whether the events of Act III represent the next day, suggested by the reference to 'tomorrow' at 414f. (cf. 379), and for which there is an analogy in Terence's *Heautontimoroumenos* (G.-S. p. 325f., Sandbach 1986), or merely a later phase of the same day (Arnott, 1977, p. 17f., 1987).

The first interpretation, a two-day timescale, is based on 1) Onesimos' promise to tell his master about the ring 'tomorrow' at 414 in Act II and the fact that when he reappears in Act III he states that he has been trying to do this; 2) Syriskos' reference to his scheduled movements at 379, and his readiness at 415 to wait till the next day – both in Act II – followed by his agitation at 442 in Act III at the fact that Onesimos has not yet shown the ring to his master, which suggests that the action promised for the next day has failed to materialise; 3) references to the duration of the party inside Chairestratos' house from Onesimos at 383 (which suggests it began the day before) and from Habrotonon at 440, where she says lit. 'It's now the third day I've been sitting around'; 4) the difficulty of accounting for offstage action (especially that of Smikrines) within the timescale of a single day.

The second view derives from 1) the apparent convention that New Comedy's action took place within the space of a single day; 2) Arnott's suggestion (1977, p. 17 n. 2, 1987, p. 25ff.) that (a) Onesimos used 'tomorrow' merely as a means of putting off an act he found unpalatable, in other words to fob Syriskos off with an excuse, a procrastinating tendency he displays elsewhere in the play, and (b) that the word 'tomorrow' in other contexts (*e.g. Dyskolos* 131, 540, *Perikeiromene* 983) is to be taken as referring to a day that comes after the end of the play; 3) the fact that at 436 Onesimos refers to having received the ring 'just now', which would hardly be appropriate in the context of the next day and would run counter to use of the Greek word elsewhere; 4) the problem of seeing Syriskos' need to go to town on an errand at 462 in the context of 'tomorrow', the day of his intended return to work (379); 5) reference to the meal inside Charisios' house in both Act II (412 – the guests assembling) and III (609f.), which suggests the same event; 6) uncertainty concerning the play's setting, which not only makes the offstage distances Smikrines travels liable to considerable variation in commentators' estimates, but also ignores the convention of New Comedy expanding and contracting the time-frame of offstage action at will; 7) the possibility that Onesimos' statement at 382–4 (comparing the lateness of today's meal compared to that of yesterday) does not in itself constitute proof that the party began only the day before; instead Habrotonon's reference to this being the third day (440) could well indicate that it actually began two days earlier. Equally, it is possible that Onesimos' complaint at 382–4 is meant simply to contrast two different cooks, one hired to prepare the meal the day before, the other Karion, hired that day – hence his enquiries at the beginning of the play.

Determining which analysis of the evidence is the more likely, however, is hampered by the varied interpretation to which Menander's language is at times open. It may indeed be the case that in contrast to modern commentators, with a printed text and ample time, the ancient audience was not concerned with such niceties, and that reference to the passage of time here was more geared to the creation of tension than absolute precision. (See further, Martina II.1, p. 35–9, Primmer p. 136–8, Blume p. 110–12, Zagagi p. 81, Blanchard 1983, p. 342 n.81, Hunter p. 159 n. 30, Furley pp. 167–9.)

419ff. At the beginning of the Act Menander skilfully exploits disappointed expectations (Blundell p. 28, Ireland 1983), as Onesimos' forceful acquisition of the ring in Act II turns into anxiety and indecision in the face of his master's hostility. Such an opening may have been designed indeed to contrast with a display of self-satisfaction expressed in the opening scenes of Act I with Karion, a pointed contrast of characterisation. No less significant is the shift in the depiction of Charisios himself, who, like his wife, is consistently seen through the eyes of others until Act IV. So far the extant text has portrayed him as someone given over to drinking and carousing with prostitutes, a picture moderated perhaps only by information given in the lost prologue. Now he appears as someone in a mood of sullen anger at the revelation of his wife's disgrace, just as with the entry of Habrotonon comes a shift away from the picture provided by Smikrines, from a young man actively squandering resources to one wasting them by failing to exploit the opportunities presented. It is important, however, not to over-emphasise the shift in depiction, since it has to be seen within the context of the audience's superior knowledge and their focus of interest, which is more concerned with how normality will eventually be restored.

424. that tell-tale: Like 'the tell-tale who knows too much' at 426f., the words form evidence for reconstructing Onesimos' role in revealing Pamphile's disgrace to his master.

425f. if he gets back together with his wife: Onesimos sees himself in a no-win situation. As the source of information that led to the breakdown of the marriage he feels threatened by his master if the estrangement from Pamphile continues. On the other hand, if marital relations are restored, he remains a constant reminder of, and danger to, a secret both husband and wife would need to maintain – the birth of a supposedly illegitimate child. The slave now realises that injecting a further factor, a ring associated with an abandoned baby, only holds out the promise of further disaster for himself.

[**425–7.** μή...ἀφανίσῃ: As the translation shows, the construction here with the subjunctive is dependent upon an implicit verb of fear of a possible future event.]

427–9. A fine thing...bad enough: Line endings are only tentatively restored, making 'wanting' a hesitant suggestion.

430. Let go of me: Habrotonon's address to those inside, who have evidently been attempting to press their attentions upon her, is an intriguing mixture of singular and plural references. Commentators suggest a momentary singling out of one young man, but the existence of a similar effect at *Dyskolos* 123 'I beg you (singular), get out (plural) of the way', suggests this may be little more than an idiom. In dramatic terms, on the other hand, such unwanted attention forms a neat contrast with the major topic of her monologue here, Charisios' aversion to her, which itself allows a thematic bridge with Onesimos' own appearance: for all their ignorance of the other's presence on stage, they are linked by the young man's hostile attitude towards them. In Habrotonon's case Charisios' reaction to her presents a strong contrast to the picture painted earlier by Smikrines. It foreshadows the theme of Charisios' continuing love for Pamphile, already implicit in Onesimos' speech at the beginning of the Act and developed with even greater force in Act IV, and it reveals Charisios' supposedly riotous lifestyle as a desperate and unsuccessful attempt to drown his sorrows. For her part Habrotonon's reaction to the situation, rather than reciprocated hostility, is a combination of confusion and sympathy at his waste of money in hiring someone like herself but signally failing to take advantage of the full range of services she expected to provide. This in turn serves as foreshadowing to the rounded personality that emerges later in the Act. (On the position of Habrotonon as *hetaira* see further Brown 1990, Hunter p. 89f., Henry pp. 57–60).

435f. Should I give...: While the idea of returning the ring to Syriskos is here rejected, its very mention forms a prelude to the slave's entry at 442.

438f. I'm qualified...basket: A reference to the Panathenaic festival, when new offerings of clothes carried by virgins were presented to the cult statue of Athena on the Acropolis. Habrotonon's words thus become comically ironic, emphasising the degree of sexual neglect she has suffered. Lape, indeed, (2004, pp. 167, 247) hints at the irony of Charisios treating his wife like a *hetaira* in that the audience knows he forced himself upon her, while Habrotonon is treated almost as a future wife – untouched.

442. The re-entry of Syriskos adds little to development of the plot in terms of the slave's own input; rather, he becomes the catalyst in bringing together Onesimos and Habrotonon through mention of the Tauropolia festival and the rape, which in turn allows Onesimos to escape the impasse in which he finds himself. In this way Menander produces a gradation of figures significant for producing the dénouement.

445. Let's have arbitration: The Greek involves the same word as used by Daos at 220, a passing link with the earlier scene before new developments.

450. You dimwit: Editors generally regard this as spoken by Syriskos, part of an exasperated question. As Arnott (1977) argues, however, it is Syriskos who is here being obtuse in not seeing the implications of the ring, and nowhere else in the scene is the slave's attitude to Onesimos lacking in formal politeness.

451. Tauropolia: A festival dedicated to Artemis and held at Halae Araphrenides on the E. coast of Attica (cf. Euripides' *Iphigenia in Tauris* 1450–61), its night-time setting making it a prime occasion for illicit sexual activity (cf. Menander's *Samia* 38ff.), hence 'a sound bet...raped', and ironic in view of its dedication to a virgin goddess. The seriousness of rape now imputed to Charisios is, of course, mitigated in stage terms for us by the as yet unknown identity of the victim, and for the original audience by its knowledge that Charisios has already made some restitution by marrying his victim (Scafuro p. 238f.). Such coincidence, essential if the play is to have a happy ending, is an important functional element of New Comedy (cf. Terence's *Hecyra*, where Pamphilus' marriage to Philumena likewise 'rectifies' his earlier raping of her).

[**452.** παννυχίδος οὔσης καὶ γυναικῶν: οὔσης here does double duty for οὐσῶν.
κατὰ λόγον ἐστὶν: the equivalent of a verb like λογίζομαι, hence the acc. and infin. that follows.]

455. if one were to find her: Onesimos' concentration here upon the mother is understandable in that he is already certain that the father is Charisios and realises that only the mother can connect the rape, the ring and the baby. At the same time, however, such concentration is also a factor in his reluctance to show the ring to his master, and by continuing to emphasise this aspect of the baby's origins Menander is then able to engineer a transfer of emphasis to Habrotonon, whose posing as the missing mother produces an ultimately more satisfactory conclusion.

462f. I've an errand to run...what needs to be done: Uncertainty surrounds the question of whether Syriskos ever returns to the stage. Wilamowitz p.76 interpreted the restoration at 462 ('I'll be back') as evidence that he does (cf. most recently Martina II.2 ad loc.), but unless such an event took place in a missing section of Act V it is difficult to locate it within the action we have. Similarly, his wish to seek advice in town on what needs to be done (a somewhat unexpected act from a charcoal-burner according to Blume p. 113) could be interpreted as a continuation of his feelings of responsibility for the child as its guardian, but essentially, with his role in the play now complete, Syriskos' statements here are probably no more than a means of signalling his departure from the stage and the action.

464. The child: As the first words in Habrotonon's question they provide a significant pointer to the focus of her attention, a contrast to 'the ring' (Onesimos' first word at 419) that may not be fortuitous. As Bain observes p. 139, though Habrotonon must have become aware of Onesimos' presence on stage virtually the moment Syriskos intervened, there is no indication of this in the text by way of aside at that point; instead we have to rely upon our own restoration of stage action.

466. so he says: As G.-S. point out ad loc., these non-committal words do not invite investigation of some hidden meaning, but simply gloss over what would otherwise have required either the inaccuracy of an affirmative response (since Syriskos did not in fact find the child) or a lengthier detailing of the truth.

469. as a slave: This would be the inevitable consequence of the child being brought up by either Syriskos or Onesimos (cf. Syriskos' account of the myth of Neleus and Pelias, 326f.n. above). As Henry points out p. 58, Habrotonon is constantly depicted as championing those who have suffered wrong (cf. 486–90, 508–10, 856).

471. no one knows the mother: Reference to the mother here serves to allow exploration of her possible identity and the pathos of the circumstances surrounding the rape before Habrotonon turns our attention instead back to Charisios at 499 in an effort to avoid resurrecting the girl's disgrace.

472. While he was drunk: The earlier reference to simply losing the ring while drunk at 407 now takes on deeper significance, but in terms of New Comedy it was a conventional means of accounting for rape, cf. Plautus *Aulularia* 745 'I did it (rape) under the influence of drink and love', 794f. 'I admit I wronged your daughter at the festival of Ceres through drink and the impulse of youth', Terence *Adelphi* 470 'Night, love, wine and youth overcame him'. To modern thinking such treatment of rape cannot but seem cavalier, but 1) it accounts for untimely pregnancies; 2) it is usually set in a period before the play has begun (with the exception of Terence's *Eunuch*); 3) it has either been already atoned for by marriage, as here and in Terence's *Hecyra*, or will result in marriage between perpetrator and victim; and 4) in contemporary thinking it was a lesser humiliation for the girl than premarital consensual sex, since it involved an unwilling victim (Fantham p. 53f., Omitowoju p. 174, Pierce p. 166, cf. Lape 2004, p. 92f.).

474. he was on his own: There is a degree of uncertainty in the Greek here, the result of one letter difference between the evidence of C and the emendation suggested by some editors, which produces 'while they (the women) were on their own' (with the implication that they were away from the communal rites and thus unprotected). The argument in support of the emendation, that there is little point in emphasising Charisios' lack of companions (G.-S. ad loc., cf. Wilamowitz p. 78), is no less valid in the case of the women, since male protectors would presumably not have been present at such a female-oriented festival. Stress upon Charisios being alone, on the other hand, automatically rules out the possibility of others' involvement in the pregnancy.

478. I was taking part: Further variation of text occurs between the reading of C given here and the emendation (or variants) accepted by many: 'she was taking part…'. Choice largely depends upon whether the emphasis is upon Habrotonon's pride at being able then to mix freely with respectable women, or on providing an explanation of the raped girl being in the group Habrotonon was playing for (cf. G.-S. ad loc.).

I didn't as yet have any experience of what men are like: A subtle piece of characterisation. Already Habrotonon has voiced concern for the child being reared as a slave; now recollection of the rape brings back memories of her own lost virginity, a loss that was probably no more her own choice, as the slave of a pimp, than it was of the rape-victim. That she counters Onesimos' doubting response with an oath by Aphrodite, goddess of love, in 480 is a nice piece of irony.

as yet: The words (οὔπω γάρ in the Greek) serve to emphasise Habrotonon's virgin state 'at the time', with the unstated yet clear implication that things changed. [ᾔδειν: An alternative form for the first person singular ᾔδη.]

483: if I saw her: A neat foreshadowing of what happens in Act IV, and the most efficient resolution of the situation once its complexities and implications have been explored. For the moment, though, her identity will be forced into the background since as yet there is nothing to connect the girl with either the ring or the baby. [**485**. τυχόν: An alternative for ἴσως and often combined with it, as at 504.]

489f. her beautiful fine dress quite ruined: Mention of damage to what is actually a high-quality light cape produced originally at Tarentum in S. Italy, has brought a variety of reaction from commentators: from sympathy for Habrotonon's simplistic view of the world, to condemnation of a negative and grasping character who places more emphasis upon ruined clothes than on the girl herself (G.-S. p. 334). Significantly, however, mention of the dress only occurs after a description of the girl's clear emotional distress, transferring the traumatic physical effects of the rape from the girl to her clothes (cf. Omitowoju p. 174, Pierce p. 166, Brown 1993, p. 196f.). At the same time, though, Menander has been careful to present a realistically rounded personality in Habrotonon. Her evident altruism and sympathy for the girl and the baby are carefully balanced by knowledge of the real world in which she finds herself – the world of slavery, where sexual favours are bought and sold – hence her reference to the girl's financial status at 485 and the hopes for freedom at 548.

[ταραντῖνον...ἀπολωλεκ[υ]ῖ': Lit. 'having ruined her dress', cf. 529.]

491. She may have: Uncertainty as to whether the girl had been able to seize the ring from her assailant is one crucial factor that prevents an immediate *prima facie* connection between Charisios and the rape (see further, Traill p. 231).

495. a free-born girl: Habrotonon here introduces a theme that is both a development upon Syriskos' earlier suggestion that the baby's parents may be of citizen status, and will have greater significance for Onesimos' later thoughts at 568–70, centred on the implications for the marriage of Charisios and Pamphile.

497f. First, let's find out who *she* is, Habrotonon: Onesimos continues the theme of 455f., perhaps combined with an unspoken resumption of his reluctance to reveal to his master information tantamount to an accusation of rape – this on top of the earlier disclosure of Pamphile's 'infidelity'. On a technical level, however, the suggestion serves both to motivate the shift from Onesimos to Habrotonon in bringing about the play's resolution and to introduce her alternative plan – the need first to confirm Charisios' paternity. This has been an implicit factor in the interpretation of events so far, but it is merely an inference based on circumstantial evidence. As Habrotonon points out at 502–7, the ring may have found its way into any number of hands before being lost during the rape.

502–6. surety…handed it over: The scenarios envisaged by Habrotonon are complicated by a degree of uncertainty as to the precise meaning of the Greek at this point, but clearly they need to be reasonably distinct, and those given in the translation have generally met with the approval of commentators.

[**511.** τί οὖν ποήσῃ τις;: A subjunctive verb in a deliberative question.]

512. what you think of it: Lit. 'if it meets with your approval'. In the plan she now outlines Goldberg p.64 emphasises Habrotonon's ability to put on an act and to manipulate Charisios by her description of the 'rape', both by-products of her profession and, like her later wistful hope for freedom, a means by which Menander imbues her with a credible personality.

515f. I'm beginning to understand: As G.-S. observe, Onesimos' claim to understand what Habrotonon plans is built on the very little information that she has actually given so far. More likely, the claim has a purely technical function, mirrored by further interjections at 520 ('Great!'), 525 ('Brilliant…') 528 ('Good'), 532 ('Heracles'), and 535 ('There's…dealing'), which divide up details of the plan into discrete sections, thus allowing the audience to grasp it more easily (cf. *Dyskolos* 94ff., *Aspis* 18ff., 328ff.). To enliven the episode, Menander provides a description of the account Habrotonon intends to give Charisios, (with emphasis upon the occasion, the violence used, and the result) through quotation of her intended statements, thus bringing the encounter with him vividly before the audience without the need for its actual portrayal on stage (Blume p. 115, Nünlist 2002, p. 240).

517. while I was still a virgin: The words are probably inserted in order to explain why someone in Habrotonon's current position could take part in a festival reserved for 'respectable' women.

524. so as not to make any mistakes: Despite having been present on the occasion of the rape Habrotonon was not a witness to the actual event and clearly knows less than the suspected perpetrator. To circumvent any difficulties this might cause her, Menander has her raise the wholly reasonable possibility of error in her account, and counter it through reference both to the loosening effect of wine on Charisios' tongue, allowing him in essence to take the lead in the story, and to the platitudes mentioned at 526. The result is a wholly natural and convincing plan of campaign.

[τοῦ διαμαρτεῖν μηδὲ ἕν: The infinitive is here converted into a noun by the addition of the definite article, and then made into a genitive of purpose dependent upon an implicit preposition such as χάριν, lit. 'for the sake of making no mistakes'. In such uses the negative is regularly μή, cf. 527.]

530ff. Before this, though: Why has Menander reversed the strictly chronological order of events envisaged inside by describing the interview before its preliminaries: Habrotonon's enquiries about the baby? Is it to continue the theme of her prime concern: to establish the connection between Charisios and the rape by means of the ring, and only then to link the baby thematically with the event? That the ring lies at the heart of her plan is suggested, indeed, by the way it is used to frame the confrontation with Charisios, with the reference to it at 535 ('what's just been found') returning to the description at 514.

541. It's what I'd like: Self-interest in the form of hoped-for freedom only emerges in Habrotonon's thinking once her concern for the child has been fully explored, and only then in response to Onesimos' mention of the possibility, a mention prompted as much by the low opinion of her motivation he expresses at 557–60 as by the evident admiration of her intelligence he has displayed so far (Hunter p. 90, cf. Ireland 1992, p. 74f.). True, she returns to the theme at 548f. ('Just let me get my freedom... Let that be the reward I get from this situation') but here too it comes in the context of what for her is a worse scenario (children). The view, therefore, that freedom is Habrotonon's prime concern (Mazon, cited by G.-S. p. 334, cf. Arnott 1979b, p. 353f., 1981, p. 222, Rosivach p. 100) is at best an exaggeration, at worst a distortion of the text. In any case, the fate of figures like Habrotonon will be determined not by their own wishes but ultimately by those of the freeborn characters, and whether freedom ever does materialise is lost in damage to the text. Why then has Menander introduced the theme at all? The answer must be to depict her as a credible personality, rather than a two-dimensional personification of virtue like Bacchis in Terence's *Hecyra*. She may be a slave with noble sentiments, but she is someone whose role in society would make total altruism unnatural. To qualify her evident generosity of spirit Menander investigates its extent: hopes for freedom exist, but they are only voiced at the prompting of another character and are set within definite limits. By raising and then rejecting the possibility of Habrotonon seeking further advantage by abandoning the search for the real mother (544–6) Menander once again explores the theme of motivation, while at the same time hinting at a further contrast, this time between the character who found the baby and the one who restores it to its rightful place. At 254f. Daos had rejected the idea of keeping the child for reasons that were wholly negative; here Habrotonon does the same, but on altogether more positive grounds – to return it to its parents (see further Brown 1990, p. 258, Henry p. 60, Goldberg p. 64).

543. By the two goddesses: Demeter and Persephone, an oath restricted to women.

552. I'll be able to do so: Onesimos' threat of retribution should Habrotonon depart from her promised course of action may be taken at face value, or, like Syriskos at the end of Act II, it may be simply bluster disguising the fact that he has by now lost control of the situation.

555. Dear Persuasion: Personification of abstractions, and invocation of them in relevant contexts, was a not infrequent factor in the thought-patterns of antiquity, as evidenced by the role of Tyche (Chance) in *Aspis* or Agnoia (Misapprehension) in *Perikeiromene*. G.-S. ad loc. point out that while the personification of persuasion was often closely linked with oratory and invoked in speeches, its association with Aphrodite was also a motif in vase-painting and a cult in Athens. Hence, it is in the context of love affairs that Habrotonon is more accustomed to invoke her, with Persuasion representing a highly relevant ally in the coming scheme. Her mention here may have been given additional irony if Persuasion had spoken the lost prologue.

557ff. Technically, Onesimos' speech is an extended exit-monologue designed to round off the previous scene, indicate the implications of Habrotonon's plan for Charisios' marriage, introduce Smikrines back onto the stage and thereby motivate Onesimos' own departure. In terms of structure it divides in two, with the first half (557–66) developing further Onesimos' distrust of Habrotonon and despair of gaining anything from the situation for himself, the second (566–71) centred on the danger that the situation poses to Pamphile (see 566f.n. below). On a dramatic level the first illustrates well Arnott's theme of cross-characterisation (1979a, pp. xxxii–v), where Menander deliberately invests a character with features running counter to those expected (*e.g.* the decidedly non-militaristic soldiers of *Perikeiromene* and *Misoumenos*). Thus, whereas in New Comedy it was often the male slave who displayed ingenuity and employed strategies to overcome difficulties (*e.g.* Daos in *Aspis* – in Roman Comedy it becomes pretty much a standard routine), here it is a woman who assumes the role, leaving Onesimos to lament his own lack of ability, his doubtful reliance on her if he is to get any advantage from the situation, and his realisation that the best he can realistically hope for is avoidance of further trouble.

557–60. When she saw...another tack: There is no evidence that Onesimos was ever aware of Charisios' neglect of Habrotonon, mentioned at 430–5. Instead, Menander simply transfers the knowledge to him in order to extend further his distrustful view of the woman: if love doesn't work, she must hope that feigning motherhood will win her freedom and perhaps establish her as Charisios' long-term mistress.

566f. mistress' position is precarious: From the implications of Habrotonon's plan for both slaves Onesimos' thoughts in the second half of the speech turn to a factor introduced only in passing at 495f. – the possibility of discovering that the mother is free-born – but an altogether more serious threat to Pamphile. For while Habrotonon might hope that posing as the child's mother will win her freedom, she could never supplant a legal wife (despite Smikrines' forecast at 792 in Act IV); nor would the child be legitimate. Identification of a free-born mother on the other hand could easily result in disgrace and divorce for Pamphile, already spurned by her husband, and her replacement by someone who has borne him the son and heir every Greek male desired (the fact that the baby is male is an assumed certainty. On the legitimisation of a child by subsequent marriage see Harrison 1968, p. 70 n.

2, Ogden p. 125). In the present context, however, what is presented by Onesimos as a threat to his mistress becomes a source of ironic comedy for the audience, aware that such a discovery will, in fact, heal the rift between the young couple by revealing their joint connection to the child and the circumstances of its conception. For the moment, however, the only positive aspect to the situation Onesimos can envisage here is that it will not be of his making, an outcome that echoes his wish at the end of the speech's first half ('Just let me steer clear of further trouble') and the problems caused earlier by his revelation of Pamphile's pregnancy.

571. The line is very fragmentary, having 'to escape' as the only whole word readable, but context suggests either the translation given, or Arnott's '[he'll]… [hope] to wriggle free of her domestic [contretemps]'.

575. sticking my nose in: the same basic word that was translated as 'nosey' in fr. 2a.

576. teeth: The reading of C for what is a problematic line marred by textual corruption. The word comes at the very end of Onesimos' grumbles about the perils of becoming involved in the affairs of his master, giving it a degree of importance and potency. Many suggest that 'cut off' raises expectations of a reference to castration only to divert attention to something more innocuous (G.-S. ad loc., Krieter-Spiro p. 185); Arnott 1979a, in contrast, asserts corruption here and emends to 'balls'.

579. Perhaps he's found out the truth: The observation, and Onesimos' desire to avoid any fallout from such a development, form the motivation for his hasty departure from the stage in the face of the old man's return. But what has Smikrines learned? For the audience a number of possibilities exist:

1) he has discovered that Onesimos' account of Charisios' whereabouts, designed to prevent the old man's entry into Chairestratos' house (hypothesised in the note on 180–216), was a fabrication;
2) he has learned about Pamphile's pregnancy;
3) he has heard the report that Charisios is the father of an illegitimate child by Habrotonon. Which of the three represents reality only becomes clear subsequently.

580ff. Unfortunately, at this point the first major section of well preserved text in the Cairo papyrus ends, and what follows until the end of the Act is a patchwork of fragments preserving only the beginnings and ends of lines partially supplemented by more recent discoveries. As a result, any reconstruction of dramatic action or interpretation of the characters' statements made must be viewed with caution. That said, however, what does remain suggests that Smikrines now launches upon a further monologue of complaint, mirroring 127ff. and centred once again upon Charisios' lifestyle (which has apparently become common knowledge) and the harp-girl Habrotonon.

584–5. The whole city…: Restored from fr. 882K (= Orion *Etymologicum Magnum* 23a 1), which attributes the words to Menander, but not specifically to *Epitrepontes*.

603ff. With Smikrines' words 'good riddance' at the end of 602 the old man's tirade apparently comes to an end, though some editors have continued his role until 608/9. This seems unlikely since his closing words have an air of finality about them, and a comment from him at 609f., on developments inside Chairestratos' house, requires such information to be first brought on stage. That the new character is Karion, the cook, is suggested by the reference at 613 ('If anyone...cook') and insertion of the name in the margin of C at 622; that he is accompanied by an assistant, Simias, played by a mute, is more than likely in view of the mention of that name at 630. The intervention of such a traditionally comic character as the cook at this point serves a double purpose: 1) it blunts the force of any fulminations from Smikrines for an audience that knows the old man's reactions are misplaced (Goldberg p. 65); 2) it leads to revelation of Habrotonon's feigned relationship to the child (hence Smikrines' comment at 645f.) and the effect this has had on the party inside. Any dialogue between the two, however, is perhaps unlikely in view of the disparity in dramatic importance between them; instead the old man may simply inject asides into the cook's monologue (see, however, Arnott 1979a, p. 467, who suggests an exchange at 622–5; cf. Martina II.1, p. 27).

610–14. As at *Aspis* 216ff. the interruption of a meal and the consequent loss of a contract by a cook form a neat variation on the usual boasting of such characters. That the mass departure of guests signalled by Karion here was actually enacted on stage is posited by Martina II.2, p. 376–7, but seems unlikely; rather; they may have been represented simply by the appearance of Chairestratos(?) at 631.

[**614.** βαλεῖτ' ἐς μακαρίαν: Lit. 'go and be blessed', a substitute for the expected imprecation ἐς ὄλεθρον or ἐς κόρακας, and long used (cf. Aristophanes' *Knights* 1151, Plato *Hippias Major* 293a). The scholiast to Aristophanes explains the usage by the fact that the dead were called οἱ μακαρῖται, 'the blessed'. As regularly in the expression the verb is intransitive.]

621. From the fact that by 645f. Smikrines believes that Charisios has had a son by Habrotonon, there is support for Sandbach's restoration of the line ('A son's been born to Charisios and the harp-girl'), of which otherwise only the first three and last five letters remain.

629. mistress of the house: It is tempting to see here a reference to the idea Habrotonon replacing Pamphile.

631ff. While a degree of uncertainty must continue to surround identification of the character who enters at this point, a role for Chairestratos is now generally favoured (his name occurs at 662 and as a marginal note at 692), rather than Simias, the choice of early editors, which was based on the occurrence of the name at 630 and interpretation of him as a friend of Charisios (wrongly, since the name is only ever found attached to slaves). No less problematic is the dramatic action at this point, though analogies elsewhere suggest an initial monologue by the young man setting out his reaction to events inside and commented upon by asides from Smikrines, followed by a possible dialogue between them.

633f. eyebrows up: While the phrase is sometimes found in the context of philosophers, more often it has implications of superciliousness (cf. *Sikyonios* 160 'I hate you and all those who raise their eyebrows', Alexis fr. 16.1–2 K-A 'Whenever I see generals with their eyebrows drawn up'). Presumably the reference is to Habrotonon, whom Chairestratos envisages as acting, or likely to act, above her former station as a result of her claim to be the mother of Charisios' son. As a result his words may provide some early indication of those feelings for her which ostensibly emerge at the beginning of Act V (Arnott 2004a, p. 275, 2004b, p. 41f.).

638f. daughter…has given birth: Uncertainty surrounds interpretation of these scattered words, evidently part of Smikrines' comment on what he has just heard. Mention of 'daughter' can only be a reference to Pamphile, but this cannot then be linked directly with 'has given birth' since it is only in Act V that the old man learns the truth of the situation. The verb, therefore, must be taken either as a reference to Habrotonon, who has reportedly given birth, or as lacking a negative, indicating that, unlike the music-girl, Pamphile has *not* had a child.

640–2. If interpretation of *paragraphi* at this point is correct, the lines belong to Chairestatos. His use of the term 'summon', with its technical sense of summoning witnesses, perhaps provides an indication of what he sees as future action by Smikrines – a complaint of misconduct on Charisios' part leading to divorce (cf. Harrison 1968, pp. 40–4). Certainly this forms the basis of Smikrines' later determination at 657ff.

645. this companion of you folk: At this point it would seem that Smikrines turns to address Chairestratos directly, but the significance of his use of the plural 'you folk' has caused unnecessary complications for commentators, who posited the continued presence of Simias, now seen as an assistant to the cook Karion rather than a friend of Charisios (see n. 631ff. above). More likely, Smikrines' words here simply extend beyond Chairestratos to include all those involved in the party (cf. 662 and Knemon's similar tendency in *Dyskolos* 166–177, Ireland 1995, 166n.).

647–56. These highly fragmentary lines may originally have contained a heated exchange between Smikrines and Chairestratos, but apart from the latter's possible echo of the old man's unsympathetic description of his son-in-law as 'wretched' there is little that can be extracted from the tattered remains.

The alignment of line beginnings and endings, where they exist in the manuscript, is variously interpreted. For the scheme adopted here see Gronewald 1986 n.4, Martina II.2 p. 389f. The traditional arrangement posits:

<u>εἰληφ</u>[	]τις	
παρ .. [	]θας	
ενη[	μ]άλα	650

658. overstepping my rights: For the question of whether a father had the legal right to remove his daughter from her marital home see Scafuro p. 307–9, Harrison 1968, pp. 30–2, Macdowell 1978, p. 88, Brown 1983, p. 420, Turner 1979, pp. 120–

3. Certainly, Pamphile's resistance to her father's attempts to remove her against her will at 714–5, Charisios' declaration at 929–31, and Smikrines' emphasis upon necessity rather than the law at 1103–4, suggest he might not, but as Just p. 33 observes, retention of some rights by a father would allow his intervention in a case of ill-treatment by the husband. On the other hand, the present instance may point a contrast between what was legally allowed and morally appropriate (Brown 1983, p. 420, cf. Smikrines' assertion of the law on *epikleroi* in *Aspis*).

664f. Take...unworthy of us: The fragmentary evidence of the text here suggests that the lines continue Smikrines' speech. However, this would require the inappropriate assignment of 665b–70., 'And don't say...' to Chairestratos, and Nünlist's suggestion (1999) that 664f. be given to the young man instead has much to recommend it.

667–70. Overlap of the papyrus remains with an otherwise unattributed fragment (Fr. Com. Adesp. 78 K-A) allows restoration of the lines, indicating the strength of the old man's disgust at Charisios' behaviour (hence the derogatory 'whore') and the scandal it has created.

680ff. Following the lacuna, in which some seven lines are altogether missing, and the tattered remnants of the next four, the text resumes with the final stages of apparent dialogue before the end of the Act. However, while assignment of speaker for the later stages is well evidenced in the manuscripts, dispute remains as to the speaker of 680–2 and whether more than one character is involved here. Suggestions have generally centred on:

1) assignment to Smikrines, possible if 680 ('Does he hate...dolce vita') is regarded as the old man's sarcastic reaction to a defence attempted in the previous lines (Arnott 1979a, Martina);
2) attribution to Chairestratos as a defence of his friend, though this founders on the inappropriate nature of their content;
3) assignment of 680 to Chairestratos, the final statement in his defence of Charisios, followed by Smikrines' barbed response in 681ff.;
4) interpretation of 680, like 688 and 692, as an eavesdropping aside from Chairestratos in what is essentially a monologue from Smikrines (cf. 127ff., Arnott 2004b, p. 41). As often, any certainty of interpretation remains elusive.

Despite continuing problems of restoring and interpreting a fragmentary text it may be that Smikrines here imagines Charisios' current lifestyle and its consequences: drinking, wenching, discord, disease, the ruination of finances and marital relations, before culminating not with the immorality of the situation, but with Pamphile's dowry (688, cf. 134f.). This in turn leads to its own consequences – the need to remove Pamphile herself from the marital home.

687. he/she wasn't convincing: Certainty of interpretation here is elusive as a result of variation in both textual reading (with Rife suggesting 'I didn't convince') and interpretation. So, for instance, in the text adopted here is the subject 'he' (*i.e.*

Charisios) or 'she' (Pamphile)? If the former, what are the circumstances involved; if the latter, is it a reference to Smikrines' earlier contact with his daughter after he entered Charisios' house at 163?

691f. he's been treating us like illegal immigants: Lit. 'He's become connected to us by marriage as if to people registered as metics'. For a marriage to be valid in Attic law both parties were required to be of full citizen status. Metics, legally registered resident aliens, were thus debarred from marriage with citizens. Hence Smikrines interprets Charisios' attitude to his wife and her family as being on a par with the contempt felt by someone who finds himself party to such an invalid marriage, (see further MacDowell 1978, pp. 76–8, Furley p. 205f., Traill p. 178 n. 5).

697–701. The passage raises a number of problematic issues. Editors vary over whether 697 ('Will Charisios...other woman') should be given to Smikrines as a statement (Martina, *i.e.* 'Thinking we don't even notice, he'll keep her and introduce the other woman'), or to Chairestratos as a question, as printed here (Arnott 2004a p. 285) – his name is found in the margin of manuscript M at 698. Arnott's attribution gains some support from the fact that giving 697 to Smikrines would essentially repeat the contents of 694–5. From Chairestratos on the other hand thoughts of a continued and permanent relationship between Charisios and Habrotonon introduce factors that, in the context of his own possible attraction towards her, might well lead to the despair of 699 ('All my expectations are turned upside down').

What is the 'task' that now forms the motive for Chairestratos leaving the stage in preparation for the choral ode? The idea that following Habrotonon's revelations Charisios had determined to purchase her freedom and had commissioned his friend to carry this out, thus motivating also his entry at 631 (Arnott 2004a, p. 275, 2004b p. 42), is tempting but finds no corroboration in the text we have.

Act IV

Despite the still fragmentary nature of the text at the beginning of the Act, recent discoveries have helped to expand the evidence provided by the Cairo papyrus, enabling us to appreciate more fully the force of a scene as powerful and significant for the action as the arbitration itself. In terms of structure Menander, as elsewhere, provides a bridge between Acts as Smikrines attempts to put into effect the plan to remove his daughter from her marital home, signalled at 689ff., bringing on stage events that we might normally expect to be played out indoors (cf. the appearance of Knemon at *Dyskolos* 909ff., Blume p. 60f.). Further appreciation of the scene's power comes from the traditional location of the major crisis within Act IV, before its subsequent resolution. In the present case indeed we see a double crisis, one involving both husband and wife, though treated separately, notwithstanding an element of interconnection as one crisis flows from the other. Significant too for the overall development is the fact that only now do we see the young couple themselves despite the fact that their marital difficulties lie at the very heart of the action – thus far (unless they figured in earlier lost scenes) they have been represented only by surrogates. Their introduction becomes all the more effective as each is brought face-to-face with the implications of the situation in which they find themselves. In Pamphile's case, she falls victim to her father as he seeks to demonstrate the impossibility of a relationship complicated by the existence of a mistress, just as she was earlier the victim of the other males in her life, whether this be her assailant or her husband in his reaction to the birth of a child. In the case of Charisios, he is brought to realise the enormity of his loss and the insensitivity of his 'moral stance' in abandoning his wife, a realisation produced more by internal reflection than by direct outside persuasion. For the audience Smikrines' picture of a double household remains rich in irony since this is far from Charisios' intentions, as was clear at the beginning of Act III. Similarly, Habrotonon will soon prove to be the agent of the marriage's restoration, rather than the reason for its failure, a factor that may have been hinted at in the lost prologue.

As it stands the dialogue between father and daughter, in many respects redolent of the debates in Greek tragedy (Arnott 2004a, p. 276, 2004b, p. 43), falls into three main sections: 1) the authority of a father over the fate of his daughter, 2) the reasons why Pamphile should abandon her marriage, 3) Pamphile's defence of her marriage. In the first section, extending as far as 715, Pamphile touches upon a topic already hinted at by Smikrines himself at 658 (see note ad loc.), questioning the extent and duration of her father's power over her as *kyrios*, her legal guardian, with its implications of limiting and conflicting with a husband's authority over his wife. The evidence of ancient legal sources on this (*e.g.* Demosthenes 41.4, P. Didot 1, 801–35n. below) is equivocal and may depend in part on whether the union had resulted in offspring. Rather than an investigation of the restrictions upon guardianship *per se*, however, the dialogue centres instead on the difference between willing obedience, achieved through persuasion, and forced compliance, inherent in her use of the term 'owner' (715), see further, Traill pp. 179–88. For her part Pamphile attempts to assert an element of her own will in the face of Smikrines' assertive instructions ('you must leave' 703), and to resist what in her eyes would be a tantamount reduction to slave status (cf. Patterson p. 200).

706f. [a donkey's] shadow: A possible restoration, based on the story of a man who hired a donkey to go to Megara, but finding the sun too strong on the journey dismounted and sat in its shadow. The driver objected that the other had hired the donkey to carry him, not to provide shade, and eventually their dispute resulted in litigation (*scholia* to Aristophanes' *Wasps* 191). The underlying message of the tale is to illustrate the triviality of some disputes, here used by Smikrines to impress upon his daughter the futility of her objections.

720. At this point Smikrines begins his threefold argument against Charisios, whose behaviour has placed him beyond redemption and may drag his daughter down with him: 1) Finance: the reference at 749–50 to double expenses for the Thesmophoria and Skira festivals (see below) suggests Charisios' need to pay for both his wife and his mistress to attend. The prominence given to the topic inevitably serves to emphasise the old man's money-oriented attitude, evident ever since 127ff. This financial aspect indeed carries on, if only by implication, into Smikrines' second argument, the establishment of an extra home in the Peiraeus; 2) Neglect by her husband (752ff.) as Charisios forsakes the house in Athens for his mistress's down by the harbour, enjoying his time with her while Pamphile is left fruitlessly hoping for his return; 3) Pamphile's inability to counter the wiles of a mistress (790ff.), whose practised skill at manipulating her lover's emotions will inevitably result in the wife being supplanted (see further Scafuro pp. 313–15).

749–50. Thesmophoria...Skira: Festivals reserved for women. The first, held in the autumn and designed to promote the fertility of the ground, was dedicated to Demeter, goddess of crops; the other, an apparent amalgamation of Athenian and Eleusinian rites in honour of Poseidon, Athena, Demeter and Persephone, was held in June at Skiron on the road to Eleusis; see further Parke.

759–86. Into the gap of *c.* 26 lines Martina inserts P. Michigan 4733.4, which with its mention of 'harp-girl', 'money', someone 'learning' and 'being mad' may well have originally formed part of Smikrines' arguments here, emphasising the continued drain on Charisios' resources to pay for his new mistress and his state of mind.

[**792.** ἐξίσακε: Placed between two future verbs (ἔσται and παραλύσει) the perfect here, with its inherent present connotations resulting from past action, takes on an almost future meaning: Habrotonon will be encouraged by the fact that through her actions she *becomes / will become* a wife in all but name, and will then edge Pamphile out.]

793–6. It's difficult...flattery: The lines are quoted by Palladius, *Dialogus de Vita S. Ioannis Chrysostomi* (Coleman-Norton p. 94) among others, and attributed to *Epitrepontes* solely on the basis of the reference to Pamphile and the rivalry with a whore that it contains.

797. Pythia: The Delphic priestess, whose utterances were regarded as coming from Apollo. Through his claim Smikrines impresses on Pamphile the need to accept the truth of what he is saying; to the audience, knowing that Habrotonon's character and intentions are totally different, the old man's claims are a fine piece of dramatic irony, illustrating his misapprehension of the situation and justifying the scale of embarrassment he will suffer in Act V when he is told the truth (cf. Lape 2004, p. 166).

801–35. Despite recent additions to the Greek text at this point and the reaction the speech produces in Charisios (878–932), there is much in Pamphile's defence of her marriage that still remains either uncertain or highly dependent upon textual restoration and interpretation. This is especially the case in her opening lines (801–5), where Pamphile seems to defer to her father's better judgement (the final exhortation of his speech) while rejecting unquestioned compliance with it, a piece of rhetorical sophistication more typical of the seasoned orator than a young wife

(Arnott 2004b, p. 44f., Traill p. 206ff.) and perhaps designed to counter Smikrines' claim in 716 that the time for persuasion has passed. Thereafter she sets out to counter her father's arguments, not with a point-by-point refutation, but rather with a line of reasoning that concentrates on vindicating her continued attachment to Charisios. Hence, in 808 'let's drop [all talk of] fallen women' she rejects the whole theme of Charisios' attachment to a whore, which formed so emphatic a factor in Smikrines' speech and which only re-emerges fleetingly at 822, even then within the context of Pamphile's loyalty to her husband. With 'Secondly' in 808 she proceeds to answer the claim that Charisios' lifestyle is totally unacceptable and the cause of all her problems, excusing some aspects, steadfast in her determination to stand by him no matter what, and in 829–35 seemingly certain that her loyalty will win through. Though total clarity of understanding is perhaps beyond our reach, and supplements to the text are included *solely* to provide a form of connected text, a better understanding of the speech's emotional content can be derived from comparison with P. Didot I (Greek text in Sandbach pp. 328–30), a fragment attributed by the copyist to Euripides but which (following G.-S. p. 723f.) is perhaps better located in comedy and which, though in some respects reflecting a situation different in terms of causation, does stem from a similarly troubled marriage:

'Father, you should be making the speech I'm making, since it's more appropriate for you to take thought than it is for me, and to speak where speech is necessary. But since you haven't taken up the opportunity, it remains for me, perhaps, to say what's right. I have no choice. If my husband has committed some dreadful offence, it's not for me to punish him for it. If he's done some wrong against me, I ought to be aware of it, but I'm not. Perhaps I'm just a silly woman: I won't deny it, and yet, father, if a woman has no intellectual ability when it comes to judging other things, she does perhaps show sense when it's her own business. Suppose you're right. Tell me what wrong he's done me. There's a law set down for husband and wife: for him to love his wife constantly to the end, and for her to do whatever pleases him. He has been to me exactly what I expected; what pleases him pleases me, father. He's good to me but he's fallen on hard times, and now, so you say, you want to give me in marriage to some rich man so that I don't suffer a life of poverty. And where is all the money, father, that will give me greater happiness than my husband does? Or how is it right and proper that I share the good things he had but not share his poverty? Suppose the man who's to get me next – dear God forbid – it certainly won't ever be with my consent or if I can help it – suppose he loses his money, will you give me to another husband? And if he too fares the same, will you give me to yet another? How far will you experiment with fate in my life, father? When I was a girl, it was for you to find a husband to give me to; the choice was then yours. But now that you've given me away in marriage, it's for me to make these decisions, and rightly so. If I make the wrong choice, it's my own life I'll be harming. That's the truth. So, by the goddess of our house and home, don't deprive me of the husband you married me to. I'm asking

you for this, father, as a favour – a favour that is humane and fair. If you refuse, you'll
be doing what you wish by force, and I shall try to bear my lot as I must, without
disgracing myself.'

(For a discussion of marital loyalty between a young couple growing within what
are essentially arranged marriages see Walcot p. 26f., Brown 1993, p. 200f.; see
further Scafuro pp. 315–17, 323–5, Traill pp. 213–23.)

807. Chance: Inclusion of the reference (see 351n.) may serve to bring into play
Pamphile's rejection of the idea that she is the victim of an unjust Fate in finding
herself married to a supposed profligate like Charisios. If so, this forms a prologue
to the defence of both his actions and their marriage.

808. Let's drop…fallen women: One is tempted to see in Pamphile's words here a
reference to her own state as a rape-victim, inserted as a pointer to audience reaction,
cf. Martina II.2, pp. 452–3.

810. [enjoy oneself] with a few people: Pamphile apparently produces a stark
contrast between the picture she here draws of Charisios' recent behaviour and that
consistently given by her father, a picture that in turn pointedly contrasts with the
audience's knowledge of how much enjoyment the young husband has actually
derived from his high living, as described by Habrotonon at 431–41.

812f. [a good friend]…[bad]: A possible supplement, reproducing a sentiment
found elsewhere: 'It's better for people to get a poor but honest father-in-law and
friend than one who's rich and base' (Euripides, *Andromache* 639–41); 'A true
friend is far better than hidden wealth you keep buried away' (Menander, *Dyskolos*
811–12).

815. As you said just now: Probably referring to a lost segment of Smikrines'
argument. Pamphile clearly contrasts her father's continuing emphasis upon the
material with her own upon the emotional ties that bind her to her marriage, cf.
Euripides' *Oedipus* fr. 545a Kannicht 'It is good too, if her husband has suffered a
setback, for his wife to put on a sad face for him and to take a share of his problems
and pleasures. Now that you are suffering, I shall bear suffering too and share your
troubles, and nothing will be harsh for me'.

820–35. While editors have suggested supplements to lines here, the extant text
offers little to inspire total confidence in what has been put forward: 1) the idea that
Smikrines has voiced his intention of giving his daughter to another husband, 2)
Pamphile's belief that in the event of Habrotonon moving into the house, she will
see Pamphile's continuing loyalty to her husband, and 3) by comparing the two
women, Charisios will see which is better. It is unfortunate that comparison with
Charisios' report at 920–2 supports only Pamphile's continuing loyalty in the face
of adversity.

Fr. 8K–T. I was…weeping: Cited in the *scholia* to Euripides' *Phoenissae* 1154
and aptly located in Pamphile's monologue following the exit of Smikrines and
before the intervention of Habrotonon. As such it marks the nadir of her situation:
abandoned by her husband and assailed by the efforts of her father to wrest her away

from the man she still loves, and perhaps too assailed by memories of the child she was forced to abandon. The resultant oxymoron of being 'burned up with weeping' is perhaps to be explained as the result of the eyes swelling and stinging through prolonged weeping, just as they do when exposed to smoke.

853. I'll go out with it (*i.e.* the baby): Attempts to explain the apparent abruptness of Habrotonon's appearance here have usually turned on events hypothesised for the gap before the resumed text: Habrotonon, on stage for some time, has seen and recognised Pamphile, and has gone indoors to bring out the child (G.-S. ad loc.). As Frost p. 74 observes, however, such a scenario is highly unlikely since it is only at 860 that Habrotonon becomes certain of Pamphile's identity. More dramatically effective in view of its inherent surprise effect would be

1) an unannounced appearance at this point, perhaps addressing 'I'll go out with it' to someone indoors (speculation as to who is addressed – Bain p. 197– serves no purpose), followed by
2) a brief quasi-dialogue establishing the women's respective emotional states, including Habrotonon's 'when will you see your mother', clearly inserted for its ironic potential,
3) a sudden confrontation with that mother. In this way instant recognition and the dialogue it inspires creates a ready escape from misery for Pamphile, but one paradoxically delayed by her own reluctance to converse with a *hetaira*.

854. something I've done: The addition of μοι suggests that Habrotonon thinks the baby's crying has been caused by some action of hers.

855. in my wretchedness: Menander neatly sets the scene within a frame of contrasting emotion: here despondency, at 873f. the happiness that revelation of the truth allows; here an appeal for divine pity, at 874 the assurance that the appeal has been heard.

858ff. One moment, madam: As G.-S. point out p. 359, there is considerable sophistication in Menander's management of the recognition-process, in particular the shifting reactions of the two women to one another, separated as they are by a considerable social gulf – visible perhaps through their respective modes of dress and perhaps too by Pamphile's recognition of Habrotonon's 'relationship' to Charisios. So, for instance, Habrotonon begins with the formal address, 'madam' (lit. 'lady') at 858 in order to establish contact and avoid any hostile reaction that her profession might attract, and it is with equal, and no doubt cooler, formality that Pamphile replies (859). Once Habrotonon is certain of the girl's identity, however, she lapses into the more colloquial and relaxed 'dear' and 'sweetheart' of 860 and 862, a show of familiarity that is not reciprocated. Instead, at 864 Pamphile continues to use formal address, with 'madam' as the important first word in the line and sentence (unparalleled elsewhere in Menander). With this comes also a shift of dramatic balance between the two women as Pamphile, who till now has merely been reacting to the other's approach, evidently recognises an item with the baby, ignores the enquiry about the Tauropolia and begins to control the dialogue with questions of her own. For her part Habrotonon, aware by now that her investigations are beginning to bear fruit, shifts back from the initial 'dear' of 865 to the formal 'madam' of 866 by way of reassurance. Ironically, once realisation of the truth begins to emerge, it is Pamphile who takes on the less formal style with 'dear' in 871.

869. to gain time: The same phrase as used at 538 ('without any distractions'), probably a deliberate echo, just as 'not to do the mother any wrong' echoes the sentiments at 499ff.

867-70. Aren't you its mother?...But who's the father?: The suddenness of the questions from Pamphile both hastens on the action to complete the recognition and indicates what lies at the centre of her anxious thoughts now that she has been brought back into contact with a baby she recognises as her own.

875. There's the neighbour's door: Lit. 'Someone is making a noise at the neighbours' door', a conventional means of announcing the imminent arrival of a character from one of the stage houses (cf. *Dyskolos* 204, 586, 689f., *Perikeiromene* 316, *Misoumenos* 206f., 282, 442f., *Samia* 567, 669, *Karchedonios* 4), and here a device for motivating the exit of the two women now that the recognition is substantially complete. Stage doors were double-leaved, meeting in the middle, and hinged with spikes at top and bottom that fitted into sockets, the resultant noise coming either from the hinges themselves or the rattling of the latch. (See further 906n., Ireland 1995 188n., Bader, Beare, pp. 285-94).

878ff. While natural justice demanded that Pamphile, the victim of rape and its consequences, should be rescued from her situation by the simple expedient of visual recognition (foreshadowed at 483f.), the process of rehabilitating Charisios in order to reunite the young couple is an altogether more complex matter – hence the scale of its presentation and the use of two sources to bring it about: Onesimos and Charisios himself. This in itself allows a wide spectrum of factors to be inserted into the process. So, for instance: 1) Onesimos' monologue is clearly introduced for the benefit of the audience – hence its narrative function of reporting indoor events and the use of the clarifying statement 'I mean my master, Charisios' (880), the blatant reference to the audience at 887 'gentlemen', and the explanation he later gives for his exit from the house. Charisios' speech in contrast has all the self-absorption of the true soliloquy, producing a considerable gain in emotional force and bringing before the audience the reality of what was previously description. 2) Onesimos' account of his master's tirade is represented in paratragic terms as insanity, its force comically intensified, as we learn at 901ff., as much by fears for his own safety as by alarm for Charisios (cf. 425-7, Blundell p. 32f.). In this respect the speech adds an interlude of partial respite between the serious tone of what went before and Charisios' own account, which is characterised throughout by caustic censure. 3) Both speeches contain direct quotation of what has been heard. However, while that from Onesimos focuses on the young man's criticism of his actions, that from Charisios is centred more on the morality underlying his reaction to the situation. This is further intensified by the quasi-objective criticism of the imagined divinity and the pathos inherent in quoting Pamphile's pointedly generous defence of her husband, an echo of the arguments she herself had earlier advanced: compare 816–21 and 920–2 (Arnott 2004a, p. 278f.).

878f. The guy's crazy…by the gods: Quadruple repetition of the same basic word in the Greek immediately sets the emotional atmosphere of what for Onesimos is a crisis, but for the audience a pointed contrast to the women's joy when they left the stage.

880f. Black depression: Lit. 'black bile', commonly seen as the cause of insanity, cf. *Dyskolos* 89, *Samia* 563, Jacques 1998b. In other contexts reference to 'bile' alone was enough to convey the idea (*Aspis* 422, *Epitrepontes* 393, *Samia* 416).

884. eavesdropping: Lit. 'stooping', but with the implication of bending over at the door in order to hear the conversation outside. Before the discovery of new text, which expanded the dialogue between Smikrines and Pamphile, Webster (1974, p. 138) imagined an on-stage appearance by Charisios in order to overhear the conversation (cf. G.-S. ad loc). That this would render otiose Onesimos' account of the young man's reaction is well demonstrated by Frost p. 73; it would also represent an unwelcome distraction of audience-attention away from the centre of interest (Nünlist 2002, pp. 241–3). In light of this Onesimos' revelation at 892 that his master 'went inside' must indicate no more than moving away from the door further into the house.

886. so it seems: The words point to the fact that Onesimos had not overheard the dialogue between Smikrines and his daughter, and hence he is only able to provide details of his master's reaction to it, in contrast to the more intense narrative soon to come from Charisios himself.

887. gentlemen: Such mild ruptures of the dramatic illusion through reference to the audience at moments of high emotion (cf. *Dyskolos* 194, 659, 666, *Samia* 269, 329, 447, 683), are hardly felt and are readily understandable in a theatre which had no means of either darkening the auditorium or highlighting the stage, where in consequence the audience and actors were constantly aware of one another. They do, however, serve to illustrate the essential artificiality of monologues, the purpose of which was exposition: to present the audience with information already known to the speaker (cf. 880 and the much longer address to the audience at *Samia* 214ff., Bain pp. 190–207, esp. 197f.).

895ff. I commit…: As at 913ff., Charisios underlines the stark contrast between his own situation and that of Pamphile: himself the agent of rape who occupied the moral high-ground when he learned that she had given birth to an ostensibly illegitimate child, Pamphile the victim of rape who suffers doubly, as a result of both the attack and her husband's reaction, and whose misfortune has attracted opprobrium rather than sympathy. For the male an extra-marital liaison with a girl like Habrotonon did not constitute adultery and any offspring would automatically be illegitimate and thus pose no threat to the family unit. For a wife on the other hand, whose function was basically to produce legitimate children, fidelity was paramount if the family line was not to be corrupted. But how would the contemporary audience view such seemingly advanced thinking as this in the context of a sullied wife, who in legal terms could apparently expect little more than automatic repudiation and return to her father? We can hardly imagine that in the stance taken by Charisios – the outpouring of scorn against the hypocrisy of his earlier behaviour – Menander was attempting a revolution in attitudes. Rather, in the context of a marriage disrupted by an obstacle the audience knows is a phantom it is an unproblematic insertion designed more to illuminate the depth of Charisios' true feelings for this wife and the fact that he deserves his ultimate rescue from the predicament he finds himself in. For the audience the young man's words thus pose no danger to accepted morality. As Omitowoju p. 181f. argues, Pamphile has had sex with only one man, her husband; the rape has already been recompensed by marriage, and the process of reuniting child and parents is underway.

898. misfortune: The same basic word as 'mess' (891), 'misfortune' (914, 921), and 'wretched' (918), and clearly intended to link the couple in their shared adversity. Commentators, though, are divided as to what is actually being equated in Charisios' reference to 'the same misfortune'. To a modern audience, sensitive to the right of any woman not to be the victim of sexual violence, emphasis automatically falls upon Charisios' implicit reference to rape ('an act like that') in 895, thus making his tirade a denunciation of double standards. Yet to equate his active commission of rape with Pamphile's victimisation would be perverse. Hence, in a wide ranging analysis of the episode and the reactions it has drawn from commentators Konstan pp. 144–9 argues that if repetition of vocabulary is designed to link the fate of the young couple, it must link factors of equal status: the fact that both have produced illegitimate offspring (certainly, Pamphile's use of 'misfortune' in the context of Charisios at 921 can only be a reference to the birth of an illegitimate child). This, rather than the theme of rape or sexual infidelity, he argues, lies at the root of the whole situation, the thread that links Charisios' abandonment of his home with his reaction here (cf. Pierce p. 166, Furley p. 233f.). While Konstan's view has met with a considerable degree of approbation, more recent commentators point to continuing issues within Menander's text:

1) the fact that Charisios' reaction to the revelation of Pamphile's illegitimate child would have automatically carried with it implications of lost virginity; indeed in the context of the implicit rape and illegitimate child mentioned at 895f. the reference to Pamphile suffering the same misfortune (898) can only be taken to include her rape (Konstan, in contrast, p. 148f., dismisses the prime importance of a girl's virginity before marriage);

2) that while both have been involved in sexual liaisons, there is a difference in the appropriateness of those liaisons: pre-marital sex for Pamphile has wrecked her marriage; pre-marital sex for Charisios carries no such catastrophic consequences (Omitowoju p.177–82, cf. Lape 2004, p. 249–52, Patterson p. 280 n. 83);

3) the situation is continually viewed from Charisios' viewpoint – even the strictures of the imagined deity at 911ff. – and it is only in Pamphile's defence of her husband at 920ff. that she comes to the fore (Rosivach p. 31f.).

It is also curious that Charisios should centre his thoughts on his wife's illegitimate child while presumably aware that it has been exposed and is probably dead, rather than upon the event that produced the child. In some respects, though, it may be that commentators are seeking within the scene a degree of consistency that is more the province of logic than of drama, or are injecting into it factors never intended by the playwright. It may well be that Menander deliberately injected an element of ambiguity into a situation which, as mentioned above, is in any case the product of pure misapprehension, and that interpretation here depends as much upon the character of the commentator as it does upon analysis of the text.

903. the guy who spilled the beans: Like 424–7, confirmation of what must have been revealed in the play's initial scenes.

906. There's the door: Lit. 'He has struck the door'. An alternative to the wording used at 875 to signal the opening of a stage door. It is tempting to see its insertion here as indicating a greater degree of haste and emotion on the part of the character emerging, though elsewhere it is found in contexts devoid of such emotion (*Samia* 301), just as the more neutral 'make a noise' occurs in contexts where the character is overwrought (*Dyskolos* 586, *Samia* 567, G.-S. p. 574).

907. There is a degree of uncertainty about Onesimos' movements between this point and 932–5, where he is specifically addressed. Though the translation suggests that he dashes into Charisios' house in order to escape the attention of his master, Bain p. 145–7 argues for retaining the slave on stage and interpreting his claim at 936, that he has just come out, as a lie designed to amuse the audience through the panic that has caused it (see further 932n., Frost p. 75, Blume p. 120, Martina II.2, p. 498, 515f., Furley ad loc.). However, like the suggestion that Charisios was visible during the exchange between Smikrines and Pamphile, such continued presence by the slave would have detracted from the audience's concentration upon the young man.

908. Charisios' entry is given no explicit motivation; nor does it need one. The young man's appearance on stage (presumably for the first time in the play) has already been prepared by Onesimos, and to have added introductory preliminaries here would have seriously weakened the tension already built up (Frost p. 75). Similarly, his speech, a true soliloquy of self-address, forms a neat continuation of that already reported by Onesimos, inserted for the benefit of the audience; but whereas the slave saw his master's outburst as symptomatic of madness, Charisios' words now become transformed into cold self-rebuke and sarcasm, an extension of the misery he earlier attempted to bury beneath a show of high-living.

reputation: While reputation was a natural ambition for a Greek, something to be derived from meritorious action, Charisios now realises that his behaviour has been based more on an obsessive concern with appearance rather than on reality, and that while his stance towards his wife has to some degree conformed to Athenian norms, it is undercut by his own past actions and by the couple's starkly contrasting responses to a similar situation, hence 920ff. (see further Traill p. 191f.).

912ff. Editors have varied in their interpretation of where quotation of the divine power's words begins, depending on whether we read 'I've shown' or 'He's shown', with the latter producing '...here the divinity has shown, "As a human, you wretch..."'. Such a scheme, however, seems unlikely in view of the strained meaning that results.

915. *you*'ve stumbled: The same verb as 'He's stumbled' (821), deliberately used to form a connection between Pamphile's defence of her husband and the criticisms here.

919. She doubtless...mind: Spoken with cutting sarcasm as Charisios contrasts his wife's loyalty with his own reaction to the situation.

921–7. Fragmentation of the text here creates problems for interpretation, though a reasonable outline can be discerned. Following the strictures of the divine force Charisios turns to recollection of what he heard earlier, his words echoing the sentiment (if not the exact wording) of Pamphile's no less fragmentary statements at 820f. From this he seemingly returns to considerations of his own behaviour, his 'high-and-mighty' mirroring exactly Smikrines' description of him at 693, before injecting a display of bravado in reaction to the old man's treatment of Pamphile.

930. My wife's not leaving me: It is difficult to accept Charisios' words here at face value, despite the young couple's evident mutual regard, since they do nothing to solve the real impediment to a resumption of their life together, Pamphile's sullied state as a result of rape and the birth of a child; this remains insoluble till the intervention once again of Habrotonon. Rather, the peremptory tone and bluster adopted seem more designed both to underline the depth of Charisios' contrition and growth in self-awareness, and to provide a forceful display of loyalty to Pamphile that matches the one earlier from her. For all its force the young man's outburst here carries no real weight; he is never called upon to put it into practice and the audience is fully aware that the problem faced is without substance (cf. Omitowoju p.214).

932. Why are you here again?: To whom is this addressed? G.-S. p. 366 see it as directed to Smikrines, part of Charisios' imagined confrontation with the old man, arguing that 'again' logically fits Charisios' understanding of the old man's comings and goings, while it would be improper for the slave to disregard the question if directed at him (cf. Bain p. 145 n.1). Others, with perhaps more justice, see it as directed at Onesimos as he sheepishly emerges from Charisios' house (Sisti, Arnott 1979a ad loc., Verdenius p. 40, Martina II.2, p. 513), on the grounds that though the question is directed at Onesimos, the slave simply does not hear his master at this point, while, if directed at Smikrines, the question would more naturally come at the beginning of any exchange, imaginary or not. On the other hand, splitting the two questions ('Why...Why'), with their deliberately balanced positioning, between two addressees might be regarded as losing some of their evident force.

Why does Onesimos emerge at this point, when it is Habrotonon who has assumed responsibility for bringing about the dénouement, and when does Habrotonon herself appear? For those like Bain who suggest Onesimos' presence throughout Charisios' soliloquy (see n. 907 above) there is no problem; Charisios simply becomes aware of the slave on stage prior to, or at the same time as, the appearance of Habrotonon, and he suggests p. 146f., that Onesimos' claim to have come out at that very moment is simply a lie intended to amuse the audience. However, this raises the problem of interpreting 935–8 if he has not been indoors to learn the truth. Thus, given that Onesimos' involvement in resolving the problem facing the young couple follows naturally from his participation in formulating Habrotonon's plan, a scenario in which he emerges with, or, more likely, slightly before her in order to reveal the truth, is both natural and dramatically effective (G.-S. p. 366f.). Indeed, his appearance first allows a brief and comic continuation of the fear he has of his master; for while he now knows the truth as a result of being inside Charisios' house with Pamphile and Habrotonon, he is also aware that in his master's eyes his earlier revelations continue to be the cause of all his misery. Is the ordering of events here, then, a gradation of effect as Charisios is brought into contact with the source of bad news before being confronted with the source of his salvation? When seen in this light, Onesimos' words at 937f. ('I've done...') form an attempt to redeem himself through good news, an attempt, however, that is not allowed to progress to completion.

While Onesimos directs his words in 933f. to Habrotonon ('And don't you.... I beg you', cf. similar thoughts at 551), she is first addressed by Charisios at 942, a remarkable gap if Habrotonon has been onstage for the whole of his period. The suggestion that the two appear on stage simultaneously, but that somehow Habrotonon remains hidden or not noticed, strains credibility. More natural is for Onesimos to address his appeal at 933f. through the open door as he emerges, and then to be accosted by his master before Habrotonon herself appears at 941 in answer to the slave's appeal not to leave him in the lurch, and ready to reveal the truth. Unfortunately, however, textual loss at this point prevents certainty.

937. I've done...: The words refer to Onesimos' part in discovering the truth, beginning with the initial recognition of the ring.

942. Who are you?: The question (if restoration is correct) cannot indicate any lack of recognition on Charisios' part since it is he who hired Habrotonon. Rather it must indicate his surprise at being confronted by her.

944ff. At this point revelation of the truth gets under way, and despite damage to the text we can gain some understanding of its progress: an initial denial that Habrotonon is the child's mother, followed by dialogue involving all three characters in which we see a final outburst of Charisios' anger against Onesimos, this time for the deception inherent in Habrotonon's plan, the slave's attempt to 'pass the buck', and Charisios' hesitation to accept the news being presented to him, their purpose as much to tantalise by retarding the truth till 953f. as to produce a comic effect.

950. You were testing [me]?: *I.e.* through the ruse of Habrotonon's claim to be the child's mother. The loss of the verb's ending makes it unclear whether this is directed at Onesimos alone or both him and Habrotonon. Certainly, the slave's attempt to shift blame onto Habrotonon in the following line suggests the former, but, like his resolve at 574ff. to steer clear of trouble in future, it could equally betoken an attempt to avoid further trouble for himself in the context of Charisios' words referring to them both.

952. you villain: Lit. 'you temple-robber'. Since the term can be applied to both men and women (cf. 1064), there is some uncertainty as to whether the jibe is directed at Onesimos or Habrotonon. Many argue for the former, and indeed Charisios has been aware since 945 that he was hoodwinked by the woman. However, it could equally be argued that, stung by Onesimos' claim '*She* persuaded me' in the previous line, Charisios now rounds on her only to be mollified by her response. Thereafter Charisios is slowly brought to realise the truth, reluctant as he is to accept the implications of what he is told, hence 'please don't raise my hopes' (958) and the need for Habrotonon to explain the motive behind her actions implicit in 971 'before knowing everything'. (For similar delay at moments of revelation cf. Smikrines' slow realisation of the truth at 1117ff., the recognition scene of *Perikeiromene* 779ff., and Terence *Hecyra* 841ff.) With the problem that has underlain the play now resolved the Act was probably brought to an end with the disappearance of Charisios indoors to be reunited with Pamphile, accompanied perhaps by Habrotonon, leaving Onesimos on stage to provide a final comment on the situation before himself disappearing (the fragmentary nature of the final six lines of the Act, however, makes attribution uncertain). That the reconciliation of husband and wife finds no overt representation on stage is understandable: its basis has been well established both by Pamphile's defence of her marriage and Charisios' subsequent reaction to it, which provide ample evidence that the only thing rupturing relations was misapprehension over parentage of the baby (cf. the complications created by Demeas' similar misinterpretation of the child's origins in *Samia* and the circumvention of any overt reconciliation between him and his mistress Chrysis just before the play's ending, Ireland 1992, p. 61). Its portrayal, moreover, would have required a degree of sentimentality Menander seems to have avoided; for while emotional attachments regularly form the basis of Menandrian plays, it is the obstacles standing in their way that constitute the basis of plots, rather than the overt demonstration of those attachments face-to-face, unless mitigated by other factors (*e.g.* the intervention of Moschion in the recognition scene at *Perikeiromene* 824 or of Getas at *Misoumenos* 617ff. Arnott). Any overt scene of reconciliation would also invite consideration of factors that have been carefully avoided by the action we have seen: Pamphile's reaction to the knowledge that her husband is also the man who brutally raped her, just as there has been no word of condemnation from either Onesimos or Habrotonon for Charisios' act, which remains outside the temporal parameters of the play.

Act V

With major issues resolved and the young couple reunited behind the scenes, analogies elsewhere suggest that Act V serves its usual function of rewarding the good and punishing the 'ogre' of the action, in this case Smikrines. The second of these is well represented in the extant text. Any reward for Habrotonon, in contrast, is complicated by the fragmentary nature of the text in the Act's opening scene (a composite of evidence from scraps of papyrus belonging to C, discussed by G.-S. p. 370f. and Martina II.2, p. 527f.) and by interpretation of what does exist, though her hopes for freedom as a reward for her efforts at 539ff. are often cited as a pointer to possible developments here. But who speaks at 979ff.? The presence of Chairestratos' name, albeit restored, at 982 gave rise in the past to a variety of suggestions, including an entry by Simias. Current interpretation of Simias' role as no more than assistant to the cook Karion, however, effectively rules this out. Others suggested Onesimos as speaker, playing the role of go-between but equally problematic (for the fanciful circumstances adduced and the difficulties created see G.-S. p. 371–3). Rather, on the basis of *Dyskolos* 214f. ('Stop moaning, Sostratos'), *Samia* 326f. ('What are you shouting for, Demeas?'), *Sikyonios* 397f. ('You mustn't even look at the girl now, Moschion'), the opening lines may well be taken as self-address, with Chairestratos, newly returned from the errand that marked his exit at the end of Act III and unaware of recent developments, lamenting the futility of his own feelings for Habrotonon, conflicting as they do with his sense of loyalty to his friend. But what evidence is there for such feelings of affection? A reference by Choricius *Apol. Mim.* XXXII, 73, 'Chairestratos loves a harp-girl' is sometimes adduced as indicating as much, but its relevance to *Epitrepontes* must remain to some extent speculative. And even the very fact of Habrotonon being rewarded cannot be guaranteed (cf. Bacchis in Terence's *Hecyra* who merely wins her ex-lover's thanks), though natural justice strongly suggests such a development.

987. But enough of that: πάξ in the Greek, an exclamation to end a discussion found elsewhere in Diphilus fr. 96 K-A, Terence *Heautontimoroumenos* 291, 717, and Plautus *Miles Gloriosus* 808.

1004ff. Following references to 'like a wolf' and 'gone away' in 1003–4, which suggest an image of frustrated hopes that might be appropriate to the young man (cf. *Aspis* 372f.), the insertion of *paragraphi* under the initial letters of subsequent lines indicates that his self-address has now come to an end. At this point either dialogue intervenes immediately with the entry on stage of one or more new characters, or there is a brief section of quasi-dialogue such as occurred at the beginning of Act III. Identification of Onesimos as speaker is confirmed by the appearance of his name in the margin at 1021, his role evidently to reveal the truth of the situation, thus allowing those subsequent developments which commentators variously infer. Whether he was accompanied by his master at this point or the young man enters later must, however, remain a moot point. Arnott 1979a, pp. 505/7, for instance, suggests that the dialogue after Chairestratos' self-address may initially have been between Charisios and Onesimos and centred on their resolve to approach Chairestratos. However, too little of the text remains to allow any certainty of restoring stage action.

1060f. For all their completeness, identification of speaker and interpretation in these lines are fraught with difficulty. *Dicola* at 1041, 1052 and 1055 suggest continued dialogue; thereafter the process of clearing the stage in readiness for the arrival of Smikrines must get underway, resulting in a single character remaining to speak the final summation of events. In what now follows the conditional sense of 'He wouldn't have been able' and the more definite 'I shall, though' (1064f.) best suit Charisios as speaker, since he certainly has no interest now in Habrotonon, the 'girl like her'. The translation assumes that he entered during the course of Chairestratos' learning the truth, assuring his friend that he was now free to indulge his feelings for her before ushering him and Onesimos inside. It is equally possible that he has been present since 1005, though in that case one might have expected some indication of his name as a marginal note.

1062ff. As elsewhere (cf. fr.1n.) Menander eases the transition between scenes by introducing the characters who now appear as if in mid-conversation. Mention of Sophrone's name at the end of 1062 brings onto the stage a figure not previously referred to in the extant text, though she may have found reference in more fragmentary sections (*e.g.* at the end of the dialogue between Smikrines and Pamphile). Even so, her name readily identifies her as the old nurse of New Comedy (cf. Menander's *Heros*, Terence's *Eunuch* and *Phormio*). Early editors, working from less complete material, variously gave the old woman a speaking part (*e.g.* 1068 'It isn't better to strike quickly'; 1070 'Make her...when you see her'; 1120 'yes'; 1123–6 'Nature willed...Smikrines'; 1130–1 'No greater...the child'). Publication of the Michigan material, however, now indicates clearly that the third speaking part was reserved for the intervention of Chairestratos at 1133, thus reducing Sophrone to a mute character, whose only communication is by gesture (Krieter-Spiro p. 36–9, G.-S. p. 381, Arnott 2001, p. 81). The awkwardness of such non-communication, though, is neatly diminished by the simple expedient of reference to offstage dialogue in 1063–9. Yet why is Sophrone introduced at all, when her role in this latest attempt to end Pamphile's marriage (hence 1070) is forestalled by the intervention of Onesimos? As often with Menander the answer is multi-faceted: 1) By the introduction of initial quasi-dialogue the playwright is able to set the scene, reiterating the old man's state of mind and knowledge (his continuing fixation with the dowry), when the audience is aware of how radically the situation has altered. 2) Sophrone's presence allows Smikrines' continuing and obtuse misapprehension to be highlighted by contrasting it with the old woman's ready appreciation of the truth. 3) This in turn heightens the comedy within his frustrated irritation at both Sophrone's resistance to his plans (*e.g.* the threat to smash her head in or stick her in the pond at the beginning and end of his initial speech) and his later failure to gain clarification in the face of evident jibes from Onesimos.

1063. as well: The reference is probably to Pamphile's own earlier resistance to her father's arguments. Smikrines here sees something of a conspiracy forming.

1073. all night long: A possible indication that in terms of stage time the play has reached late afternoon (G.-S. ad loc.).

1075f. The door's locked: Since house doors were not normally locked during the day (cf. Plautus' *Mostellaria* 444 'What's this? The door's locked in daytime?', *Dyskolos* 427–9), use of the device serves to ensure that the coming scene of burlesque is played out on stage and is no more in need of special pleading (*e.g.* part of Charisios' attempt to prevent Smikrines taking his daughter away – Wilamowitz p. 109) than the bringing of Knemon on stage in *Dyskolos* Act V. At the same time, however, Menander exploits the comic potential of the stock routine for attracting the attention of those inside by emphasising Smikrines' annoyance – his use of 'hammer' rather than 'knock' – and the lack of deference in Onesimos' response.

1079. his dowry and his daughter: The order may not be fortuitous, reflecting the priorities of the old man's thinking throughout the play. In what follows Onesimos' response, in particular the reference to embezzlement, flows naturally from the topic in Smikrines' opening speech at 1065f., obviating the need for repetition of its theme here. That Onesimos did not in fact hear Smikrines' earlier words passes without notice, of course, as Menander simply transfers knowledge from the audience to the stage character.

1083. By the gods…: Smikrines' retort forms the cue for Onesimos' sermon, a patchwork of political and philosophical ideas, some vaguely Epicurean (the separation of the gods from concern with the workings of the world), others Stoic or Peripatetic (the guiding role of character: see further, G.-S. on 1091, Krieter-Spiro p. 151–5, Gaiser 1967, pp. 26–30), designed not to present any consistent theme but to raise a smile at the thought of a slave dabbling in the subject (cf. Sostratos' similarly incongruous lecture to his father on the correct use of wealth at *Dyskolos* 797ff.).

1084–6. Do you think…good and ill…Smikrines?: The idea of the gods being overwhelmed by the effort of attending to the deserts of each individual is mirrored in Euripides' *Melanippe* fr. 506 Kannicht 'Do you think that wrongdoings leap up to the gods on wings, that someone then writes them in the folds of Zeus' writing tablet, and that he then looks at them and passes judgement on mortals? Even the whole sky would not be enough if Zeus wrote down the sins of men, nor, if he examined them, could he send punishment to each man. Rather, Justice is somewhere here, nearby, if you want to see her,' and in Epicurean thought at Cicero, *De Natura Deorum* I, 52 'Your (Stoic) god seems very overworked…But if there is some god in the world who rules over it…how surrounded he is with irksome and laborious work'.

[**1088.** ὅμοιον εἰπεῖν: 'roughly speaking', an idiomatic expression expressing approximation, which may be traced back to Aeschylus *Agamemnon* 1403f. 'Whether you wish to praise or blame me is *all the same*'.]

a thousand cities: A patent exaggeration, as Onesimos' addition of 'roughly speaking' suggests, but designed to illustrate the impossibility of outside interference by the gods in the affairs of each individual. Similarly, the reference to 30,000 inhabitants (cf. Aristophanes' *Ecclesiazusae* 1132) is given not to represent any form of reality, but simply to emphasise what becomes a ridiculously large figure.

1090. How could they?: Lit. 'How?' Interpretation here is open to question. C places a *dicolon* before the word but omits the *paragraphus* at the beginning of the line that would normally be expected to produce the order of speech in the translation. Some editors, therefore (*e.g.* Arnott 1979a), disregard the *dicolon* and continue with Onesimos throughout, making this a question he poses himself before himself answering it with 'You're implying...drudgery'.

1093f. his character as guardian: A variation on the idea that everyone has a *daimon* or guardian spirit (Menander fr. 500.1–3 K-A 'Each man has a *daimon* at his side from the moment of his birth, a beneficent guide throughout life', Epictetus I, 14, 12 'He (Zeus) has nonetheless set by each man's side as a guardian his *daimon*, and has committed the man to his care, a guardian who does not sleep and cannot be deceived'), cf. Heracleitus fr. 119 DK 'His character is a man's *daimon*', Epicharmus fr. 266 K-A 'A man's character is his *daimon*, for some good, for others ill', Seneca *Epistulae Morales* 41.2 'A holy spirit resides within us, observer and guard of our deeds, good and ill. As we treat it, so it treats us'. G.-S. p. 378 see an element of inconsistency in Onesimos' argument: 1) an individual's character brings him good or ill; 2) everyone has a guardian spirit which rewards what is good and punishes what is bad. However, this relies too much upon logic in what is essentially a mishmash of ideas from a slave.

1100f. So is my character...stupid: Smikrines' question allows Onesimos to focus on both the stupidity and wrongness of the old man's actions – attempting to remove his daughter from her marital home – but this within the context of both his and the audience's superior knowledge. Hence, Smikrines is seen as rushing towards disaster because of his misinterpretation of the evidence and his impetuosity, and is only saved by 'mere chance' (ταὐτόματον 1108), with Menander perhaps emphasising through use of this term the intervention of a more impersonal force than *tyche*. Smikrines is being saved *by accident* rather than by the design of some superior force, just as the simple coincidence of rapist and victim now being husband and wife removes any need for the planned divorce by showing it to be totally irrelevant to the current situation (cf. 351n. above, G.-S. 1108n. who note the fluidity in the ancient view of chance and accident: Philemon fr.125 K-A 'There is for us no god Chance, there isn't; rather accident, which just happens to people, is given the name chance' and Menander *Samia* 163 'Accident is somehow a god, it seems.').

1110f. So don't let me find...again: The warning from a slave to a citizen is comic by virtue of its very incongruity and illustrates well the gulf between the knowledge of the one and the continuing ignorance of the other, cf. *Dyskolos* 932ff., the lecture of Sikon the cook to Knemon).

[ὅπως μὴ λήψομαί: A regular elliptical construction based on a presumed verb of precaution (*e.g.* φυλάττω). The tense of the dependent verb becomes naturally future.]

1112. take your daughter's baby: The instruction forms the sting in the tail of Onesimos' strictures and is comic precisely because of its sudden addition. Onesimos' criticism so far here has concentrated upon condemnation of Smikrines' plans as wrong-headed and the fact that all his complaints are now without substance. Suddenly the old man is presented with what the audience knows is the solution to the problem, but a solution of which he has no prior knowledge and which is presented to him like a bombshell, without the essential intervening factors that explain how the solution has been reached. As a result it is clearly designed to raise Smikrines' blood-pressure further, allowing demonstration of his blindness to the truth when contrasted with the acuity of a humble character like Sophrone (cf. Chairestratos' inability to understand Daos' plan at *Aspis* 346f. and the slave's comment on the old man's 'denseness' at 353, Krieter-Spiro p. 60f.).

1114. thicky: Lit. 'thick-skinned' but with clear connotations of mental incapacity, cf. Plautus' *Miles Gloriosus* 235 'My master's enclosed within an elephant's hide, not his own. He has no more sense than a stone'.

1115. taking care...marriageable age: The sarcasm inherent in Onesimos' words here contrasts with the importance to any family in antiquity that claimed respectability of maintaining the unblemished reputation of its marriageable females (cf. Daos' complaint against Knemon in *Dyskolos* 222–4, Ireland 1995 218n.). The difficulty of protecting women from unwanted sexual advances was also a standard comic theme: Alexis fr. 340.2 K-A 'There's nothing harder to protect than a woman'; Apollodorus of Carystus fr. 6 K-A 'The door's bolted, but no builder has made a door so strong that a weasel and seducer can't get through'; Plautus' *Epidicus* 404f. 'One can never be too careful in preserving the chastity of one's daughter'.

1116. four months premature: Lit. 'five-months children'. Such foetuses would not be capable of survival, hence a baby born five months after marriage could not have been conceived in wedlock, as Pamphilus realises in Terence's *Hecyra*. That Sophrone grasps the significance marks the point of divergence between her understanding and Smikrines' and serves to isolate the old man in his continuing misapprehension – he's the last to find out the truth.

1119–20. The presence of paragraphi at the beginning of these lines and of dicola before and after 'Sophrone', before and after 'Do you understand?' and after 'Yes' indicates that the copyist interpreted his text here as involving both Smikrines and Sophrone as well as Onesimos. As G.-S. observe ad loc., however, the dicola are better taken as signifying change of addressee, with Onesimos turning momentarily from the old man to Sophrone. Thus, 'Do you understand?' neatly avoids the more obvious conclusion to Onesimos' narrative of events: '... and raped her'. Furley in contrast, taking the manuscript at face value translates:

(On)   ...It was at the Tauropolia that my master –
(Sm)   Sophrone –
(On)   caught the girl alone, separated from the dancers.
(Sm)   you understand?
(On)   Oh yes...

1123–4. Nature willed…for this: The quotation, from Euripides' *Auge* fr. 265a
Kannicht, in which Heracles raped Auge during a night-time festival and left a ring
with her by which he later recognised the baby that was subsequently born, continues
the theme of the old man's inability to draw conclusions from evidence presented
to him unless that evidence is blatantly obvious. This becomes doubly ironic in the
context of someone whom Syriskos earlier flattered for his knowledge of tragic plots
– as Onesimos points out with: 'Why are you so dim?' and the offer to recite the
whole speech in order to make his point. (See further Cusset pp. 158–62, and Hunter
p. 135f., who suggests that by reference to the *Auge* Menander is reminding his
audience that they are watching a play with a long ancestry.) A *paragraphus* at the
beginning of the 1124 and *dicola* before and after the question, suggesting a change
of speaker, once again indicate a misunderstanding by the copyist rather than any
involvement of Smikrines here, *e.g.* Smikrines: 'What? Are you stupid?' Attempts
by some commentators to involve Sophrone: Smikrines: 'What?' Sophrone: 'You're
so dim', predate evidence of Chairestratos' approaching intervention.

1128. The line in C is textually problematic, lacking a syllable which is variously
restored, *e.g.* Onesimos: 'She knows. Rest assured that the [old woman] got <it>
first' (Sandbach, Arnott 1979a); '<but> rest assured that…' (de Falco); . The fact
that the Michigan papyrus overlaps from 1127, however, now reveals that the text
originally must have repeated 'she knows', which C had reduced to a single instance.
This produces either the form given in the translation (cf. Arnott 2004a, p. 280) or
Martina's Smikrines: '…Does she know?' Onesimos: 'She knows. Rest assured…'.

1132–44. The Michigan papyrus now supplies additional, and important, information
on the play's closing scenes, in particular the arrival of Chairestratos, whose name
occurs as a marginal note in 1133, and who thus occupies the third speaking part that
early editors had assigned to Sophrone. The abruptness of his intervention suggests
that he here interrupts and completes the old man's train of thought (*e.g.* Smikrines:
'the child from the unmarried woman with Charisios…' Chairestratos: 'You can say
is your daughter's'). Thereafter the double reference to Smikrines in 1138 and 1140
and the mention of quarrelling in 1136 (with the implication of inherent futility)
suggest he provides further confirmation of what Onesimos has revealed, diverts
him from further trouble-making ('you're quarrelling *to no purpose*'), and perhaps
finally invites him inside to join his now reunited family (cf. Callidamates' role at
the end of Plautus' *Mostellaria*). Whether yet another scene intervenes is, of course,
impossible to divine.

With the end of the play missing and much of the Act's beginning fragmentary a
number of loose ends exist either in the play or in the minds of commentators:

1. What is the fate of Habrotonon? On the analogy of *Dyskolos*, where the help
    Gorgias has given in bringing about Sostratos' marriage is rewarded with a
    wedding of his own, we might expect her to gain the freedom she hoped for
    earlier at 541–9, linked perhaps to Chairestratos' apparent affection for her

(cf. Krieter-Spiro p. 127–9, Henry p. 56, Traill p. 239f.). Whether this is given any more prominence in the text than the restoration of Chrysis to her former position in Demeas' household in Act V of *Samia* (line 730), however, must remain a moot point (cf. Arnott 2004a, p. 281).

2. What is the fate of Onesimos? With the problem of the child resolved there is no need for his continuing fears with regard to his master's attitude. Any remaining resentment at the thought of what his earlier revelations caused must be counterbalanced by recognition that this intervening trouble has led ultimately to the restoration of the child to its rightful parents. He, like Sophrone and Smikrines, will ultimately disappear indoors to join whatever festivities are taking place, perhaps with a parting expression of relief that all has turned out well, though probably forever a slave. It may, in fact, be Onesimos who speaks the final formulaic appeal for the audience's favour found in *Dyskolos*, *Misoumenos*, *Samia* and *Sikyonios*.

3. What is the fate of Smikrines? As noted above (1132–44n.), the reintegration of Smikrines into the family-circle is a likely hypothesis, following a suitable humbling at the hands of Onesimos. For while the old man has been a major source of trouble for his daughter, this has been the result not of innate badness but of misinterpreting Charisios's behaviour and his own money-orientated thinking (a stock fault of old men as Micio recognises in Terence's *Adelphi* 833f., 'Old age introduces only this one fault to men: we're all excessively concerned with money.'). As MacCary 1971, p. 307 observes, 'he is not evil, only misguided', and his role in the arbitration scene had been pivotal in assuring the ultimate happy ending.

4. What is the fate of Syriskos? At 462 his threatened return, for all that this exists as textual restoration, suggested to some his reappearance later in the action (see n. ad loc.). This, however, seems highly unlikely, and with his dramatic role by then exhausted, any hypothesised return is best dismissed to the realms of imagination.

Unplaced book fragments

Orion, *Antholognomici* VII 8: Cited by a number of ancient authors but only by Orion as coming from *Epitrepontes* (as a correction for the first ascription to Menander's *Georgos*). The line in itself provides little clue as to context and is variously located by commentators (in the prologue, in the dialogue between Smikrines and Pamphile, in the lacuna after 958). However, it may find a place in Chairestratos' advice to Smikrines in the play's closing sections, along the lines of Demeas' explanation of Plangon's motherhood to her father Niceratos at *Samia* 588ff., *i.e.* What has happened cannot be undone; the wrong has been righted; so accept reality even if this requires some constructive logic (cf. Arnott 1979a, p. 521, who sets it in the final scenes but places it instead into the mouth of Onesimos).

Stobaeus *Eclogae* 4, 29, 58: The lines seem suited to the end of the play and to form part of Smikrines' realisation of his earlier foolishness. Furley, in contrast, places the fragment at or near the beginning of Smikrines' speech at 127ff. He also includes with it Stobaeus 4, 29, 59, 'I don't think it's the mark of a free man to put up with pleasure when it's associated with insolence.'

Unplaced Papyrus fragments

P. Berol. 21142 (= Martina fr. 5, Arnott fr. 12): The text is attributed to *Epitrepontes* only through mention in line 3 of Charisios' name, which occurs nowhere else in extant comedies. The collocation, albeit in successive lines, of πίνειν and βινεῖν, mirroring Aristophanes *Frogs* 740 'drinking and screwing', suggests a low level of vocabulary that might well fit the opening scene between Onesimos and Karion discussing events indoors, as in Martina's text (cf. Sandbach 1990, p. 343, Arnott 1979a, p. 525f.) Connection with the play at all must, however, remain contentious.

P. Oxy. 2829 (= Martina fr. 13, Arnott fr. 11): Ten fragments, the first four of which overlap with the evidence of C. The remaining six, while possibly from the same general area as the others, provide little more than scraps of words and virtually nothing in terms of context, with the exception of fr. VI, where the restoration 'sleeping away from home' in line 2 can only refer to Charisios (cf. line 136 where the same word is used) and a *dicolon* after 'to me' in line 4 indicates dialogue. Attempts to associate the letters in fr. IX with 364 have proved unsuccessful since vague traces of letters in the line above do not accord with those of 363.

P. Oxy. 4023 (= Martina fr. 14): The extreme fragmentation of the text makes restoration and context a vain hope.

P. Mich. 4733 fr.1 (= Martina fr. 16): Mention of the name Karion strongly suggests a association with 603–31 where he is on stage. The existence of a *dicolon* before the name indicates either dialogue, with Smikrines a possible interlocutor (if one supposes he knows the cook's name), or a character turning to address a different character.

P. Mich. 4733 fr.6 (= Martina fr.15): Extracting anything from the few extant letters is impossible.

Pap Mich. 4801g fr.1 (= Martina fr.17): The lack of any text in lines 2 and 3 suggested to the editors that they may mark the interchange between Acts, though this seems unlikely since there is no evident overlap between what the fragment does preserve and the Act openings we have. The mention of witnesses in line 8 resonates with similar vocabulary in 661. However, speaker and context remain elusive, as does the presence or absence of dialogue, and problems of word-restoration make any reconstruction hazardous.

P. Mich. 4800 B26/B17F (= Martina fr.18): The few letters that are readable provide no clues as to meaning, though the presence of a *dicolon* in line 6 may indicate dialogue and be followed by the initial letter of a name (Charisios / Chairestratos).

P. Mich. 4807c (= Martina fr.19): The absence of any discernible words makes the extraction of information impossible.

BIBLIOGRAPHY

Editions, Commentaries and Textual Studies
General
G.-S. = Gomme A. W. and Sandbach F. H. *Menander, A Commentary*, Oxford 1973.
Sandbach F. H. 1990 *Menandri Reliquiae Selectae*, 2nd ed. Oxford 1990.

Aspis
Arnott W. G. 1979a *Menander* vol. 1, Cambridge MA and London.
Austin C. 1969–70 *Menandri Aspis et Samia*, Berlin.
Beroutsos D. C. 2005 *A Commentary on the 'Aspis' of Menander, Part One: Lines 1–298*, Göttingen.
Borgogno A. 1972 *Menandri Aspis*, Milan.
Del Corno D. 1970a 'Note all' *Aspis* di Menandro', *Zeitschrift für Papyrologie und Epigraphik* 6, 213–25.
Del Corno D. 1971 'Ancora sull' *Aspis* di Menandro', *Zeitschrift für Papyrologie und Epigraphik* 8, 29–32
Gronewald M. 1992 'Zu Menander's *Aspis*', *Zeitschrift für Papyrologie und Epigraphik* 90, 50–54.
Groton A. H. 1982 *A Commentary on Menander's Aspis 1–163*, Diss. Michigan.
Handley E. W. 1995 'Menander, Aspis (and Other Plays?)', *The Oxyrhynchus Papyri* 61, London, 6–13.
Jacques J.-M. 1998a *Ménandre: le Bouclier*, Paris.
Kasser R. and Austin C. 1969 *Papyrus Bodmer XXVI, Ménandre: le Bouclier*, Geneva.
Sbordone F. 1970 *Menandro Aspis*, Naples.
Sisti F. 1971 *Menandro Aspis*, Rome.
Willis W. H. 1990 'Un nouveau fragment du codex Bodmer de Ménandre', in Handley E. and Hurst A. (eds), *Relire Ménandre*, Geneva, 167–171.

Epitrepontes
Arnott W. G. 1977 'Four Notes on Menander's *Epitrepontes*', *Zeitschrift für Papyrologie und Epigraphik* 24, 16–20.
Arnott W. G. 1979a *Menander* vol. 1, Cambridge MA and London.
Arnott W. G. 2004a 'Menander's *Epitrepontes* in the Light of the New Papyri', in Cairns D. L. and Knox R. (eds), *Law, Rhetoric and Comedy in Classical Athens: Essays in Honour of D. M. MacDowell*, Swansea, 269–92.

266 *Bibliography*

Arnott W. G. 2004b 'New Menander from the 1990s', in Bastianini G. and Casanova A. (eds), *Menandro: cent' anni di papyri*, Firenze, 35–53.

Furley W. G. 2009 *Menander Epitrepontes*, London.

Gronewald M. 1986 'Menander, *Epitrepontes*, neue Fragmente aus Akt III und IV', *Zeitschrift für Papyrologie und Epigraphik* 66, 1–13.

Handley E. W. 2009 'Menander *Epitrepontes*', *The Oxyrhynchus Papyri* 73, London, 25–31.

Martina A. 1997 *Menandri Epitrepontes* I (*Text*), Rome, 2000 II.1 (*Prolegomena*), II.2 (*Commentary*), Rome.

Nünlist R. 1999 'Ein neu identifiziertes Buchfragment aus Menanders *Epitrepontes*', *Zeitschrift für Papyrologie und Epigraphik* 128, 54–6.

Nünlist R. 2003 'Notes on P. Oxy 4021, Fr. 3 (Menander, *Epitrepontes*)', *Zeitschrift für Papyrologie und Epigraphik* 144, 59–61.

Nünlist R. 2004 'The Beginning of *Epitrepontes* Act II', in Bastianini G. and Casanova A. (eds), *Menandro: cent' anni di papyri*, Firenze, 95–106.

Parsons P. J. 1994 'Menander, *Epitrepontes* 150–164 etc.', *The Oxyrhynchus Papyri* 60, London, 30–35.

Parsons P. J. 1994a 'Menander, *Epitrepontes* 290–301, 338–345, 376–400, 421–447', *The Oxyrhynchus Papyri* 60, London, 35–39.

Parsons P. J. 1994b 'Menander, *Epitrepontes* 655–65 etc.', *The Oxyrhynchus Papyri* 60, London, 39–41.

Pintaudi R. and López-García A. L. 1999 'Menander *Epitrepontes* 662–666; 688–691 (S) in un Papiro Laurenziano (PL III.3 10 A; TAV. I)', *Zeitschrift für Papyrologie und Epigraphik* 124, 15–16.

Sandbach F. H. 1986 'Two Notes on Menander (*Epitrepontes* and *Samia*)', *Liverpool Classical Monthly* 11.9, 156–60.

Turner E. G. 1983a 'Menander *Epitrepontes*', *The Oxyrhynchus Papyri* 50, London, 36–41.

Turner E. G. 1983b 'Menander *Epitrepontes*', *The Oxyrhynchus Papyri* 50, London, 42–48.

Verdenius W. J. 1974 'Notes on Menander's *Epitrepontes*', *Mnemosyne* 37, 17–43.

Weinstein M. E. 1971 'Menander *Epitrepontes*', *The Oxyrhynchus Papyri* 38, London, 19–27.

Wilamowitz-Moellendorff U. von 1925 *Menander, das Schiedsgericht*, Berlin.

Secondary Literature

Anderson, W. S. 1970 'A New Menandrian Prototype for the *Servus Currens* of Roman Comedy', *Phoenix* 24, 229–36.

Arnott W. G. 1972 'From Aristophanes to Menander', *Greece and Rome* 19, 65–80.

Arnott W. G. 1975 'The Modernity of Menander', *Greece and Rome* 22, 140–55.

Arnott W. G. 1979b 'Time, Plot and Character in Menander', in Cairns F. (ed.), *Papers of the Liverpool Latin Seminar II*, Liverpool, 343–60.

Arnott W. G. 1981 'Moral Values in Menander', *Philologus* 125, 215–27.

Arnott W. G. 1986 'Menander and Earlier Drama', in J. H. Betts *et al.* (eds), *Studies in Honour of T. B. L. Webster* I, Bristol, 1–9.

Arnott W. G. 1987 'The Time-Scale of Menander's *Epitrepontes*', *Zeitschrift für Papyrologie und Epigraphik* 70, 19–31.

Arnott W. G. 1995 'Menander's Manipulation of Language for the Individualisation of Character', in de Martino F. and Sommerstein A. H. (eds), *Lo spettacolo delle voci* II, Bari, 147–64.

Arnott W. G. 2001 'Visible Silence in Menander', in Jäkel S. and Timonen A. (eds), *The Language of Silence I*, Turku, 71–85.

Astorga J. A. 1990 *The Art of Diphilus: a Study of Verbal Humor in New Comedy*, Diss. Calif.

Bader E. 1971 'The ψόφος of the House-Door', *Antichthon* 5, 35–48.

Bain D. 1977 *Actors and Audience: A Study of Asides and Related Conventions in Greek Drama*, Oxford.

Bastianini G. and Casanova A. 2004 *Menandro: cent' anni di papyri*, Firenze.

Beare W. 1964 *The Roman Stage*, 3rd ed., London.

Belardinelli A. M. 2000 'A proposito dell' uso et della funzione dell' *ekkyklema*: Eur. *Hipp.* 170–266, 808–1101, Men. *Asp.* 309–399, *Dysk.* 689–758a', *Seminari Romani di Cultura Greca* 3, 243–265.

Blanchard A. 1983 *Essai sur la composition des comédies de Ménandre*, Paris.

Blanchard A. 2007 *La comédie de Ménandre: politique, éthique, esthétique*, Paris.

Blänsdorf J. 1982 'Die Komödienintrige als Spiel im Spiel', *Antike und Abendland* 28, 131–154.

Blundell J. 1980 *Menander and the Monologue*, Göttingen.

Blume H.-D. 1998 *Menander*, Darmstadt.

Borgogno A. 2002 'Per un'analisi dell' *Aspis* di Menandro', *Maia* 54, 243–58.

Brown P. G. McC. 1983 'Menander's Dramatic Technique and the Law of Athens', *Classical Quarterly* 33, 412–20.

Brown P. G. McC. 1987 'Masks, Names and Characters in New Comedy', *Hermes* 115, 181–202.

Brown P. G. McC. 1990 'Plots and Prostitutes in Greek New Comedy', *Papers of the Leeds Intenational Latin Seminar* 6, 241–66.

Brown P. G. McC. 1993 'Love and Marriage in Greek New Comedy', *Classical Quarterly* 43, 189–205 = Segal 2001, 42–64.

Cohen E. 1992 *Athenian Economy and Society*, Princeton.

Cohoon J. W. 1914 'Rhetorical Studies in the Arbitration Scene of Menander's *Epitrepontes*', *Trans. of the American Philological Association* 45, 141–230.

Collard C. and Cropp M. 2008 *Euripides Fragments* (Loeb vol.VII), Cambridge Ma. and London.

Cox C. A. 2002 'Assuming the Master's Values: The Slave's Response to Punishment and Neglect in Menander', *Mouseion* 2, 23–38.

Csapo E. and Slater W. J. 1994 *The Context of Ancient Drama*, Ann Arbor.

Cusset C. 2003 *Ménandre ou la comédie tragique*, Paris.

Damen M. L. 1985 *The Comedy of Diphilus Sinopeus in Plautus, Terence, and Athenaeus*, Diss. Texas.

Del Corno D. 1970b 'Il nuovo Menandro: 'Lo Scudo' et 'la Donna di Samo', *Atene e Roma* 15, 65–79.

Dohm H. 1964 *Mageiros: Die Rolle des Kochs in der griechischen-römischen Komödie*, München.

Dworacki S. 1973a 'The Presentation of Persons in Menander's *Shield*', *Symbolae Philologorum Posnaniensium* I, 33–45.

Dworacki, S. 1973b 'The Prologues in the Comedies of Menander', *Eos* 61, 33–47.

Fantham E. 1975 'Sex, Status and Survival in Hellenistic Athens: A Study of Women in New Comedy', *Phoenix* 29, 44–74.

Feneron J. S. 1975 *Some Elements of Menander's Style*, Diss. Stanford.

Ferrari F. 2001 *Menandro e la commedia nuova*, Turin.

Frost K. B. *Exits and Entrances in Menander*, Oxford 1988.

Gaiser K. 1967 'Menander und der Peripatos', *Antike und Abendland* 13, 8–40.

Gaiser K. 1971 *Der Schild oder die Erbtochter*, Zurich and Stuttgart.

Gaiser K. 1973 'Menanders Komödie "Der Schild"', *Grazer Beiträge* 1, 111–136a.

Gaiser K. 1983 'Ein neues Fragment aus Menanders 'Aspis', *Zeitschrift für Papyrologie und Epigraphik* 51, 37–43.

Goldberg S. 1980 *The Making of Menander's Comedy*, London.

Halliwell S. 1983 'The Staging of Menander *Aspis* 299ff.', *Liverpool Classical Monthly* 8.2, 31–2.

Handley E. W. 1965 *The Dyskolos of Menander*, London.

Handley E. W. 1969 'The Conventions of the Comic Stage and their Exploitation by Menander', in Turner E. G. (ed.), *Ménandre*, 3–26. = Segal 2001, 27–41.

Handley E. W. 1987 'Acts and Scenes in the Comedy of Menander', *Dioniso* 57, 299–312.

Handley E. W. 1990 'The Bodmer Menander and the Comic Fragments', in Handley E. and Hurst A. (eds), *Relire Ménandre*, Geneva, 123–48.

Harrison A. R. W. 1968 *The Law of Athens I: The Family and Property*, Oxford, 1971 *II: Procedure*, Oxford.

Holzberg N. 1974 *Menander, Untersuchungen zur dramatischen Technik*, Nürnberg.

Hunter R. L. 1979 'The Comic Chorus in the Fourth Century', *Zeitschrift für Papyrologie und Epigraphik* 36, 23–38.

Hunter R. L. 1985 *The New Comedy of Greece and Rome*, Cambridge.

Hurst A. 1990 'Ménandre et la tragédie', in Handley E. and Hurst A. (eds), *Relire Ménandre*, Geneva, 93–122.

Hurst A. 2000 'Wie schickt Menander den Artz weg', in Gödde S. and Heinze T. (eds), *Skenika: Beiträge zum antiken Theater und seiner Rezeption. Festschrift zum 65. Geburtstag von Horst-Dieter Blume*, Darmstadt, 103–11.

Hurst A. 2004 'Ménandre en ses recoins', in Bastianini G. and Casanova A. (eds), *Menandro, cent' anni di papiri*, Florence, 55–70.

Ireland S. 1981 'Prologues, Structure and Sentences in Menander', *Hermes* 109, 178–88.

Ireland S. 1983 'Menander and the Comedy of Disappointment', *Liverpool Classical Monthly* 8.3, 45–7.

Ireland S. 1992 *Menander, Dyskolos, Samia and Other Plays*, Bristol.

Ireland S. 1995 *Menander, The Bad-Tempered Man*, Warminster.

Iversen P. A. 2001 'Coal for Diamonds', *American Journal of Philology* 122, 381–403.

Jacques J.-M. 1978 'Mouvement des acteurs et conventions scéniques dans l'acte II du Bouclier de Ménandre', *Grazer Beiträge* , 37–56.

Jacques J.-M. 1996 'La figure de l'étranger dans la Comédie Nouvelle: à propos du *Bouclier* de Ménandre', *Littératures Classiques* 27, 323–32.

Jacques J.-M. 1998b 'La bile noire dans l'antiquité grecque: médecine et littérature', *Revue des Études Anciennes* 100, 217–34.

Jacques J.-M. 2000 'La comédie nouvelle a-t-elle utilisé l'eccyclème?', *Pallas* 54, 89–102.

Just R. 1989 *Women in Athenian Law and Life*, London.

Kahil, L. 1969 'Remarques sur l'iconographie des pièces de Ménandre', in Turner E. G. (ed.), *Ménandre*, 231–51.

Karabelias E. 1970 'Une nouvelle source pour l'étude du droit attique: le *Bouclier* de Ménandre', *Revue Historique de Droit Français et Étranger* 48, 357–89.

Karnezis J. E. 1977 'Misrepresentation of Attic Law in Menander's *Aspis*', *Platon* 29, 152–5.

Katsouris A. G. 1975a *Tragic Patterns in Menander*, Athens.

Katsouris A. G. 1975b *Linguistic and Stylistic Characterisation: Tragedy and Menander*, Ioannina.

K.-A. = Kassel R. and Austin C. 1983–2001 *Poetae Comici Graeci*, Berlin.

Konet R. J. 1976 'The Role of *Tuche* in Menander's *Aspis*', *Classical Bulletin* 52, 90–2.

Konstan D. 1995 *Greek Comedy and Ideology*, New York and Oxford.

Krieter-Spiro M. 1997 *Sklaven, Köche und Hetären: das Dienstpersonal bei Menander: Stellung, Rolle, Komik und Sprache,* Stuttgart.

Lacey W. K. 1968 *The Family in Classical Greece*, London.

Lane Fox R. 1985 'Aspects of Inheritance in the Greek World', in Cartledge P. A. and Harvey F. D. (eds), *Crux, Essays in Honor of de Ste Croix*: *History of Political Thought* 6, 208–32.

Lape S. 2004 *Reproducing Athens: Menander's Comedy, Democratic Culture, and the Hellenistic City*, Princeton and Oxford.

Lape S. 2006 'The Poetics of the *Kômos*-Chorus in Menander's Comedy', *American Journal of Philology* 12, 89–109.

Leisner-Jensen, M. 2002 'Vis Comica; Consummated Rape in Greek and Roman New Comedy, *Classica et Mediaevalia* 53, 173–96.

Lloyd-Jones H. 1971 'Menander's *Aspis*', *Greek, Roman and Byzantine Studies* 12, 175–95.

Lombard D. B. 1971 'New Values in Traditional Form: A Study in Menander's *Aspis*', *Acta Classica* 14, 123–45.

MacCary W. T. 1969 'Menander's Slaves: their Names, Roles and Masks', *Trans. of the American Philological Association* 100, 277–94.

MacCary W. T. 1970 'Menander's Characters: Their Names, Roles and Masks', *Trans. of the American Philological Association* 101, 277–90.

MacCary W. T. 1971 'Menander's Old Men', *Trans. of the American Philological Association* 102, 303–25.

MacDowell D. M. 1978 *The Law in Classical Athens*, London.

MacDowell D. M. 1982 'Love Versus the Law: an Essay on Menander's *Aspis*', *Greece and Rome* 29, 42–52.

Munteanu D. 2002 'Types of Anagnorisis: Aristotle and Menander, a Self-Defining Comedy', *Wiener Studien* 115, 111–26.

Nünlist R. 2002 'Speech within Speech in Menander', in Willi A. (ed.), *The Language of Greek Comedy*, Oxford, 219–59.

Ogden D. 1996 *Greek Bastardy in the Classical and Hellenistic Periods*, Oxford.

Omitowoju R. 2002 *Rape and the Politics of Consent in Classical Athens*, Cambridge.

Paduano G. 2004 'Ridere con Menandro', in Bastianini G. and Casanova A. (eds), *Menandro: cent' anni di papyri*, Firenze, 9–33.

Parke H. W. 1977 *Festivals of the Athenians*, London.

Patterson C. B. 1998 *The Family in Greek History*, Harvard.

Pierce K. F. 1997 'The Portrayal of Rape in New Comedy', in Deacy S. and Pierce K. F. (eds), *Rape in Antiquity*, London, 163–84.

Pöhlmann E. 1991 'Die Funktion des Chores in der neuen Komödie', in *Studi di filologia classica in onore di G. Monaco*, Palermo, 349–59.

Poole M. 1977 'Menander's Comic Use of Euripides' Tragedies', *Classical Bulletin* 54, 56–62.

Primmer A. 1986 'Karion in den *Epitrepontes*', *Wiener Studien* 99, 123–41.

Raven D. S. 1968 *Greek Metre, An Introduction*, 2nd ed., London.

Rosivach V. J. 1998 *When a Young Man Falls in Love; the Sexual Exploitation of Women in New Comedy*, London.

Sandbach F. H. 'Menander's Manipulation of Language for Dramatic Purposes', in Turner E. G. (ed.), *Ménandre*, 111–36.

Sbordone F. 1970 'Due Note sul nuovo Menandro', *Rend. dell'Accad. di Arch.* 45, 41–56.

Scafuro A. C. 1997 *The Forensic Stage*, Cambridge.

Schaps D. M. 1979 *Economic Rights of Women in Ancient Greece*, Edinburgh.

Segal E. (ed.) 2001 *Oxford Readings in Menander, Plautus and Terence*, Oxford.

Sifakis G. M. 1967 *Studies in the History of Hellenistic Drama,* London.

Sifakis G. M. 1971 'Aristotle *E.N.* IV, 1, 1123a19–24, and the Comic Chorus in the Fourth Century', *American Journal of Philology* 92, 410–32.

Taplin O. 1977 'Did Greek Dramatists Write Stage Instructions?', *Proc. of the Cambridge Philological Soc.* 23, 121–32.

Traill A. 2008 *Women and the Comic Plot in Menander*, Cambridge.

Turner E. G. (ed.) 1969 *Ménandre*, Vandeouvres- Genève.

Turner E. G. 1979 'Menander and the New Society of his Time', *Chronique d'Egypte* 54, 106–26.

Vogt-Spira G. 1992 *Dramaturgie des Zufalls: Tyche und Handeln in der Komödie Menanders*, München.

Walcot P. 1987 'Romantic Love and True Love: Greek Attitudes to Marriage', *Ancient Society* 18, 5–33.

Walton J. M. and Arnott P. D. 1996 *Menander and the Making of Comedy*, Westport.

Webster T. B. L. 1950 *Studies in Menander*, Manchester.

Webster T. B. L. 1974 *An Introduction to Menander*, Manchester.

Wiles D. 1991 *The Masks of Menander: Sign and Meaning in Greek and Roman Performance*, Cambridge.

Zagagi N. 1990 'Divine Interventions and Human Agents', in Handley E. and Hurst A. (eds), *Relire Ménandre*, Geneva, 63–91.

Zagagi N. 1994 *The Comedy of Menander, Convention, Variation and Originality*, London.